MULTINATIONAL FIRMS AND IMPACTS ON EMPLOYMENT, TRADE AND TECHNOLOGY

For decades, governments, politicians, and trade unions have feared that firms investing abroad involved a loss of employment and a decline in wages for the home country, the implied assumption being that global production and consumption are somehow fixed. Similarly, research on multinational firms has tended to present them as having a number of alternatives – export, licensing or foreign direct investment – for the exploitation of fixed foreign markets.

In actuality, the complex relationships between parent companies and their foreign affiliates must be examined very carefully and with the most disaggregated statistics available if we are to get an accurate understanding of their impacts. A major obstacle to this research has been the confidential nature of the necessary data. This collection, with contributions from many distinguished writers in the field, presents work that has been able to exploit relevant data for countries such as the United States, France, Italy, Belgium and Japan. The essays show, for the first time with a large sample, the high degree of complementarity between foreign direct investment (FDI) and home exports, especially for intra-firm trade, and the exact evolution in the nature of employment between mother companies and affiliates.

Another important debate has revolved around the impact of foreign multinationals on the host countries. It is shown here that the impacts of multinational firms are mediated by their ability to create linkages with the host economy. Foreign direct investment generates backward and forward linkages in the host economy. Increased competition, technology transfer, increased access to world markets due to spillovers to local firms, and worker training are among the positive effects for FDI.

This book is the first volume of selected work first presented at the seventh Sorbonne International Conference on Multinational Firms' Strategies. The companion volume, also published by Routledge, is *Multinational Firms: The Global–Local Dilemma*, edited by John H. Dunning and Jean-Louis Mucchielli.

Robert E. Lipsey is a Research Associate of the National Bureau of Economic Research, and Professor Emeritus of Economics at Queens College and the Graduate Center of The City University of New York.

Jean-Louis Mucchielli is Professor of Economics at the University of Paris I Panthéon-Sorbonne, France.

STUDIES IN GLOBAL COMPETITION
Edited by John Cantwell,
The University of Reading, UK
and
David Mowery,
University of California, Berkeley, USA

JAPANESE FIRMS IN EUROPE
Edited by Frédérique Sachwald

TECHNOLOGICAL INNOVATION, MULTINATIONAL
CORPORATIONS AND NEW INTERNATIONAL
COMPETITIVENESS
The case of intermediate countries
Edited by José Molero

GLOBAL COMPETITION AND THE LABOUR MARKET
Nigel Driffield

THE SOURCE OF CAPITAL GOODS INNOVATION
The role of user firms in Japan and Korea
Kong-Rae Lee

CLIMATES OF GLOBAL COMPETITION
Maria Bengtsson

MULTINATIONAL ENTERPRISES AND
TECHNOLOGICAL SPILLOVERS
Tommaso Perez

GOVERNANCE OF INTERNATIONAL
STRATEGIC ALLIANCES
Technology and transaction costs
Joanne E. Oxley

STRATEGY IN EMERGING MARKETS
Telecommunications establishments in Europe
Anders Pehrsson

GOING MULTINATIONAL
The Korean experience of direct investment
Edited by Frédérique Sachwald

MULTINATIONAL FIRMS AND IMPACTS ON
EMPLOYMENT, TRADE AND TECHNOLOGY
New perspectives for a new century
Edited by Robert E. Lipsey and Jean-Louis Mucchielli

MULTINATIONAL FIRMS
The global–local dilemma
Edited by John H. Dunning and Jean-Louis Mucchielli

MULTINATIONAL FIRMS AND IMPACTS ON EMPLOYMENT, TRADE AND TECHNOLOGY

New perspectives for a new century

Edited by
Robert E. Lipsey
and
Jean-Louis Mucchielli

London and New York

First published 2002
by Routledge
11 New Fetter Lane, London EC4P 4EE

Simultaneously published in the USA and Canada
by Routledge
29 West 35th Street, New York, NY 10001

Routledge is an imprint of the Taylor & Francis Group

© 2002 Routledge

Typeset in 10/12 pt Times by
Newgen Imaging Systems (P) Ltd, Chennai, India
Printed and bound in Great Britain by MPG Books Ltd, Bodmin

British Library Cataloguing in Publication Data
A catalogue record for this book is available
from the British Library

Library of Congress Cataloging-in-Publication Data
Multinational firms and impacts on employment, trade, and technology:
new perspectives for a new century/edited by Robert E. Lipsey and
Jean-Louis Mucchielli.
p. cm. – (Studies in global competition; v. 11)
"This book is the first volume of a collection selected papers from a
conference held in la Sorbonne, Paris, June 17–18, 1999" –
Acknowledgements.
Includes bibliographical references and index.
1. Foreign trade and employment–Congresses. 2. International business
enterprises–Congresses. 3. Investments, Foreign–Congresses.
4. International division of labor–Congresses. 5. Employees–Effect of
technological innovations on–Congresses. 6. Unemployment–Congresses.
7. Labor economics–Congresses. 8. Industrial policy–Congresses.
9. Economic policy–Congresses. 10. Full employment policies–Congresses.
11. Globalization–Economic aspects–Congresses. I. Lipsey, Robert E.
II. Mucchielli, Jean Louis. III. Series.

HD5710.7M852001   338.8′8–dc21   2001041839

ISBN 0-415-27053-7

CONTENTS

List of contributors　　　　　　　　　　　　　　　　　vii

Introduction　　　　　　　　　　　　　　　　　　　　ix

PART I

Multinational firms, international production and home employment　　　　　　　　　　　　　　　　　**1**

1　**Foreign production by US firms and parent firm employment**　　　　　　　　　　　　　　　　　**3**

　ROBERT E. LIPSEY

2　**Foreign direct investment and employment: home country experience in Italy**　　　　　　　　**24**

　SERGIO MARIOTTI AND LUCIA PISCITELLO

PART II

Multinational firms and international trade: FDI and export, FDI and intra-firm trade　　　　　**41**

3　**Relationships between trade and FDI flows within two panels of US and French industries**　　**43**

　LIONEL FONTAGNÉ AND MICHAËL PAJOT

4　**Intra-firm trade and foreign direct investment: an empirical analysis of French firms**　　　　**84**

　SÉVERINE CHÉDOR, JEAN-LOUIS MUCCHIELLI AND
　ISABELLE SOUBAYA

5 Foreign investment transactions and international trade
   linkages   101
   DEBORAH L. SWENSON

6 Intra-firm trade and market structure   119
   STÉPHANE BECUWE, CLAUDE MATHIEU AND PATRICK SEVESTRE

PART III
Multinational firms, linkages and
spillovers effects   137

7 Linkages, multinationals and industrial
   development   139
   AMY JOCELYN GLASS, VASILIOS D. KOSTEAS AND KAMAL SAGGI

8 Local procurement by Japanese manufacturing affiliates
   abroad   154
   RENÉ BELDERBOS, GIOVANNI CAPANNELLI AND KYOJI FUKAO

PART IV
Multinational firms, structure and diffusion of
technology and innovation: how globalization is
structured   175

9 The effectiveness of intellectual property rights:
   an exploration of French survey data   177
   EMMANUEL COMBE AND ETIENNE PFISTER

10 The innovative activities of multinational firms in
   Italy   197
   GIOVANNI BALCET AND FRANCESCA CORNAGLIA

11 Innovative strategies and know-how flows in
   international companies: some evidence from
   Belgian manufacturing   220
   REINHILDE VEUGELERS AND BRUNO CASSIMAN

12 Foreign direct investment as a technology sourcing strategy:
   the case of Korean multinationals   244
   LUIS MIOTTI AND FRÉDÉRIQUE SACHWALD

Index   269

CONTRIBUTORS

Robert E. Lipsey Professor, Queens College and Graduate Center, CUNY and National Bureau of Economic Research, New York

Sergio Mariotti Professor at the Politecnico di Milano, Dipartimento di Economia e Produzione, Italy

Lucia Piscitello Assistant Professor at the Politecnico di Milano, Dipartimento di Economia e Produzione, Italy

Lionel Fontagné Director of the CEPII and Professor at the Université Paris 1 Panthéon – Sorbonne TEAM (University of Paris 1 and CNRS), France

Michaël Pajot Researcher at the Direction de la Prévision, Université Paris 1 Panthéon – Sorbonne TEAM (University of Paris 1 and CNRS), Paris, France

Séverine Chédor Associate Professor at the University of le Maine, TEAM Université Paris I CNRS, GAINS Université du Maine

Jean-Louis Mucchielli Université de Paris I Panthéon – Sorbonne TEAM, France

Isabelle Soubaya TEAM University Paris 1 & CNRS, Université de Paris I Panthéon – Sorbonne Maison des Sciences Economiques TEAM, France and Université de la Réunion, Faculté des Sciences Economiques Ceresur, France

Deborah L. Swenson Associate Professor of Economics, UC Davis and NBER, Department of Economics, University of California, CA

Stéphane Becuwe Directeur de Recherche au CNRS, Maison des sciences de l'homme et de la société, Université de la Rochelle, France

Claude Mathieu Professor of Economics, Université de Tour and Erudite-Université Paris XII – Val de Marne, France

Patrick Sevestre Professor at the University Paris XII Val de Marne, France

CONTRIBUTORS

Amy Jocelyn Glass Assistant Professor of Economics, Department of Economics, Texas A&M University, Bush Academic Building West, College Station, TX 77843-4228, USA

Vasilios D. Kosteas Graduate Associate, Ohio State University, Department of Economics, OH

Kamal Saggi Associate Professor at the Southern Methodist University, Department of Economics, Dallas, USA

René Belderbos Royal Netherlands Academy of Arts and Science Research Fellow, University of Maastricht, Faculty of Economics and Business Administration, The Netherlands

Giovanni Capannelli Professor, University of Malaya European Studies Programme, Asia–Europe Centre, University of Malaya, Kuala Lumpur, Malaysia

Kyoji Fukao Professor, Institute of Economic Research, Hitotsubashi University, Tokyo, Japan

Emmanuel Combe Professor at the University Paris XII Val' de Marne, Université du Havre, France

Etienne Pfister TEAM-CNRS-Université de Paris 1, Maison des Sciences Economiques, 106-112, Boulevard de l'hôpital, 7501, Paris, France

Giovanni Balcet Professor of International Economics, University of Turin, Italy

Francesca Cornaglia Junior Researcher at the Labotorio R. Revelli, University of Turin, Turin, Italy

Reinhilde Veugelers Professor Katholieke Universiteit Leuven, Belgium & CEPR Fellow, London UK

Bruno Cassiman Assistant Professor IESE Business School, Universidad de Navarra, Avenida Pearson 21, 08034 Barcelona, Spain

Luis Miotti is Assistant Professor at University Paris XII (Centre de Recherche en Economie Industrielle)

Frédérique Sachwald is Senior Research Fellow at ifri and adjunct professor at University Paris XIII (Centre de Recherche en Economie industrielle)

INTRODUCTION

For several decades governments, politicians, and trade unions have feared that investments abroad by home multinational firms, especially manufacturing ones, involved replacing home workers by foreign workers with a resulting loss of home employment and a decline in wages. The implied assumption was that total world production and consumption were fixed, and that production abroad would reduce home production by replacing home country by local production and increasing imports from manufacturing foreign affiliates.

According to these hypotheses, production abroad is a substitute for production at home and the impacts on home country production and employment are necessarily negative. Similarly, recent theoretical approaches, including multinational firm theory, often tend to picture firms as having alternative ways to exploit a fixed and given foreign market: export, licensing or foreign direct investment (FDI). The multinational firm maximizes its profit by selecting the lowest cost combination of licensing, exporting or producing abroad to meet a fixed demand. More recently, in the strategic approach, FDI is viewed as a means to preempt local markets and to avoid entry or expansion by local or rival foreign firms.

These approaches, because of the restrictiveness of the assumptions involved, and the neglect of macroeconomic determinants of production and employment, do not reveal much about the impacts of FDI. The analysis of the impacts on parent firms is enriched by an examination of the complex relationships between parent companies and their foreign affiliates. With the establishment of a foreign affiliate, a wide variety of events may follow. The firm as a whole may increase its share of a host country market, earn a share where there was none before, as is often the case in a service industry, or create a market where there was none before. Intra-firm trade is created; a parent company may export to its subsidiaries capital goods, skilled labor, equipment, intermediate products or even final products of a different type or quality from those produced locally. Affiliates can also export to their parent companies or to third countries inside or outside the multinational's network of affiliates. The network links give many opportunities for exports and FDI to be more complements than substitutes. This has been a major result of empirical researches.

To find these complementarities it has been important to examine data at an individual firm level in order to evaluate the relationships between each parent company and its foreign affiliates. For a long time it was not possible for economists to work on large samples of such data because of the confidential information involved. Even now, many national statistical institutes deny access to individual firm data even though no individual information would emerge from the final statistical results. Economists are then constrained to build their own samples with the help of information from the newspapers or yearly reports of certain firms. However, it is impossible to build large samples of thousands of firms with such precise features as are provided by the official questionnaire sent by the national statistical institute to almost all the resident enterprises.

With samples from countries where these individual data can be exploited, the knowledge of links, in terms of volume and nature, inside the multinational firms' network can be improved. It is also possible to combine data from several inquiries concerning enterprises, such as inquiries on financial links, on geographical location of foreign subsidiaries, number of foreign employee, and on real and financial indicators for parent firms.

1. Multinational firms, international production, and home employment

In the first two papers attention is focused on the link between FDI and home employment. If complementarity is demonstrated, it is underlined also that in the case of FDI in LDCs, the nature of the home production can change, becoming more skilled or capital intensive than before. For Robert Lipsey (Chapter 1) there is no indication in aggregate data that movements of production from the United States to foreign affiliates of US firms have had any negative effect on employment of parent firms or in the United States as a whole. A regression analysis of individual firm data does point to some effects of foreign production on employment within firms. Higher levels of affiliate production in developing countries are associated with lower parent employment for any given level of parent production at home.

Sergio Mariotti and Lucia Piscitello (Chapter 2) provide some statistical evidence on the relationship between FDI and the home country labor intensity. The variation of the employment in foreign affiliates by Italian manufacturing firms, in the period 1985–95, significantly influenced the labor intensity of the domestic production: an increase of foreign employment in less developed countries, characterized by low labor cost, reduced the labor intensity of the domestic production. The impact on the domestic labor intensity is positive when FDI is directed towards advanced countries. Results obtained corroborate the interpretation which distinguishes between horizontal investments driven by market seeking strategies, that constitute the bulk of FDI in more advanced countries, and vertical investments led by strategies of allocating labor-intensive portions of the output or labor-intensive stages of production, which represent the great part of FDI towards less developed countries.

2. Multinational firms and international trade: FDI and export, FDI and intra-firm trade

In the second part of the book, the analysis concerns the link between trade and FDI. The authors provide explanations over the generally observed complementarity between FDI and trade. In Chapter 3, Lionel Fontagné and Michael Pajot challenge the traditional complementarity relationship in several respects for the French and American cases. They examine in particular whether the macroeconomic complementarity they observe is a statistical artefact resulting from linkages between industries. The authors use data broken down by industry and partner to assess this issue. They observe complementarity for both French and American data even at the sectoral level. It appears, however, for the case of France for instance, that about 50% of the complementarity between exports and outward FDI is in fact due to exports from other industries than the investing one.

In Chapter 4, Séverine Chedor, Jean-Louis Mucchielli and Isabelle Soubaya offer a new study of the link between FDI and trade though an examination of intra-firm trade. A former study (Chédor and Mucchielli 1998) concluded that there was a complementarity between French exports and French FDI; the main objective here is to deepen this first analysis. First of all, could the global relationship of complementarity between trade and FDI be explained by intra- and inter-firm trade? Second, to what extent are imports more or less influenced by FDI than exports? The results confirm a positive relationship between FDI and global trade. However, it appears that French FDI and intra-firm trade are much stronger complements than French FDI and inter-firm trade. This result provides an explanation of the usually opposite findings of empirical and theoretical analysis on the ground of complementarity/substitution between trade and FDI. Furthermore, this positive relationship between trade and FDI seems to be stronger for exports compared to imports, which tends to show that potential trade deficit cannot be generated by FDI.

Deborah Swenson goes further in Chapter 5, by examining, with US data, how different types of foreign investment affect trade flows. When investment is broken down by function, Swenson finds that the strongest complementary effects of foreign investment on trade appear in manufacturing. The apparent strength of this effect is smaller in services or trade, and non-existent in the resource sector. Then she breaks down manufacturing investment. She finds that some foreign investment types stimulate trade linkages, while others supplant previous trade flows. What this suggests is that understanding the consequences of foreign investment flows will be aided by greater focus on their composition.

Stéphane Becuwe, Claude Mathieu and Patrick Sevestre, in Chapter 6, go back to an imperfect competition model in order to analyze the theoretical evolution of trade realized inside multinational firms and the intensity of intra-industry trade according to the competitive degree of markets. They show that the quantities produced by subsidiaries can be complementary to intra-firm trade, for example, they can have the same positive evolution with respect to the number of

MNFs, highlighting in that way a positive relationship between exports and direct investments even when trade barriers exist.

3. Multinational firms, linkages, and spillovers effects

In the third part of the book, it is shown that the impacts of multinational firms have to be underlined by the ability to create linkages with the rest of the host economy. Amy Glass, Vasilios Kosteas and Kamal Saggi explore, in Chapter 7, the arguments that FDI encourages industrial development through linkages. In general, there is strong theoretical support for the idea that FDI can play a crucial role in industrial development by generating backward and forward linkages in the host economy. On the empirical side, the evidence is mixed. While some studies support the linkage effects of FDI, others fail to find such effects. Finally, linkages are only one of the potential channels through which FDI impacts a host economy. The authors conclude that any policy formulation based primarily on the notion of linkages would be misguided. Increased competition, technology transfer, increased access to world markets due to spillovers to local firms, and worker training are some of the other channels through which FDI can benefit the host economy, and such benefits can be realized despite the absence of linkages.

René Belderbos, Giovanni Capanelli and Kyoji Fukao, in Chapter 8, examine more empirically the extent to which Japanese firms establish vertical linkages in host economies, by analyzing the local procurement ratio of 272 Japanese manufacturing affiliates in the electronics industry. Affiliates of parents that belong to vertical keiretsus with intensive intra-keiretsu supplier relationships reach significantly *higher* local procurement levels. Membership of a vertical keiretsu facilitates this achievement of higher local procurement levels through co-ordinated investments in overseas manufacturing operations by the "core" firm and its suppliers within the keiretsu. Keiretsu firms were found to achieve higher local procurement levels only in case of a large presence of Japanese suppliers provided that these locally established Japanese suppliers sell on the local market.

At the same time, a greater relative presence of Japanese firms in the local supplier base (in particular, Japanese firms with local market-oriented operations) was found to facilitate higher local procurement levels. The establishment mode of the affiliate was found to have a major impact on vertical linkages. Greenfield affiliates recorded significantly lower local procurement ratios than acquired affiliates, due to the latter's pre-acquisition embeddedness in the local economy. The sales strategy of the affiliates was also found to affect local procurement behavior. Affiliates that sell a larger share of output on local markets recorded higher local procurement.

4. Multinational firms, structure and diffusion of technology and innovation: how it is structured inside the globalization

In the last part of the book, linkage effects are also viewed through technological spillovers effects and the propensity to diffuse abroad new technologies. But several types of technological behavior can emerge. First, a multinational would like to protect itself by patents or secrecy against imitation. Second, multinational firms will have in some host countries more R&D activities than local firms, and the problem is to know if this R&D spreads inside the host economy. Third, multinational firms can proceed to strong technological exchanges by intra-firm, but also inter-firm, trade, improving thereby the diffusion to the host countries. Finally, some firms can invest abroad in order to acquire innovation and R&D unavailable at home. This implies "upward investments".

Emmanuel Combe and Etienne Pfister present, in Chapter 9, the results of two surveys conducted on two samples of French firms. The first one analyzes the effectiveness and limitations of patent motivations. Patent effectiveness seems particularly high for very large firms. Patenting is driven by the fear of imitation, by the search for negotiating power, and by the desire to avoid future legal problems. The most important limitation of patents is the ease of inventing around them. Patent application, renewal and enforcement costs come second. The second survey looks at industrial property rights in an international context. In particular, they look at the patent strategies of firms with an international activity. They find that the distribution of applications across countries closely matches the distribution of activities across countries. The use of trademarks is more frequent than the use of patents in Asia and other developing countries; the opposite is true for industrialized countries. For foreign countries outside Europe, it looks as if protection was sought preventively before entering a market. The most interesting conclusions come from the analysis of IPR limitations. The authors find that the costs of litigation and of counseling are significantly higher in the US than anywhere else; however, the damages awarded are also higher there. Asia fares particularly badly on average, but the most important limitations come from the inability of firms to detect and sue the infringers and then to get an appropriate level of compensation. Legislation itself appears to be only a minor obstacle. Last, when we look at the determinants of such obstacles, it appears that country effects dominate individual firm effects.

Giovanni Balcet and Francesca Cornaglia, in Chapter 10, make a first attempt to shed light on the innovative activities of foreign multinationals in Italy. At the beginning of the 1990s 23 percent of total industrial R&D in Italy was by foreign affiliates, while in the same year they accounted for less than 10 percent of total industrial employment. Different typologies and diversified strategies of multinationals emerge with respect to innovative behavior. In some sectors the market-orientation strategies in Italy go along with the location of relevant R&D facilities, aiming to adapt the range of products to domestic market features. In other sectors, on the contrary, high innovation indicators go along with high export intensity and intra-group outflows of technology. The first group of industries includes communications equipment and pharmaceuticals: R&D intensity and intra-group technology inflows are higher than average, while export intensity is lower. The main strategy of multinational firms in this case seems to be accessing the Italian domestic market, mainly through acquisitions, and the exploitation of innovative advantages created abroad and transferred from the home country or from other affiliates to Italy.

A second group of high-tech industries, on the contrary, shows higher export-intensity indicators than average (in the case of computers, scientific instruments and other transport equipment, higher than average intra-group technology out-flows can be observed). This cluster includes multinational firms with European or global strategies, which are able to export both innovative goods and new tech-nologies from Italy. In this case, R&D activities are not only connected to the local manufacturing units, but are also related to international research networks. IBM Italia is a relevant example of this typology.

For Belgium as host country, Reinhilde Veugelers and Bruno Cassiman, in Chapter 11, demonstrate that the EUROSTAT/CIS survey results clearly indi-cate that internationally operating firms are more innovation-active. They access not only local but also international external technology sources, through buying strategies as well as cooperative R&D agreements. The analysis further suggests an important role for reciprocity in know-how flows, through the prevalence of cooperation which relies on mutual exchange. In addition, there is a strong com-plementarity between selling and buying technology. Interestingly those firms receiving know-how are also more likely to transfer know-how, But the results pre-sented here also strongly suggest a complementarity between technology transfers occurring internally within the MNE and transfers to the local economy. Foreign affiliates that are receiving internal know-how, when they are integrated in the multinational innovative process, are more likely to generate local transfers and to cooperate with local partners. This result suggests that for subsidiaries to play a more integrative role in the multinational innovations is not necessarily detrimen-tal for the host economy; at least it is able to benefit from the spillovers of this know-how.

Finally, Luis Miotti, and Frédérique Sachwald indicate in Chapter 12 that technological spillovers can come from a sort of "upward investment" done by multinational firms belonging to emerging economies. They can invest in the most developed countries in order to realize "technology sourcing investments". But it thus seems that they have no ownership-specific advantages able to give them some advance compared to the local firms. In their study, the authors show that Korean firms are attempting to tap into the American technological resources through minority ventures. Moreover, they clearly tend to locate these technology sourcing ventures in specific clusters where adequate resources and partners are concentrated. Taken together, the empirical analyses suggest that the American comparative advantage (both at the national and local level) interacts with R&D intensity in attracting Korean investments.

For the authors, these empirical results are to be considered in the context of globalization, where multinational firms have become a much more heterogeneous crowd. Comparisons between American, European and Japanese multinationals have already suggested that national characteristics have a long-lasting impact on firms' advantages and behavior. The Korean case represents yet another source of heterogeneity since Korean multinationals are typically latecomers.

The general feeling emanating from all these studies is that FDI has in general a positive impact on host and home countries. The impacts are quite complex and depend on many variables. Even if FDI increases the volume of trade, employment and technology, it changes the nature of a lot of these flows. For instance, labor-intensive foreign production in LDCs may hurt unskilled labor in home countries, intra-trade firm is more complementary to FDI than inter-firm trade and even if technological spillover effects are positive, they depend to a great extent upon the analyzed industry. These studies show the richness of the statistical approaches but also the fact that we are only at the beginning of new results permitted by these new individual firm and establishment datasets.

5. Acknowledgments

This book is the first volume of a collection of selected papers from a conference held in la Sorbonne, Paris. This conference was prepared and organized by Professor Jean-Louis Mucchielli and the International Pole of the TEAM-CNRS research center (University of Paris 1). Sponsors of this conference included the Commissariat Général du Plan and the University of Paris 1. Special thanks should be extended to Soledad Zignago and Isabelle Soubaya who were particularly active, among many others, in the organization of the conference. The collection, revision and processing of the papers in this volume has been brilliantly done by Tek-Ang Lim.

Part I

MULTINATIONAL FIRMS, INTERNATIONAL PRODUCTION AND HOME EMPLOYMENT

1

FOREIGN PRODUCTION BY US FIRMS AND PARENT FIRM EMPLOYMENT*

Robert E. Lipsey

1.1. Introduction

There has long been a suspicion in the United States that investment abroad by US firms, especially manufacturing firms, involves replacing US workers by foreign workers, with a resulting loss of employment and decline in wages for the firms' workers in the United States. That suspicion was probably at its peak during the late 1960s and the 1970s, and has declined somewhat since then, but it still exists. Worries about the impact of outward foreign direct investment (FDI) led to Congressional proposals to restrict it and to administration measures to limit its financing in the United States.

The adverse effect on home labor was thought to occur through two main channels. One was the replacement of home production for the US market by imports from the affiliates and the other was the replacement of home production for export by affiliate production in the host countries. Since imports into the United States from manufacturing affiliates abroad were relatively small, most attention was focused on export replacement. However, a series of studies of export replacement failed to find evidence that it had taken place. Most studies, including parallel ones for Swedish firms, seemed to find that the net effect of affiliate production on parent exports was positive, if there was any effect at all. For the most part, these studies have found little or no effect or found that production abroad, on

*This paper was prepared for presentation at the Seventh International Conference of the Sorbonne, at the University of Paris I Pantheon-Sorbonne. Partial support for the paper was provided by the Commissariat Général du Plan of France under Contract No. 4/1998. I am indebted for helpful comments on the paper to Deborah Swenson, of the University of California-Davis, the discussant at the Sorbonne Conference, to other participants at that meeting, and to Johan Norbeck, of the Research Institute of Industrial Economics, Stockholm, the discussant at a session of the Western Economic Association in July 1999. I am also indebted to Shachi Chopra-Nangia and Li Xu for skillful assistance in preparing the paper.

net balance, promoted parent exports, and presumably parent employment in the United States.

Much of the concern over outward FDI arose from the impression that production and employment abroad had been rising rapidly. That was the case from the 1950s through the mid-1970s, but in the ten years after 1977, employment in foreign affiliates of US firms outside banking fell by almost a million. It has recovered since then, but did not reach the 1977 level again until 1995. Most of this decline took place in manufacturing affiliates, and the number of these employees was still below the 1977 level in 1995.

It is clear from the data, as is demonstrated more fully below, that there has been no aggregate shift of production or employment by US multinationals out of the United States to their foreign affiliates, at least in the past twenty or twenty-five years. If there is any impact of foreign operations by US firms on US labor markets, it must be through some different mechanism. The issue we explore here is a different one. We take the level of production by US multinationals in the United States as given, determined by each firm's judgment as to the optimal geographical allocation of its worldwide production. We then ask whether these geographical allocations affect the firms' home employment or wage levels by altering the labor intensity or the skill intensity of the firms' home production. They might do so if, for example, firms allocated their most labor-intensive or least skill-intensive activities or products to their foreign affiliates or to their affiliates in low-wage countries.

FDI is one vehicle by which production is allocated among countries, or real-located over time. The basic long-term forces behind these reallocations are the rising per capita incomes of home countries, which force their comparative advantages up the capital-intensity and skill-intensity scales, and the economic growth of foreign markets. For some countries, the depletion of a natural resource alters comparative advantages. In other cases, major changes in currency values induce investment abroad. Often, home country firms have acquired, over a long time, firm-specific advantages in the industries that are seen to be inevitably declining at home. They may have built up technological skills, marketing skills, networks of trade, and brand names that provide market access at home and abroad. In that case, these firms can retain some of the rents on their firm-specific skills by FDI, establishing or acquiring production facilities in the countries to which comparative advantages in production, or in parts of a production chain, are migrating. Some familiar examples are US petroleum industry firms that invested in crude production abroad as the cost of US petroleum resources increased, and Swedish firms in the forest products and forest product machinery industries.

These shifts in the location of production are presumably reflected in the composition of a firm's home production. We would expect that home production within a firm would shift away from industries, or segments of industries, in which the home country was losing comparative advantage. Thus, we would expect that US firms with foreign production facilities would allocate the more labor-intensive

4

segments of their production to locations where labor, or unskilled labor, was relatively cheap. The result at home would be a shift toward more capital-intensive or skill-intensive types of production.

The data for the individual firm regressions used in this study are from the confidential individual firm responses to the benchmark survey of US direct investment abroad in 1989 conducted by the Bureau of Economic Analysis (BEA) of the US Department of Commerce. The calculations had to be performed at the BEA to preserve the confidentiality of the responses.

1.2. Have US firms moved their production and employment to foreign countries?

There are several ways to measure the importance of foreign production and employment by US firms relative to economic activity at home. The two measures we use here are production, as represented by gross product, and employment. Activity abroad can be compared with parent production and employment at home or with production and employment in the whole domestic US economy. The comparison with parent activity describes the choices made by the multinational firms themselves and the comparison with the US as a whole describes the potential impact on the US economy. The gross product data for parents begin only in 1977, after the major part of the expansion of overseas production, and are available only for benchmark survey years until 1994. The gross product data for the MNCs' foreign operations apply only to majority-owned affiliates (MOFAs).

From 1977 to 1982 the share of foreign operations in the output of US MNCs declined, by more than 10 per cent. After that there was some recovery, to the point that the 1997 share was almost identical to the 1977 level:

Gross product of US MOFAs
as per cent of gross product
of parents and MOFAs, 1977–97

1977	24.7
1982	21.9
1989	23.4
1995	25.4
1996	25.2
1997	24.8

Source: Table A1.1.

Over these twenty years, taken as a whole, US MNCs seem to have increased home and foreign production more or less in step with each other, without any substantial shift in or out of the United States.

The comparison with production in the United States as a whole, as represented by Gross Domestic Product (GDP), can be carried back to the earlier period of rapid growth in production abroad by US firms:

Gross product of
US MOFAs as per cent of
US GDP, 1966–97

1966	4.89
1970	6.88
1977	7.95
1982	6.90
1989	5.88
1995	6.40
1996	6.50
1997	6.40

Source: Table A1.1.

We can describe this comparison as measuring the shift to foreign production by all US firms, including non-multinationals. After the large increase in the relative importance of overseas production between 1966 and 1977, over 60 per cent, as compared with total US domestic output, the foreign share fell back for more than a decade, although not to its 1966 level. After 1989, MOFA production rose again, relative to total US production, by more than 10 per cent, but in 1997 it still remained almost 20 per cent smaller relative to US domestic production than in 1977.

Employment has the advantage over production as a measure of foreign and domestic activity that it is not distorted by exchange rate changes, and lends itself to examination of absolute, as well as relative, movements. The number of employees of foreign affiliates of US MNCs grew by almost 3.5 million between 1957 and 1977, more than doubling (Table A1.2). After that, there was a reduction by almost a million foreign workers over the next decade. That pullback was followed by a recovery that did not pass the 1977 level until 1995. Over the whole twenty years since 1977, only about 800,000 overseas employees were added by US firms, a negligible number compared with the up to 40 million added by the US economy as a whole. However, parent firms increased their home employment only slightly; their employment in 1997 was only a million more than in 1977, and their share of total US employment dropped from 21 to 15 per cent between 1977 and 1997. The MNCs were clearly occupying a different universe from that of the United States as a whole.

The affiliate share of MNC employment, which we can observe only since the peak in 1977, declined until the late 1980s, and then recovered, passing the 1977 level in 1995:

Employment in US affiliates abroad as per cent
of employment in nonbank MNCs, 1977–97

	MOFAs	*All affiliates*
1977	22.1	27.6
1982	21.2	26.2
1985	21.0	26.2
1989	21.4	26.1
1995	24.2	28.3
1996	24.4	28.6
1997	24.7	28.8

Source: Table A1.2.

Thus, within the multinationals, there was a small shift in the location of employment from the United States to foreign locations.

Relative to the whole domestic US economy, US firms' affiliate employment has not come near to returning to its 1977 levels:

Employment in US affiliates abroad as
per cent of total US employment, 1957–97

	All affiliates	*MOFAs*
1957	5.2	n.a.
1966	n.a.	5.3
1977	8.0	5.9
1982	6.8	5.1
1985	6.1	4.5
1989	5.7	4.4
1995	5.9	4.8
1996	5.9	4.8
1997	6.2	5.0

Source: Table A1.2.

After growing by over 50 per cent relative to total domestic US employment between 1957 and 1977, foreign employment by US firms then declined by over 30 per cent to a level not far above that of 1957. The ratio began to rise again during the 1990s, but remained far below that of the late 1970s.

All in all, it seems safe to conclude that there has been no shift of employment in the aggregate from the domestic US economy to the foreign operations of US firms.

1.3. Have US firms moved their manufacturing production and employment to foreign countries?

Since manufacturing and petroleum are much more important in the internation-alized output of US firms than in domestic output, the internationalized shares of output are much larger in these two sectors than in others. The share of the petroleum output of US firms that is produced abroad has increased greatly as US domestic reserves of petroleum have declined or become more expensive to exploit, relative to those abroad. In manufacturing too, the foreign share of US multinationals' production has risen even since 1977, the year in which the share of foreign production in general reached a peak and began to decline:

Gross product of MOFAs of US manufacturing
parents as per cent of manufacturing
parents and MOFAs gross product

1977	21.2
1982	22.4
1989	26.1
1995	29.4
1996	28.6
1997	29.2

Source: Table A1.3.

In 1977, 21 per cent of the total output of US manufacturing MNCs was produced outside the United States, and that share had risen to 29 per cent by 1997. Thus, US manufacturing MNCs have allocated more of their worldwide output to their foreign operations.

Since these MNCs are a large, though declining, part of US manufacturing output, their foreign production was large also relative to total US manufacturing output.

Gross product of MOFAs of
US manufacturing MNCs as per cent of
US manufacturing gross product

1977	17.5
1982	18.7
1989	20.4
1995	23.4
1996	23.4
1997	22.9

Source: Table A1.3.

Since 1977, US manufacturing firms' production outside the United States has increased from 17.5 to 23 per cent of all manufacturing production in the US including that of non-multinational and foreign-owned firms. Since 1977, the share of the MNC parent firms in US manufacturing output has fallen from 65 to 55 per cent. This does not mean that non-multinational firms are taking over US manufacturing. Instead, the share of US manufacturing affiliates of foreign multinational firms has increased. Foreign-owned manufacturing affiliates in the United States, which produced only 3.5 per cent of US manufacturing output in 1977, accounted for 12.5 per cent in 1997 (Zeile 1999 and Table A1.3). Thus, both US and foreign manufacturing firms were increasing their degree of internationalization; each group was producing more in the other's home market.

Affiliate employment of US manufacturing
MNCs as per cent of total manufacturing
MNC employment

1977	30.9
1982	31.4
1989	30.8
1994	33.9
1995	34.3
1996	34.8
1997	36.7

Source: Table A1.4.

The data on employment show that from 1977 through the 1980s, there was essentially no change in the share of foreign employment in the total employment of US manufacturing MNCs. Then the foreign share began to creep up during the 1990s, reaching 37 per cent in 1997. As can be seen in Table A1.4, the number of employees outside the United States in 1997 remained below the 1977 level, but while foreign employment fell by about 250,000, the parents' domestic employment fell by over 3 million.

The comparison with total manufacturing employment in the United States can be made for a longer period, and puts the 1980s and 1990s in a different perspective (see table on p. 10). The move to overseas manufacturing employment took place mainly between 1957 and 1977, when about 300,000 foreign employees were added, almost tripling the number. Domestic manufacturing employment was also rising during those two decades by 2.6 million, so that the growth of foreign employment was not a matter of reducing employment in the United States.

Employment in foreign affiliates of US manufacturing
MNCs as per cent of total manufacturing employment
in the United States 1957–97

1957	10.9
1966	19.1
1977	26.0
1982	25.7
1989	23.3
1994	25.4
1995	25.6
1996	26.0
1997	26.9

Source: Table A1.4.

The absolute number of affiliate employees fell sharply in the decade after 1977, by something like 850,000, and the ratio to domestic US manufacturing employment fell also. Then, the number of foreign employees increased again, but in 1997 it remained below the 1977 level. Relative to domestic employment, foreign employment regained its earlier level, and by 1997, was slightly above it.

While the extent of internationalization of US manufacturing MNCs was about the same in 1996 as in 1977, the parent share of US manufacturing employment has declined steadily, from 60 per cent in 1977 to 46 per cent in 1997. As was the case for production, the parents' place as employers was mostly taken by foreign manufacturing firms. Employment in US affiliates of foreign manufacturing firms jumped from 3.5 per cent in 1977 to more than 12 per cent in 1997 (Zeile 1999; Table 8). Thus, US and foreign manufacturing MNCs were both internationalizing; each group increased its employment in the other group's region. In the US at least, the main result was a shift of manufacturing employment from US MNCs operating at home to foreign MNCs operating in the United States.

1.4. The geographical allocation of production and employment

Even if there had been no major growth in the overall importance of foreign production or employment, there could have been geographical shifts that might have affected domestic labor markets, such as an increase in the proportion of employment in developing, or low-wage, countries. If we divide the affiliate locations roughly into developed and developing, treating Canada, Europe, Japan, Australia, and New Zealand as developed, we find the following trend:

Gross product of MOFAs in developed countries as
per cent of total MOFA gross product, 1977–97

1977	65.9
1982	72.4
1989	81.8
1995	79.9
1996	78.5
1997	77.5

Source: Mataloni and Goldberg (1994); Mataloni
(1998, 1999).

Until the end of the 1980s, production by US MOFAs was increasingly
concentrated in developed countries. After that, a small rise occurred in the developing country share, but it still remains less than a quarter of the worldwide total,
a considerably smaller proportion than in 1977 and 1982.

US affiliate employment in developed countries
as per cent of total affiliate employment

	All affiliates	*MOFAs*
1966		71.5
1977	69.2	71.1
1982	67.0	67.9
1989	67.4	69.6
1995	63.8	66.4
1996	64.2	66.7
1997	62.8	65.7

Source: US Department of Commerce (1972),
(1981), Tables II.G3 and III. G3; (1985), Tables II.F3
and III.F3; (1992), Tables II.G3 and III.G3; Mataloni
(1998, 1999).

The developing countries' shares of US firms' foreign employment are somewhat larger than their shares of production, because output per worker is lower
in developing countries than in developed ones. The fluctuations in shares are
much smaller, however, perhaps because the influence of exchange rate changes
is eliminated. The trend seems to be toward a larger share of employment in
developing countries, especially in the 1990s, but most employment continues to

be in developed countries. The developing country share of MOFA employment rose from a little under 30 per cent in 1966 to 34 per cent thirty years later, probably not enough for major effects on US labor markets.

On the whole, it does not appear that aggregate movements in the location of production by US MNCs have been of a type or size to have any major effects on US labor markets as a whole. If that is the case, the place to look for possible impacts may be within the individual firm, rather than in aggregates of employment.

1.5. Parent employment in individual firms

Since the aggregate movements in production and employment, especially since 1977, do not appear likely to have had major domestic labor market effects in the United States, we turn next to studying possible impacts of overseas production on an individual firm's home employment. And since, as pointed out in the introduction, there are no indications from past studies that foreign production by a US firm reduces the firm's exports, and therefore its total production, we look for possible impacts elsewhere. We ask whether, even given the total level of production by a parent firm, its level of employment is affected by its choices about the allocation of different types of production to its home and foreign operations. Two firms with the same total parent firm (home) output might have different levels of home employment if they had made different allocations of their worldwide production. For example, one firm may have placed its labor-intensive operations abroad and retained only its capital-intensive operations at home while the other firm either had no foreign operations or did have them but did not split production between home and abroad by this criterion. The first firm would then have lower home employment for the same home production level. Another possibility might be that one firm places all the supervisory activity and research and marketing support for its worldwide production at home while the other firm spreads them around to its production locations. In that case, the first firm would have a higher level of home employment, given its home production.

A study for an earlier period (Lipsey *et al.* 1982) found strong evidence that capital intensities in US affiliates differed among locations in response to differences in factor prices. Capital intensities were much higher in developed country affiliates than in those in developing countries, where wages were far lower. That was true for affiliate aggregates within industries, and remains true, according to the latest BEA survey (US Department of Commerce 1998b).

It was also true among affiliates within individual US multinationals, and it was pointed out that a positive relationship between the price of labor and the capital intensity of affiliate production could represent several different phenomena. One is adaptation to factor price differences by choosing different factor proportions along a single isoquant. Another is adaptation by choosing different technologies to produce the same product in different countries. A third is various types of allocation or, as described there, selection of products or sub-industries from among those in the firm's repertoire.

The first two explanations of the relationship would not imply any impact on an MNC's home production, but the third one would, if the allocation included the firm's home country operations. The earlier study could not distinguish among these alternative explanations because home country operations were not covered, but they are included in this paper.

We examine this question here by running a set of regression equations in which parent employment (PEMP) is related to parent production (PNS), proxied by parent net sales (sales minus imports from affiliates abroad) and affiliate production (ANS), proxied by affiliate net sales (affiliate sales minus imports from the parent). We also have experimented with variants separating different types of affiliates. The equations presented here for all affiliates are similar to those for manufacturing alone in Blomström *et al.* (1997), and in some respects to those in Kravis and Lipsey (1988).

The first equation (with constant term suppressed, *t*-values in parentheses) suggests that there is some allocation of labor-intensive activities to foreign operations, since the coefficient for ANS is negative.

$$PEMP = 5.55PNS(53.7) - 1.10ANS(8.9)$$

$$RSQ(corr.) = 0.666 \quad No. Obs. = 2,054 \tag{1}$$

However, the same equation in log form gives the opposite result:

$$Ln\ PEMP = 0.867\ Ln\ PNS(75.4) + 0.020\ Ln\ ANS(1.9)$$

$$RSQ(corr.) = 0.815 \quad No. Obs. = 2,054 \tag{2}$$

The log form gives a heavier weight to the differences at the lower end of the size scale, and the difference in the signs of the coefficients suggests that the negative influence comes from the largest affiliates. That suspicion is confirmed to some degree by arithmetic equations omitting the 150 largest affiliates, which produce positive, but only marginally significant, coefficients for ANS.

If we divide parent firms into manufacturing and non-manufacturing parents, we find the overall negative effect in both groups:

$$MPEMP = 5.95PNS(55.8) - 0.775ANS(5.56)$$

$$RSQ(corr.) = 0.853 \quad No. Obs. = 1,296 \tag{3}$$

$$NMPEMP = 5.03PNS(26.3) - 1.446ANS(6.9)$$

$$RSQ(corr.) = 0.495 \quad No. Obs. = 759 \tag{4}$$

Despite the emphasis on reallocation in manufacturing, the effect seems to be stronger in the non-manufacturing sector. One problem is the heterogeneity of that sector. A major part of production there is in the Petroleum industry, which includes all activities of firms in that group, whether they are in extraction, refining, transportation, or retailing.

If we separate affiliate net sales into those by manufacturing affiliates (ANSM) and those by affiliates in non-manufacturing industries (ANSNM), the negative effect on home employment appears, somewhat surprisingly, to be concentrated in the non-manufacturing affiliates.

$$PEMP = 5.52PNS(53.6) - 0.37ANSM(1.7) - 2.25\ ANSNM(7.2)$$

$$RSQ(corr.) = 0.668 \quad No.\ Obs. = 2,054 \tag{5}$$

However, if we examine manufacturing parents separately, it is clear that the negative coefficient for non-manufacturing affiliates comes entirely from the non-manufacturing sector:

$$MPEMP = 6.02PNS(56.9) - 1.63ANSM(8.2) + 1.66ANSNM(3.9)$$

$$RSQ(corr.) = 0.866 \quad No.\ Obs. = 1,295 \tag{6}$$

Among manufacturing MNCs, the negative association is only with the sales of manufacturing affiliates; higher sales by non-manufacturing affiliates are associated with higher home employment. The allocation of labor-intensive activities to foreign affiliates by manufacturing firms mainly involves manufacturing operations themselves.

If firms are reallocating production to take advantage of factor price differences, and in particular, labor price differences, it would be reasonable to expect that production in developing countries would reflect this motivation more than production in developed countries. Average wages in developed country affiliates of manufacturing parents in 1989, the year of this cross-section, were only 10 per cent below parent firm averages. Average wages in developing country affiliates, however, were about 75 per cent below the parent level. It would therefore be to such countries that production would be allocated for labor cost saving. We therefore test whether the negative influence on parent employment, given parent production, comes mainly from production by affiliates in developing countries (ANSLDC) or from production by affiliates in developed countries (ANSDC).

$$PEMP = 5.46PNS(53.8) + 0.472ANSDC(2.3) - 10.1ANSLDC(10.5)$$

$$RSQ(corr.) = 0.679 \quad No.\ Obs. = 2,054 \tag{7}$$

That expectation is strongly confirmed by equation (7). Production in developed countries adds to parent employment per unit of home output while production in developing countries reduces it.

It should be noted that the log version of the equation does not suggest this type of allocation of production.

$$Ln\ PEMP = 0.849\ Ln\ PNS(77.1) + 0.036\ Ln\ ANSDC(6.5)$$

$$+\ 0.004\ Ln\ ANSLDC(0.9)$$

$$RSQ(corr.) = 0.818 \quad No.\ Obs. = 2,054 \tag{8}$$

The log equation, giving heavier weight to the smaller affiliates, suggests that affiliate production in developed countries adds to parent employment, given parent production, but that production in developing countries has no effect on parent employment.

If we examine the impact separately for manufacturing and non-manufacturing parents, the strong influence of the production in developing countries is evident:

$$MPEMP = 5.96PNS(56.1) - 0.286DCANS(1.31) - 4.806LDCANS(3.47)$$

$$RSQ(corr.) = 0.864 \quad No. \ Obs. = 1,296 \tag{9}$$

$$NMPEMP = 5.02PNS(26.7) + 0.185DCANS(0.5) - 9.47LDCANS(5.9)$$

$$RSQ(corr.) = 0.511 \quad No. \ Obs. = 759 \tag{10}$$

Given the supposed non-tradability of many of the services included in the non-manufacturing sector, the large negative coefficient for production in developing countries is surprising, because the MNCs could not allocate production to developing countries for sale in developed countries. However, if the petroleum industry is important in the results, the negative coefficient would be more understandable, although the motivation would in that case involve mainly resource costs other than labor. Only a disaggregation of the non-manufacturing sector could answer this question.

The ability of MNCs to allocate production in response to factor price differences might be affected by host country characteristics, including trade policies. To test this possibility, we divided developing countries into two groups, one we thought of as outward-oriented, and the other inward-oriented. The former group includes Asian countries, except for India, and Mexico, and the latter group includes other developing countries. The coefficients for sales by the two groups were sharply different, despite the crudeness of the classification:

$$MPEMP = 6.15PNS(54.7) + 0.11ANSDC(0.5) + 0.86ANSLDCO(0.3)$$

$$- 23.50ANSLDCI(10.2)$$

$$RSQ(corr.) = 0.876 \quad No. \ Obs. = 1,296 \tag{11}$$

All of the effects on parent employment appear to be associated with production in countries with relatively inward-looking trade policy. Neither production in developed countries nor production in outward-oriented developing countries affected home employment. These results raise the possibility that some allocation in response to factor costs may be a consequence of production location biased by host country rules.

Within manufacturing, it is possible to examine some of these relationships in several major groups of industries. A listing of only the ANS coefficients from equations explaining parent employment, given parent production, shows that negative coefficients, which we interpret as indicating allocation by degree of capital intensity, are not ubiquitous.

	ANS	t	RSQ(corr.)
Foods	−0.28	0.8	0.44
Chemicals	−0.67	1.6	0.87
Metals	−0.40	0.7	0.87
Non-Elect. Mach.	0.83	5.7	0.97
Elect. Mach. & Equip.	4.03	6.1	0.97
Transp. Equip.	−7.53	26.5	0.99

In two major industries of US manufacturing direct investment abroad, the two machinery industries, the relationship of affiliate production to home employment is positive; more affiliate production means more home employment, given the level of home production. Only in Transport Equipment, mainly motor vehicles, is there strong evidence for the allocation of labor-intensive production to affiliates.

If we characterize the affiliates by the distinctions made in equation (11), there is considerably more evidence of effects on home employment in the various ANS coefficients:

	DC	LDC-Outward	LDC-Inward	RSQ(corr.)
Foods	−7.87(2.8)	98.9(4.7)	−96.4(3.2)	0.601
Chemicals	−1.13(1.6)	−16.0(3.2)	9.4(2.3)	0.873
Metals	−7.29(4.9)	112.3(8.4)	−11.0(2.8)	0.890
Non-Elect. Mach.	0.68(4.0)	3.7(1.1)	−12.8(2.1)	0.969
Elect. Mach. & Equip.	6.70(5.4)	4.1(1.5)	−15.1(3.5)	0.973
Transp. Equip.	−8.07(13.1)	−28.0(3.9)	9.6(3.2)	0.993

For only one industry group, Foods, was the equation substantially improved by this breakdown of affiliate locations. In three of the industry groups, Foods, Metals, and Transport Equipment, the coefficients for developed country affiliate net sales are negative and significant, suggesting some allocation of labor-intensive activities to affiliates, but in the two machinery industries, the coefficients are positive. Food industry affiliates are particularly oriented to their host country markets, as are, to a smaller extent, affiliates in Chemicals and Metals, but those in the Transport Equipment group are export-oriented, as are those in the two machinery groups. Thus, the apparent allocation effect is not associated with export orientation, as we expected, but more with orientation to local sales among these developed country affiliates, Transport Equipment being a conspicuous exception.

Among developing country affiliates, the evidence for allocation of labor-intensive production is mainly in the countries classified here as inward-oriented, the exceptions being Chemicals and Transport Equipment, where the affiliates in outward-oriented developing countries showed the negative coefficients we associate with allocation by the MNCs. On the whole, it appears that it is the outward-oriented industries and locations that require complementary employment at home and the inward-oriented ones that involve the allocation of labor-intensive activities to affiliates.

In general, the coefficients for sales by developed country affiliates are smaller than those for affiliates in developing countries. One reason may be that the wage differences between the United States and many other developed countries were not large in 1989, and some developed countries had higher nominal wages. The motivation for allocating labor-intensive production to developed countries was therefore slight.

A possible ground for skepticism about some of these coefficients is the fact that when squared terms for affiliate sales are added to the equations, the coefficients for ANS change considerably. For example, in foods, both ANS terms turn positive while the squared terms are negative and significant. The Chemicals equation is not affected much but the large positive coefficient in Metals is much reduced and becomes insignificant, while the squared term is positive and significant. In the two machinery industries, the terms for inward-oriented countries become positive and significant. In fact, no significant negative term for ANS remains. It is difficult to judge without access to the data, but the effects of including the squared terms suggest that the results are heavily influenced by the largest affiliates. Taken literally, the coefficients could imply that small affiliates tend to lead to higher home employment for supervision or other headquarters functions while large affiliates are used as locations for labor-intensive activities.

1.6. Affiliate production and parent wage levels

If foreign operations affect the labor intensity of a firm's home operations, they might also affect the skill intensity of the parent firm. Again, there are at least two possible avenues for such effects. One is that low-skill operations may be allocated to foreign affiliates, particularly those in developing countries, resulting in a higher skill mix, and presumably a higher average wage, at home. The other avenue is that higher levels of foreign activity may require more staff at home for supervision and financial oversight. In this case, both effects go in the same direction; more foreign production should lead to higher wages at home.

Average parent wages increase with size of parent, as represented by parent net sales (PNS). However, the effect does not appear to be linear, but declines as parent firms are larger, and we therefore include in the equations a term for PNS squared:

$$PW = 0.055PNS(2.43) - 0.011PNSSQ(3.34) + 0.082ANS(2.78)$$

$$RSQ(corr.) = 0.025 \tag{12}$$

Not much of wage variation among parents is explained by this equation, but larger foreign production is associated with higher average earnings, presumably from a higher average skill level, at home.

To the extent that allocation of low-skill activities to low-wage countries was an important element of this effect, production in developing countries should have a greater impact than production in developed countries:

$$PW = 0.05PNS(2.17) - 0.11PNSSQ(3.33) + 0.054ANSDC(1.53)$$
$$+ 0.0039ANSLDC(1.81)$$
$$RSQ(corr.) = 0.026. \tag{13}$$

If anything, production in developed countries seems to have a greater impact on parent wage levels than production in developing countries, but neither coefficient is significant and too much weight should not be placed on them. Similar equations with dummy variables for three-digit industries do not alter the results.

Wage equations for the individual industry groups produced few coefficients for affiliate sales that were even marginally significant. In Chemicals and in the miscellaneous collection called 'Other manufacturing,' coefficients for sales by developing country affiliates were a positive influence on parent average wages, but the coefficients for the squared terms were negative. In metals, the coefficient for production in affiliates in inward-oriented regions was positive and significant.

The weak evidence we find on wages points to positive relations between affiliate production and parent wage levels. However, there is hardly any evidence to support the idea that allocation of low-skill operations to affiliates, rather than requirements for headquarters services, is the crucial factor.

1.7. Conclusions

There is no indication in aggregate data that movements of production from the United States to foreign affiliates of US firms have had any negative effect on employment by parent firms or in the United States as a whole, at least in the past twenty years. Even if such movements in production by US MNCs could have that effect, they cannot explain recent labor force developments because there has been almost no shift of production or employment by US firms. Some continued shifts to foreign locations have taken place in US manufacturing firms, but these have been offset by matching shifts into the United States on the part of foreign manufacturing firms.

A regression analysis of individual firm data does point to some effects of foreign production on employment within firms. Higher levels of affiliate production in developing countries are associated with lower parent employment for any given level of parent production at home. The allocation by MNCs of the more labor-intensive segments of their production to their developing country affiliates and the more capital-intensive segments to their home operations reduces the labor intensity of their home production and thus their demand for labor for any given level of home production. There is only weak evidence for a wage or skill effect. If there is any effect it is that foreign operations are associated with higher wages at home.

We do provide at least a partial answer to the question raised in an earlier paper by Lipsey *et al.* (1982). That is whether the low-capital intensities of affiliates in developing countries involve simply responses to low-labor costs by changing factor pro portions for identical products or processes. The answer here is that at least some of the reason for low-capital intensities is the MNCs' choice of which products to produce in low-wage countries.

Appendix

Table A1.1 Gross product of nonbank US multinational firms and US GDP

	Parents and MOFAs ($ million)	Parents ($ million)	MOFAs ($ million)	US GDP ($ billion)
1966	n.a.	n.a.	36,752	787.8
1970	n.a.	n.a.	54,720	1,035.6
1977	651,665	490,529	161,136	2,026.9
1982	1,019,734	796,017	223,717	3,242.1
1983	n.a	n.a	216,683	3,514.5
1984	n.a	n.a	220,331	3,902.4
1985	n.a	n.a	220,074	4,180.7
1986	n.a	n.a	231,644	4,422.2
1987	n.a	n.a	269,734	4,692.3
1988	n.a	n.a	297,556	5,049.6
1989	1,364,878	1,044,884	319,994	5,438.7
1990	n.a	n.a	356,033	5,743.8
1991	n.a	n.a	355,963	5,916.7
1992	n.a	n.a	361,524	6,244.4
1993	n.a	n.a	359,179	6,558.1
1994	1,717,488	1,313,792	403,696	6,947.0
1995	1,831,046	1,365,470	465,576	7,269.6
1996	1,978,948	1,480,638	498,310	7,661.6
1997	2,089,796	1,570,490	519,306	8,110.9

Sources: Howenstine (1977), Table 1; Lipsey *et al.* (1998), Table 1; Mataloni and Goldberg (1994); Mataloni (1998); Seskin (1998), Table 1; Mataloni (1999), Table 1; US Department of Commerce (1999), Table 1.1.

Table A1.2 Employment of nonbank US multinational firms and total US employment (thousands)

	MNCs		Parents	Affiliates		Total employment US
	Parents and all affiliates	Parents and MOFAs		All affiliates	MOFAs	
1957				3,178		61,308
1966					3,874	73,516
1977	26,081	24,254	18,885	7,197	5,369	90,421
1982	25,345	23,727	18,705	6,640	5,022	97,763
1983	24,783	23,253	18,400	6,383	4,854	98,529
1984	24,548	22,973	18,131	6,418	4,842	103,123
1985	24,532	22,923	18,113	6,419	4,810	105,804
1986	24,082	22,543	17,832	6,250	4,711	107,737
1987	24,255	22,650	17,986	6,270	4,664	110,751
1988	24,141	22,498	17,738	6,404	4,761	113,906
1989	25,388	23,879	18,765	6,622	5,114	116,642
1990	25,264	23,786	18,430	6,834	5,356	117,557
1991	24,837	23,345	17,959	6,878	5,387	116,630
1992	24,190	22,812	17,530	6,660	5,282	117,116
1993	24,222	22,760	17,537	6,685	5,223	118,772
1994	25,670	24,273	18,565	7,105	5,707	121,695
1995	25,921	24,500	18,576	7,345	5,924	124,576
1996	26,334	24,867	18,790	7,544	6,077	127,015
1997	27,885	26,392	19,867	8,018	6,525	129,980

Sources: Lipsey (1989), Mataloni (1992, 1998, 1999), Seskin (1998), US Department of Commerce (1998a), Vol. 2, Table 6.4, and (1999), Table B.8.

Table A1.3 Gross product of US multinational manufacturing firms and US manufacturing gross product

	Parents and MOFAs ($ million)	Parents ($ million)	MOFAs ($ million)	US gross manufacturing output ($ billion)
1977	382,280	301,286	80,994	462.6
1982	542,689	421,050	121,639	649.8
1989	793,771	586,568	207,203	1,013.5
1995	1,023,697	723,182	300,515	1,282.2
1996	1,071,324	764,725	306,599	1,309.1
1997	1,080,824	765,122	315,702	1,378.9

Sources: Lum and Yuskavage (1997); Mataloni and Goldberg (1994); Mataloni (1998, 1999); US Department of Commerce (1999), Table B.3.

Table A1.4 Employment of US multinational manufacturing firms and total US manufacturing employment 1957, 1966, 1977 and 1982–97 (thousands)

	MNCs		Parents and MOFAs by industry of		Parents	All affiliates by industry of		MOFAs by industry of		US part-time & full time employment in manufacturing[a]
	Parents and all affiliates by industry of									
	Parent	Affiliate	Parent	Affiliate		Parent	Affiliate	Parent	Affiliate	
1957	15,347					(1,846)[b]	1,700			17,009
1966		16,630	14,247			(3,654)[c]			2,615	19,138
1977				15,548	11,775	(5,272)[b]	4,855	3,714	3,773	19,601
1982	15,104	14,966		13,890	10,533	4,814	4,433		3,358	18,750
1983	15,350	14,723		13,694	10,493	4,611	4,230		3,201	18,366
1984	15,194	15,030		13,906	10,660	4,689	4,370		3,245	19,329
1985	14,849	14,852		13,705	10,503	4,692	4,349		3,202	19,207
1986	14,606	14,552		13,523	10,431	4,418	4,121		3,092	18,901
1987	14,292	14,314		13,226	10,196	4,410	4,118		3,030	18,951
1988	14,640	13,964		12,878	9,820	4,473	4,144		3,058	19,321
1989		14,318	13,791	13,374	10,127	4,513	4,191	3,664	3,247	19,365
1990		14,138	13,458	13,182	9,805	(4,586)[d]	4,333	3,741	3,377	18,984
1991		13,773	13,293	12,814	9,514	(4,612)[d]	4,259	3,779	3,300	18,374
1992		13,255	13,012	12,515	9,246	(4,575)[d]	4,009	3,766	3,269	18,023
1993		12,999	12,684	12,245	9,019	(4,430)[d]	3,980	3,664	3,226	18,025
1994	13,692	13,313	12,908	12,565	9,049	4,643	4,263	3,858	3,516	18,281
1995	13,811	13,423	13,224	12,685	9,080	(4,731)[e]	4,344	4,144	3,606	18,448
1996	13,745	13,353	13,044	12,626	8,960	(4,785)[e]	4,393	4,084	3,666	18,436
1997	13,625	13,216	12,843	12,503	8,623	(5,002)[e]	4,593	4,220	3,880	18,621

Sources: Lowe and Mataloni (1991); Mataloni (1992, 1993, 1994, 1995, 1996, 1997, 1998, 1999); Mataloni and Fahim-Nader (1996); Seskin (1998); US Department of Commerce (1999), Table B.8; Whichard (1989).

a Excluding Petroleum and Coal Products.
b Extrapolated from 1982 by employment by industry of affiliate.
c Extrapolated from 1977 by MOFA employment by industry of affiliate.
d Extrapolated from 1977 by employment by industry of affiliate.
e Interpolated between 1989 and 1994 by employment by industry of affiliate.
e Extrapolated from 1994 by employment by industry of affiliate.

References

Blomström, M., Fors, G. and Lipsey, R. (1997) 'Foreign direct investment and employment: home country experience in the United States and Sweden', *Economic Journal*, 107: 1787–97.

Howenstine, Ned G. (1977) 'Gross product of foreign affiliates of US companies', *Survey of Current Business*, 57: 17–28, February.

Kravis, I. and Lipsey, R. (1988) 'The effect of multinational firms' foreign operations on their domestic employment', NBER Working Paper No. 2760, November.

Lipsey, R. (1989) 'The internationalization of production', NBER Working Paper No. 2293, Cambridge, MA, National Bureau of Economic Research.

Lipsey, R., Blomström, M. and Ramstetter, E. (1998) 'Internationalized production in world output', in R. Baldwin, R. Lipsey and J. Richardson (eds), *Geography and Ownership as Bases for Economic Accounting*, Studies in Income and Wealth, Vol. 59, Chicago: University of Chicago Press for the NBER, pp. 83–135.

Lipsey, R., Kravis, I. and Roldan, R. (1982) 'Do multinational firms adapt factor proportions to relative factor prices?', in A. Krueger (ed.), *Trade and Employment in Developing Countries: 2. Factor Supply and Substitution.* Chicago: University of Chicago Press, pp. 215–55.

Lowe, J. and Mataloni, R. Jr (1991) 'US direct investment abroad: 1989 benchmark survey results', *Survey of Current Business*, 71: 29–55, October.

Lum, S. and Yuskavage, R. (1997) 'Gross product by industry, 1947–1996', *Survey of Current Business*, 77: 20–35, November.

Mataloni, R. Jr (1992) 'US multinational companies: operations in 1990', *Survey of Current Business,* 72: 60–78, August.

Mataloni, R. Jr (1993) 'US multinational companies: operations in 1991', *Survey of Current Business,* 73: 40–58, July.

Mataloni, R. Jr (1994) 'US multinational companies: operations in 1993', *Survey of Current Business,* 74: 42–62, June.

Mataloni, R. Jr (1995) 'US multinational companies: operations in 1993', *Survey of Current Business,* 75: 31–51, June.

Mataloni, R. Jr (1996) 'US multinational companies: operations in 1994', *Survey of Current Business,* 76: 31–51, June.

Mataloni, R. Jr (1997) 'US multinational companies: operations in 1995', *Survey of Current Business,* 77: 44–68, October.

Mataloni, R. Jr (1998) 'US multinational companies: operations in 1996', *Survey of Current Business,* 78: 47–73, September.

Mataloni, R. Jr (1999) 'US multinational companies: operations in 1997', *Survey of Current Business,* 79: 8–35.

Mataloni, R. Jr and Fahim-Nader, M. (1996) 'Operations of US multinational companies: preliminary results from the 1994 benchmark survey', *Survey of Current Business,* 76: 11–37, December.

Mataloni, R. Jr and Goldberg, L. (1994) 'Gross product of US multinational companies 1977–91', *Survey of Current Business*, 74: 42–63, April.

Seskin, E. (1998) 'Annual revision of the national income and product accounts', *Survey of Current Business,* 78: 7–166, August.

US Department of Commerce (1972) *US Direct Investment Abroad, 1966: Final Data*, A Supplement to the Survey of Current Business, Washington, DC, Bureau of Economic Analysis, US Department of Commerce, no date.

US Department of Commerce (1981) 'US direct investment abroad: 1977', Washington, DC, Bureau of Economic Analysis, April.

US Department of Commerce (1985) 'US direct investment abroad, 1982', *Benchmark Survey Data*, Washington, DC, Bureau of Economic Analysis, December.

US Department of Commerce (1992) 'US direct investment abroad: 1989', *Benchmark Survey Final Results*, Washington, DC, Bureau of Economic Analysis, October.

US Department of Commerce (1998a) 'National income and product accounts of the United States 1929–1994', Washington, DC, Bureau of Economic Analysis, US Department of Commerce, April.

US Department of Commerce (1998b) 'US direct investment abroad: 1994', *Benchmark Survey Final Results*, Washington, DC, Bureau of Economic Analysis, May.

US Department of Commerce (1999) 'National data'. *Survey of Current Business*, 79: D-2-50.

Whichard, O. G. (1989) 'Us multinational companies: operations in 1987, *Survey of Current Business*, 69: 27–39, June.

Zeile, W. (1999) 'Foreign direct investment in the United States: preliminary results from the 1997 Benchmark Survey', *Survey of Current Business,* 79: 21–54.

2

FOREIGN DIRECT INVESTMENT AND EMPLOYMENT*

Home country experience in Italy

Sergio Mariotti and Lucia Piscitello

2.1. Introduction

In the context of the increasing multinationalization of firms and markets, foreign direct investment (FDI) is considered more and more responsible for welfare in the host country because of advantages related to the introduction of new technologies and innovation, new managerial techniques, skills (Caves 1974; Blomström 1989; Cantwell 1989; Wang and Blomström 1992; Perez 1997), capital, new jobs created/safeguarded and the establishment of local industrial sectors (Blomström 1991; Haddad and Harrison 1993; Markusen and Venables 1999). Likewise, the impact of international activities on the home country economy has been largely debated although predominantly through anecdotal evidence and case studies. In particular, the relationship between firms' foreign production activities and domestic employment attracted the most interest in the international literature. As a consequence, the theoretical debate about the impact of the firms' foreign activities on their home country employment is lively and it mainly focuses on three fundamental issues: (i) whether production by foreign affiliates of a home country's firms is a substitute or a complement to home country production by the parent firms or by other home-country firms (e.g. Frank and Freeman 1978; Jordan and Vahlne 1981; Glickman and Woodward 1989; Blomström and Kokko 1994; Krugman 1994; Lawrence 1994, 1996; Lipsey 1994; Messerlin 1995; Agarwal 1996); (ii) the impact of foreign activities on the domestic employment structure and on the wage differentials (e.g. Kravis and Lipsey 1988;

*The financial support of a Fondo di Ricerca Ateneo (Evoluzione del processo di internazionalizzazione dell'industria italiana) is gratefully acknowledged. The authors wish to express their thanks to Salvatore Baldone, Massimo Colombo, Paola Garrone, Fabio Sdogati for their useful comments and suggestions. The paper is a joint effort by the authors. Nonetheless, Sergio Mariotti drafted Sections 2.2 and 2.6, and Lucia Piscitello Sections 2.1, 2.3, 2.4 and 2.6.

Brainard and Riker 1997); and (iii) the impact of foreign activities on the labour intensity of home production (e.g. Blomström *et al*. 1997; Fors and Kokko 1999; Lipsey 1999).

Most existing literature refers to the US case (e.g. Hawkins 1972; US Tariff Commission 1973; Frank and Freeman 1978; Glickman and Woodward 1989; Lipsey 1994; Almeida 1997; Brainard and Riker 1997; Lipsey 1999), while more recent studies have begun to raise the issue with reference to some European countries too (e.g. Blomström *et al*. 1997; Fors and Kokko 1999, for Sweden; Messerlin 1994, for France; Agarwal 1996, Nunnenkamp 1998, for Germany). However, evidence proposed with reference to the Italian case has been quite scanty and limited to some explorative studies about de-localization of production by Italian firms towards developing countries (Mutinelli and Piscitello 1997; Faini *et al*. 1998; Barba *et al*. 1999).[1]

The present paper belongs to approach (iii), addressing the issue of the impact of FDI on the labour intensity of home production. Empirical evidence is provided with reference to the Italian case in the decade 1985–95, a period in which FDI undertaken by Italian firms experienced a noteworthy upsurge while, on the contrary, domestic employment experienced a relevant reduction.

The remaining of the paper is organized as follows. In Section 2.2 we discuss the theoretical framework and develop hypotheses as to the effects of FDI on the labour intensity of domestic production. In Section 2.3 we present data employed in the empirical study. Section 2.4 illustrates the model and the variables and Section 2.5 presents the empirical findings. Some summarizing remarks in Section 2.6 conclude the paper.

2.2. International growth and domestic employment: the theoretical framework

Traditional literature states that firms expanding their production in low cost, less developed countries tend to substitute domestic employees with employees in foreign affiliates. In particular, firms which undertake *vertical* investment actually dismantle the structure of their value chain through the re-localization of labour-intensive activities in low-cost countries. As a consequence, the typology of domestic production changes, since both the capital and the highly skilled labour intensity increase. The effect on the domestic market would be, *ceteris paribus*, a net decrease in the employment level. Nonetheless, because of other compensatory effects the *ceteris paribus* condition does not hold. In fact, the increased efficiency associated with the new structure of the production chain can enhance the parent company's competitive position and increase its (domestic and foreign) market share through positive externalities exerted on domestic production and demand. Additionally, some complementarities between foreign and domestic production can arise thanks to the foreign trade flows stimulated by the presence *in loco*, which facilitates commercial penetration.[2]

Moreover, we argue that this is only part of the story. Vertical de-localization can have effects not just on the parent company's domestic employment, but even on the business environment in which it operates, with particular reference to subcontracting relations and the local externalities induced by the demand (originated by the parent company) for specialized inputs, services, managerial and operative skills (Rodriguez-Clare 1996). Indeed, production in foreign affiliates could induce: (i) *substitutive* effects on domestic employment, whenever it causes the write-off of previous subcontracting relations and/or the reduction of the local demand for goods and services; (ii) *complementary* effects, whenever the enhanced competitive position (and innovativeness) of the parent company and its additional demand for specialized inputs increase the local externalities.

Summarizing the effects just mentioned, the canonical interpretation states that an increase of foreign production in less developed countries implies a contraction in the labour intensity of domestic production both at the level of the parent company itself and at the level of the environment in which it operates. On the contrary, it seems difficult to state anything about the absolute levels of domestic employment. The literature suggests different arguments when FDI is undertaken in advanced countries (for a survey see Agarwal 1997), namely that FDI mainly pursues horizontal market seeking strategies, and several mechanisms can increase the labour intensity of domestic production. In particular, the expansion into large international markets requires more supervision, coordination and control over the activities geographically dispersed, as well as the extension of the activities and functions (i.e. R&D, marketing) generally centralized at the parent level (Blömstrom *et al.* 1997; Fors and Kokko 1999). As a consequence, the parent company's requirements for highly skilled and white collar workers increase; and such effects could extend to the whole economic area in which the parent operates, because of the externalities generated by the induced demand for specialized inputs and skilled labour. Lastly, the net employment level could rise because of several complementary activities induced by the FDI which often compensate substitution between foreign production and foreign trade.[3]

Within this theoretical framework, the present paper aims to investigate the relationship between the variation that occurred in the labour intensity of domestic production in the manufacturing industry in the period 1985–95, and the variation of employees in foreign affiliates by Italian firms in the same interval. The model developed, far from being a micro-founded structural model, suggests a descriptive equation which focuses on the effects induced by FDI on the factor proportion in domestic production, once controlling for domestic production itself has been taken into account. In particular, the hypotheses advanced are the following:

(1) FDI undertaken in less developed countries – generally associated with vertical investment – tends to reduce the labour intensity of the home country domestic production;

26

(2) FDI undertaken in advanced countries – horizontal investment – tends to increase the labour intensity of the home country domestic production.

The approach employed stretches back to a previous approach suggested by Blomström *et al.* (1997) which deals with the issue of factor proportions in US and Swedish home operations, asking whether production abroad tends to raise or lower the labour intensity of home production. Nonetheless, the present paper extends it because:

(a) the observation unit is not the single firm, but the *industrial region*, defined as the ensemble of firms operating in the same industrial macro-sector – constituted by interdependent sectors belonging to the same industrial filière – and localized in the same geographical region; and
(b) it refers to the variation of domestic and foreign employment, rather than to their absolute stock levels.

As far as the observation unit is concerned, the analysis at the single-firm level would not allow us to take into account how foreign production affects the parent's relevant business environment. The fundamental hypothesis is that the lion's share of such impact is sectorally and spatially circumscribed within the industrial region (as previously defined) in which the firm operates and carries out most of its external relations. As far as the Italian case is concerned, the hypothesis is corroborated by the distinctive nature of the Italian industrial system in which competitiveness is grounded on a specific structure based on industrial districts (Becattini 1990), which allows us to exploit agglomerative advantages and to capture the efficiency of proximity between suppliers and users (Porter 1992).

Concerning the temporal dimension, the analysis of the variation – rather than the stock levels – of domestic and foreign employment constitutes a richer and more precise approach. Indeed, it also allows us to rule out time-invariant omitted variables and to take into account any lagged and leaded effects.

2.3. Data

Data considered relate to employment in foreign manufacturing affiliates by Italian firms, and to domestic employment in Italy in manufacturing sectors, in the decade 1985–95. In particular, two different data sets have been employed:

(i) the data set of the Italian National Institute for Social Security, which records employment in Italy, at both the sectoral (manufacturing sector) and geographical (administrative region) levels;
(ii) the data set Reprint, which provides censuses of foreign manufacturing affiliates by Italian firms.[4]

Table 2.1 Employment in the manufacturing foreign affiliates and national employment in manufacturing sectors

Year	No. of Italian parents	No. of foreign affiliates	No. of employees in the foreign affiliates	Total no. of employees in Italy	Ratio of foreign to domestic (%)
1985	282	697	244,188	4,808,375	4.96
1987	295	843	364,495	4,731,711	7.58
1989	340	1,075	435,690	4,933,086	7.20
1991	444	1,394	551,565	4,849,981	11.21
1993	619	1,709	578,294	4,420,743	13.05
1995	723	1,950	589,438	4,515,891	13.19
1997	804	2,034	606,266	n.a.	n.a.

Source: Data set Reprint (CNEL–R&P–Politecnico di Milano) and INPS (Italian National Institute for Social Security).

The dynamics of the two phenomena are illustrated in Tables 2.1 and 2.2. In particular, the first section of Table 2.1 shows the number of Italian parent companies investing abroad in manufacturing sectors, as well as the number of their foreign affiliates and employees, in the period considered. In the second section of Table 2.1 is reported the total number of domestic employees in manufacturing in Italy, as well as the percentage ratio of foreign to domestic employment in manufacturing, in the same period. It emerges that employees in foreign manufacturing affiliates of Italian firms more than doubled in the decade considered (from nearly 244,000 to almost 590,000 employees). International growth concerned both advanced and less developed countries (Table 2.2). As far as the former is concerned, the 1980s witnessed the greatest increase, particularly in Western Europe; while the 1990s recorded a noteworthy contraction in foreign employment both in Western Europe and in North America. Concerning less developed countries, foreign initiatives by Italian firms in Eastern Europe and Asia rose, while remaining more stable in Latin America and Africa. Summarizing, at the end of 1995 the geographical division of foreign employees in Italian affiliates is the following: 40.1 per cent in Western Europe, 17.1 per cent in Eastern Europe, 14.8 per cent in Latin America, 12.2 per cent in Asia, 10.4 per cent in North America, 5.3 per cent in other residual areas.

During the same period, the number of employees in manufacturing firms in Italy decreased from nearly 4.8 million to little more than 4.5 million (see Table 2.1). As a consequence, in the period under examination the percentage ratio of foreign to domestic employment increases from 5.1 to 13.1 per cent.

The concomitance of the two opposite trends does not allow us to infer any conclusions about the relationship between foreign and domestic employment; the illustration of data just provides the quantitative scenario in which to posit the following analyses. Nevertheless, the data sources employed allows us to break down information about employment both by sectors and by geographical region in order to operationalize the idea that the relationship between foreign and

Table 2.2 Evolution of the geographical distribution of foreign affiliates of Italian firms, 1985–95

	1985		1992		1996	
	No.	%	No.	%	No.	%
Foreign affiliates (no.)						
Western Europe	318	45.6	740	53.1	890	45.6
Central and Eastern Europe	4	0.6	101	7.2	346	17.7
North America	112	16.1	195	14.0	209	10.7
Latin America	124	17.8	151	10.8	184	9.4
Asia	53	7.6	104	7.5	195	10.0
Oceania	8	1.1	11	0.8	17	0.9
Africa	78	11.2	92	6.6	109	5.6
Total	697	100.0	1,394	100.0	1,950	100.0
Employees of foreign affiliates (no.)						
Western Europe	88,256	36.1	262,972	47.7	236,456	40.1
Central and Eastern Europe	2,100	0.9	30,862	5.6	100,628	17.1
North America	32,868	13.5	73,082	13.2	61,388	10.4
Latin America	66,062	27.1	91,134	16.5	87,253	14.8
Asia	26,405	10.8	62,782	11.4	72,189	12.2
Oceania	1,010	0.4	1,443	0.3	1,794	0.3
Africa	27,487	11.3	29,290	5.3	29,730	5.0
Total	244,188	100.0	551,565	100.0	589,438	100.0

Source: Data set Reprint (CNEL–R&P–Politecnico di Milano).

domestic employment should be better analyzed at the industrial region level. In particular, as a proxy for the industrial region, we considered the combination of the 20 Italian administrative regions (defined at the NUTS2 level), and of nine sectors (see Table 2.3).[5] Such a definition allows us to capture most of the interdependencies between the multinational firm and its business environment with reference to both intersectoral relations and their spatial dimension. The 180 observations (see Appendix 1) thus obtained assure good statistical significance for the model developed.

2.4. The model

The model developed investigates the relationship between the variation of domestic employees and the variation of employees in foreign affiliates by Italian manufacturing firms, given the variation in the domestic production level and accounting for the effects of technical progress upon the productivity of labour.

The estimated equation is the following:

$$\Delta EMPH_i = f(\Delta PRODH_i, \Delta EMPF_i, R\&D_i, \Delta PRODH_i^2) \tag{1}$$

$$i = 1, \ldots, 180$$

Table 2.3 Macro-sectors and administrative regions constituting the 180 'industrial regions'

#	Sectors	#	Administrative regions
1	Food, drinks and tobacco	1	Piemonte
2	Textile, clothing, leather and shoes	2	Valle d'Aosta
3	Paper, printing and publishing	3	Liguria
4	Chemicals and pharmaceuticals	4	Lombardia
5	Non-metallic products	5	Trentino A.A.
6	Metals	6	Veneto
7	Metal products and machinery	7	Friuli V.G.
8	Transport equipments	8	Emilia Romagna
9	Other manufacturing	9	Toscana
		10	Umbria
		11	Marche
		12	Lazio
		13	Campania
		14	Abruzzo
		15	Molise
		16	Puglia
		17	Basilicata
		18	Calabria
		19	Sicilia
		20	Sardegna

where, for each industrial region i (defined as in Section 2.3) in the period 1985–95:

- $\Delta EMPH_i$ is the variation in the number of domestic employees in region i;
- $\Delta EMPF_i$ is the variation in the number of employees in foreign affiliates by Italian firms belonging to region i;
- $\Delta PRODH_i$ is the variation in the added value produced in each industrial region i;
- $\Delta PRODH_i^2$ and $R\&D_i$ take into account: (i) the effects of scale economies which could induce possible non-linear effects in the relationship between labour intensity and production; (ii) the autonomous effects engendered by technological progress, which can cause a contraction in domestic employment via an improvement in labour productivity. The variable $\Delta PRODH_i^2$ is the square of the variation in the added value, while the innovative intensity $R\&D_i$ is the ratio between R&D expenditures and the added value produced by the firms in region i; the latter is a *proxy* for the level of technological opportunities of increasing labour productivity, enjoyed by each region i.[6]

Moreover, given the often complex nature of multinational firms and their related structural composition and geographical dislocation, the impact of foreign activities upon the labour intensity of domestic production can differ when the parent firm's activities pertain to one or several industrial regions. Therefore, we distinguished between:

- *single-region* firms, that is, single-sector single-plant firms, and single-sector multi-plant firms with the different plants located in the same geographical region;
- *multi-region* firms, that is, multi-sector and/or multi-plant firms with plants located in several Italian regions.

Accordingly, the variable $\Delta EMPF_i$ has been detailed as follows:

- $\Delta EMPF1_i$ is the variation of the number of employees in foreign affiliates by *single-region* firms pertaining to region i;
- $\Delta EMPF2_i$ is the variation of the number of employees in foreign affiliates by *multi-region* firms whose headquarters pertain to region i;
- $\Delta EMPF3_i$ is the variation of the number of employees in foreign affiliates by *multi-region* firms whose plants pertain to region i (excluding headquarters' plants).

The distinction between $\Delta EMPF2_i$ and $\Delta EMPF3_i$ allows us to take into account that foreign initiatives undertaken by multi-plant and multi-sector diversified firms can impact not just on the industrial region in which the parent's headquarters is located but also – although in different ways – on the regions where its industrial plants are placed. It is worth observing that large firms are more likely to assume the just-mentioned characteristics while, on the contrary, small firms are generally single-region.

Finally, in order to evaluate the impact of different FDI typologies, each variable $\Delta EMPF_i$ has been specified according to the country in which foreign affiliates are active (Blomström *et al.* 1997; Braunerhjelm and Oxelheim 1998; Fors and Kokko 1999; Lipsey 1999). The variables have been specified under the hypothesis that advanced countries are more likely to host horizontal market seeking investments, while developing countries are more likely to attract vertical investment mainly aiming at accessing low-cost manpower. In particular, since Central and Eastern Europe (CEE) countries, as well as the countries belonging to the Mediterranean basin, have been the favourite target for Italian investment mainly aimed at reducing labour cost, especially by small and medium enterprises (see Mutinelli and Piscitello 1997), it seems crucial to investigate FDI in that area separately. The variables considered are the following:

- the variation of employment in foreign affiliates localized in advanced countries ($\Delta EMPF1\_ADV_i$; $\Delta EMPF2\_ADV_i$; $\Delta EMPF3\_ADV_i$);
- the variation of employment in foreign affiliates localized in CEE and Mediterranean basin countries ($\Delta EMPF1\_EAST_i$; $\Delta EMPF2\_EAST_i$; $\Delta EMPF3\_EAST_i$); and

– the variation of employment in foreign affiliates localized in developing countries ($\Delta EMPF1\_DEV_i$; $\Delta EMPF2\_DEV_i$; $\Delta EMPF3\_DEV_i$).

The estimated model then became:

$$\Delta EMPH_i = f(\Delta PRODH_i; \Delta EMPF1\_ADV_i; \Delta EMPF2\_ADV_i;$$
$$\Delta EMPF3\_ADV_i; \Delta EMPF1\_EAST_i; \Delta EMPF2\_EAST_i;$$
$$\Delta EMPF3\_EAST_i; \Delta EMPF1\_DEV_i; \Delta EMPF2\_DEV_i;$$
$$\Delta EMPF3\_DEV_i; R\&D_i; \Delta PRODH_i^2) \quad i = 1, \ldots, 180$$

2.5. Empirical findings

Results of the econometric analysis – run through multiple OLS regression – are reported in Table 2.4. In particular, the most general model in which the whole set of variables is considered (Model 1) as well as the best specification of the model itself (Model 2) are reported. Estimates provide satisfactory results as more than 50 per cent of the variance is explained in both cases (the adjusted R^2 is indeed 0.54 in both the models). The estimation results for Model 1 suggest that the variation experienced in the period 1985–95 by employment in Italian multinationals' foreign affiliates does influence the variation in the labour intensity of home production. However, the impact on local employment differs according to the target foreign country and the geographical/sectoral spread of the Italian parent companies.

Results confirm that the impact on the variation of domestic labour intensity is significantly positive for advanced countries (ADV), while it is significantly negative when FDI refers to less developed countries (DEV and EAST). In particular, that is true for single-region firms (the coefficient of $\Delta EMPF1\_ADV$ is indeed positive and significantly different from zero at $p < 0.05$ in Model 1 and at $p < 0.01$ in Model 2) and even more for FDI undertaken by multi-region firms, which induces positive effects both on the headquarters' region ($\Delta EMPF2\_ADV$ is always significantly positive at $p < 0.01$) and in the industrial regions where other plants are located ($\Delta EMPF3\_ADV$ is also always positive at $p < 0.01$). A similar effect, although opposite in sign, is observed for the variation of employment in foreign affiliates by Italian firms in CEE and Mediterranean countries. $\Delta EMPF1\_EAST$, $\Delta EMPF2\_EAST$ and $\Delta EMPF3\_EAST$ are always significantly negative at least at $p < 0.05$, thus meaning that investment undertaken abroad to exploit the low cost of labour and de-localize the most labour-intensive stages of production actually induce a contraction in the domestic intensity of labour in each Italian region involved in the process, even only indirectly. Interestingly, foreign employment in developing countries negatively

Table 2.4 Results of the econometric analysis

	Model 1		Model 2	
Constant	273.89		92.81	
	(0.356)		(0.124)	
ΔPRODH	2.048		3.563	
	(2.857)	***	(3.009)	***
ΔEMPF1_ADV	5.07		6.091	
	(2.031)	**	(2.667)	***
ΔEMPF2_ADV	0.938		0.941	
	(2.778)	***	(3.702)	***
ΔEMPF3_ADV	0.441		0.421	
	(6.778)	***	(6.961)	***
ΔEMPF1_DEV	−9.901		−9.457	
	(−6.425)	***	(−6.396)	***
ΔEMPF2_DEV	0.217			
	(0.639)			
ΔEMPF3_DEV	0.109			
	(0.959)			
ΔEMPF1_EAST	−3.537		−3.591	
	(−4.529)	***	(−4.684)	***
ΔEMPF2_EAST	−3.156		−2.829	
	(−4.849)	***	(−8.393)	***
ΔEMPF3_ EAST	−0.374		−0.209	
	(−1.884)	*	(−2.094)	**
R&D	−23.017		−24.111	
	(−4.465)	***	(−4.784)	***
ΔPRODH^2	0.000			
	(0.925)			
No obs.	180		180	
R^2	0.572		0.564	
R^2 adj	0.538		0.541	
Test F	17.058	***	24.448	***

Legenda: t-values in brackets.
***: significant at $p < 0.01$; **: significant at $p < 0.05$; *: significant at $p < 0.10$.

influences labour intensity of domestic employment when undertaken by single-region firms (ΔEMPF1_DEV is negative and significantly different from zero at $p < 0.01$ both in Model 1 and Model 2) while it does not come out significant in influencing labour intensity at home when undertaken by multi-region firms (ΔEMPF2_DEV and ΔEMPF3_DEV are not significant in Model 1 and therefore they have been eliminated in the best specification, i.e. Model 2).[7] A possible interpretation can be referred to strategies adopted in developing and less developed countries by large firms. The latter are indeed likely to pursue mixed strategies, especially in the farthest large markets (e.g. Brazil, China, India), where market seeking reasons go with labour seeking strategies. Moreover, large firms seem to pursue exclusively de-localization of labour-intensive stages of production to neighbouring less developed areas (CEE and Mediterranean countries).[8]

As far as the control variables are concerned, the estimates obtained highlight – besides the obvious positive correlation between the variation of domestic employment and domestic production – the significant role of the proxy for changes engendered by technical progress, which allows for a contraction in domestic employment mainly due to innovation in the period considered (R&D is indeed significant at $p < 0.01$ both in Model 1 and in Model 2). On the contrary, $\Delta PRODH^2$ does not appear to be statistically different from zero, thus showing that the reduction of domestic labour intensity is not influenced by economies of scale in production.

We can summarize the results as follows. Given the variation in domestic production as well as the innovative intensity in the industrial region i, each additional employee in foreign affiliates localized in advanced countries is associated with an increase of six employees in the region, when FDI is undertaken by single-region firms; of one employee when FDI is undertaken by multi-region firms with headquarters in region i, and 0.5 employees when FDI is undertaken by multi-region firms with plants in region i.[9]

Similarly, each additional employee in foreign affiliates in Eastern and Mediterranean countries is associated with a loss of four employees in the industrial region in case of single-region firms, and of three employees in the region where the headquarters of multi-region parent companies is located. Again, in order to determine a loss of one employee in the Italian industrial regions where multi-region firms own plants, five employees abroad are necessary. As far as the developing countries are concerned, only FDI undertaken by single-region firms has a significant negative impact on domestic employment. Indeed, an increase of one foreign employee means a loss of nine domestic employees.

It is necessary to stress that such results can be interpreted as a measure of variation of labour intensity, and not as a net effect of FDI on the domestic employment level. Indeed, the model does not take into consideration any relationships between FDI, foreign trade, domestic production and employment level.[10] Nevertheless, compared to earlier studies in which there appears to be a generalized consensus that the quantitative effects of foreign production on domestic employment are not dramatic, this study seems to suggest that internationalization undertaken by Italian firms induces remarkable changes in the labour intensity of domestic production,[11] associated with a likely noteworthy restructuring in the competence profile of domestic employment.[12]

2.6. Conclusions

This paper provides some empirical – statistically robust – evidence on the relationship between FDI and home country labour intensity. It allows us to state that the variation of employment in foreign affiliates by Italian manufacturing firms, in the period 1985–95, significantly influenced the labour intensity of the domestic production. In particular, once we have controlled for the variation in domestic production as well as for the effects of technical progress occurring in the period, econometric findings confirm that an increase in foreign employment in less developed countries, characterized by low labour cost, reduces the labour intensity of domestic production, with the exception of FDI undertaken by large firms in less developed extra-European countries, which show in fact a non-significant relationship. The impact on domestic labour intensity is positive when FDI is directed towards advanced countries.

Results obtained corroborate the canonical interpretation which distinguishes between horizontal investments driven by market seeking strategies, which constitute the bulk of FDI in more advanced countries, and vertical investments led by strategies of allocating labour-intensive portions of the output or labour-intensive stages of production, which represent most FDI towards less developed countries. In particular, horizontal investments induce in the home country additional requirements for skilled labour, mainly due to additional supervision and coordination activities, R&D and marketing activities by the parent company, and to the positive externalities engendered in its relevant environment. On the contrary, vertical investments lead to a reduction of domestic labour intensity, as they respond to de-localization strategies of low-skilled production stages towards low-wage countries. The exception represented by FDI undertaken by the largest Italian firms in less developed extra-European countries reflects their hybrid strategies combining traditional de-localization with penetration of the local market. Moreover, the larger the market size and the geographical distance, the stronger is the latter.

The empirical exercise developed does not allow us to infer anything about the net impact of FDI on the absolute level of domestic employment. That would require a micro-founded structural model able to take into account all the complex relationships between foreign production, domestic employment and production, foreign trade and the variations in the investing firms' competitive advantages. Nonetheless, it is possible to draw some considerations on the issue. First, the econometric model highlights the noteworthy quantitative reduction in the domestic labour intensity associated with vertical FDI directed towards less developed countries. Therefore, a lasting and loose increase of vertical investment, causing such a depressive impact on mass domestic employment, would become unsustainable in the long-term unless adequately balanced by horizontal investments. Second, the relevant changes induced on domestic labour intensity by both vertical and horizontal investment imply systematic and flexible adjustments in the labour market. In particular, this concerns the greater supply of higher vocational profiles and the consequent need for additional investment in human capital. The lack of such structural adjustment processes would cause other fatal consequences for the competitiveness of the country, and the stability and growth of domestic employment.

Appendix: sectoral classification adopted in Reprint and the nine sectors considered

Data set reprint	Sectors
Supplier dominated industries	
Primary food	Food, drinks and tobacco
Textiles	Textiles, clothing, leather and shoes
Clothing	Textiles, clothing, leather and shoes
Leather products and shoes	Textiles, clothing, leather and shoes
Wood and wooden products	Other industrial products
Printing and publishing	Paper, printing and publishing
Other manufacturing	Other industrial products
Scale intensive industries	
Processed food	Food, drinks and tobacco
Drinks	Food, drinks and tobacco
Tobacco	Food, drinks and tobacco
Paper products	Paper, printing and publishing
Base chemicals	Chemicals and pharmaceuticals
Cosmetics and toiletries	Chemicals and pharmaceuticals
Fibers	Chemicals and pharmaceuticals
Rubber products	Other industrial products
Plastic products	Other industrial products
Glass and glass products	Non-metallic products
Other non-metallic minerals	Non-metallic products
Metals	Metals
Metal products	Metal products and machinery
Household appliances	Metal products and machinery
Cables	Metal products and machinery
Electrical automotive components	Metal products and machinery
Other electrical products and components	Metal products and machinery
Automotive	Transport equipments
Mechanical automotive components	Transport equipments
Specialized suppliers industries	
Mechanical machinery and equipment	Metal products and machinery
Electrical machinery	Metal products and machinery
Other transport equipment	Transport equipments
Science based industries	
Fine chemicals	Chemicals and pharmaceuticals
Pharmaceuticals	Chemicals and pharmaceuticals
Information technology	Metal products and machinery
Electronics, telecommunications	Metal products and machinery
Instruments	Metal products and machinery
Aerospace	Transport equipments

Notes

1 Greater attention has been devoted to the relationship between foreign trade and domestic employment (Bella and Quintieri 1995; De Nardis and Malgarini 1996; De Nardis and Paternò 1997; Scarlato 1999).
2 This aspect refers to the well-known issue about the relationship between FDI and foreign trade (Jordan and Vahlne 1981; Aitken *et al.* 1994; Lawrence 1994, 1996; Lipsey 1994; Messerlin 1995; UNCTAD 1996; WTO 1996). With reference to the Italian case, see the recent survey in Mori e Rolli (1998).
3 See Note 2.
4 The data set Reprint has been developed at Politecnico di Milano in cooperation with the National Council for Economics and Labour. For further details, see Cominotti *et al.* (1999).
5 Foreign activities in petroleum extraction have not been considered, owing to the very limited number of employees in such industry in Italy.
6 The hypothesis is that regions with higher R&D intensity experienced higher productivity increase. Nonetheless, it is worth noting that R&D expenditures are not exclusively devoted to process innovation (which are more likely to cause a productivity increase). Moreover, data on R&D expenditures are available only at the regional level and from 1991 onwards. Therefore the variable has been calculated in the interval 1991–95.
7 The sign of the estimated coefficients seems to suggest a positive, although not statistically significant, impact upon $\Delta EMPH_i$
8 Examples are provided by the initiatives undertaken by the largest Italian groups (Fiat, Pirelli, Montedison, Eni, Parmalat, Merloni, etc.) in China and in the Mercosur area, where the penetration of the market as well as the search for low production costs were the fundamental determinants.
9 It is worth noting that the remarkable difference between the impacts in terms of number of employees for single- and multi-region firms is explained by the fact that in the latter case the effect is spread over the several regions in which they are active. Moreover, the greater stability in the region where the firm's headquarters is located refers both to the presence of activities hardly replaceable (e.g. coordination and control activities), and to the major care the firm adopts toward the context where its head office is active.
10 Incidentally, it is worth observing that a positive (negative) variation of one billion Italian lira in domestic added value induces an increase (decrease) of four employees in domestic employment.
11 Similar results have been recently achieved by Fors and Kokko (1999) in a study based on seventeen of the largest Swedish MNCs in the period 1985–94.
12 The effects induced by FDI on the qualitative structure of domestic employment have not been tested in the present model. Concerning the impact of a globalization process on the competence profile in advanced countries, see Baldwin (1995), Slaughter (1995), Brainard and Riker (1997), OECD (1997).

References

Agarwal, J. P. (1996) 'European integration and German FDI: implications for domestic investment and Central European Economies', *National Institute Economic Review*, 160.
Agarwal, J. P. (1997) 'Does foreign direct investment contribute to unemployment in home countries? An empirical survey', Kiel Working Paper No. 765, Institute für Weltwirtschaft, Kiel.
Aitken, B., Hanson, G. H. and Harrison, A. E. (1994) 'Spillovers, foreign investment, and export behaviour', NBER Working Paper No. 4927, National Bureau of Economic Research, Cambridge, MA.

Almeida, B. (1997) 'Are good jobs flying away? US aircraft engine manufacturing and sustainable prosperity', Working Paper No. 206, Center for Industrial Competitiveness, University of Massachussets.

Baldwin, R. E. (1995) 'The effects of trade and foreign direct investment on employment and relative wages', *OECD Economic Studies*, 23, OECD, Paris.

Barba Navaretti, G., Falzoni, A. M. and Turrini, A. (1999) 'Italian multinationals and de-localisation of production', Paper presented at the *Conference on 'Integrazione internazionale e mercato del lavoro'*, Università Commerciale L. Bocconi, Milano, May 7–8.

Becattini, G. (1990) 'The marshallian industrial districts as a socio-economic notion', in F. Pyke, G. Becattini and W. Sengenberger (eds), *Industrial Districts and Inter-firm Cooperation in Italy*. Geneva: ILO.

Bella, M. and Quintieri, B. (1995) 'Employment determination in an open economy: the impact of trade on industry employment in italy', in B. Quintieri (ed.), *Patterns of Trade, Competition and Trade Policies*. London: Avebury.

Blomström, M. (1989) *Foreign Investment and Spillovers: A Study of Technology Transfer*. London: Routledge.

Blomström, M. (1991) 'Host country benefits of foreign direct investment', in D. G. McFetridge (ed.), *Foreign Investment Technology and Economic Growth*. Toronto: University of Toronto Press.

Blomström, M. and Kokko, A. (1994) 'Home country effects on foreign direct investment: evidence from Sweden', NBER Working Paper No. 4639, National Bureau of Economic Research, Cambridge, MA.

Blomström, M., Fors, G. and Lipsey, R. E. (1997) 'Foreign direct investment and employment: home country experience in the United States and Sweden', *The Economic Journal*, 107.

Brainard, S. L. and Riker, D. A. (1997) 'Are US multinationals exporting US jobs?', NBER Working Paper No. 5958, National Bureau of Economic Research, Cambridge, MA.

Braunerhjelm, P. and Oxelheim, L. (1998) 'Does FDI replace home country investment? The effects of European integration on the location of Swedish investment', CEPR – Symposium on New Issues in Trade and Location.

Cantwell, J. A. (1989) *Technical Innovation and Multinational Corporations*. Oxford: Basil Blackwell.

Caves, R. E. (1974) 'Multinational firms, competition and productivity in host-country markets', *Economica*, 32: 176–93.

Cominotti, R., Mariotti, S. and Mutinelli, M. (eds) (1999) *Italia Multinazionale*. Roma: Documenti CNEL 17.

De Nardis, S. and Malagarini, M. (1996) 'Commercio estero e occupazione in Italia: una stima con le tavole intersettoriali', Centro Studi Confindustria 3, Roma.

De Nardis, S. and Paternò, F. (1997) 'Scambi con l'estero e posti di lavoro: l'industria italiana nel periodo 1980–95', Centro Studi Confindustria 13, Roma.

Faini, R., Falzoni, A. M., Galeotti, M., Helg, R. and Turrini, A. (1998) 'Importing jobs and exporting firms? A close look at the labour market implications of Italy's trade and foreign direct investment flows', Development Studies Working Paper No. 120, Centro Studi Luca d'Agliano, Milan.

Fors, G. and Kokko, A. (1999) 'Home country effects of FDI: foreign production and structural change in home country operations', Paper presented at the *Seventh Sorbonne International Conference*, 17–18 June, Paris.

38

Frank, R. H. and Freeman, R. T. (1978) 'The distributional consequences of direct foreign investment', US Department of Labour, Bureau of International Labour Affairs, Washington, DC.

Glickman, N. J. and Woodward, D. P. (1989) *The New Competitors. How Foreign Investors are Changing US Economy*. New York: Harper Collins.

Haddad, M. and Harrison, A. (1993). 'Are there positive spillovers from direct foreign investment?', *Journal of Development Economics*, 42: 51–74.

Hawkins, R. G. (1972) 'US multinational investment in manufacturing and domestic economic performance', Occasional Paper 1. Center for Multinational Studies, Washington, DC.

Jordan, G. L. and Vahlne, J. E. (1981) 'Domestic employment effects of direct investment abroad by two Swedish multinationals', Working Paper No. 13, Multinational Enterprises Programme, ILO, Geneva.

Kravis, I. B. and Lipsey, R. E. (1988) 'The effect of multinational firms' foreign operations on their domestic employment', NBER Working Paper No. 2760, National Bureau of Economic Research, Cambridge, MA.

Krugman, P. (1994) 'Does third world growth hurt first world prosperity?', *Harvard Business Review*, July–August.

Lawrence, R. Z. (1994) 'Trade, multinationals and labor', NBER Working Paper No. 4836, National Bureau of Economic Research, Cambridge, MA.

Lawrence, R. Z. (ed.) (1996) *Single World Divided Nations? International Trade and OECD labor Markets*. Harrisonburg: Brookings Institution Press.

Lipsey, R. E. (1999) 'Foreign production by US firms and parent firm employment', Paper presented at the *Seventh Sorbonne International Conference*, 17–18 June, Paris.

Lipsey, R. E. (1994) 'Outward direct investment and the US economy', NBER Working Paper No. 36/4671, National Bureau of Economic Research, Cambridge, MA.

Markusen, J. R. and Venables, A. J. (1999) 'Foreign direct investment as a catalyst for industrial development', *European Economic Review*, 43.

Messerlin, P. A. (1995) 'The impact of trade and capital movements on labor: evidence on the French case', *IECD Economic Studies*, 24.

Mori, A. and Rolli, V. (1998) 'Investimenti diretti all'estero e commercio: complementi o sostituti?', Temi di discussione del Servizio Studi 337. Banca d'Italia, Roma.

Mutinelli, M. and Piscitello, L. (1997) 'Understanding the strategic orientation of Italian foreign investment in Central and Eastern Europe', *International Business Review*, 6.

Nunnenkamp, P. (1998) 'German direct investment in Latin America. Striking peculiarities, unfounded fears, and neglected issues', Kiel Working Paper No. 861, Institute für Weltwirtschaft, Kiel.

OECD (1997) 'Trade, earnings and employment: assessing the impact of trade with emerging economies on OECD labor market', *Employment Outlook*, OECD, Paris.

Perez, T. (1997) 'Multinational enterprises and technological spillovers: an evolutionary model', *Evolutionary Economics*, 7: 169–92.

Porter, M. (1992) *The Competitive Advantages of Nations*. New York: The Free Press.

Rodriguez-Clare, A. (1996) 'Multinationals, linkages, and economic development', *American Economic Review*, 86.

Scarlato, M. (1999) 'The impact of international trade on employment and wage differentials: some evidence from the Italian macro-regions', Paper presented at the *Conference on Integrazione internazionale e mercato del xlavoro*, Università Commerciale L. Bocconi, Milan, 7–8 May.

Slaughter, M. (1995) 'Multinational corporations, outsourcing and American wage diversion', NBER Working Paper No. 5253, National Bureau of Economic Research, Cambridge, MA.

UNCTAD (1996) 'Investment, trade and international policy arrangements', *World Investment Report 1996*, United Nations, Geneva.

US Tariff Commission (1973) *Implications of Multinational Firms for World Trade and Investment and for US Trade and Labor*, Washington DC: US Government Printing Office.

Wang, C. and Blomström, M. (1992) 'Foreign investment and technology transfer: a simple model', *European Economic Review*, 36: 137–55.

WTO (1996) 'Trade and foreign direct investment', *Annual Report 1996*, WTO, Geneva.

Part II

MULTINATIONAL FIRMS AND INTERNATIONAL TRADE
FDI and export,
FDI and intra-firm trade

3

RELATIONSHIPS BETWEEN TRADE AND FDI FLOWS WITHIN TWO PANELS OF US AND FRENCH INDUSTRIES*

Lionel Fontagné and Michaël Pajot

3.1. Introduction

Foreign direct investment (FDI) and international production are developing at a high pace. FDI flows have recorded a 19 per cent increase in 1997, and 10 per cent in 1998, to reach roughly USD 440 billion. Around 50,000 parent and 450,000 affiliates operate worldwide (UNCTAD 1998). These affiliates account for 6 per cent of world GDP, compared with 2 per cent in 1982. Intra-firm trade (noticeably trade in goods-in-process) accounts for one-third of world exports and foreign affiliates' sales grow faster than world exports. Global exports of foreign affiliates reached USD 2 trillion in 1997, and their sales 9.5 trillion.

The recent increase in FDI flows is twofold:

1 Developing countries are currently liberalizing foreign inward investment. The conclusion of numerous bilateral agreements on FDI has provided the institutional framework for this increase. UNCTAD (1998) reports that such an agreement was signed every two and a half days in 1997 on average. Actually 1,500 agreements are in force all over the world. Thus, developing countries accounted for 37 per cent of total flows in 1997, a 20-point increase since 1990.
2 The second engine of FDI growth is Mergers and Acquisitions. They accounted for half of FDI flows in 1997, banking, insurance, pharmaceuticals and telecommunications being the leading sectors. Key determinants of such overseas operations are the firms' reaction to the increased global competition, the liberalization of capital flows among developed countries,

*We acknowledge for OECD-DSTI support to this research programme since 1996. The French Ministry of Finance and the CEPII have also provided support at different stages.

Table 3.1 Inward and outward FDI flows as a per cent of gross capital formation; selected countries

	1986–91	1996		1986–91	1996
World					
in	3.6	5.6			
out	4.1	5.5			
Developed			Developing		
in	3.5	3.6	in	3.4	8.7
out	4.5	5.2	out	1.3	3.3
USA			Africa		
in	6.5	7	in	3.9	7.3
out	3.4	6.9	out	1.4	0.4
Canada			Latin America + Carrib.		
in	5.3	6.2	in	5.3	12.8
out	5.3	8.2	out	0.7	0.7
UK			CEECs		
in	13.6	14.6	in	0.4	19.9
out	17.1	19.1	out	.	1.8
France			Asia		
in	4.5	8.2	in	2.8	7.4
out	8.7	11.3	out	1.5	4.3

Source: UNCTAD (1998) Appendices.

the deregulation of key sectors such as telecommunications, and a further step towards integration in Europe.

A good measure of the magnitude of globalization is the ratio of international to domestic investment (Table 3.1). On average, this ratio has been stable in the recent period for developed economies, even for outward flows, with the exception of USA and France. In the UK, outward FDI accounts for one-fifth of domestic investment. In contrast, the increase is very sharp for developing countries, noticeably for Central Europe where one-fifth of domestic investment is inward FDI.

Taking these transformations of the world economy as a motivation, this paper aims to examine the relationships between trade and FDI. More precisely, we investigate whether FDI flows displace or complement trade flows. From the point of view of the investing country, if FDI displaces trade, exports will be crowded out by local sales on foreign markets, detrimental to the domestic industry. In contrast, if trade and FDI are confirmed as complements, investing abroad might lead to greater competitiveness on foreign markets. Reciprocally, from the point of view of the host country, inward FDI would have, in case of complementarity, detrimental effects on the current balance.

Given their relevance for economic policy, these relationships have recently been addressed in the debate on the opportunity to implement a multilateral agreement on FDI. Having surveyed the empirical literature, Drabek (1998) concluded that the links between FDI and trade were ascertained; hence this issue of the debate about a multilateral agreement on FDI was no longer questionable:

> One of the frequently heard arguments against an MAI among politicians is that the linkages between trade and FDI are not known. (...) This view is clearly incorrect in that the empirical evidence already exists (...). I have compiled what I believe to be all the major studies that address the question of the extent to which trade and FDI are substitutable or complementary from both home and host countries' perspectives (...). Most of the literature points to the case of complementarity.
>
> (p. 11)

This complementarity is, however, challenged in the literature. At the level of the firm, such complementarity is questionable. In addition, unobserved macroeconomic factors such as country size, per capita income, etc., can be the foundation of the observed macroeconomic complementarity. Lastly, results differ by large according to the type of FDI data used. Stressing some key dimensions of this relationship will clarify the debate:

- First, it must be kept in mind that FDI flows, FDI stocks, local sales, and local production are different measures of foreign activity. Substituting one proxy for another leads to different results.
- In addition, the level of analysis matters: a substitution at the level of the firm may be associated with a complementarity at the industry level, spillovers[1] between firms being taken into account in the latter case. In the same way, spillovers between industries within the manufacturing sector provide an additional opportunity for complementarity.
- Lastly, total FDI is subject to very large complementarity effects. Therefore, a comparison between both extremes of the spectrum is illustrative: an investment in wholesale trade will lead to increased industrial exports, whereas production abroad, at the individual firm level, may at least partially substitute for previous or potential exports.

To our knowledge, these complex relationships have never been addressed in the literature in a systematic manner using data broken down by sector, country and partner in an international comparative perspective. The rest of the paper is organized as follows. Mechanisms linking trade and FDI are examined in a first section based on a brief survey of the literature. A second section provides an evidence of the magnitude of complementarity effects at the macroeconomic level, among OECD countries. A new approach to complementarity – substitution relationships, based on sectoral and bilateral trade and FDI data, is presented in the third section, and applied to France and the United States. In a last section, we build on the previous results in order to clarify the mechanisms leading to the observed macroeconomic complementarity between trade and FDI flows.

3.2. Mechanisms linking trade to FDI

Following Stevens and Lipsey (1992), it has become usual to distinguish between *financial* and *production* implications of FDI. The former has a rather indirect impact on trade flows, whereas the second are direct.

Financial interactions refer to the *possible substitution between domestic and foreign investment.* Concerning implications for production, the question is *whether FDI displaces trade, output and employment*, through the intermediate of trade flows. Outward FDI may displace trade at the level of the firm, since foreign affiliates' local sales substitute at least partially for exports. It is, however, not necessarily the case at the level of industries or at the macroeconomic level. In addition, investing abroad induces intra-firm imports if labour-intensive or resource-intensive activities are relocated abroad. Hence, trade is not necessarily displaced by outward FDI.

Most empirical studies of the relationship between trade and FDI aim to estimate the direction and the magnitude of the impact of FDI on trade. Such estimates provide a direct measurement of substitution versus complementarity effects. Explaining exports (imports) as a function of FDI and different control variables, one is interested in the sign and magnitude of the parameter estimate associated with foreign investment.

If a negative parameter on FDI is obtained in export equations, exports are at least partially replaced by local sales on foreign markets and this is detrimental to the domestic industry of the investor. Production and employment can be negatively affected in the home country. Reciprocally, the trade balance in the host country would benefit from this substitution effect.

If a positive parameter is obtained, trade and FDI are complements. Investing abroad leads to greater competitiveness in foreign markets, to the benefit of the investing country's exports and industry and to the detriment of the host country's trade balance.

Accordingly, depending on the type of FDI data mobilized (firm, industry, manufacturing sector, total), results will change dramatically.

At the microeconomic level, the economic literature generally refers to trade and FDI as alternative strategies. Firms can alternatively produce at home and export, or produce abroad and substitute foreign affiliates' local sales for exports. The new trade theory, building on imperfect competition, emphasizes that economies of scale and transportation costs are key elements in this decision process. Increasing returns to scale limit the number of efficient plants, whereas transportation costs and more generally trade barriers act in the opposite direction. The so-called 'proximity – concentration trade-off' (Brainard 1993a) is the key issue explaining if, and how, FDI substitutes for trade. A comprehensive view is given by the introduction of firm-specific fixed costs as opposed to plant-specific fixed costs. When the former are high and the latter are low, FDI spreads largely if transportation costs are not negligible: multinationals locate different subsidiaries near their different markets and local production displaces trade (Markusen and Venables 1995).

In addition to these bilateral effects, it must be noticed that third country competitors may lose market shares in the host country to the benefit of the investing country. Hence, in contrast to MITI (1997), it cannot be considered that each dollar of sales abroad substitutes for one dollar of exports. For example, the business literature surveyed in Blomström and Kokko (1994) makes a comparison between the effects of alternative ways of exploiting firm-specific advantages. The main result is that the dominant effect is an increase in the foreign market share associated with FDI. Second, exports of intermediate products towards foreign subsidiaries are compensating for lost exports. Lastly, there is good evidence that foreign affiliates export less and import more than US firms (the benchmark study recently realized by the French Ministry of Industry reaches the same conclusion). In total, the impact on trade could be (slightly) positive.

Accordingly, Lipsey and Weiss (1984) highlight that one dollar of local production induces 9–25 cents of additional exports from the investing country. They explain exports of individual firms towards each market (five zones), using the size of the parent, the production and sales of local affiliates, and the size of the host economy (its GDP) as explaining variables. Not surprisingly, the elasticity linking trade and local output is three times larger using statistics at the industry level than for individual firms' data, as a result of externalities between firms within industries.

Sweden, to the benefit of the database provided by the Industrial Institute for Economic and Social Science Research (Stockholm), has generally been taken as a good case study.[2] Swedenborg (1979) concludes that FDI has no significant effect on the parent exports, as local sales substitute these exports, while new exports are induced (intermediate goods or complements of supply). This result was confirmed in 1982 by a study finalized by the same author: each dollar of local sales substitutes only 2 cents of exports but 'creates' 12 cents of new exports, the net effect being a positive complementarity of 10 cents. Blomström et al. (1988) conclude a limited effect of complementarity.

However, taking into account that foreign production can substitute for exports not only to the host country but also to third markets, Svensson (1993) found a trade displacement effect for the 1980s, which can be explained by unfavourable conditions of industry in Sweden in this period.

Finally Andersson (1993) and Blomström and Kokko (1994) suggest that the structure of Swedish exports might be more affected than the value of these exports as a result of outward FDI. Rikker and Brainard (1997) stress the vertical splitting up of processes that is associated with FDI: FDI does not displace output, it splits the production process worldwide. Hence, FDI complements trade in intermediate products.

In total, the empirical validation of the microeconomic hypothesis of substitution is poor.

Turning to data at the industry level, contrasting results have been obtained so far. Lipsey and Weiss (1981) consider forty-four foreign markets in which US firms compete against thirteen other exporting countries. Without US FDI, US exports to these markets would have been smaller: one dollar of local sales leads to 2–78 cents of additional exports to the corresponding market (depending on the industry).

Brainard (1993b) explains the respective share of exports and local sales in total international involvement (defined as export plus sales) for twenty-seven US markets, by industry. Transportation costs and tariffs promote local sales, detrimental to exports. When the income per capita of the destination market catches up with the US one, US multinationals tend to substitute FDI for exports, in accordance with Markusen's convergence hypothesis.

Fontagné and Pajot (1997) run econometric estimates on bilateral and sectoral data. Using disaggregated data, the diagnosis of complementarity between trade and FDI flows was validated for a pooling of industries. Interestingly, the impact of FDI on trade is much larger when spillovers between sectors are taken into account.

Lastly, the relationship between FDI and trade can be tackled at the macroeconomic level. Eaton and Tamura (1994) use a model controlling for country determinants in order to explain either bilateral total exports or bilateral FDI flows of Japan and the USA for a 100 countries over the period 1985–90. Each variable of internationalization (export, import, inward FDI or outward FDI) is explained by the population of the partner country, its income per capita, its density, its endowment in human capital and dummies accounting for 'natural regions' of integration. Certain factors jointly determine trade and FDI. For example, FDI and trade flows increase in proportion to the income per capita to the partner country, while regionalism also has a positive impact on trade and FDI bilateral relationships. *There is a large and positive relationship between outward FDI and exports, as well as imports, for Japan and the US*. This relation is not verified for inward FDI.

Using time-series analysis, Andersen and Hainaut (1998) find, however, contrasted evidence of complementarity effects between exports and outward FDI flows: there is a complementarity for the United States, Japan, and Germany, but not for the United Kingdom for which no significant relationship was found.

3.3. Complementarity at the macroeconomic level

In this section, export equations for twenty-one OECD countries are estimated using FDI data at the aggregated level. These equations build on Bergstrand (1989), a methodology largely used in the empirical literature on trade flows. Details concerning the variables are provided in Appendix 1. With the exception of FDI, the explanatory variables used here are traditional: country share in total GDP[3] of the sample, difference in GDPs per capita between exporter and destination market, geographic distance proxying for transport costs, dummies for adjacency and membership of the EU, inward and outward FDI flows.

A traditional problem with FDI data is the difference in records of a given FDI flow according to the reporting country. We choose to consider declarations of FDI flows reported by the exporting country. In addition, as the model is log-linearized, a problem arises with zero values or net divestments corresponding to negative values. The solution adopted here is to define a new variable having satisfactory properties. The transformed variables (see Appendix 2) are referred to below as TOUT and TIN.

A database of bilateral trade flows over the 1980–95 period has been built for a sample of reporting OECD countries. We obtain a panel of observations with three indexes: i for the reporting OECD country, j for its partner and t for the year of observation. The selected countries are: Germany, Belgium-Luxembourg, Denmark, France, Ireland, Italy, Netherlands, the United Kingdom, Greece, Sweden, Spain, Portugal, Austria, Finland, Norway, Switzerland, Canada, the United States, Australia, Japan and New Zealand.

A trade equation between the twenty-one selected OECD countries is estimated using i as a reporting country.

$$\ln(X_{ij}) = 12.76 + 0.689 * \ln(GDPPN_j) - 0.291 * DFGDPP_{ij}$$
$$\underset{(t)}{} \quad \underset{(120.19)}{} \quad \underset{(85.36)}{} \quad \underset{(-7.95)}{}$$

$$- 0.048 * \ln(DFGDPPCP_{ij}) - 0.718 * \ln(DIST_{ij})$$
$$\underset{(-6.21)}{} \quad \underset{(-58.51)}{}$$

$$+ 0.838 * \ln(ADJ_{ij}) + 0.109 * \ln(EU)$$
$$\underset{(18.90)}{} \quad \underset{(2.87)}{}$$

$$+ 0.529 * \ln(TOUT_{ij}) + 0.438 * \ln(TIN_{ij}) + e_i + e_t \quad (1)$$
$$\underset{(8.29)}{} \quad \underset{(6.25)}{}$$

n: 3011   condition number: 28.90 [15.60, without intercept]
adjusted R^2: 89.43%   LM test: 71558
F-value: 653.63   Hausman test: 133
prob > F: 0.0001 t: statistics in parentheses.

Parameters obtained in equation (1), using both reporting country (i) and time fixed effects, confirm those traditionally assessed in the empirical literature on international trade. The (relative) size of the market, adjacency and regionaliza-tion promote exports. Difference in country sizes, or trade impediments, such as transport costs, have an opposite impact. More interestingly, the economic distance does not promote bilateral trade, in contrast to the predictions of the classical the-ory of international trade. This is not very surprising since we assess trade flows between industrialized countries, generally referred to as countries trading on the basis of new theories of international trade.

FDI-related parameter estimates are positive, in coherence with the hypothesis of complementarity at the aggregated level.

The comparison of simulated bilateral trade flows, corresponding to an *anti-monde* without FDI, and observed bilateral trade flows, can be performed. It provides good information on the magnitude of 'FDI-induced' trade flows. Nevertheless, given the transformation adopted for FDI variables, this result must be handled cautiously. The largest increase in trade is associated with the US–Japan relationship. Japanese exports to the US are 'increased' by a 150 per cent factor. The following tightest bilateral relationships are USA–UK, US–Canada,

49

Table 3.2 Increase (%) in trade flows associated with bilateral FDI, 1994 (X_{ij})

i \ j	usa	jap	ger	uk	fra	ita	nld	blx	dnk	fin	nor	swe	irel	aus	swi	spa	port	gre	can	austra	nzl
USA	—	86	70	98	63	35	0	32	7	4	9	14	15	4	47	18	2	0	99	17	6
Japan	149	—	12	22	5	2	16	9	.	0	0	1	4	0	2	.	.	.	8	13	1
Germany	9	1	—	38	21	-7	20	12	0	-2	-1	-3	10	7	.	8	4	1	0	0	0
UK	101	3	21	—	14	9	62	6	2	1	7	9	5	1	-1	8	3	.	-3	33	6
France	42	2	19	35	—	14	15	26	1	1	0	-2	4	0	6	.	1	1	2	0	.
Italy	6	1	4	7	11	—	14	6	1	0	0	0	1	0	3	7	1	1	1	0	.
Netherlands	17	0	17	38	7	6	—	17	1	1	3	20	9	2	20	4	.	.	3	3	.
Belg-Lux	-1	-4	44	-26	35	-5	14	—	2	0	-1	30	1	-13	-7	-13	-1	-1	4	-3	0
Denmark	11	0	3	13	2	0	5	4	—	3	11	9	7	0	2	10	0	0	-3	0	0
Finland	3	.	4	10	3	0	10	2	15	—	2	5	.	.	-1	.	.	0	0	0	.
Norway	14	1	1	3	0	0	3	0	7	3	—	0	0	0	1	0	0	0	1	0	.
Sweden	10	1	-4	6	-10	0	58	0	0	5	-2	—	-5	2	7	.	.	.	0	.	.
Ireland	.	.	.	.	.	.	.	.	.	.	.	.	—	.	.	.	.	.	.	.	.
Austria	1	0	7	1	0	0	0	1	.	.	.	0	.	-1	1	.	0	.	1	.	.
Switzerland	47	-2	16	23	11	1	11	4	1	.	.	8	.	.	—	-1	.	.	.	0	.
Spain	21	3	15	-1	14	9	12	10	0	1	0	0	1	0	6	—	5	0	0	0	.
Portugal	1	.	3	0	1	0	1	1	.	.	.	0	.	.	.	2	—	.	0	.	.
Greece	.	.	.	.	.	.	.	.	.	.	.	.	.	.	.	.	.	—	.	.	.
Canada	86	6	.	-14	.	.	.	.	.	.	.	.	.	.	.	.	.	.	—	2	.
Australia	20	2	0	29	3	.	3	2	.	.	.	.	0	.	.	.	.	.	2	—	4
New Zealand	7	0	0	2	.	.	11	0	.	.	.	.	.	.	.	.	.	.	12	12	—

Source: Simulation based on equation (1).

UK–Netherlands, US–France and Sweden–Netherlands.[4] Finally, the impact is highly asymmetric in the US–Germany case: the complementarity is high for German exports to the US, but conversely the complementarity is negligible for US exports to Germany. The latter asymmetry may be due either to a contrasted sectoral composition of FDI flows, US investment being relatively more important in service activities, or to differences in US and German firms' strategies (see Table 3.2).

3.4. Evidence based on sectoral and bilateral data

As highlighted by the literature review above, different data generally lead to contrasting results concerning the relationship between trade and FDI. At the macro level a strong complementarity is expected, whereas this is not the case at more disaggregated levels of analysis. Having ascertained the macroeconomic complementarity in the previous section, we must now examine this relationship at the level of industries.

In this section, we focus on the United States and France, which provide the best bilateral FDI data at the sectoral level. We will match both data sets with trade data in order to estimate Bergstrand-type equations for panels of industries. We consider separately each country and its different partners. In order to compare estimates, it has been necessary to finalize a data set in a common nomenclature. Lastly, this FDI data set had to share a common nomenclature with bilateral trade flows. The identified sector refers to the sector of inward investment flow and the sector of outward investment flow.

3.4.1. Database

Concerning French data, the Balance of Payments Appendices have been collected over 1984–95. Contrary to US data, reinvested earnings are not reported until 1996. Hence, it has been impossible to extend our database and to integrate new data compiled with new principles.

Finally, we built two sets of databases: France using the French (disaggregated) nomenclature (Table 3.3), and France and United States using the US classification (Table 3.4).

The database for French FDI flows entails 20,812 observations:

- forty-three countries;
- forty-four sectors of which nineteen are manufacturing sectors;
- twelve years: 1984–95 of which eleven years (1984–94) have been matched with trade data.

Since the sectoral breakdown is more detailed for French data, the latter can be used at its finest level of disaggregation or re-aggregated in order to come back to the twenty-two sectors of the US classification.

Table 3.3 Data for France

No.	Sectors	Chelem (CEPII)
1	Agriculture	JA, JB, JC
2	Energy	(3 + 4 + 5)
3	Coal, lignite, crude oil, natural gas	IA, IB, IC
4	Refined products	IG, IH
5	Other	II
6	Manufacturing	(7 + 10 + 13 to 23)
7	Ferrous and non-ferrous metals	(8 + 9)
8	Quarrying	HA, HB
9	Products	CA, CB, CC
10	Minerals	(11 + 12)
11	Quarrying	HC
12	Products	BA, BB, BC
13	Chemicals products	GA, GB, GC, GD, GE, GF, GG
14	Foundry and forging metals	FA, FB
15	Industrial and agricultural machinery	FC, FD, FE, FF, FG, FH
16	Office machinery, computers, instruments	FI, FJ, FK, FO
17	electric and electronic equipment	FL, FM, FN, FP, FQ, FR
18	Transport equipment	FS, FT, FU, FV, FW
19	Food, beverages, tobacco	KA, KB, KC, KD, KE, KF, KG, KH, KI
20	Textiles and wearing	DA, DB, DC, DD, DE
21	Wood, publishing, printing	EC, ED
22	Rubber and plastic products	GH, GI
23	Other manufacturing	EA, EB, EE, NA, NB, NV
24	Construction	
25	Services	
26	Trade and repairs	
27	Hotels and restaurants	
28	Land transports	
29	Other transports	
30	Sea transports	
31	Coastal water transport	
32	Air transport	
33	Auxiliary services of transports	
34	Communications	
35	Banking	
36	Insurance	
37	Autres services marchands	
38	Medical, cultural, social, etc	
39	Other	
40	Other services	
41	Real estate	
42	Holdings	
43	Unallocated	
44	Total	

Table 3.3 (*Continued*)

No.	Partners
	All countries
1	Algeria
2	Argentina
3	Australia
4	Austria
5	Belgium-Luxembourg
6	Brazil
7	Canada
8	Chile
9	China
10	Denmark
11	Egypt
12	Finland
13	Germany
14	Greece
15	Hong Kong
16	Hungary
17	Indonesia
18	Ireland
19	Israel
20	Italy
21	Japan
22	Korea Republic of
23	Malaysia
24	Mexico
25	Morocco
26	Netherlands
27	New Zealand
28	Norway
29	Philippines
30	Poland
31	Portugal
32	Singapore
33	Spain
34	Sweden
35	Switzerland
36	Taiwan
37	Thailand
38	Tunisia
39	Turkey
40	United Kingdom
41	United States
42	Ex-USSR
43	Venezuela

Concerning US investment abroad, we have information on flows over 1982–95. Foreign investment in the United States is available over 1980–94. This has led us to exploit the US database only partially:

- thirty-eight countries are used in estimates;
- only eleven years (1984–94) have been used in estimates, since 1980–83 were not available for France. In addition, the trade database covered the years until 1994 only;
- twenty-three industries aggregated into twelve sectors.

Table 3.4 Patterns of the joint US–French database

No.	Industries	Inward FDI 80/86	Inward FDI 87/94	Outward FDI 82/95
1	All industries			
2	Petroleum			
3	Tot manuf			
4	Food and kindred products			
5	Chemicals and allied products			
6	Primary and fabricated metals			
7	Machinery			calc
8	Industrial machinery and equipment	n.a.	n.a.	
9	Electronic and other electric equipment	n.a.	n.a	
10	Other manufacturing			calc
11	Transportation equipment	n.a.	n.a.	
12	Other manufacturing except transportation equipment	n.a.	n.a.	
13	Wholesale trade			
14	Depository institutions			
15	Finance (e]xcept depository institutions), insurance and real estate	calc	calc	
16	Finance except depository institutions			n.a.
17	Insurance			n.a.
18	Real estate			n.a.
19	Other industries gl	calc	calc	calc
20	Mining		n.a.	n.a.
21	Retail trade			
22	Services	n.a.		n.a.
23	Other industries*			

Table 3.4 (Continued)

No.	FDI in 80/86	FDI in 87/94	FDI out 82/95	Country
	All countries	All countries	All countries	All countries
1			Argentina	Argentina
2		Australia	Australia	Australia
3		Austria	Austria	Austria
4	Belgium	Belgium	Belgium	Belgium
				Belgium +Luxemb.
5		Brazil	Brazil	Brazil
6	Canada	Canada	Canada	Canada
7			Chile	Chile
8			China	China
9		Denmark	Denmark	Denmark
10			Ecuador	Ecuador
11			Egypt	Egypt
12		Finland	Finland	Finland
13	France	France	France	France
14	Germany	Germany	Germany	Germany
15			Greece	Greece
16		Hong Kong	Hong Kong	Hong Kong
17			Indonesia	Indonesia
18		Ireland	Ireland	Ireland
19	Israel	Israel	Israel	Israel
20	Italy	Italy	Italy	Italy
21	Japan	Japan	Japan	Japan
22		Korea	Korea Republic of	Korea Republic of
	Luxembourg	Luxembourg	Luxembourg	Luxembourg
23		Malaysia	Malaysia	Malaysia
24		Mexico	Mexico	Mexico
25	Netherlands	Netherlands	Netherlands	Netherlands
26		New Zealand	New Zealand	New Zealand
27		Norway	Norway	Norway
28		Philippines	Philippines	Philippines
29			Portugal	Portugal
30		Singapore	Singapore	Singapore
31		Spain	Spain	Spain
32	Sweden	Sweden	Sweden	Sweden
33	Switzerland	Switzerland	Switzerland	Switzerland
34		Taiwan	Taiwan	Taiwan
35			Thailand	Thailand
36			Turkey	Turkey
37	United Kingdom	United Kingdom	United Kingdom	United Kingdom
38		Venezuela	Venezuela	Venezuela

For the United States, partners differ according to periods.
*Heterogenous industry defined as follows: Inward fdi 80/86: other indust. + services; Inward fdi 87/94: other indust. + mining; Outward fdi 82/95: other indust. + mining + retail trade.
n.a.: non-available; calc: calculated.

3.4.2. Methodology

Three sets of explanatory variables are introduced in the estimates: country variables, sectoral variables, and FDI variables, as detailed in Appendix 5.

- Country variables are: the size of markets, proxied by the average GDP[5] of the reporting country and its partner (AVRGDP), the Balassa–Bauwens measure of differences in GDPs (DIFFGDPW), the demand for variety proxied by the average income per capita of the reporting country and its partner (AVRGDPPC), the economic distance and the difference in human capital endowment both proxied by the difference in income per capita between the reporting country and its partner (DIFFGDPPC), the transportation costs proxied by the geographical distance (DIST), the existence of a common border (adjacency, ADJ) and the regionalization proxied by the existence of preferential commercial schemes (dummy CPOL).
- Turning to sectoral variables, which have no country dimension, concentration, economies of scale, share of white-collar workers in employment, capital intensity, or capital ratio (barriers to entry) can be used. Given the high level of industry aggregation, it has been decided to introduce economies of scale only. A 'representative economy' has been constructed, pooling British, French, German and Italian firms, by size. Calculation is carried out at the three-digit level of the NACE. The relative productivity of larger firms (>500 employees) is computed.
- Lastly, FDI is disentangled into outward and inward flows, in bilateral relations between the reporting country k and its partner k' and relations of k with all other countries: thus the notations will be OUT and IN, OUTOTH and INOTH.

The log-linearization of FDI was a problem in the previous section, due to zero or negative values. Turning in this section to a panel of industries, this problem is even more difficult. It would be possible to adopt the same transformation (see Appendix 2). But at such a level of detail, results would be highly sensitive to the choice of the constant used in the transformation process. Hence we used raw data. A tentative estimate with transformed FDI flows is provided in Fontagné and Pajot (1998).

We consider each panel as a sequence of (annual) periods and systematically introduce fixed effects on periods as far as statistical tests support models with effects. In addition, different combinations of specific effects are introduced in order to account for unobserved industry and partner effects.[6]

First, we estimate bilateral import and export equations (equations (2)), using the classical vector of macroeconomic variables plus our four bilateral variables of FDI flows; in addition, a variable of economies of scale (having no time dimension) plus a fixed effect on partners account for the proximity–concentration trade-off. For example, distance is captured by such fixed effects. But the existence of a common border, language, culture, etc. is also captured.

$$Z_{ijkt} = \alpha_1 \text{AVRGDP}_{ijt} + \alpha_2 \text{DIFFGDPW}_{ijt} + \alpha_3 \text{CPOL}_{ijt}$$
$$+ \alpha_4 \text{SCALE}_k + \alpha_5 \text{FOUT}_{ijkt} + \alpha_6 \text{FIN}_{ijkt}$$
$$+ \alpha_7 \text{FOUTOTH}_{ikt} + \alpha_8 \text{FINOTH}_{ikt} + e_j + e_t \quad (2)$$

$$Z = X, M$$

Second, we estimate bilateral import and export equations (equation (3a)), using the same vector of macroeconomic variables plus our four bilateral variables of FDI flows. The industry dimension is no longer captured by a measure of economies of scale, but by a fixed effect on industries hence, remaining industry specificity (e.g. capital intensity or market structures) is controlled for. Reciprocally, the fixed effect on the partner country is dropped, and country specificity is captured by the traditional distance and adjacency variables.

$$Z_{ijkt} = \alpha_1 \text{AVRGDP}_{ijt} + \alpha_2 \text{DIFFGDPW}_{ijt} + \alpha_3 \text{CPOL}_{ijt}$$
$$+ \alpha_4 \text{DIST}_{ij} + \alpha_5 \text{ADJ}_{ij} + \alpha_6 \text{FOUT}_{ijkt} + \alpha_7 \text{FIN}_{ijkt}$$
$$+ \alpha_8 \text{FOUTOTH}_{ikt} + \alpha_9 \text{FINOTH}_{ikt} + e_k + e_t \quad (3a)$$

$$Z = X, M$$

Then we estimate bilateral import and export equations excluding economies of scale, distance and adjacency, but integrating alternatively industry fixed effects (equation (3b)), or country fixed effects (equation (3c)).

$$Z_{ijkt} = \alpha_1 \text{AVRGDP}_{ijt} + \alpha_2 \text{DIFFGDPW}_{ijt} + \alpha_3 \text{CPOL}_{ijt}$$
$$+ \alpha_4 \text{FOUT}_{ijkt} + \alpha_5 \text{FIN}_{ijkt} + \alpha_6 \text{FOUTOTH}_{ikt}$$
$$+ \alpha_7 \text{FINOTH}_{ikt} + e_k + e_t \quad (3b)$$

$$Z = X, M$$

$$Z_{ijkt} = \alpha_1 \text{AVRGDP}_{ijt} + \alpha_2 \text{DIFFGDPW}_{ijt} + \alpha_3 \text{CPOL}_{ijt}$$
$$+ \alpha_4 \text{FOUT}_{ijkt} + \alpha_5 \text{FIN}_{ijkt} + \alpha_6 \text{FOUTOTH}_{ikt}$$
$$+ \alpha_7 \text{FINOTH}_{ikt} + e_j + e_t \quad (3c)$$

$$Z = X, M$$

$$Z_{ijkt} = \alpha_1 \text{AVRGDP}_{ijt} + \alpha_2 \text{DIFFGDPW}_{ijt} + \alpha_3 \text{CPOL}_{ijt}$$
$$+ \alpha_4 \text{FOUT}_{ijkt} + \alpha_5 \text{FIN}_{ijkt} + \alpha_6 \text{FOUTOTH}_{ikt}$$
$$+ \alpha_7 \text{FINOTH}_{ikt} + e_j \quad (3d)$$

$$Z = X, M$$

Lastly, the latter equation is estimated excluding the period fixed effects by stake of comparison (equation (3d)).

Countries with which France or the United States trades the most are also countries with which links are the strongest: culture, history, language, geographic proximity. Hence, if such source of variance remains unobservable, this influence is captured by the FDI variable in the absence of fixed effects on the partners: we get a biased estimator. The lower the emphasis on macroeconomic variables, the stronger the bias.

Accordingly, fixed effects on partners are good substitutes for adjacency or transport costs variables. Consider, for example, the French case. Having controlled for FDI, average market size, difference in market sizes (export equation), or in income per capita (import equation), and trade agreements, the geography of French exports (Table 3.5) and imports (Table 3.6) is easily characterized. Germany is *ceteris paribus* the most preferred French trade partner for exports and imports, followed by Italy, Belgium, United Kingdom, etc. Mediterranean historical partners are in a very good relative position. At the opposite of the spectrum, countries for which the geography of trade costs is the most detrimental are the United States and Japan.

Turning to industries, variables related to transaction costs (adjacency and distance) are integrated in the equations, in order to capture only the specialization of the reporting country. In the export equation, for instance, the largest positive effects are obtained for transport equipment, chemicals, food, machinery and agriculture. This is to be compared with the negative effects associated with coke and petroleum, minerals, quarrying, refined petroleum, etc. This is precisely the French specialization to export.

In total, models with effects have to be preferred to OLS estimates largely used in the related literature; and period plus partner fixed effects should be introduced systematically. We are, however, constrained by two outcomes. First, since we must[7] maintain a fixed effect on periods, we cannot add more than one fixed effect, which will be alternatively associated with partners or industries. Second, when the industry disaggregation is weak, a large, part of the variance is associated with characteristics of the partner country. Hence, partners' fixed effects largely capture such variance: the parameter estimates for FDI variables are reduced. In addition, the significance level of our parameter estimates is much lower for FDI variables.

As an illustrative example of the latter outcome, Table 3.7 considers two sets of estimates, with and without country fixed effects. Only two bilateral macroeconomic variables are introduced (referred to in the first column). The first set of rows considers the relationship between total bilateral FDI and total bilateral trade. The second and third sets consider respectively such relations for the panel of nineteen French industries and for the same industries aggregated in the six-sector US nomenclature. The influence of fixed effects is strongest in the import equation. If we aggregate this data in the US nomenclature, the statistical significance of the related parameters sinks. Notice the difference in parameter estimates between both

Table 3.5 Fixed effects on partners and industries: French exports 1984–94

Fixed effects on partners (equation (3c))			Fixed effects on industries (equation (3a))		
Partner	Effect	t-stat	Industry	Effect	t-stat
Germany	928	17.02	18	395	25.09
Italy	544	10.07	13	217	12.87
Belgium +Luxemb.	511	12.08	19	146	8.38
United Kingdom	363	6.76	15	89	5.65
Switzerland	223	7.80	1	76	4.80
Spain	177	4.19	17	66	3.73
Netherlands	90	2.05	20	40	2.53
Algeria	75	2.50	9	40	2.54
Morocco	72	1.89	16	5	0.30
Tunisia	67	1.60	22	−2	−0.13
Singapore	25	0.71	23	−44	−2.80
Egypt	12	0.40	14	−48	−3.10
Israel	−3	−0.08	21	−88	−5.55
Hungary	−4	−0.11	12	−121	−7.73
Chile	−7	−0.18	4	−132	−8.36
Austria	−11	−0.43	5	−142	−9.05
Hong Kong	−12	−0.41	8	−153	−9.65
Malaysia	−14	−0.42	11	−166	−10.46
Sweden	−19	−0.67	3	−176	−10.49
New Zealand	−19	−0.57			
Philippines	−21	−0.63			
Venezuela	−27	−0.91			
Turkey	−31	−1.18			
Norway	−31	−1.19			
Finland	−31	−1.18			
Thailand	−32	−1.16			
Poland	−39	−1.46			
Indonesia	−53	−2.02			
Taiwan	−61	−2.30			
Portugal	−61	−1.44			
Argentina	−85	−3.15			
Korea Republic of	−86	−2.90			
Mexico	−111	−3.51			
Australia	−112	−3.40			
China	−145	−3.59			
Canada	−148	−3.38			
Greece	−152	−3.26			
Ireland	−153	−2.94			
Brazil	−164	−4.14			
Denmark	−173	−3.99			
Ex-USSR	−204	−4.40			
Japan	−531	−9.94			
United States	−551	−6.46			

Table 3.6 Fixed effects on partners and industries: French imports 1984–94

Fixed effects on partners (equation (3c))			Fixed effects on industries (equation (3a))		
Partner	Effect	t-stat	Industry	Effect	t-stat
Germany	1337	23.88	18	287	14.27
Italy	620	11.61	20	125	6.25
Belgium +Luxemb.	567	10.44	15	123	6.11
United Kingdom	359	6.80	13	121	5.59
Spain	189	4.34	17	87	3.83
Netherlands	177	3.28	16	78	3.89
Switzerland	100	3.16	19	70	3.15
Morocco	63	1.83	23	66	3.25
Algeria	56	1.69	9	15	0.73
China	28	0.80	22	−15	−0.74
Tunisia	25	0.73	3	−26	−1.21
Thailand	4	0.11	1	−44	−2.15
Indonesia	3	0.09	14	−49	−2.44
Egypt	2	0.06	21	−50	−2.44
Philippines	1	0.04	4	−108	−5.32
Malaysia	−8	−0.23	12	−133	−6.68
Chile	−9	−0.26	8	−174	−8.59
Turkey	−10	−0.29	11	−181	−8.92
Poland	−14	−0.40	5	−192	−9.60
Ex-USSR	−22	−0.64			
Hungary	−25	−0.75			
Brazil	−26	−0.79			
Venezuela	−38	−1.15			
Mexico	−45	−1.36			
Korea Republic of	−55	−1.72			
Taiwan	−65	−2.06			
Portugal	−67	−1.52			
Norway	−72	−2.14			
Argentina	−75	−2.35			
Sweden	−101	−2.90			
Israel	−133	−4.02			
Ireland	−142	−2.73			
Singapore	−160	−4.62			
New Zealand	−162	−4.80			
Finland	−164	−4.61			
Greece	−169	−3.27			
Hong Kong	−172	−5.00			
Austria	−191	−5.03			
Australia	−216	−6.23			
Denmark	−233	−4.38			
Canada	−253	−7.23			
Japan	−389	−6.43			
United States	−518	−4.95			

Table 3.7 Comparison of parameter estimates for specifications including or excluding effects. France (1984–94), no fixed effect on periods

		Excluding country fixed effects		Including country fixed effects	
		X	M	X	M
France – French nom.: Total	FOUT	1.517***	1.293***	1.164***	1.278***
Macro: $AVRGDP_{ij}$, $DIFFGDPPC_{ij}$		(4.50)	(3.21)	(7.00)	(7.58)
	FIN	4.641***	4.586***	1.820***	1.392***
		(9.87)	(8.15)	(7.92)	(5.97)
France – French nom.: Industries	FOUT	0.545***	0.220**	0.503***	0.241***
macro: $AVRGDP_{ij}$, $DIFFGDPW_{ij}$		(7.12)	(2.34)	(7.43)	(2.92)
	FIN	0.492***	0.677***	0.288***	0.402***
		(4.34)	(4.86)	(2.89)	(3.31)
France – US nom.: Industries	FOUNT	0.422*	0.653**	0.344*	0.266
macro: $AVRGDP_{ij}$, $DIFFGDPW_{ij}$		(1.898)	(2.04)	(1.77)	(0.99)
	FIN	1.243***	1.840***	0.623**	0.911**
		(3.82)	(3.927)	(2.25)	(2.39)

Significant at 1% (***), 5% (**), 10% (*).

levels of data aggregation (when these parameters are significant): as expected, a smaller number of industries leads to higher complementarity effects due to the 'internalization' of spillovers. The parameter estimate is even much larger in the first set of rows concerning the equation 'total'.

Another issue is the choice between fixed and random effects. Generally, models with fixed effects have a better fit (Figure 3.1) for equations concerning the manufacturing sector as a whole. In contrast, the Hausman test generally discriminates in favour of random effects as far as the panel of individual industries is concerned. Given the structural nature of the related effects, fixed effects have been chosen. The magnitude of the parameters is generally unaffected by this choice, as illustrated in Table 3.8.

Systematically, macroeconomic variables have the right sign in our equations. The average size of markets, average income per capita, economic distance (intensity of the comparative advantage), adjacency and regional integration have a positive impact on the value of trade flows; and reciprocally for the difference in market sizes. Such results are extensively replicated in the literature and deserve much attention. We will focus in the following on the specific role of FDI, returns to scale and transaction costs.

3.4.3. Results for France

On the whole, the diagnosis of complementarity between trade and FDI flows is validated by our methodology, even at the sectoral level. Let us consider this result in detail (Tables 3.9 and 3.10), bearing in mind that country determinants of trade are controlled for, and that we have a panel of nineteen industries.

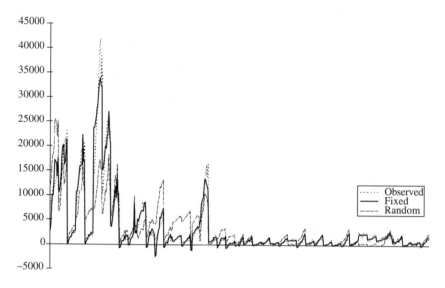

Figure 3.1 Observed and fitted values for the equation 'total'. France 1984–94.

Considering the 'industry + scale' estimates (equation (2)), a one dollar outward FDI flow is associated with 54 cents of additional exports and with only 24 cents of additional imports, in the industry considered, *vis-à-vis* the country of investment. Thus, three conclusions can already be drawn.

First, notwithstanding possible substitution effects at the level of individual firms, our panel of nineteen industries validates the complementarity between trade and outward FDI flows. That does not mean that such complementarity is necessarily observed for each industry; such outcome will be investigated further below. That does not mean that other proxies of the multinational activity would give the same result: FDI stocks or foreign subsidiaries' production abroad could give a different assessment.

Second, outward FDI is not complementary with exports only. Outward FDI is also associated with additional imports. It could be the case that France imports more (is disadvantaged) in certain industries: facing import pressure, French firms would relocate their production abroad, leading to a positive relationship between outward FDI flows and imports in our panel. The only way to control for such outcome is to introduce fixed effects on industries: this, however, will force us to drop economies of scale.

Third, conditional to the previous remark, we get provisional information on the magnitude, and not only the direction of the relationship between trade and FDI flows within industries. Here, each dollar of French investment abroad is associated with a 30-cent trade surplus in the industry of the investment, *vis-à-vis* the country of investment.

Table 3.8 Comparison of fixed and random effect specifications in the panel of French industries

	Total		Manufacturing sector		Industries	
	Fixed effect	Random effect	Fixed effect	Random effect	Fixed effect	Random effect
FOUT	1.164***	1.174***	0.782***	0.778***	0.503***	0.503***
FIN	1.821***	1.943***	0.821*	0.939***	0.288***	0.293***
FOUTOTH	−0.008	−0.008	0.034	0.037	0.038***	0.038***
FINOTH	0.014	0.024	0.058	0.075	0.149***	0.149***
AVRGDP	0.005***	0.005***	0.007***	0.006***	0.0003***	0.0003***
DIFFGDPPC	−0.142***	−0.140***	−0.215***	−0.209***		
DIFFGDPW					−292.76***	−321.40***
CPOL	3017.7***	4089***	2830.5***	3950.5***	133.42***	203.17***
CSTE		−256.94		−557.31		86.799*

Significant at 1% (***), 5% (**), 10% (*).

Table 3.9 Export equations for France (1984–94, nineteen industries)

	Effect on partners only (3d)	Effect on periods and			
		Partners (3c)	Industry (3b)	Industry (transaction costs) (3a)	Partners (economies of scale) (2)
FOUT	0.503***	0.497***	0.487***	0.491***	0.541***
	7.431	7.336	6.706	7.232	7.767
FIN	0.288***	0.293***	0.388***	0.284***	0.111
	2.898	2.950	3.626	2.841	1.124
FOUTOTH	0.038***	0.042***	0.002	0.002	0.082***
	4.467	4.561	0.168	0.174	8.173
FINOTH	0.149***	0.154***	0.032*	0.034**	0.085***
	10.476	10.476	1.854	2.141	5.506
AVRGDP	0.0003***	0.0004***	0.0003***	0.0002***	0.0005***
	15.144	11.499	20.926	24.258	12.646
DIFFGDPW	−292.76***	−173.65**	−367.77***	−183.06	−199.41**
	−3.759	−2.052	−21.840	−11.036	−2.111
AVRGDPPC					
DIFFGDPPC					
CPOL	133.42***	166.20***	409.33***	247.95***	189.12***
	2.993	3.642	41.399	22.612	3.713
SCALE					100.84***
					5.725
ADJ				490.55***	
				35.343	
DIST				−0.0029***	
				−3.297	
Cste		−77.47	124.65***	18.382	−233.75***
		−1.439	8.858	1.225	−3.669
R^2 adj	0.481	0.482	0.40	0.48	0.55
F	171.28	140.55	167.37	217.24	143.78
nobs	8987	8987	8987	8987	7095
LM	49721	49723	24055	30919	47222
Hausman	—	37.18	6.97 (0.4)	3.34 (0.9)	—
cond. numb.	7.5 (2.7)	7.5 (2.7)	7.5 (2.7)	9.1 (3.6)	16.4 (6.5)

Significant at 1% (***), 5% (**), 10% (*).

Unfortunately, turning to inward FDI, the equation controlling for economies of scale is not significant. It is rather difficult to assess the magnitude of the parameter we are interested in, even if the sign remains positive. Hence a specification with fixed effects on periods and on industries must be preferred.[8]

Using equation (3a), we control the individual specificity of the nineteen industries in the panel: economies of scale, market structures, comparative advantage, etc. The adjacency variable controls for transaction costs, while geographic distance enters successfully in the export equation only. Since we now control for the

Table 3.10 Import equations for France (1984–94, nineteen industries)

	Effect on partners only (3d)	Effect on periods and			
		Partners (3c)	Industry (3b)	Industry (transaction costs) (3a)	Partners (economies of scale) (2)
FOUT	0.241***	0.235***	0.177*	0.197**	0.245***
	2.923	2.843	1.920	2.270	2.930
FIN	0.402***	0.407***	0.606***	0.465***	0.153
	3.317	3.356	4.469	3.641	1.285
FOUTOTH	0.053***	0.047***	0.007	0.006	0.046***
	5.024	4.229	0.386	0.380	3.826
FINOTH	0.083***	0.088***	0.009	0.012	0.046***
	4.823	4.930	0.420	0.609	2.512
AVRGDP	0.0004***	0.0003***	0.0003***	0.0003***	0.0004***
	15.488	8.035	23.953	23.960	9.472
DIFFGDPW					
AVRGDPPC					
DIFFGDPPC	−0.014***	−0.015***	−0.011***	−0.008***	−0.019***
	−8.366	−7.214	−11.607	−8.685	−8.037
CPOL	99.443*	91.421*	467.25***	281.53***	93.976
	1.840	1.667	35.132	20.634	1.561
SCALE					145.43***
					6.882
ADJ				570.40***	
				34.121	
DIST					
Cste		59.367	1.512	−42.93***	−120.14**
		1.380	0.092	−2.720	−2.242
R^2 adj	0.44	0.44	0.30	0.38	0.56
F	147.41	120.36	109.29	151.62	147.31
Nobs	8987	8987	8987	8987	7095
LM	54817	54819	5993	7626	67253
Hausman	—	21.60	11.91 (0.11)	9.65 (0.29)	—
cond. numb.	6 (2.9)	6 (2.9)	6 (2.9)	6 (3)	16 (5.4)

Significant at 1% (***), 5% (**), 10% (*).

level of comparative advantage of individual industries, the value of the parameter estimate for FOUT shrinks to 49 cents per dollar. In the same way, the value of the parameter estimate for FOUT shrinks in the import equation: we get 20 cents additional imports to be compared with 25 cents in the previous estimation. As expected, France exports more and invests more abroad in industries which have a competitive advantage: this accounts roughly for 10 per cent of the complementarity between outward FDI and exports observed at the industry level. The same remark can be made for imports: France imports and invests abroad in industries which suffer a competitive disadvantage: this accounts for roughly 20 per cent of the observed complementarity between outward FDI and imports observed at the industry level. Turning to inward FDI, the relationship is significant in equation (3a). We get the following magnitudes: 47 cents of additional imports per dollar of hosted FDI, compared with only 28 cents additional exports.

Equation (3b) has fixed effects on industries and periods, but does not control for transaction costs. Hence, the parameters for FDI are inflated by such an outcome in the import equation. This equation is provided by stake of comparison but results are clearly unreliable for the import equation.

Equation (3c) has fixed effects on partners and periods but does not control for economies of scale. Results are similar to equation (2) as far as the export equation is concerned. In contrast, the import equation has a better fit and this is why we are interested in such specification. Parameter estimates are similar to those obtained with equation (3a).

In total, the reliable magnitude of the parameter estimates is the following. Each dollar of outward FDI is associated with roughly 50 cents additional exports to the host country and 20 cents additional imports from the host country. Reciprocally, each dollar of inward FDI is associated with 40 cents of additional imports from the investing country and 30 cents additional exports to the investing country. This suggests a negative impact of inward FDI on the trade balance in the industry considered, in coherence with the trade surplus associated with outward FDI. From a policy point of view, this result leads to the conclusion that outward FDI enhances the competitiveness of the investing industry. We will examine this issue in detail below.

Concerning third countries, our estimates fail to identify anything but a rather negligible positive impact. The impact of French outward FDI toward third countries on bilateral French exports is only marginal (though positive and statistically significant). In addition, it is roughly balanced by the reciprocal impact on imports. The impact of inward investment from third countries on bilateral French exports is larger: 15 cents per dollar.

3.4.4. Comparison with the United States

The principle of estimates is identical to the one referred to above. It must be noticed, however, that the quality of the model is smoothed by the aggregation of industries. We tentatively estimated three specifications with effects: one specification with fixed effects on partners only (equation (4)), one with fixed effects on periods only (equation (5)), and one with fixed effects on periods controlling for economies of scale (equation (6)). Equation (4) is accepted by the Lagrange Multiplier test, whereas equations (5) and (6) are rejected. Hence, an OLS specification (equation (7)) must be preferred, incorporating economies of scale within the vector of explanatory variables in order to maintain the link with the underlying proximity–concentration trade-off. Equation (6) is not reported in Tables 3.11 and 3.12 below: equation (5) is reported by stake of comparison only. Once again, the complementarity relationship between trade and FDI flows is ascertained.

Table 3.11 Export equations for a panel of six industries (France and United States, 1984–94)

		Fixed effect on partners only (4)	Fixed effect on periods only (5)	OLS + Scale (7)
France	FOUT	0.344*	0.362*	0.381**
		1.777	1.785	2.013
	FIN	0.623**	0.850***	0.493*
		2.252	2.885	1.772
	FOUTOTH	0.006	−0.067	0.030
		0.202	−1.483	1.005
	FINOTH	0.422***	0.510***	0.119***
		9.982	9.601	2.568
	R^2 adj	0.524	0.458	0.514
	F	63.68	115.62	288.26
	nobs	2442	2442	2442
	LM	6360	0.01 (0.92)	1.92 (0.16)
	Hausman	—	3.39 (0.91)	—
	cond. numb.	6.3 (3.7)	6.46 (3.82)	59.37 (6.41)
USA	FOUT	2.788***	2.749***	2.655***
		8.463	8.588	8.681
	FIN	0.255	0.359**	0.524***
		1.587	2.351	3.641
	FOUTOTH	0.242***	0.251***	−0.083*
		5.206	5.177	−1.790
	FINOTH	0.066**	0.089**	0.047*
		2.174	2.496	1.645
	R^2 adj	0.45	0.44	0.49
	F	25.92	48.22	121.30
	nobs	1004	1004	1004
	LM	407.65	10.31	2.66 (0.10)
	Hausman	43.23	11.60 (0.11)	8.05 (0.43)
	cond. numb.	13.9 (3.2)	14.32 (3.37)	58.61 (13.55)

Significant at 1% (***), 5% (**), 10% (*).

$$Z_{ijkt} = \alpha_1 \text{AVRGDP}_{ijt} + \alpha_2 \text{DIFFGDPPC}_{ijt} + \alpha_3 \text{CPOL}_{ijt} + \alpha_4 \text{FOUT}_{ijkt}$$
$$+ \alpha_5 \text{FIN}_{ijkt} + \alpha_6 \text{FOUTOTH}_{ikt} + \alpha_7 \text{FINOTH}_{ikt} + e_j \qquad (4)$$

$$Z = X, M$$

$$Z_{ijkt} = \alpha_1 \text{AVRGDP}_{ijt} + \alpha_2 \text{DIFFGDPPC}_{ijt} + \alpha_3 \text{CPOL}_{ijt} + \alpha_4 \text{ADJ}_{ij}$$
$$+ \alpha_5 \text{FOUT}_{ijkt} + \alpha_6 \text{FIN}_{ijkt} + \alpha_7 \text{FOUTOTH}_{ikt}$$
$$+ \alpha_8 \text{FINOTH}_{ikt} + e_t \qquad (5)$$

$$Z = X, M$$

Table 3.12 Import equations for a panel of six industries (France and United States, 1984–94)

		Fixed effect on partners only (4)	Fixed effect on periods only (5)	OLS + Scale (7)
France	FOUT	0.266	0.088	0.118
		1.000	0.310	0.436
	FIN	0.912**	1.310***	0.890**
		2.391	3.171	2.245
	FOUTOTH	0.057	−0.019	0.081*
		1.379	−0.310	1.936
	FINOTH	0.431***	0.526***	0.072
		7.405	7.066	1.088
	R^2 adj	0.467	0.369	0.416
	F	51.83	80.36	193.95
	nobs	2442	2442	2442
	LM	9447	1.12 (0.29)	4.39 (0.04)
	Hausman	—	—	—
	cond. numb.	5.5 (3.5)	6.46 (3.82)	59.37 (6.41)
USA	FOUT	3.374***	2.728***	2.600***
		5.409	4.482	
	FIN	0.898***	0.721**	1.277***
		2.957	2.451	
	FOUTOTH	0.357***	0.393***	−0.317***
		4.058	4.202	
	FINOTH	0.093*	0.134**	0.109*
		1.609	1.946	
	R^2 adj	0.362	0.33	0.313
	F	18.31	30.36	58.18
	nobs	1004	1004	1004
	LM	954.65	45.34	37.40
	Hausman	31.74	15.15 (0.03)	10.37 (0.24)
	cond. numb.	13.9 (3.2)	14.32 (3.37)	58.61 (13.55)

Significant at 1% (***), 5% (**), 10% (*).

$$Z_{ijkt} = \alpha_1 \text{AVRGDP}_{ijt} + \alpha_2 \text{DIFFGDPPC}_{ijt} + \alpha_3 \text{CPOL}_{ijt} + \alpha_4 \text{ADJ}_{ij}$$
$$+ \alpha_5 \text{SCALE}_k + \alpha_6 \text{FOUT}_{ijkt} + \alpha_7 \text{FIN}_{ijkt} + \alpha_8 \text{FOUTOTH}_{ikt}$$
$$+ \alpha_9 \text{FINOTH}_{ikt} + e_t \tag{6}$$
$$Z = X, M$$

$$Z_{ijkt} = \alpha_1 \text{AVRGDP}_{ijt} + \alpha_2 \text{DIFFGDPPC}_{ijt} + \alpha_3 \text{CPOL}_{ijt} + \alpha_4 \text{ADJ}_{ij}$$
$$+ \alpha_5 \text{SCALE}_k + \alpha_6 \text{FOUT}_{ijkt} + \alpha_7 \text{FIN}_{ijkt} + \alpha_8 \text{FOUTOTH}_{ikt}$$
$$+ \alpha_9 \text{FINOTH}_{ikt} \tag{7}$$
$$Z = X, M$$

Using this more aggregated nomenclature, outward French FDI has no significant impact on French bilateral imports. In contrast, its positive impact on French exports is ascertained: 34–38 cents per dollar.

This is to be compared with the parameter estimates obtained for US outward FDI, which are by far larger. Hence, the complementarity between trade flows and FDI outward flows is much higher at the industry level for the United States. It does not prove, however, that there is any benefit for the US trade balance. In particular, when fixed effects on partners are introduced, the induced trade deficit associated with US outward FDI is large. This is potentially due to importation from subsidiaries located in low-wage countries. The comparison of the parameter estimates in the import equation with and without fixed effects has the following explanation: when one controls for the general structure of US imports, outward US FDI leads to more imports than otherwise. Hence, relatively marginal exporters to the US market provide the bulk of US imports associated with foreign investment.

Turning to inward FDI, the negative impact on the French trade balance is assessed only when we introduce fixed effects on partners. It must be noticed, however, that the magnitude of the complementarity relation is much larger than in the export case. Such outcome is not observed in the US case: inward FDI has a limited impact on trade flows. Noticeably, the relationship between inward FDI and exports is much weaker in the US than in the French case. Foreign firms invest in the US in order to enter a huge domestic market: they do not aim to export from the subsidiary. However, the net impact on the trade balance remains negative.

Such relations may, however, differ by industry and we have to turn to estimates for individual industries.

The industry specificity of the relation between trade and FDI can be addressed, estimating the model industry by industry. Using the disaggregation of industry into six sectors on French and US data gives a rough overview of such sector specificity (Table 3.13).

As expected, it is not only the magnitude of the relation that changes across industries, but also the sign of the parameter estimates associated with FDI. In addition, it can also change according to the reporting country. Consider petroleum, for example. French FDI abroad is substitutive to French exports, and more surprisingly substitutive to French imports. Turning to the United States, there is in contrast a complementarity relationship of inward and outward flows of FDI with imports.

With the exception of the latter sector, the relationship between trade and FDI is positive when significant, but we could hardly give an example of a significant and positive impact of FDI on the trade balance of the investor or of the investing country.

Table 3.13 Parameter estimates for FDI in individual industries trade
equations (France and Unites States 1984–94)

	France		USA	
	FOUT	*FIN*	*FOUT*	*FIN*
Exports				
Petroleum	−0.070**	−0.050	−0.019	−0.018
Food	0.347***	0.287**	−0.100	0.015
Chemicals	−0.070	1.250***	0.111	0.018
Metals	0.282**	4.130***	0.130	0.370***
Machinery	0.183	−0.290	−0.030	0.146
Transport eqpt. other manuf	0.850*	−0.595	0.890***	−0.200*
Imports				
Petroleum	−0.345**	0.144	0.279***	0.149***
Food	0.126	0.076	0.126	0.075
Chemicals	0.091	1.520***	−0.021	0.347
Metals	0.300*	4.320***	0.138	0.503***
Machinery	−0.218	−0.286	0.703	0.441
Transport eqpt. other manuf	0.848	−0.560	1.219**	0.185

Significant at 1% (***), 5% (**), 10% (*).

3.5. Is the macroeconomic complementarity between trade and FDI an artefact?

It must lastly be examined if the complementarity observed at the macroeconomic level is a statistical artefact. In order to tackle this criticism, two issues have to be considered: the extent of spillovers between industries, and the potential joint determination of trade and FDI flows at the sectoral level by the sectoral competitiveness.

3.5.1. The observed complementarity is partly due to spillovers

Let us first consider trade and FDI data for the manufacturing sector and for the economy as a whole. It is expected that spillovers between industries increase the (absolute value of) parameter estimates associated with FDI: but how important are such spillovers?

We consider here a model with fixed effects on partners only: it is impossible to introduce fixed effects on industries since we run estimates not only on the panel of nineteen industries but also on the manufacturing sector as a whole or on the whole economy. We are interested in doing a comparison of parameters between these estimates. Hence the specification must remain the same in the three sets of estimates. In total, three equations of bilateral exports are estimated: first within the panel of the individual industries (equation (10)); second at the manufacturing level using FDI within the manufacturing sector as an explanatory variable (equation (9)); third at the manufacturing level using total FDI as an explanatory variable (equation (8)). Three equations for imports are estimated in the same way. Our estimates highlight positive spillovers, since the impact on trade is much higher in the equations for 'Total industry'.

$$Z_{ijt} = \alpha_1 AVRGDP_{ijt} + \alpha_2 DIFFGDPPC_{ijt} + \alpha_3 CPOL_{ijt}$$
$$+ \alpha_4 ADJ_{ij} + \alpha_5 FOUT_{ijt} + \alpha_6 FIN_{ijt} + e_t \qquad (8,9)$$

$$Z = X, M$$

$$Z_{ijkt} = \alpha_1 AVRGDP_{ijt} + \alpha_2 DIFFGDPPC_{ijt} + \alpha_3 CPOL_{ijt}$$
$$+ \alpha_4 ADJ_{ij} + \alpha_5 FOUT_{ijkt} + \alpha_6 FIN_{ijkt} + e_t \qquad (10)$$

$$Z = X, M$$

All but one parameter estimates for our variables FIN and FOUT are significant for France[9] (Table 3.14). The last three columns identify respectively the spillovers of FDI in services on trade in goods (1)/(2), the spillovers between total FDI and individual industries exports and imports (1)/(3) and the spillovers of FDI in individual industries on the rest of the manufacturing sector (2)/(3).

The spillover ratio for outward FDI is 1.87 between industries as far as bilateral exports are concerned: a dollar of outward FDI in a given industry is associated with only 58 cents additional exports in this industry and 1.09 dollar additional exports in the manufacturing sector as a whole. To put it differently, *58 cents additional exports are registered in the industry that invests one dollar abroad and 50 cents in addition throughout the rest of the manufacturing sector*.[10] Even if the comparison of the first and third columns highlights large spillovers, these results stress that the 30 cents positive trade imbalance associated with each dollar invested abroad is independent of the level of analysis and of the magnitude of the spillovers.[11]

The spillover ratio for inward FDI is much larger as far as exports are concerned. The expected negative trade imbalance reaches 13 cents per dollar at the industry level, but 46 cents for the manufacturing sector as a whole. To put it differently, each dollar of foreign investment in France is associated with 13 cents additional imports from the investor's country in the industry of investment, and to 33 cents additional imports from the investor's country in the remaining industries.[12]

3.5.2. Trade and FDI are the two faces of the same coin

Countries invest abroad and export more in industries in which they are advantaged. Reciprocally, countries invest abroad and *import* more in industries in which they are disadvantaged. Lastly, foreign firms invest more in the domestic economy in

71

Table 3.14 An assesment of the magnitude of spillovers for France and FDI

	Total (1) (8)	Manuf (2) (9)	Indus (3) (10)	(1)/(2)	(1)/(3)	(2)/(3)
Export						
FOUT	1.072***	1.087**	0.580***	0.99	1.85	1.87
	4.098	2.264	7.933			
FIN	3.645***	2.576***	0.432***	1.42	8.44	5.96
	9.975	3.157	3.994			
R^2 adj	0.807	0.739	0.390			
F	124.86	84.96	348.43			
nobs	473	473	8987			
LM	3.65 (0.056)	2.55 (0.11)	1.10 (0.29)			
Hausman	1.61 (0.95)	3.22 (0.78)	7.49 (0.27)			
cond. numb.	6.39 (4.09)	6.05 (3.63)	5.62 (2.68)			
Import						
FOUT	0.768**	0.167	0.276***	ns	2.783	ns
	2.309	0.277	3.095			
FIN	3.542***	3.040***	0.564***	1.17	6.28	5.39
	7.626	2.959	4.270			
R^2 adj	0.756	0.716	0.335			
F	92.71	75.54	284.95			
nobs	473	473	8987			
LM	4.65 (0.03)	2.99 (0.08)	0.01 (099)			
Hausman	0.81 (091)	2.81 (0.83)	6.35 (0.385)			
cond. numb.	6.39 (4.09)	6.05 (3.63)	5.62 (2.68)			

Significant at 1% (***), 5% (**), 10% (*).
ns: not significant.

sectors for which the domestic economy is disadvantaged. Introducing effects on sectors is expected to reduce the magnitude of the complementarity between trade and FDI flows. In total, the measurement of the relationship between FDI flows and the changes in sectoral trade balances can be affected by the introduction of effects on industries or partners in the estimates. Various combinations of panel estimates have to be introduced in order to check this point. This is done in Table 3.15 for the French panel of nineteen industries and in Table 3.16 for the US–French panel of six industries.

In the French case, using the nineteen-industry panel, estimates of trade imbalances are robust to the change of specification. Fixed effects on partners only, or a combination of fixed effects on periods and partners or industries do not change fundamentally the parameter estimate concerning outward FDI. Each dollar invested abroad is associated with a 26–30 cents export surplus according to the equation estimated. Such amount takes into account the fact that advantaged French industries export and invest more abroad in order to assess their competitiveness. Reciprocally, it takes into account the fact that disadvantaged industries may invest abroad in order to relocate some production capacities in low-cost countries

Table 3.15 Trade imbalance associated with FDI flows, panel of nineteen industries, France 1984–94

	Effect on partners only (3a')	Effect on periods and			
		Partners (3c)	Industries (3b)	Industries (transaction costs) (3a)	Partners (economies of scale) (2)
FOUT	0.262	0.262	0.310	0.294	0.296
FIN	−0.114	−0.114	−0.218	−0.181	ns
FOUTOTH	−0.015	−0.005	ns	ns	0.036
FINOTH	0.066	0.066	ns	ns	0.039

ns: not significant.

Table 3.16 Trade imbalance associated with FDI flows, panel of six industries, France and USA 1984–94

	Fixed effect on partners	Fixed effect on periods	OLS + Scale
France			
FOUT	ns	ns	ns
FIN	−0.289	−0.460	−0.397
FOUTOTH	ns	ns	ns
FINOTH	−0.009	−0.016	ns
USA			
FOUT	−0.586	0.021	0.055
FIN	ns	−0.362	−0.753
FOUTOTH	−0.115	−0.142	0.234
FINOTH	−0.027	−0.045	−0.062

ns: not significant.

and partially import the output at home. Concerning the trade imbalance associated with inward FDI, the results are more sensitive to the specification. When one takes into account the fact that disadvantaged industries import more and are largely subject to inward investment, we get roughly 20 cents of net imports per dollar of inward FDI. But controlling for geographic structure of French imports, we get only 11 cents. This means that countries that export the most toward France are also those that invest the most.

Turning to the panel of six industries, this aggregation reduces the quality of the estimates in the French case. Hence, there is no significant relationship between trade imbalances and outward FDI. This is not the case, however, for inward FDI in France: 30–40 cents of net imports are associated with each dollar of inward FDI. Interestingly, in the US case, the benefits of investing abroad disappear if one controls for the geographic structure of US imports and exports. Here, each dollar of outward FDI is associated with 58 cents net imports if one uses fixed effects on partners. In addition, the impact of inward FDI is also negative when significant (between 36 and 75 cents according to the specifications).

3.6. Conclusion

The WTO working group on the relationship between trade and investment has concluded that the relationship between trade and FDI was a complementarity (WTO 1998). However, this complementarity is challenged in the literature. At the level of the firm, such complementarity is questionable; and unobserved macroeconomic factors can be the very foundation of the observed macroeconomic complementarity. Complementarity might be a simple artefact.

This paper aimed at addressing this issue in a systematic manner using, first, proper macroeconomic modelling and data broken down by sector, country and partner in an international comparative perspective.

Our estimates highlight a complementarity at the macroeconomic level and provide an order of its magnitude. *Bilateral* export equations are estimated using a panel of twenty-one OECD countries. FDI-related parameter estimates are positive, in coherence with the hypothesis of complementarity at the macroeconomic level. The comparison of simulated bilateral trade flows, corresponding to an *anti-monde* without FDI, and observed bilateral trade flows, highlights that the largest increase in trade is associated with the US–Japan relationship, followed by USA–UK and USA–Canada.

Then, we turned to a sectoral and bilateral approach for France and the United States, examining two panels of industries and partner countries over 1984–94. Even at the sectoral level, the diagnosis of complementarity between trade and FDI flows is validated by this methodology. In the French case, controlling for economies of scale, a one-dollar outward FDI flow is associated with 54 cents of additional exports and with only 24 cents of additional imports, in the industry considered *vis-à-vis* the country of investment. The complementarity between trade flows and FDI outward flows is larger at the industry level for the United States. That does not prove, however, that there is any benefit for the US trade balance: when fixed effects on partners are introduced, the induced trade deficit associated with US outward FDI is large.

In total, a large share of the complementarity between trade and FDI at the macroeconomic level can be explained by large spillovers between industries.

Lastly, the introduction of various combinations of specific effects is required in order to check that results are not biased. Estimates of trade imbalances are robust to this change of specification: each dollar invested abroad is associated with roughly 30 cents of net export. The results concerning inward FDI are more sensitive to the specification since countries that export the most to France are also those that invest the most. In the US case, the benefits of investing abroad disappear if one controls for the geographic structure of US trade: each dollar of outward FDI is associated with 58 cents net imports. In addition, the impact of inward FDI is also negative and large when significant.

In total we have demonstrated why, and how much, trade and FDI are complements at the macroeconomic level. This is partially due to spillovers between firms within industries and between industries within the manufacturing sector. It is also partially due to biased estimates when models do not control for the fact that competitiveness is a whole: France exports more and invests more abroad in industries which benefit a competitive advantage: this accounts roughly for 10 per cent of the observed complementarity between outward FDI and exports observed at the industry level. Reciprocally, under-competitive industries are largely contested by foreign entries and may invest abroad in order to relocate production facilities in more advantaged countries.

The following limitations of this analysis must, however, be stressed. First, correlation does not mean causality; hence, we do not consider that FDI causes trade imbalances. Second, our estimates miss long-run benefits generally associated with FDI, notably inward FDI. More generally, alternative variables of foreign activity, such as FDI stocks, should be considered before drawing definitive conclusions.

Appendix 1: variables used in trade equations for 21 OECD countries

X_{ij} Total exports from i to j; unit: US$ million.

$\text{GDPC}_{i(j)}$ GDP of country i (j) in current US$; unit: US$ million.

$\text{GDPPN}_{i(j)}$ Share of country i (j) in the total PPP – GDP of the sample.

$$\text{GDPPN}_i = \frac{\text{GDPP}_i}{\sum_{k=1}^{21} \text{GDPP}_k} \times 100$$

The PPP – GDP is estimated using constant international prices in 1990 US$.

$\text{GDPC}_{i(j)}$ Per capita GDP at current prices in US$ for country i (j).

DFGDPP_{ij} Difference in size between country i and country j, proxied by the difference in PPP – GDPs between the two countries. The absolute value between these GDPs is replaced by a normalization proposed by Balassa and Bauwens (1987). The latter indicator is not sensitive to the absolute size of the countries, in contrast to the former. It takes values ranging from 0 to 1. The more the countries are similar, the more w tends to 0.5, the more the indicator tends to 0.

$$\text{DFGDPP} = 1 + \frac{[w \ln w + (1 - w) \ln(1 - w)]}{\ln 2}$$

$$\text{with } w = \frac{\text{GDPP}_i}{\text{GDPP}_i + \text{GDPP}_j}$$

DFGDPPCP$_{ij}$ Economic distance between i and j proxied by the difference in PPP per capita incomes. Generally, a high per capita income is associated with a larger relative endowment in human and physical capital and in technology. The absolute value of this difference is directly considered here.

$$\text{DFGDPPCP} = |\text{GDPPCP}_i - \text{GDPPCP}_j| \; ; \text{ unit: US\$.}$$

DIST$_{ij}$ Geographic distance between the capitals of countries i and j; unit: kilometer; source: Pc-Globe©.

ADJ$_{ij}$ Dummy for adjacency between i and j; if i and j have a common frontier, then ADJ = 2, else ADJ = 1.

EU   Dummy assessing for the common membership of i and j in the EU (2,1).

TOUT$_{ij}$ Transformation of US\$ million net flows of FDI from country i to country j. Since outward net investments can be either positive (investments exceeding divestments) or negative, the transformation guaranties positive values. See Appendix 2.

TIN$_{ij}$ Transformation of US\$ million net flows of FDI from country j to country i. Since these inward net investments can be either positive (investments exceeding divestments) or negative, the transformation guaranties positive values. See Appendix 2.

All variables were taken in logarithm, with the exception of DFGDPP.

Appendix 2: the transformation of FDI flows

In our sample, the larger net divestment is −US\$ 4,600 million. Thus, the new variable is constrained to be positive for this value. All observations being greater than −US\$ 5,000 million, the ratio fdi/5000 is never larger than −1, and thus the transformed variable is always larger than 0, a value that can be log-linearized:

$$\text{lfdi} = \ln\left(1 + \frac{\text{fdi}}{5000}\right); \qquad \text{lfdi} = (\text{TIN, TOUT})$$

This transformation allows negative, nil or positive values to be obtained when the observed flows are respectively negative, nil or positive:

$$\text{fdi} < 0 \quad \Rightarrow \quad 1 + \frac{\text{fdi}}{5000} < 1 \quad \Rightarrow \quad \text{lfdi} < 0$$

$$\text{fdi} = 0 \quad \Rightarrow \quad 1 + \frac{\text{fdi}}{5000} = 1 \quad \Rightarrow \quad \text{lfdi} = 0$$

$$\text{fdi} > 0 \quad \Rightarrow \quad 1 + \frac{\text{fdi}}{5000} > 1 \quad \Rightarrow \quad \text{lfdi} > 0$$

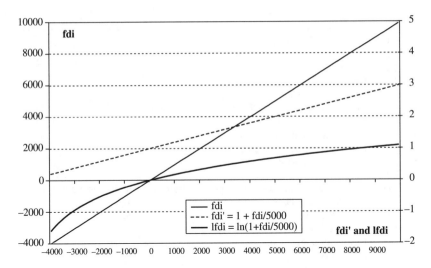

Figure A.1 The transformed FDI flows.

Appendix 3: CHELEM classification

1	BA	Cement and derived products
2	BB	Ceramics (including manufactured mineral articles n.e.s.)
3	BC	Glass (flatware and hollow-ware)
4	CA	Iron and steel-making (including pig iron and sheet steel)
5	CB	Tubes and first-stage processing products
6	CC	Non-ferrous metals
7	DA	Yarns and fabrics
8	DB	Clothing (with fabrics as the main input)
9	DC	Knitwear (made directly from yarns)
10	DD	Carpets and textile funishings
11	DE	Leather furskins and footware
12	EA	Articles in wood
13	EB	Furniture (made of wood or other materials)
14	EC	Paper and pulp
15	ED	Printing and publications
16	EE	Toys, sports equipment and miscellaneous manufactured articles
17	FA	Large metallic structures
18	FB	Miscellaneous hardware
19	FC	Engines, turbines and pumps
20	FD	Agricultural equipment
21	FE	Machine tools
22	FF	Construction and public works equipment
23	FG	Specialized machines
24	FH	Arms and weaponary
25	FI	Precision instruments

26	FJ	Watch and clockmaking
27	FK	Optics and photographic and cinematographic equipment
28	FL	Electronic components
29	FM	Consumer electronics
30	FN	Telecommunications equipment
31	FO	Computer equipment (including office equipment)
32	FP	Domestic electrical appliances
33	FQ	Heavy electrical equipment
34	FR	Electrical apparatus (including passive devices)
35	FS	Vehicle components
36	FT	Cars (including motorcycles)
37	FU	Commercial vehicles and transport equipment (including public transport vehicles and railway equipment)
38	FV	Ships (including oil rigs)
39	FW	Aeronautics
40	GA	Basic inorganic chemicals
41	GB	Fertilizers
42	GC	Basic organic chemicals
43	GD	Paints, colorings and intermediate chemical products n.e.s.
44	GE	Toilet products, soaps and perfumes (including chemical preparations n.e.s.)
45	GF	Pharmaceuticals
46	GG	Plastics, fibers and synthetic resins
47	GH	Plastic articles
48	GI	Rubber articles (including tires)
49	HA	Iron ores and scrap
50	HB	Non-ferrous ores and scrap
51	HC	Unprocessed minerals
52	IA	Coal (including lignite and other primary energy products)
53	IB	Crude oil
54	IC	Natural gas (including all petroleum gases)
55	IG	Coke
56	IH	Refined petroleum products
57	II	Electricity
58	JA	Cereals
59	JB	Other edible agricultural products
60	JC	Non-edible agricultural products
61	KA	Cereal products
62	KB	Fats (of vegetable or animal origin)
63	KC	Meat and fish
64	KD	Preserved meat and fish products
65	KE	Preserved fruit and vegetable products
66	KF	Sugar products (including chocolate)
67	KG	Animal foodstuffs
68	KH	Beverages
69	KI	Manufactured tobaccos
70	NA	Precious stones, jewelry, works of art
71	NB	Non-monetary gold
	NV	Not elsewhere specified
	TT	Total

Appendix 4a: disaggregation for the US FDI data

Trade (CHELEM)	FDI classification of the model	US FDI classification (CITIrev3)	CHELEM/US FDI
HA, HB, HC	1 – All industries (2 + 3 + 13 + 14 + 15 + 19)	Total	
IA, IB, IC, IG, IH	20 – Mining	Mining and quarrying	HA, HB, HC, IA
	2 – Petroleum	Oil	IB, IC
		Coal and petroleum products	IG, IH
	3 – Total manufacturing (= 4 + 5 + 6 + 7 + 10)	Secondary	
KA, KB, KC, KD, KE, KF, KG, KH, KI	4 – Food and kindred products	Food, beverages and tobacco	KA, KB, KC, KD, KE, KF, KG, KH, KI
GA, GB, GC, GD, GE, GF, GG	5 – Chemicals products	Chemical products	GA, GB, GC, GD, GE, GF, GG
CA, CB, CC, FA, FB	6 – Primary and fabricated metal	Metal products	CA, CB, CC, FA, FB
FC, FD, FE, FF, FG, FH, FO	8 – Machinery except electric	Mechanical equipment	FC, FD, FE, FF, FG, FH, FO, FP
FL, FM, FN, FP, FQ, FR	9 – Electric and electronic	Electric and electronic equipment	FL, FM, FN
	7 – Machinery (= 8 + 9)		
FS, FT, FU, FV, FW	11 – Transport equipment	Motor vehicles	FS, FT, FU
		Other transport equipment	FV, FW
BA, BB, BC, DA, DB, DC, DD, DE, EA, EB, EC, ED, EE, FI, FJ, FK, GH, GI, NA, NB, NV	12 – Other manufacturing	Textiles, leather and clothing	DA, DB, DC, DD
		Paper, printing and publishing	EA, EC, ED
		Non-metallic products	GH, GI
		Other manufacturing	BA, BB, BC, DE, EB, EE,
	10 – Transp eqpt and other manuf (= 11 + 12)		FI, FJ, FK, FQ, FR, NA, NB, NV
II, JA, JB, JC	23 – Other industries	Agriculture	JA, JB, JC
		Electricity, gas and water	II

Appendix 4b: disaggregation for the French FDI data

Trade (CHELEM)	FDI classification of the model	French FDI classification (APE)	CHELEM/French FDI
HA, HB, HC	1 – All industries (2 + 3 + 13 + 14 + 15 + 19)	Total	
	20 – Mining	Quarrying of ferrous and non-ferrous metal	HA, HB
		Quarrying of non-metallic minerals	HC
IA, IB, IC, IG, IH	2 – Petroleum	Coal, lignite, crude oil, natural gas	IA, IB, IC
		Refined petroleum	IG, IH
	3 – Total manufacturing (= 4 + 5 + 6 + 7 + 10)	Manufacturing	
KA, KB, KC, KD, KE, KF, KG, KH, KI	4 – Food and kindred products	Food, beverages and tobacco	KA, KB, KC, KD, KE, KF, KG, KH, KI
GA, GB, GC, GD, GE, GF, GG	5 – Chemicals products	Chemical products	GA, GB, GC, GD, GE, GF, GG
CA, CB, CC, FA, FB	6 – Primary and fabricated metal	Ferrous and non-ferrous metal products	CA, CB, CC
		Foundry and forging metals	FA, FB
FC, FD, FE, FF, FG, FH, FO	8 – Machinery except electric	Industrial and agricultural machinery	FC, FD, FE, FF, FG, FH
		Manuf of office, computing, precision instruments	FI, FJ, FK, FO
FL, FM, FN, FP, FQ, FR	9 – Electric and electronic 7 – Machinery (= 8 + 9)	Electric and electronic equipment	FL, FM, FN, FP, FQ, FR
FS, FT, FU, FV, FW	11 – Transport equipment	Transport equipment	FS, FT, FU, FV, FW
BA, BB, BC, DA, DB, DC, DD, DE, EA, EB, EC, ED, EE, FI, FJ, FK, GH, GI, NA, NB, NV	12 – Other manufacturing	Manufacturing of non-metallic minerals	BA, BB, BC
		Mauface of textiles, wearing apparel	DA, DB, DC, DD, DE
		Paper, paperboard articles, printing, publishing	EC, ED
	10 – Transp eqpt and other manuf (= 11 + 12)	Rubber and plastics products	GH, GI
		Other manufacturing	EA, EB, EE, NA, NB, NV
II, JA, JB, JC	23 – Other industries	Agriculture	JA, JB, JC
		Other energy	II

Appendix 5: variables used in trade equations for France and United States

X (M)	US or French exports (imports) to (from) individual partners (US\$ million)
FOUT	US or French outward FDI flows to individual partners (US\$ million)
FIN	US or French inward FDI flows from individual partners (US\$ million)
FOUTOTH	Total US or French outward FDI flows excluding bilateral flows with the partner country taken into consideration (US\$ million)
FINOTH	Total US or French inward FDI flows excluding bilateral flows with the partner country taken into consideration (US\$ million)
AVRGDP	Average of US of French GDP with partner country's GDP (US\$ million)
DIFFGDPPC	Economic distance between i and j proxied by the absolute value of the difference in per capita incomes. DFGDPPC = $|GDPPC_i - GDPPC_j|$; unit: US\$.
DIFFGDPW	Difference in size between country i and country j, proxied by the difference in GDPs between the two countries.

$$\text{DFGDPW} = 1 + \frac{[w \ln w + (1 - w) \ln(1 - w)]}{\ln 2}$$

$$\text{with } w = \frac{GDP_i}{GDP_i + GDP_j}$$

See Appendix 1 for other variables.

Notes

1 We will use the following definition of spillovers: if exports of a firm (industry) A to a given country are boosted by an investment of a firm (industry) B in this country, there is a spillover from B to A.
2 See Andersson *et al.* (1996).
3 All GDPs are at PPP prices.
4 Negative values account for net divestments.
5 In contrast with the former section, we consider GDPs at current prices.
6 Hummels (1998) provides the theoretical framework for such fixed effects.
7 This is a binding constraint with LIMDEP-7.
8 Economies of scale are controlled with such fixed effect.
9 We use the French classification.
10 The model fails to capture any additional exports associated with trade in services. This may be due to the fact that outward investment is reported within the industry of investment, not in the industry of destination. Hence, an investment in a commercial subsidiary realized by the pharmaceutical industry is reported as an investment in the pharmaceutical sector.
11 0.58–0.28 at the individual industry level versus 1.07–0.77 at the total level.
12 Such trade imbalance disappears at the total level: this is an unexpected and unexplained result.

References

Andersen, P. S. and Hainaut, P. (1998) 'Foreign direct investment and employment in the industrial countries'. Bank for International Settlements Working Paper No. 61.

Andersson, T. (1993) 'Nya villkor för ekonomichi och politik. Ekonomikommissions förslag', *SOU*, 16, bilaga 3 (s85–107).

Andersson, T., Fredriksson, T. and Svensson, R. (1996) *Multinational Restructuring, Internationalization and Small Economies: The Swedish Case.* London: Routledge.

Bergstrand, J. H. (1989) 'The generalized gravity equation, monopolistic competition, and the factor-proportions theory of international trade', *Review of Economics and Statistics*, 23: 143–53.

Blomström, M. and Kokko, A. (1994) 'Home country effects of foreign direct investment: evidence from Sweden', CEPR Discussion Paper No. 931, April.

Blomström, M., Lipsey, R. and Kulchycky, K. (1988) 'US and Swedish direct investment and exports', in R. Baldwin (ed.), *Trade Policy Issues and Empirical Analysis.* Chicago: Chicago University Press.

Brainard, S. L. (1993a) 'An empirical assessment of the factor proportions explanation of multinational sales', NBER Working Paper No. 4580.

Brainard, S. L. (1993b) 'An empirical assessment of the proximity-concentration tradeoff between multinational sales and trade. NBER, Working Paper No. 4583.

Drabek, Z. (1998) 'A multilateral agreement on investment: convincing the sceptics', *WTO Staff Working Paper*, ERAD-98-05.

Eaton, J. and Tamura, A. (1994) 'Bilateralism and regionalism in Japanese and US trade and direct foreign investment patterns', NBER Working Paper No. 4758.

Fontagné, L. and Pajot, M. (1997) 'How foreign direct investment affects international trade and competitiveness – an empirical assessment', Working Paper CEPII No. 97-17, December.

Fontagné, L. and Pajot, M. (1998) 'Trade, competitiveness and FDI: a new appraisal', *DSTI/EAS/IND/SWP(98)9*, OECD, Paris.

Hummels, D. (1998) 'Toward a geography of trade costs', *Miméo*, University of Chicago.

Lipsey, R. E. and Weiss, M. E. (1981) 'Foreign production and exports in manufacturing industries, *Review of Economics and Statistics*, 66(2): 304–8.

Lipsey, R. E. and Weiss, M. E. (1984) 'Foreign production and exports of individual firms', *Review of Economics and Statistics*, 63(4): 488–94.

Markusen, J. R. and Venables, A. J. (1995) 'Multinational firms and the new trade theory', NBER Working Paper No. 5036, February.

MITI (1997) 'Impact of Japanese overseas business activities on Japan's domestic economy', DSTI/EAS/IND/SWP(97)17 OECD.

Riker, D. A. and Brainard, L. S. (1997) 'U.S. multinationals and competition from low wage countries', NBER Working Paper No. 5959.

Stevens, G. and Lipsey, R. (1992) 'Interaction between domestic and foreign investment', *Journal of International Money and Finance*, 11: 40–62.

Svensson, R. (1993) 'Production in foreign affiliates – effects on home country exports and modes of entry', Licentiate thesis, Gothenburg University.

Swendenborg, B. (1979) *The Multinational Operations of Swedish Firms*. Stockholm: Almqvist & Wicksell International.

UNCTAD (1998) *World Investment Report: Trends and Determinants*. United Nations, Geneva.

WTO (1998) 'Report of the working group on the relationship between trade and investment to the general council', WT/WGTI/2, December.

4

INTRA-FIRM TRADE AND FOREIGN DIRECT INVESTMENT*

An empirical analysis of French firms

Séverine Chédor, Jean-Louis Mucchielli and Isabelle Soubaya

4.1. Introduction

The great importance given to foreign direct investment (FDI) is part of a general interest in internationalization. Apart from the relative regular increase in the international trade to GDP ratio, the growing importance of production and distribution of affiliates is a tangible proof of the globalization process. Since the exceptional increase in FDI[1] during the past ten years, trade and FDI have become the two ways – sometimes interpreted as substitute or complementary – to serve foreign markets. Indeed, several studies discuss the substitution–complementarity relationship between FDI and exports. Theoretical approaches generally tend to conclude a substitution relationship, contrary to empirical studies.

Moreover, international trade is increasingly dominated by multinational firms. Actually, intra-firm trade (i.e. trade between a parent company and its affiliates) represents, in 1998 (UNTCAD 1999), 30 per cent of world trade and also 30 per cent of total French trade[2] (Mathieu 1998). In that context, it seems necessary to divide global trade into two classes: intra-firm and inter-firm trade (or arm's length transactions). The relationship between FDI and each of these categories of trade has to be tested in order to highlight the potential impact of establishment of affiliates abroad on trade. Our paper deals with this concern for French intra-firm trade, which has never been explored in these terms. Indeed, individual databases for French multinational firms are exploited here for the first time.

In this paper, we discuss our results on FDI/trade relationships according to the type of trade (intra-firm or arm's length trade). Therefore, we try to see to what extent the volume exchanged in arm's length trade is more a complement or substitute to FDI than the volume of intra-firm trade. At the same time, we study

*This paper received support from the Commissariat Général au Plan, convention no. 4–98.

the relationships between FDI and exports and between FDI and imports. Those two issues are rarely studied together. This point will allow us to show whether FDI can imply a trade balance deficit (see Mucchielli and Chédor 1999).

After a statistical analysis of the different types of trade realized by French multinational firms, we introduce a selection of some assumptions relative to the complementarity–substitution discussion between FDI and trade. Then we present our econometric results.

4.2. Stylized facts for French multinational firms

4.2.1. French FDI abroad

In 1995, there were over 2,500,000 persons working in 16,000 foreign affiliates of enterprises located in France[3] (Bonnaud 1998), including 1,134,173 persons[4] working abroad for French groups.[5]

When we examine employment in French enterprises abroad, we can see that two-thirds of the investment is made in industrialized countries (see Table 4.1). The presence of French firms in developing areas remains weak, even if, currently, those countries record the strongest rate of increase in settlement abroad (more than 20 per cent from 1992 to 1996) compared to industrialized countries (8.4 per cent).

Owing to this strong presence in developed countries, our econometric analysis, in this paper, will deal only with those countries.

4.2.2. Main characteristics of French intra-firm trade

French databases allow us to distinguish three different levels of firms: head of groups, parent companies and affiliates abroad. Head of groups can control several enterprises (firms) located in France. Among those firms we retain only industrial one with production activities. Those firms 'directly' possess subsidiaries abroad.

Table 4.1 French location abroad (persons in thousands)

	1996		Variation 1992–96		Variation 1995–96	
	Stock of employment	%	Employment created	%	Employment created	%
World	2548	100.0	276	12.1	40	1.6
Industrialized countries	1647	64.7	138	8.4	5	0.3
EU	1133	44.5	48	4.4	25	2.3
Outside of Europe	462	18.1	−11	1.2	−22	−4.6
Other countries	901	35.3	234	21.8	36	4.1
Emergent countries[6]		20.5	215	70.1	38	7.7

Source: DREE, *Enquête Filiale 1996*, table in J. P. Bonnaud (1998).

It is the reason why we call them parent companies. Our final sample is composed of 421 parent companies for which we know exactly the number of subsidiaries abroad and for which we can distinguish between their arm's length trade and intra-firm trade.

Intra-firm trade reflects the integration of the parent company and its affiliates within an internal worldwide network system. The parent company and its affiliates exchange final products, components, services, information flows, knowledge and so on. The more firms are multinational, the more intra-firm and international trade can be exploited. For France, intra-group trade is almost as high as in the United States or Japan, and represents a third of exports and a fifth of imports (Hannoun and Guerrier 1998).

An original source of information by the French Ministry of Industry gives us data on trade between parent firms and their affiliates. This database, named 'Mondialisation' (Globalization inquiry) allows us to retain 421 French parent companies. This database, mixed with that of the 'French Directory of International Economic Relations' (DREE), gives employment abroad for each affiliate by host country. Then, this information combined with that of the French Customs will allow us to compare intra-firm trade with global trade and also with arm's length trade (inter-firm trade). The addition of a last base, 'Yearly Enterprises Inquiry' (EAE), will complete our information to characterize the 421 parent companies concerning their own specificity and their products. The groups of this sample of 421 firms realize more than half of total intra-firm exports and only a quarter of intra-firm imports.[7] This corresponds to a surplus of 125 billion Francs.

As Hannoun and Guerrier (1998) wrote in their study on agro-industry, the more French groups have affiliates abroad in a considered geographical zone, the less they export to non-affiliated firms. It is notably the case for Europe (see Table 4.2). Europe is effectively the first area of settlement abroad for French firms and it registers the strongest rate of intra-firm trade (64 per cent for intra-firm exports and 33 per cent for intra-firm imports). It also shows the integration effect of the European Community.

In that context, we will try to determinate whether production abroad can explain this intra- or inter-firm trade situation.

Table 4.2 Share of intra- and inter-firm trade in global trade by geographical zone

Zone of trade	Employees abroad (%)	Intra-firm exports (%)	Inter-firm exports (%)	Intra-firm imports (%)	Inter-firm imports (%)
All industrialized countries	70	60	40	26	74
EC	44	64	36	33	67
OECD	26	48	52	6	94
Low wage countries	30	15	85	22	78
Total	1,123,330				

4.2.3. Relationship between trade and FDI: theoretical and empirical background

As stated in the introduction, we distinguish here different types of trade: global trade, inter-firm trade (arm's length trade) and intra-firm trade. Global trade is composed of inter- and intra-firm trade. This latter represents trade between a parent company and its affiliates, while global trade includes trade that one firm makes with each host country whether or not it has an affiliate in that country. When it has no affiliate abroad or in a specific country, global trade is equivalent to inter-firm trade.

These three types of trade can be explained with general and specific determinants. We will now study the volume of these different types of trade.

4.2.4. Trade and FDI: the volume relationship for global export

4.2.4.1. The substitution case

The substitution case is often presented in traditional trade theory and also in some of the new trade theory developments. In the traditional general equilibrium $2 \times 2 \times 2$ trade model, FDI is integrated in a logic *à la* Mundell: FDI is a substitute for exports, especially because products or factors of production are alternatively internationally mobile or immobile. In the behavioural approaches focusing on the growth of the firm, international investment appears as a consequence of the growth process (Penrose 1995). The more the firm grows, the more it seeks to diversify, in particular on the geographical level, so as to reduce risks and increase its profits. The firm may choose to internalize its organizational activities and necessary inputs that were formerly supplied by the market.

All these approaches attempt to demonstrate that any foreign firm willing to invest in a new country has an intrinsic disadvantage compared to local firms. FDI then takes place only if this relative disadvantage is offset by a specific advantage of the foreign firm. In the firm theory, FDI is an element of the decision to undertake an internationalization process. Exports and FDI thus correspond to alternative modes of entry to the foreign market. Hirsch (1976) represents the decision concerning FDI versus exports as a trade-off between the different components of the firm's cost function. Firms can enter a foreign market in several ways: exports, foreign direct investments or licensing. The choice between FDI and exports is made by comparing the respective costs of the two alternatives. FDI is chosen to exploit a foreign market with high firm-specific advantages and transfer costs and weak control costs. Furthermore, in dynamic terms, penetration channels vary with time (Buckley and Casson 1981) because of the evolution of those different costs.

Recently, in the strategic behaviour models, the analysis of the trade-off between FDI and exports became more complex. FDI transforms the structure of the host sector's market. Multinational firms try to use FDI to modify this market's structure to their advantage. Some models (Smith 1987; Horstman and Markusen 1992; Motta 1992) develop a strategic choice of the means of internationalization. In these models, the multinational firm already has a specific advantage due to the existence of a production unit in its home country (initial investment in R&D). To invest abroad, the firm has only to support the fixed cost specific to FDI (such as building a new plant). Therefore any potential entrant which does not yet have a factory, suffers two disadvantages (not having established a firm and not having plant).

Models of strategic FDI underline once more the asymmetric cost between firms. The strategic behaviour of a multinational firm can then prevent a local firm from entering the same market by pre-empting the host market. In most of the new models of imperfect competition and strategic behaviour, FDI appears as a substitute for exports for cost reasons linked to the decision to invest or to export abroad. On the one hand, FDI has a pre-emptive virtue and represents a credible threat with sunk costs; on the other, exports do not possess these characteristics.

Following the conclusions of most of these theories, we should have a substitution relationship between FDI and trade.

This substitution effect can be direct or indirect. For instance, in the case of relocation, firms produce abroad instead of producing at home. Furthermore, the subsidiary may export to third countries, and these exports may have an obvious negative effect on the parent company exports to these third countries. For instance, Svensson (1996) notes that exports from subsidiaries create a strong substitution effect on third countries' markets.

Although most of the theories tend to conclude a relationship of substitution, there can be many reasons and explanations for finding a complementarity relationship. Some theoretical and empirical analyses tend to highlight these cases of complementarity between trade and FDI.

4.2.4.2. *The complementarity cases*

On the theoretical level, some authors tend to develop complementary links between FDI and trade. On a general equilibrium aspect, by example, Purvis (1972), Kojima (1978), and also Markusen (1983) and some others introduce a difference of technology in the model of Heckscher and Ohlin with international mobility of the capital factor. Then a country can export capital-intensive goods but also technology and the capital factor in the labor-intensive sector to less developed countries. These factors' transfers are pro-trade creating. The specific factors model has also been used to show that FDI and exports can be complements (Mucchielli and Mayer 1998).

On the firm's theory side, there are analyses like the internalization based on transaction cost theory. Applied to the multinational firm, there is obviously a complementary link between FDI and intra-firm trade. As a multinational firm is going to internalize an arm's length relationship by investing abroad, in fact it will internalize trade which was previously arm's length trade.

The complementarity hypothesis is more often found in empirical studies or case studies. This relationship of complementarity can be explained by different elements. For instance, foreign production can strengthen exports of the products themselves by facilitating the penetration of the foreign market as a direct effect. The volume of market share can therefore increase. This complementarity can also be explained by some indirect effects as the increase in exports of intermediate goods or equipment or as a sort of international economies of scope by facilitating the export of other products of the firm belonging to the same family or not, and so on. Empirical analyses of individual firms' data have already been undertaken, especially of American, Swedish and Japanese data (see Swedenborg 1979, 1982; Lipsey and Weiss 1981, 1984; Svensson 1996; or Head and Ries 2000). They generally conclude a relationship of complementarity between FDI and exports, except for Svensson (1996) and Noguchi (1997). The results collected by Swedenborg (1979, 1982) at the firm level are among the first to indicate a complementarity between FDI and exports. The author finds that an increase of $100 in FDI has a positive impact on the parent company exports of about $6 to $10. This complementarity is also sometimes underlined at a more aggregated level of analysis due to the spillover effects. Indeed, complementarity can be reinforced because of possible effects of spillovers from one firm to another.

Lipsey and Weiss (1984) indicate a complementary relationship which is three times more important when tests are undertaken at the sector level. It is due to the positive externalities between firms and sectors.[8] Thus, production abroad/export elasticities that indicate the intensity of the relationship of complementarity are stronger on aggregated industry data than on individual data. This result suggests that the positive effect of investment on trade includes a strong proportion of country-specific externalities. More precisely, the FDI of a firm can have a positive influence on the level of exports performed by firms from the same home country and directed to the same host country (Fontagné 1995).

These different possibilities correspond to the following result: the more FDI we have, the more we trade.

The first two relations, quoted previously, concern global trade which can be further analyzed by underlying relations between intra-firm trade and FDI.

4.2.5. Trade and FDI: the volume relationship in the case of intra-firm trade

Why can intra-firm trade be a substitute or complement to FDI?

4.2.5.1. The substitution case

In this case we can find the same elements as before. But this assumption particularly concerns links between parent companies and their affiliates. According to the dependency (or not) of the affiliate regarding its parent company, different degrees of relationship between FDI and trade can be observed. As before, if the affiliate produces abroad instead of producing domestically we have of course a substitution effect. But parent–affiliate relationships depend also on several organizational elements that we can express in terms of a relationship of autonomy/dependency.

Autonomy can come with the age of the affiliate or by way of mergers and acquisitions and its position inside the organization. An affiliate settled abroad for a long time will have more autonomy. It has more contacts with local or foreign firms compared to relations with its parent company. A firm which is acquired should also have great autonomy. It has its own habits in terms of supply, which means that autonomy is quite important. On the contrary, autonomy will be less important for greenfield affiliates.

There are other reasons which contribute to affiliates' autonomy, like the objective to serve the local market. As autonomy increases, substitution between FDI and trade will take place. Furthermore, Bergsten *et al.* (1983) have shown that FDI could be substitute for trade over a certain threshold of investment abroad. It is possible that once affiliates are really integrated into the local market, they no longer import from their parent company. Besides, Noguchi (1997) argued a positive relationship in the short run and a decreasing positive effect in the long run. Japanese exports are increasingly replaced by goods produced by Japanese affiliates. In addition, there are more and more re-exports from those affiliates to Japan. In that case, exports of capital goods or components are not enough to compensate the substitution effects. This could be essentially due to the increase in the percentage of local content in purchases of affiliates abroad (Swenson 1997).

Kravis and Lipsey (1988) had a similar approach. They attempted to underline the difference between production of affiliates reserved for sale in the local market and production for export. For the latter, there are no clear results, whereas for the former, this would have rather a negative impact on the activity of the parent company. To distinguish these two types of behaviours, authors differentiated majority affiliates (for access to the local market) from minority affiliates (for exports).

4.2.5.2. *The complementarity case*

Other elements concerning the organization of affiliates can generate complementarity relations between trade and FDI. Indeed, in terms of organization, affiliates can have a strong complementarity of their production with that of their parent company. That depends on the nature of the role attributed to each affiliate. In a hierarchical network, an affiliate can specialize in part of the production process, like components, while another can be an assembly plant. Intra-firm trade will depend on and correspond to this organization (implying intra-firm trade of intermediate and final products, see Helpman 1984).

Another group of models (Krugman 1983; Brainard 1993) analyzes the possibility of horizontal FDI between several countries. In this type of model, the decision to create a subsidiary abroad, rather than continue with exports, is a trade-off between the advantages and costs related to foreign market proximity and the scale economies derived from concentration of production in a single factory within the investor country. This set of models certainly leads to a substitution relation. Nevertheless, horizontal integration can also imply complementary relationships when affiliates and parent companies produce different varieties of final goods (Baldwin and Ottaviano 1998).

Those results of complementarity can also be interpreted in terms of quality effects and research on economies of scale. A parent company can relocate its more common (or low-quality) products in the host country and continue to export its high-quality products. The local production of the former will lead to a brand effect and increase the parent company's exports of higher quality goods. Each affiliate can also specialize in one product in order to get economies of scale or economies of scope. Each produces one product and serves a global zone from its plant. Trade between countries and intra-firm trade can then be trade in differentiated goods (Barry and Bradley 1997).

4.3. Objectives and tests

4.3.1. Objectives

Econometric analysis follows a previous analysis done on the substitution–complementarity debate between FDI and trade (Chédor and Mucchielli 1998). In this previous study we found a positive impact of FDI on exports for developed countries contrary to some developing areas. Here, we concentrate the analysis on industrialized countries, themselves separated into two sub-zones, namely the European Union (EU) and the rest of the OECD countries. Indeed, settlement abroad and also intra-firm trade are more concentrated in these countries (see Table 4.2).

Moreover, we study here not only imports and exports but also the two main components of global trade: arm's length trade and intra-firm trade. We could therefore be able to determine whether complementarity comes from arms' length trade or from intra-firm trade.

4.3.2. Econometric model

Our econometric model is composed of variables corresponding either to determinants of volume of trade, or to determinants concerning the type of trade.

In the first group of variables, there are macroeconomic variables. They are used in order to control possible bias of proximity. The characteristics of trading partners are given by GDP (gdp) and geographical distance (dist). The first variable should imply a positive impact on firms' exports. The bigger the country to which one exports (gdp), the higher the chances to export are. Geographical distance (dist), on the contrary, may negatively influence trade to this country because of increasing costs implied by transport or information costs.

The second type of variable characterizes firms' foreign activity, measured by the number of persons employed abroad. It is the only information we can get from the statistical sources as a proxy of subsidiaries' activity abroad and then of FDI. We can assume that foreign production grows with the number of employed people (an assumption also made by Blönigen 1999).

The last set of variables are micro-economic ones. Roberts and Tybout's analysis (1997), as well as the one by Bernard and Jensen (1997), identifies a certain number of variables involving a significant impact on parent companies' exports. Intensity in R&D (rd) and capital intensity are, for instance, variables which are used as indicators of firm-specific advantages. They should have a positive impact on firms' exports (a firm relatively more intensive in capital would have a positive influence on its trade). The average manpower size can be a proxy of firm size. A big enterprise measured in terms of employees can have more chance to export than a middle-sized firm (see Head and Ries 2000). Another variable, corresponding to the theory of internalization, can be added to explain the type of trade. This is advertising (adv), which relates to product-specific advantages.

Concerning literature of determinants of intra-firm trade, results seem to be unanimous. Intra-firm trade is strongly linked to the R&D intensity of the parent company (Lall 1978; Buckley and Pearce 1979; Helleiner and Lavergne 1979; Sleuwaegen 1985). Goods with strong technology content and advertising are rather internalized within a multinational firm network (that is also the conclusion of the internalization theory). A strong degree of R&D and advertising should indicate a strong degree of innovation, technology content, or differentiation. All these elements should favour internalization because of the specificity of the product traded and the high transaction costs involved in arm's length trade.

The tested detailed equation is then the following:

$$\text{TRADE}_{ic} = F \text{ (activities abroad of firm } i \text{ in country } c, \text{ gravitational variables of country } c, \text{ firm } i \text{ or products of firm } i \text{ specific advantages)}$$

where TRADE_{ic}: global, intra- or inter-firm trade, $i = 1, \ldots, n$ firms, $c = 1, \ldots, 21$ countries.[9] We present all the variables quoted previously in Table 4.3.

4.3.3. Econometric results

We implement two types of specification. The first is ordinary least squares (OLS). Thereafter, we introduce panel data specification in order to catch possible firms' or countries' heterogeneity. In traditional analysis with panel data, it is usual to have an individual dimension and a temporal one. In our paper, we have two individual dimensions corresponding to firms and countries and only one year of observation. Thus, we want to take into account possible biases due to firms' heterogeneity or countries' specificity which can affect one FDI versus trade relationship. Thanks to within and between estimators, this representation of trade and FDI will return information due only to the chosen dimension.

Table 4.3 Variables used in regressions

Variable	Name and measure	Expected sign
Dependent variable	Global, intra-firm or inter-firm exports or imports (Douanes, Mondialisation, 1993)	
Independent variables		
Firm i's own variables		
Size of firm	size: number of employees in average (EAE, SESSI, 1993)	+
Capital intensity	kl: capital = capital/number of employees (EAE, SESSI, 1993)	+
Advertising	adv = advertising expenditures/ turnover (EAE, SESSI, 1993)	+
Research and development	rd = R&D budget/turnover (Groupe, SESSI, 1993)	+
Firm abroad activity's variables		
Production abroad	fdi country: Number of persons employed abroad per country (DREE, Enquête filiale, 1994)	±
Production abroad in the zone	fdi zone: Number of persons employed per zone (DREE, Enquête filiale, 1994)	±
Host country's macro-economic variables		
Host country market size	GDP: GDP as a proxy of host country market size (CHELEM, CEPII, 1993)	+
Country distance	dist: geographic distance between Capital of partners countries	−

Table 4.4 Intra-, inter-firm and global exports: results with OLS specification

	Global exports	Intra-firm exports	Inter-firm exports
fdi country	0.24* (0.018)	1.34* (0.018)	−0.12* (0.018)
fdi zone	0.09* (0.013)	0.01 (0.013)	0.08* (0.013)
size	0.33* (0.026)	−0.14* (0.026)	0.42* (0.027)
rd	−0.1* (0.016)	−0.05* (0.016)	−0.08* (0.017)
kl	0.16* (0.02)	0.04** (0.021)	0.15* (0.021)
adv	0 (0.018)	0.14* (0.019)	−0.05* (0.019)
GDP	0.51* (0.023)	0.25* (0.025)	0.44* (0.025)
dist	−0.48* (0.026)	−0.2* (0.026)	−0.45* (0.026)
c	−9.53* (0.744)	−3.29* (0.756)	−8.89* (0.780)
R^2	0.28	0.57	0.17

*,** means that it is significant at 1% and 5%.
Standard errors are presented in parentheses.

4.3.3.1. OLS results

With OLS specification, we obtained the same results as in a previous study (Chédor and Mucchielli 1998). We observe a complementarity relationship between global exports and FDI without distinguishing intra- or inter-firm trade. Decomposition of trade into two components shows that inter- and intra-firm trade are correlated differently to FDI. We conclude that the global relationship between trade and FDI is influenced by a stronger complementarity relationship of intra-firm trade. Inter-firm exports are effectively substituted. Results indicate that a subsidiary presence in one country of a given zone (EU or OECD) has a strong positive impact. The analysis by zone demonstrates that the link between trade and FDI is bigger in countries where parent companies already have affiliates than in countries which are only export partners without production facilities for those parent companies (that is, 0.24 against 0.09 for global exports). Access to the local market seems thus more enhanced when the firm is already established in it.

Concerning other variables,[10] the sign and the influence of the size variable differs significantly according to the three types of trade. Indeed, it has a negative sign for intra-firm trade instead of the positive correlation for total trade and inter-firm trade. Further explanations have to be found for this phenomenon. For instance, it is possible that smaller multinational firms tend to give priority to trade with their affiliates abroad, while bigger multinationals have inter-firm networks and may be independent affiliates. In those circumstances inter-firm trade could be more developed. But this assumption needs to be tested. There is also a negative sign for the R&D variable. This may be due to the fact that this variable is a measure of all the multinational groups' R&D expenditures and not only those of the production parent company. Thus possible bias observed on the R&D variable can be due to the fact that R&D is often concentrated in only one laboratory[11] – which is may not be listed in our sample. But also, for a lot of firms belonging to our sample, we have no information concerning their R&D expenditures, which gives us a zero in the column for this variable and the risk of an information bias.

The other variables have the expected sign. Capital intensity has the same positive correlation with trade whatever it is. On the other hand, advertising expenditures have no relationship with global trade, a positive one with intra-firm trade and a negative one with inter-firm trade. In that sense, it seems to confirm our assumption.

The relative size of host market and the geographic distance, measured respectively by the gdp and dist variables, are similarly linked to the three types of trade. Whereas the first variable promotes trade whatever it is, the second seems to have the opposite influence.

4.3.3.2. Panel data results

As we have already mentioned, earlier results presented with the OLS specification can effectively be biased due to firms' heterogeneity or countries' specificity.

Table 4.5 Intra-, inter-firm and global exports: results with panel data specification

	Global exports	Intra-firm exports	Inter-firm exports
Country dimension			
fdi country	0.26* (0.014)	1.34* (0.014)	−0.11* (0.015)
fdi zone	0.09* (0.01)	0.01 (0.010)	0.08* (0.011)
size	0.29* (0.021)	−0.14* (0.021)	0.38* (0.022)
rd	−0.1* (0.013)	−0.05* (0.013)	−0.08* (0.014)
kl	0.16* (0.016)	0.04** (0.017)	0.15* (0.017)
adv	0 (0.015)	0.14* (0.015)	−0.04** (0.016)
GDP	0.12* (0.012)	0.13* (0.013)	0.059* (0.013)
dist	−0.30* (0.040)	−0.12* (0. 041)	−0.28* (0.042)
c	0.70* (0.052)	−0.27* (0.054)	1.06* (0.055)
R^2	0.66	0.53	0.6
Lagrange	2037*	10.5*	1511*
Hausman	64*	19**	58.5*
Firm dimension			
fdi country	0.32* (0.013)	1.39* (0.015)	0.06* (0.014)
fdi zone	0.092* (0.012)	0.01 (0.013)	0.08* (0.013)
size	−0.16* (0.032)	−0.27* (0.034)	−0.06*** (0.03)
rd	−0.04** (0.024)	−0.02 (0.026)	−0.01 (0.025)
kl	0.18* (0.028)	0.04 (0.03)	0.16* (0.029)
adv	0.036 (0.025)	0.1* (0.027)	0.01 (0.026)
GDP	0.38* (0.012)	0.19* (0.012)	0.31* (0.012)
dist	−0.59* (0.019)	−0.23* (0.021)	−0.56* (0.020)
c	1.22* (0.07)	−0.11 (0.075)	1.56* (0.07)
R^2	0.70	0.56	0.64
Lagrange	3259*	1107*	2701*
Hausman	179*	70*	157*

*,**,*** means that it is significant at 1%, 5% and 10%.
Standard errors are presented in parentheses.

Relatively small flows from relatively under-competitive or small firms can constitute noise involving biased results on FDI/trade relationships. This is why we present our results with panel data. The Lagrange specification test confirms that panel data is more adapted to the estimation of our sample owing to its heterogeneity. Furthermore, the Haussman test indicates that 'within' estimators which take into account fixed individuals' effects have to be used (see Table 4.5).

Results with panel data show that an increase of 1 per cent FDI will imply an increase of 0.32 per cent of global trade (without distinguishing an inter- or intra-firm trade). This complementarity can be decomposed into two impacts, intra-firm one and an inter-firm one. One can observe a complementarity relationship (1.39) for intra-firm trade, but a substitution one (−0.06) (whatever is the chosen dimension) for inter-firm trade. An interesting result is the constancy of correlation even if firms' or countries' heterogeneities are taken into account, thanks to panel data. It indicates that our model is robust. Concerning control variables, results are globally the same as with the OLS specification.

Table 4.6 Intra-, inter-firm and global imports: results with OLS specification

	Global imports	Intra-firm imports	Inter-firm imports
fdi country	0.09* (0.019)	0.64* (0.015)	−0.03 (0.019)
fdi zone	−0.02 (0.015)	−0.02** (0.012)	−0.02 (0.015)
size	0.7* (0.031)	0.02 (0.025)	0.72* (0.031)
rd	−0.05** (0.02)	−0.03** (0.016)	−0.04** (0.019)
kl	0.11* (0.026)	−0.01 (0.021)	0.11* (0.026)
adv	−0.07* (0.022)	−0.08* (0.018)	−0.06* (0.022)
GDP	0.84* (0.03)	0.07* (0.024)	0.86* (0.03)
dist	−0.75* (0.032)	−0.19* (0.026)	−0.74* (0.032)
c	−22.46* (0.931)	−1.48** (0.751)	−23.23* (0.919)
R^2	0.28	0.33	0.27

*,** means that it is significant at 1% and 5%.
Standard errors are presented in parentheses.

If we now examine the links between FDI and imports, the results underline that global imports are also complementary with FDI. This positive correlation seems to be determined mostly by complementarity between intra-firm import and FDI, as the relationship is not significant or weak for inter-firm imports (see Tables 4.6 and 4.7). Comments concerning other explanatory variables are globally the same as for exports. Results show also that FDI influences exports relatively more than imports. As a result, if a parent company's trade deficit is seen as the difference between exports and imports, FDI would not contribute to a potential trade deficit.

With panel data specification, taking into account individual heterogeneity (firm or country), results are improved: the relationship is a better one as R^2 is higher and confirms our previous conclusions.

4.4. Conclusion

Our main concern was to highlight the relationship between trade and settlement abroad. From a first study (Chédor and Mucchielli 1998) which concluded a complementarity relationship between global exports and FDI for industrialized countries, our main objective was to deepen the former analysis with the following points.

First of all, we wished to find out whether the global relationship of complementarity between trade and FDI could be explained by intra- and inter-firm trade. Second, the integration of imports into our analysis may tell us to what extent imports are more or less influenced by FDI than exports. Furthermore, the risk of data heterogeneity encouraged us to use econometrics of panel data. Our results confirm a positive relationship between FDI and global trade (whatever imports or exports). This complementarity concerns intra-firm trade since FDI and intra-firm trade are strongly complementery and FDI and arm's length trade are more

Table 4.7 Intra-, inter-firm and global imports: results with panel data specification

	Global exports	Intra-firm exports	Inter-firm exports
Country dimension			
fdi country	0.14* (0.014)	0.64* (0.011)	0.03** (0.014)
fdi zone	−0.04* (0.011)	−0.02* (0.009)	−0.03* (0.011)
size	0.58* (0.023)	0.014 (0.017)	0.59* (0.022)
rd	−0.05* (0.014)	−0.03* (0.011)	−0.05* (0.014)
kl	0.10* (0.019)	−0.01 (0.015)	0.1* (0.019)
adv	−0.06* (0.016)	−0.07* (0.01)	−0.05* (0.016)
GDP	0.18 (0.014)	0.01 (0.011)	0.01 (0.014)
dist	−0.56* (0.045)	−0.19* (0.035)	−0.53* (0.044)
c	1.179* (0.05)	0.70* (0.039)	1.25* (0.049)
R^2	0.58	0.32	0.56
Hausman	303*	21*	458*
Lagrange	7723*	10*	8506*
Firm imports			
fdi country	0.26* (0.015)	0.67* (0.012)	0.15* (0.015)
fdi zone	−0.01 (0.014)	−0.02 (0.011)	−0.01 (0.014)
size	0.04 (0.032)	−0.05** (0.025)	0.04 (0.031)
rd	−0.04*** (0.022)	−0.01 (0.017)	−0.04*** (0.022)
kl	0.14* (0.028)	0.02 (0.022)	0.13* (0.028)
adv	0.039 (0.025)	−0.07* (0.019)	0.06* (0.024)
GDP	0.29* (0.013)	0.02* (0.01)	0.30* (0.013)
dist	−0.66* (0.025)	−0.17* (0.02)	−0.65* (0.025)
c	1.01* (0.066)	0.61* (0.05)	1.1* (0.065)
R^2	0.67	0.33	0.67
Hausman	204*	41*	223*
Lagrange	309*	281*	320*

*,**,*** means that it is significant at 1%, 5% and 10%.
Standard errors are presented in parentheses.

substitutes. This result tends to explain the opposite main conclusion usually found between empirical results and theoretical analysis. Furthermore, this positive relationship between trade and FDI seems to be stronger for exports compared to imports.

Notes

1 An increase from 60 billion dollars in 1985 to 315 billion dollar in 1995.
2 This rate comes from a French survey made in 1993.
3 Those firms are composed of enterprises which belong to French multinational firms and also to foreign groups which are settled in France.
4 127,143 persons work in their commercial affiliates, 65,539 in their services affiliates and the rest in units of production.
5 French groups correspond to groups held predominantly (over 50 per cent) by French direction. They constitute a sample of 913 multinational firms for which we know their location abroad as well as their activities in France.

6 These twenty-four countries represent 27 per cent of affiliates and 20 per cent of total employment, but 43 per cent of affiliates were created in 1995 (Bonnaud 1998).
7 It appears not surprising since foreign groups settled in France participate more in flows of intra-group imports.
8 This positive result is verified for all sectors except for three: medicines, components electronics, equipment and automotive transportation.
9 These countries are countries of the EC, except France and OECD.
10 These variables must be considered, in addition to information they can bring, as a means of taking into account possible bias and thus being used as control variables. For example, the larger a company is, the more it will trade. Also, in order to avoid a positive link between trade and the IDE, mainly due here to the size of the company taking into account in the size of the IDE, we incorporate the size of the firm as a control variable.
11 Approximately 20 per cent of the R&D expenditures of French industrial groups are carried out by subsidiaries in France which have only R&D activities. So they do not produce goods and are classified separately from the industry sector, which can accentuate our statistical bias here (Sessi and Chiffres Clés 1999).

References

Baldwin, R. E. and Ottaviano, G. I. P. (2001) 'Multiproducts multinationals and reciprocal FDI dumping', *Journal of International Economics*, 54(2): 429–48.

Barry, F. and Bradley, J. (1997) 'FDI and trade: the Irish host-country experience', *The Economic Journal*, November.

Bergsten, C. F., Horst, T. and Moran, T. (1978) *American Multinationals and American Interests*. Washington, DC: The Brookings Institution.

Bernard, A. and Jensen, J.-B. (1997) 'Exceptional exporter performance: cause, effect or both?', NBER Working Paper No. 6272.

Blonigen, B. A. (2001) 'In search of substitution between foreign production and exports', *Journal of International Economics*, 53: 81–104.

Bonnaud, J.-P. (1998) 'Filiales à l'étranger: forte progression des pays émergents', in *Industrie et Mondialisation*. SESSI, French Ministry of Industry.

Brainard, S. L. (1993) 'A simple theory of multinational corporations and trade with a trade-off between proximity and concentration', NBER Working Paper Series No. 4269.

Buckley, P. J. and Casson, M. (1981) 'The optimal timing of a foreign direct investment', *Economic Journal*, 91: 75–87.

Buckley, P. J. and Pearce, R. D. (1979) 'Overseas production and exporting by the world's largest enterprises; a study in sourcing policy', in Casson (ed.), *Multinational Corporations*. Cheltenham, UK: Edward Elgar, pp. 325–36.

Chédor, S. and Mucchielli, J.-L. (1998) 'Implantation à l'étranger et performance à l'exportation: une analyse empirique sur les implantations des firmes françaises dans les pays emergents', *Revue Economique*, May.

Fontagné, L. (1995) 'The links between foreign direct investment and trade', *OCDE*, Workshop No. 9 Industry Committee, October 11th, Paris.

Hannoun and Guerrier (1998) 'Les échanges internes aux groupes industriels', in *Industrie et Mondialisation*. SESSI, Ministère de l'Economie, des Finances et de l'Industrie.

Head, K. and Ries, J. (2000) 'Overseas investment and firms exports', *Review of International Economics*, forthcoming.

Helleiner, G. K. and Lavergne, R. (1979) 'Intrafirm trade and the developing countries: an assessment of the data', *Journal of Development Economics*, 6(3): 341–406.

Helpman, E. (1984) 'A simple theory of international trade with multinational corporations', *Journal of Political Economy*, 31: 451–71.

Hirsch, S. (1976) 'An international trade and investment theory of the firm', *Oxford Economic Papers*, 28(2): 258–70.

Horstmann, I. J. and Markusen, J. R. (1992) 'Endogenous market structure in international trade', *Journal of International Economics*, 32: 109–29.

Kojima, K. (1978) *Direct Foreign Investment: A Japanese Model of Multinational Business Operations*. London: Croom Helm, NY: Praeger.

Kravis, I. B. and Lipsey, R. E. (1988) 'The effect of multinational firms' foreign operations on their domestic employment', NBER Working Paper No. 2760.

Krugman, P. R. (1983) 'The new theory of international trade and the multinational enterprise', in D. B. Audretsch and C. Kindleberger (eds), *The Multinational Corporations in the 1980s*. Cambridge: MIT Press.

Lall, S. (1978) 'The pattern of intra-firm exports by US multinationals', *Oxford Bulletin of Economics and Statistics*, 40(3).

Lipsey, R. E. and Weiss, M. Y. (1981) 'Foreign production and exports in manufacturing industries', *Review of Economics and Statistics*, LXIII(4): 488–94.

Lipsey, R. E. and Weiss, M. Y. (1984) 'Foreign production and exports of individual firms', *Review of Economics and Statistics*, LXVI(2): 304–9.

Markusen, J. R. (1983) 'Factor movements and commodity trade as complements', *Journal of International Economics*, 13: 341–56.

Mathieu, E. (1998) 'La production industrielle française à l'étranger', in *Industrie et Mondialisation, Chiffres Clés*. SESSI, pp. 63–72.

Motta, M. (1992) 'Multinational firms and the tariff-jumping argument. A game theoric analysis with some unconventional conclusions', *European Economic Review*, 36(8): 1557–71.

Mucchielli, J.-L. and Mayer, T. (1998) 'Les déterminants des investissements directs à l'étranger', in B. Lassudrie Duchêne (ed.), *Connaissance Économique*. Paris: Economica.

Mucchielli, J.-L. and Chédor, S. (1999) 'Foreign direct investment, export performance and the impact on home employment: an empirical analysis of French firms', in Lee Sang-Gon and P. B. Ruffini (eds), *The Global Integration of Europe and East Asia*. Cheltenham, UK: Edward Elgar, pp. 19–36.

Mundell, R. (1957) 'International trade and factor mobility,' *American Economic Review*, 47: 321–55.

Noguchi, S. (1997) 'Impacts of Japanese overseas business activities on Japan's domestic economy', OCDE, DSTI/EAS/IND/WP17.

Penrose, E. (1995) *The Theory of the Growth of the Firm*, 3rd edition. Oxford and New York: Oxford University Press.

Purvis, D. D. (1972) 'Technology, trade and factor mobility', *The Economic Journal*, 82(327): 991–9.

Roberts, M. and Tybout, J. (1997) 'The decision to export in Columbia: an empirical model of entry with sunk costs', *American Economic Review*, 87(4): 545–64.

Smith, A. (1987) 'Strategic investment, multinational corporations and trade policy', *European Economic Review*, 31: 89–96.

Svensson, R. (1996) 'Effects of overseas production on home country exports: evidence based on Swedish multinationals', *Welwirtschaftliches Archiv*, 132(2): 304–30.

Swedenborg, B. (1979) *The Multinational Operations of Swedish Firms*. Stockholm: Industriens Utredningsinstitut.

Swenson, D. L. (1997) 'Explaining domestic content: evidence from Japanese and US automobile production in the United States', in R. C. Feenstra (ed.), *Effects of US Trade Protection and Promotion Policies*. Chicago: University of Chicago Press, pp. 33–53.

UNCTAD (1999) *World Investment Report*. New York: United Nations Publication.

5

FOREIGN INVESTMENT TRANSACTIONS AND INTERNATIONAL TRADE LINKAGES*

Deborah L. Swenson

5.1. Introduction

Recent work on network ties suggests that the intensity of trade between nations may depend on linkages that have been established by managerial connections, immigration, or other types of trader exchange. While it is well known that foreign direct investment (FDI) and trade appear to be complements at the gross level, this paper considers the related issue of how the strength of the complementarity depends on the type of foreign investment.[1] These linkages are provided whenever foreign investment disseminates information between country pairs and provides a new conduit for personal and managerial information flows that may reduce the transaction costs that characterize a target country and its investors. Lipsey (1995) suggests that just such ties have affected the trade flows originating from US multinational affiliates located in Asia.[2] Lipsey finds that exports by the Asian affiliates of US firms are larger when the export destination is served by a high level of affiliated exports from their US parent.

While much work speculates on the possibility of ties between trade and investment, little work has examined how the *type* of foreign investment affects trade flows. One of the few papers on this topic is Yamawaki (1991). Yamawaki examines how Japanese investment in distribution, as measured by workers employed in the distribution sector, affects Japanese exports. Yamawaki uses a framework that recognizes the simultaneity between trade and investment, and discovers that distribution investments do affect the level of trade. This paper also explores the importance of distribution efforts, which I call 'trade sector' foreign investment, but will also examine the linkage effects that are associated with foreign investment types considering those in the manufacturing, service, and resource areas.

*This paper received support from the Commissariat Général au Plan, convention no. 4–98.

Finally, changes in the structure of foreign investment provide another reason for studying disaggregated foreign investment. In particular, a notable feature of foreign investment in recent years is the growing prevalence of transactions that take the form of mergers and acquisitions, as opposed to greenfield investments in new plants. This trend emerged during the 1980s, and has become more pronounced in the 1990s. In the US, for example, the percentage of foreign investment outlays devoted to mergers and acquisitions rose from 69.7 to 90.8 percent.[3] Such increase in cross-border foreign investments was not limited to the US. Over the same general time frame, cross-border acquisition deals in Europe grew from 26.6 billion dollars in 1991 to 149.8 billion dollars in 1998.[4] Dunning (1997a) provides further evidence on recent expansion of cross-border acquisitions in Europe. In a companion article that analyzes these trends, Dunning (1997b) speculates that the increase in European cross-border acquisitions has been spurred by the increasing economic integration in Europe, as well as increases in rivalry and reduced costs of completing such cross-border transactions.[5] It should be noted, however, that the interest in cross-border acquisitions is not limited to Europe. Firm surveys reveal a general interest in the expansion of market presence through mergers and other combinations including joint ventures, rather than the use of greenfield investment, or the expansion of current facilities.[6]

What is not clear is whether the change in transaction form represents a change in the structure of foreign investment activities, or whether the change in transaction form represents a mere change in name only. In my project I will analyze how the form of FDI transactions affects subsequent trade linkages. I will also study whether the intensity of trade activity is affected by the mode of manufacturing foreign investment.

In general I find that complementary linkages appear to be strongest for manufacturing foreign investment, followed by service and trade foreign investment. At the same time, resource foreign investments exert no comparable influence. I also explore how the mode of manufacturing investment correlates with the strength of subsequent trade flows. These results are weaker, though they suggest that plant expansions stimulate both US imports and exports while mergers and acquisitions reduce US exports. Finally, I discuss other economic determinants of trade and investment.

5.2. Background

There is a well-established literature on the linkages between trade and investment that originates with work including Lipsey and Weiss (1981, 1984) and Blomstrom *et al.* (1988). More recent work on foreign investment and trade has considered how multinational decision-making affects the choice of foreign investment versus trade. This work is reviewed in Markusen (1995) and forms a consensus that firms weigh the fixed costs of investment against the reduction of variable costs that occur as the firm reduces its tariff payments and avoids the transportation costs associated with exporting.[7] Much less attention has been paid to the question of how the type of investment affects trade linkages, though this question has been raised in recent work. Studies in this area include Head and Ries (1997) who utilize information on Japanese firm ties. Head and Ries find that firm exports are stimulated when foreign investments are made by vertically linked partners of the firm, and speculate that this indicates that firm exports are used as intermediate inputs in the vertically related firm's overseas production activities. Blonigen (2000) finds evidence of a similar nature for the Japanese auto industry. In particular, Blonigen shows how US imports of Japanese car parts rose as Japanese production facilities in the US expanded. That Japanese investment in distribution facilities has yet other effects is documented by Yamawaki (1991), who finds that Japanese exports to the US have increased with the expansion of Japanese investments in US distribution networks.

None of these studies has addressed whether the *mode* of entry into the host market affects subsequent trade flows. One difference that may cause target market acquisitions to have different trade repercussions than new plant creation is the fact that the two entry modes may entail different technological characteristics. The overall effects on trade depend substantially on the technological decisions made by the firm. For example, if we assume that a foreign firm uses its own technology when it develops new production facilities in the US, we may expect that the plant investment will stimulate US imports of the foreign parts that complement the foreign firm's technological choices. If the foreign firm decides to acquire a US target instead, it may passively operate the US target in the same manner as it was operated under its former US ownership. If so, the acquisition alters the ownership of the US facility, but has no effect on trade. In contrast, if the foreign firm acquires the US plant because it possesses superior production techniques, the method of future operations is likely to change as the foreign acquirer replaces the old US firm's operations with methods that are brought over from abroad. Since the foreign firm presumably relies on more intense use of inputs from its home country, the technology transfer causes the plant to become more reliant on imports than the plant was under US ownership.

In addition to technological differences, different modes of entry may entail very different life cycle characteristics. When a foreign firm builds a new plant, the firm is likely to expand at a later date if the plant is profitable. In contrast, the firm may be less likely to expand when the investment begins with an acquisition, as the acquisition gives the firm control of a more mature facility.

While there is no previous research that examines how the mode of entry affects subsequent trade flows, in other contexts mergers and acquisitions have been shown to differ from greenfield investments. Froot and Stein (1991) and Blonigen (1997) show that the depreciation of a country's exchange rate stimulates inbound international mergers while greenfield investments are much more weakly affected. In a similar vein, Sholes and Wolfson (1990) show that tax reforms may potentially exert different effects on mergers and acquisitions and new plant expansion – an idea that finds empirical support in Swenson (1994). Because the monetary value of acquisition foreign investment transactions is much larger than the monetary value of other foreign investment transactions, we may suspect that the two types of activity are distinct.

However, it is possible that acquisition foreign investment exerts no effect on subsequent trade flows, since the simplest of acquisitions could entail a change in ownership, and no other substantive element. On the other hand, if the acquisition allows foreign firms to promote their own products more effectively, or if the functioning of the newly acquired facilities involves the adoption of the foreign firm's production methods, trade flows are likely to change as a result of the acquisition. Dunning (1997b) notes that in the case of US acquisitions in Europe, as well as European mergers and acquisitions in Europe, the sectors receiving the most merger activities are those that are most affected by imports. While Dunning cautions that the ownership effects associated with these cross-border acquisitions are ambiguous, it is common for the acquisitions to be followed by restructuring of the acquired entity. Since there is little evidence on the post-acquisition operation of foreign-acquired firms, the overall effect of cross-border acquisitions is a matter of empirical estimation.

5.3. Data and analysis method

To study the effects of entry mode on trade flows, I use a data set of foreign investment transactions for the US. The transaction database is created by the International Trade Administration (ITA) of the Department of Commerce and covers the years from 1974 to 1994. Over this interval the ITA recorded all planned foreign investments in the US. The data set includes the foreign investment activities of almost seventy countries, and for each transaction, the ITA collected information on the location, industry, and financial size. The ITA also provides the national and corporate identity of the foreign investor. What is valuable for this study is that the ITA also collected information on the method of transaction, and whether the foreign investor performed a greenfield investment, plant expansion, joint venture, or merger and acquisition. I use this information to create investment data series for each of the countries investing in the US that distinguish the flow types by transaction method.

I use two sets of classifications to implement this project. First, I disaggregate investment into the categories: (1) manufacturing, (2) service, (3) trade, and (4) resource. Manufacturing foreign investment encompasses all foreign investment transactions that occurred in two-digit SIC industries 20–39. Investments in SIC code categories 1–14, 18–19 (Agriculture, Mining, Resource) and 40–49 (Utilities) were assigned to the category Resource foreign investment. Service foreign investment includes construction, SICs 15–17, finance, insurance and real estate, SICs 60–67, general services, SICs 70–88, and administration. Trade foreign investment includes the retail and wholesale sectors, SIC 50–59.

Second, I disaggregate manufacturing foreign investment by the form of the transactions, and identify the categories: (1) new plant, (2) plant expansion, (3) acquisition, (4) joint venture, and (5) other.

The tables included in the data appendix show the frequency and volume for each of the transaction types in the full sample and for the early and later time periods. Because the volume of foreign investment increased over the sample period, transactions completed in the late 1980s and early 1990s exert a strong influence on the averages.

Since a handful of countries perform the bulk of all investments, individual country investment is computed only for the twelve largest investors – Belgium, Canada, Finland, France, Germany, Italy, Japan, Korea, the Netherlands, Sweden, Switzerland, and the UK. The remaining investments are aggregated on a regional basis for Africa, Australia with New Zealand and surrounding island nations, the Middle East, South America, Other Asia, and Other Europe.

The trade variables of interest are US imports and exports. Here I use the US trade data compiled by Feenstra (1996). For comparability, the trade data are aggregated along the same country and regional clusterings. The final form of the data set contains investment and trade series for the twelve large investor nations and six regions for the years 1974–94. Further descriptions of the data are included in the data appendix.

5.4. Estimation framework

Since I am interested in the network ties forged by foreign investment, my estimation strategy involves regressions of trade flows on foreign investment stocks. However, since there are strong reasons to suspect that trade and foreign investment are simultaneously determined, I adopt an estimation framework that accommodates this potential. In particular, I simultaneously estimate a system of equations. The trade equations relate US imports and exports to foreign investment stocks, while the additional equations relate annual foreign investment flows to underlying economic conditions.

The first equation describes US imports I_{ct} that originate from country c in year t. In accordance with gravity treatments of trade, the log of GDP of the foreign investor is included as an explanatory variable.[8] To test the effects of foreign investment on trade flows, the next regressors are country foreign investment stocks summed to year $t - 1$ for a number of FDI categories k.[9] The last terms in the estimating equation are a set of year dummies γ_t, country dummies Π_c, and the regression error term ε_t. Similarly the second equation for exports E_{ct} measures the level of shipments emanating from the US as they relate to GDP, time, country fixed effects, and the foreign investment stocks of country c.

$$\ln(I_{ct}) = \alpha_I \ln(\text{GDP}_{ct}) + \beta_k \sum_k \ln(\text{FDI\_Stock}_{k,t-1}) + \gamma_t + \Pi_c + \varepsilon_t$$

$$\ln(E_{ct}) = \alpha_E \ln(\text{GDP}_{ct}) + \phi_k \sum_k \ln(\text{FDI\_Stock}_{k,t-1}) + \lambda_t + \Gamma_c + \eta_t$$

Because it is likely that foreign investment and trade are simultaneously determined, for each type of foreign investment flows, I estimate the responsiveness of current year foreign investment to GDP, previous year imports, transportation costs, the foreign investment activities of other countries, and year and country dummies. Here too, there is an equation error term v_t.

$$\ln(F)_{k,ct} = \alpha_F \ln(\text{GDP}_{ct}) + \sigma \ln(\text{imports}_{t-1}) + \rho \ln(\text{TC}_{ct})$$
$$+ \pi \ln(F_{k,c' \neq c,t}) + \phi^* \text{year} + \Omega_c + v_t$$

To encompass the four types of foreign investment flows, I have separate estimating equations for manufacturing, service, resource, and trade foreign investment. I use three stage least squares to estimate the four foreign investment equations simultaneously with the equations for US imports and US exports.

5.5. Results

Table 5.1 presents the results for the twelve investor nations over the twenty-two-year interval of my sample. I discuss the results of Table 5.1 in great detail since the results here are largely mirrored in the following estimation work. As a result, I only provide short comments on the following tables, to point out the places where the later results diverge from my baseline findings. Following Eaton and Tamura (1994), I have included GDP in the estimated trade as well as the foreign investment equations. As typically found in studies based on the gravity estimation framework, GDP significantly enters both the US import, US export equations, and in both cases, its coefficient is close to one in magnitude.

Stocks of foreign investment are included as explanatory variables in the US import and US export equations to see how different types of foreign investment affect the intensity of trade. In the US import equation, the stock of manufacturing foreign investment is the one explanatory variable that shows a positive and statistically significant effect. This finding of a complementary effect is in accord with most of the literature on the topic. I also find a positive relationship between the stocks of service and trade foreign investment and US imports. Though neither of these effects is statistically significant, these coefficients suggest that such investment provides an infrastructure that increases US imports from the investing countries.

On the exporting side, two types of foreign investment appear to play a role. In particular, the US exports equation shows that the US exports more to countries that have placed larger manufacturing investments in the US and to countries that have invested more in US trade facilities. When foreign countries manufacture in the US, they create products that can be exported home. This effect may be most pronounced in cases of manufactured differentiated products, since as many theories of consumer behavior predict, consumers may choose to buy some of each product variety. As long as the foreign country uses its US investments to expand its product lines, this increase in product diversity will stimulate sales back home (which are served by exports from the US). The positive coefficient on trade

Table 5.1 3SLS estimates of US trade and foreign investment in the US: 1975–94

	Dependent variables					
	US imports	US exports	MFG FDI	Service FDI	Resource FDI	Trade FDI
GDP	0.831[a]	1.175[a]	1.286	0.466	−0.302	−0.165
	(0.148)	(0.066)	(0.902)	(0.988)	(0.997)	(0.896)
MFG	0.051[b]	0.013				
stock FDI_{t-1}	(0.025)	(0.011)				
Service	0.026	−0.015				
stock FDI_{t-1}	(0.023)	(0.010)				
Resource	−0.004	−0.007				
stock FDI_{t-1}	(0.018)	(0.008)				
Trade	0.023	0.013[c]				
stock FDI_{t-1}	(0.017)	(0.007)				
Year dummies	Yes	Yes				
Country dummies	Yes	Yes	Yes	Yes	Yes	Yes
$Imports_{t-1}$			0.073	0.076	0.037	0.118
			(0.065)	(0.072)	(0.072)	(0.064)
Transport costs			0.126[b]	0.001	−0.045	−0.032
			(0.050)	(0.054)	(0.054)	(0.049)
Other country			0.064	0.123[a]	0.198[a]	0.135[a]
FDI – same type			(0.046)	(0.051)	(0.047)	(0.046)
Trend			0.119[a]	0.121[a]	0.110[a]	0.052
			(0.033)	(0.037)	(0.040)	(0.033)

Notes: All variables measured in logs. Each regression has 263 observations. All equations have country dummy variables. Standard errors in ( ).

a   denotes statistical significance at the 1 per cent level;
b   denotes statistical significance at the 5 per cent level;
c   denotes statistical significance at the 10 per cent level.

facilities suggests that some foreign investors set up trading facilities, not only to tap into US markets, but also to arrange new sales at home of US-origin goods.

Separate regressions for manufacturing, service, resource, and trade foreign investment flows were estimated along with the trade equations. A few interesting findings emerge. First, transportation costs provide explanatory power in the manufacturing foreign investment equation, but not in the other foreign investment equations. Transportation costs are an important economic element of theories of multinational firm activity, as it is posited that the impetus for doing foreign investment will be higher when foreign investment enables firms to avoid sizable costs of transportation. Since manufacturing foreign investment provides an alternative mode of providing products, and because this foreign investment allows the firm to avoid costs of transportation, the positive transportation cost coefficient accords with theory. In contrast, it is not likely that traditional transportation costs present a large impediment to the provision of services. I find that previous import levels are positively associated with the volumes of manufacturing, service, and trade foreign investment, while there is almost no discernible relationship between previous country import levels and resource foreign investment. This too, is consistent with substitution theories of the multinational firm. The high fixed costs associated with foreign investment are thought to deter FDI.

However, as firms weigh the fixed costs of FDI against the benefits of proximity and reduced marginal costs of serving the market, the fixed costs are most likely to be justified when the firms can supplant large import flows. This would explain the correlation observed for manufacturing investment. If the manufacturing investment exerts a positive pull for accompanying trade or service foreign investment, this would generate the other positive correlation. Since resource foreign investment is more likely to depend on cross-country differences in endowments, it is not surprising that there is little association between resource foreign investment and overall import levels.[10]

There are two commonalties that run across all types of foreign investment. First, countries are more likely to invest in the US when other countries are investing in similar sectors. For example, UK investment in manufacturing is higher in periods where manufacturing investment by other countries is elevated. This effect occurs because the US becomes either more or less desirable as an investment location for services, trade, manufacturing, or resources at different times. The effect is reinforced further if firms feel pressed to emulate the decisions of their competitors as postulated by Knickerbocker (1973). The second commonality for the foreign investment equations is that they all include strong trend effects, reflecting increased foreign investment over time, controlling for other national factors.

The foreign investment equations include the effects of the foreign country GDP. Here the estimated coefficients are mixed. The strongest connection between GDP and foreign investment is found for manufacturing foreign investment. As with the trade equations, the estimated coefficient is close to one, though the estimate is not statistically significant. For the other sectors, the coefficients are much smaller.

The regressions in Table 5.1 include GDP, because GDP is a good control for country size. As with gravity equation models based on differentiated goods, larger country size implies the growth in the available types of differentiated goods from which consumers may choose, presumably creating a stronger impetus for foreign trade and investment. In Table 5.1 I focused on the twelve separate countries in my analysis. Since investment is less frequent for many countries, the remaining investments were assigned to one of six regional aggregates. When I use these regional aggregates, I cease to use country GDP. In its place, I now include transportation costs in the trade equations.[11] My set of twelve country dummies is now augmented to include six region dummies for the trade flows that have been attributed to regions rather than to countries. As I would expect, all else equal, transportation costs reduce both imports to, and exports from the US. In the case of imports, a 10 per cent increase in transportation costs is associated with a 2.3 per cent reduction in imports, while the same 10 per cent increase in transportation costs is predicted to reduce US exports by 1.9 per cent. Statistically, I cannot reject that the two coefficients are equal in magnitude.

Table 5.2 3SLS estimates of US trade and foreign investment in the US: 1975–94

	Dependent variables					
	US imports	US exports	MFG FDI	Service FDI	Resource FDI	Trade FDI
Transport costs	−0.233[a]	−0.189[c]	0.079[c]	−0.004	−0.035	−0.024
	(0.064)	(0.042)	(0.041)	(0.041)	(0.042)	(0.038)
MFG	0.037	0.013				
stock FDI$_{t-1}$	(0.021)	(0.014)				
Service	0.022	0.028[b]				
stock FDI$_{t-1}$	(0.019)	(0.013)				
Resource	−0.047[a]	−0.032				
stock FDI$_{t-1}$	(0.016)	(0.011)				
Trade	0.025	0.001				
stock FDI$_{t-1}$	(0.017)	(0.001)				
Year dummies	Yes	Yes				
Country dummies	Yes	Yes	Yes	Yes	Yes	Yes
Imports$_{t-1}$			0.052	0.105[c]	−0.001	0.075
			(0.054)	(0.056)	(0.057)	(0.050)
Other country			0.080[b]	0.071[c]	0.174[a]	0.085[b]
FDI – same type			(0.036)	(0.040)	(0.037)	(0.036)
Trend			0.172[a]	0.120[a]	0.129[a]	0.084[a]
			(0.019)	(0.020)	(0.023)	(0.018)

Notes: All variables measured in logs. Each regression has 396 observations. All equations have country dummy variables. Standard errors in ( ).

a   denotes statistical significance at the 1 per cent level;
b   denotes statistical significance at the 5 per cent level;
c   denotes statistical significance at the 10 per cent level.

What is interesting in Table 5.2 regressions is that transportation costs affect foreign investment differently than trade. While transportation costs reduce trade, they are associated with higher levels of manufacturing foreign investment, and they have no discernible effect on the other categories of foreign investment. Again, this suggests that the substitution hypothesis applies to multinationals who are deciding whether to sell to consumers through exports, or transplant production while transportation costs are not an influential determinant of other types of foreign investment.

The remaining regression coefficients generally have the same signs as they did in Table 5.1. Trade, manufacturing, and service foreign investment are all weakly associated with the intensification of US imports from the foreign investment performing countries or regions. The one significant export coefficient shows that US exports are higher for countries that have large stocks of service FDI. As argued earlier, this is consistent with network explanations of trade.

In Tables 5.3 and 5.4, I use the same basic set of equations to estimate trade and investment effects first for the twelve big investor countries, and then for the twelve investors plus six regions. In Tables 5.3 and 5.4, however, the trade equations now

Table 5.3 3SLS estimates of US trade and foreign investment in the US: 1975–94

	Dependent variables					
	US imports	*US exports*	*MFG FDI*	*Service FDI*	*Resource FDI*	*Trade FDI*
GDP	0.927[a]	1.155[a]	1.282	0.466	−0.302	−0.164
	(0.154)	(0.068)	(0.902)	(0.988)	(0.997)	(0.896)
New plant	−0.014	0.005				
stock FDI$_{t-1}$	(0.024)	(0.011)				
Plant exp	0.058[c]	0.034[b]				
stock FDI$_{t-1}$	(0.033)	(0.014)				
M&A	0.018	−0.005				
stock FDI$_{t-1}$	(0.016)	(0.007)				
Joint venture	−0.017	−0.018				
stock FDI	(0.032)	(0.014)				
Equity increase	−0.029	0.029[c]				
stock FDI$_{t-1}$	(0.035)	(0.015)				
Other MFG	0.033	0.009				
stock FDI$_{t-1}$	(0.044)	(0.019)				
Service	0.043[b]	−0.016[c]				
stock FDI$_{t-1}$	(0.021)	(0.009)				
Resource	−0.002	−0.003				
stock FDI$_{t-1}$	(0.019)	(0.008)				
Trade	0.022	0.014[c]				
stock FDI$_{t-1}$	(0.018)	(0.008)				
Year dummies	Yes	Yes				
Country dummies	Yes	Yes	Yes	Yes	Yes	Yes
Imports$_{t-1}$			0.074	0.074	0.037	0.117[c]
			(0.065)	(0.072)	(0.072)	(0.064)
Transport costs			0.125[b]	0.002	−0.045	−0.031
			(0.050)	(0.054)	(0.054)	(0.049)
Other country			0.065	0.124[b]	0.197[a]	0.134[a]
FDI – same type			(0.046)	(0.051)	(0.047)	(0.046)
Trend			0.119[a]	0.121[a]	0.110[a]	0.052
			(0.033)	(0.037)	(0.040)	(0.033)

Notes: All variables measured in logs. Each regression has 263 observations. All equations have country dummy variables. Standard errors in ( ).

a denotes statistical significance at the 1 per cent level;
b denotes statistical significance at the 5 per cent level;
c denotes statistical significance at the 10 per cent level.

examine more finely disaggregated manufacturing investment flows. In particular, the manufacturing investments are now split into six groups; new plant, plant expansion, acquisition, joint venture, equity increase, and other. The remaining investment categories, service, trade, and resource, are left as they were before. In contrast, mergers and acquisitions appear to depress exports from the US to the country that performs the acquisition.[12]

Table 5.4 3SLS estimates of US trade and foreign investment in the US: 1975–94

	Dependent variables					
	US imports	US exports	MFG FDI	Service FDI	Resource FDI	Trade FDI
Transport costs	−0.261[a]	−0.197[a]	0.080[b]	−0.004	−0.034	−0.023
	(0.063)	(0.041)	(0.041)	(0.041)	(0.042)	(0.038)
New plant	−0.041[c]	−0.016				
stock FDI_{t-1}	(0.024)	(0.016)				
Plant exp	0.059	0.029				
stock FDI_{t-1}	(0.037)	(0.024)				
M&A	0.003	−0.025[a]				
stock FDI_{t-1}	(0.013)	(0.008)				
Joint venture	0.043	0.035[c]				
stock FDI_{t-1}	(0.031)	(0.020)				
Equity increase	−0.088	0.009				
stock FDI_{t-1}	(0.029)	(0.019)				
Other MFG	0.048	0.019				
stock FDI_{t-1}	(0.040)	(0.026)				
Service	0.036[c]	0.032[a]				
stock FDI_{t-1}	(0.019)	(0.013)				
Resource	−0.039[b]	−0.028[a]				
stock FDI_{t-1}	(0.016)	(0.011)				
Trade	0.028[c]	0.007				
stock FDI_{t-1}	(0.017)	(0.011)				
Year dummies	Yes	Yes				
Country dummies	Yes	Yes	Yes	Yes	Yes	Yes
$Imports_{t-1}$			0.050	0.104[b]	−0.003	0.072
			(0.053)	(0.056)	(0.057)	(0.051)
Other country			0.079[b]	0.072[c]	0.173[a]	0.084[b]
FDI – same type			(0.036)	(0.040)	(0.037)	(0.036)
Trend			0.173[a]	0.120[a]	0.129[a]	0.084[a]
			(0.019)	(0.020)	(0.023)	(0.018)

Notes: All variables measured in logs. Each regression has 396 observations. All equations have country dummy variables. Standard Errors in ( ).
a   denotes statistical significance at the 1 per cent level;
b   denotes statistical significance at the 5 per cent level;
c   denotes statistical significance at the 10 per cent level.

When manufacturing foreign investment is disaggregated by type, plant expansion emerges as the one type of manufacturing investment that exhibits a positive and significant influence on US imports and US exports.[13] In contrast, mergers and acquisitions in manufacturing are related to diminished US exports to the investing country. The effect appears in both Tables 5.3 and 5.4, though the effect is significant only in Table 5.4.

Other more general effects continue in Table 5.3 regressions. GDP plays a positive role in imports, exports, and manufacturing FDI, while it shows no particular relationship with the other types of foreign investment. Transportation costs also have the dichotomous effect that was identified earlier. High transportation costs appear to spur greater manufacturing foreign investment, while they have no identifiable effects on other types of foreign investment. In general, Tables 5.3 and 5.4 show that imports and exports are fostered by foreign investment in the trade or service sectors, suggesting that the creation of market infrastructure magnifies inter-country trade flows. Finally, other country foreign investment appears to be strongly related to own country foreign investment decisions. Once again, investors are either mimicking each other's decisions, or uniformly availing themselves of changes in the US market that are favorable for one type of investment or the other.

If anything, the one limitation of the results in Tables 5.3 and 5.4 is that the effects of the different manufacturing types are not statistically identified. In hopes of increasing the precision of the estimates, I attempted to group the investment types more tightly. New plant and plant expansion activities are assigned to the category 'greenfield investment'. As before, acquisitions stand alone. The remaining investment types are assigned to 'Other Investment'.

The foreign investment results in Tables 5.5 and 5.6 suggests that service FDI and trade FDI enhance import to and exports from the US to the country that is the source of the foreign investment. In this set of specifications, the effects of mergers are again associated with diminished US exports to the FDI-performing country. At the same time, the new greenfield investment aggregate is imprecisely estimated, and shows no general tendency towards positive or negative effects. I do not discuss the coefficients on GDP, transportation costs, imports, or other country FDI, since they all echo the findings I discuss earlier.

5.6. Conclusions

In this paper I examine how the type of foreign investment type affects the linkages between trade and foreign investment. Because it is likely that trade and foreign investment are simultaneously determined, I perform a regression analysis that jointly estimates a number of equations that pertain to US imports and US exports as well as foreign investment.

When investment is broken down by function, I find that the strongest complementary effects of foreign investment on trade appear in manufacturing. The apparent strength of this effect is smaller in services or trade, and non-existent in the resource sector. I later break down manufacturing investment according to the method of transaction selected. Here I find that plant expansions appear to be correlated with the expansion of US exports and imports, while foreign acquisitions in the US are associated with the reduction of US exports to the investing countries. Although the results are not always significant at conventional levels, they suggest that not all foreign investments are equal. Some foreign investment types stimulate trade linkages, while others supplant previous trade flows. What this suggests is that understanding the consequences of foreign investment flows will be aided by greater focus on their composition.

Table 5.5 3SLS estimates of US trade and foreign investment in the US: 1975–94

	Dependent variables					
	US imports	US exports	MFG FDI	Service FDI	Resource FDI	Trade FDI
GDP	0.964[a]	1.161[a]	1.283	0.467	−0.302	−0.162
	(0.152)	(0.068)	(0.902)	(0.988)	(0.997)	(0.895)
Greenfield	0.007	0.016				
stock FDI$_{t-1}$	(0.023)	(0.010)				
M&A	0.023	−0.011				
stock FDI$_{t-1}$	(0.016)	(0.007)				
Other MFG	−0.016	0.015				
stock FDI$_{t-1}$	(0.027)	(0.012)				
Service	0.043[b]	−0.013				
stock FDI$_{t-1}$	(0.021)	(0.009)				
Resource	−0.007	−0.004				
stock FDI$_{t-1}$	(0.019)	(0.008)				
Trade	0.023	0.012				
stock FDI$_{t-1}$	(0.019)	(0.008)				
Year dummies	Yes	Yes				
Country dummies	Yes	Yes	Yes	Yes	Yes	Yes
Imports$_{t-1}$			0.074	0.074	0.036	0.116[c]
			(0.065)	(0.072)	(0.072)	(0.064)
Transport costs			0.125[b]	0.002	−0.044	−0.031
			(0.050)	(0.053)	(0.054)	(0.049)
Other country			0.065	0.124[b]	0.198[a]	0.134[a]
FDI – same type			(0.046)	(0.051)	(0.047)	(0.046)
Trend			0.118[a]	0.121[a]	0.110[a]	0.052
			(0.033)	(0.037)	(0.040)	(0.033)

Notes: All variables measured in logs. Each regression has 263 observations. All equations have country dummy variables. Standard errors in ( ).

a denotes statistical significance at the 1 per cent level;
b denotes statistical significance at the 5 per cent level;
c denotes statistical significance at the 10 per cent level.

The regression analysis also sheds light on the economic determinants of trade and foreign investment. GDP exerts a positive inducement for imports as well as exports, and is positively associated with FDI in the manufacturing sector. I also find that transportation costs are linked to reduced imports or exports, at the same time that high transportation costs stimulate foreign investment in manufacturing sectors. Finally, the evidence shows that countries perform foreign investment at the same time as other countries make similar investments, i.e. German firms are most likely to make service (manufacturing, trade) investments in the years that other countries are making service (manufacturing, trade) investments. While this is consistent with a number of interpretations, it would be interesting to know whether this final effect reflects characteristics of the US market, or whether it arises from the nature of competition among multinational firms.

Table 5.6 3SLS estimates of US trade and foreign investment in the US: 1975–94

	Dependent variables					
	US imports	US exports	MFG FDI	Service FDI	Resource FDI	Trade FDI
Transport costs	−0.250[a]	−0.202[a]	0.080[b]	−0.003	−0.035	−0.024
	(0.063)	(0.041)	(0.041)	(0.041)	(0.042)	(0.038)
Greenfield	−0.001	−0.005				
stock FDI_{t-1}	(0.022)	(0.014)				
M&A	0.006	−0.031[a]				
stock FDI_{t-1}	(0.014)	(0.009)				
Other MFG	−0.012	0.061[a]				
stock FDI_{t-1}	(0.027)	(0.017)				
Service	0.034[c]	0.031[a]				
stock FDI_{t-1}	(0.019)	(0.012)				
Resource	−0.051[a]	−0.031[a]				
stock FDI_{t-1}	(0.016)	(0.010)				
Trade	0.031[c]	0.005				
stock FDI_{t-1}	(0.017)	(0.011)				
Year dummies	Yes	Yes				
Country dummies	Yes	Yes	Yes	Yes	Yes	Yes
$Imports_{t-1}$			0.051	0.103[c]	−0.001	0.073
			(0.054)	(0.056)	(0.057)	(0.051)
Other country			0.078[b]	0.071[c]	0.174[a]	0.085[b]
FDI − same type			(0.036)	(0.040)	(0.037)	(0.036)
Trend			0.173[a]	0.121[a]	0.129[a]	0.084[a]
			(0.019)	(0.020)	(0.023)	(0.018)

Notes: All variables measured in logs. Each regression has 396 observations. All equations have country dummy variables. Standard errors in ( ).

a denotes statistical significance at the 1 per cent level;
b denotes statistical significance at the 5 per cent level;
c denotes statistical significance at the 10 per cent level.

Data appendix

Foreign investment data

The FDI data are collected from the annual Department of Commerce publications 'Foreign Direct Investment in the United States: Transactions' for the years 1974–94. The ITA of the Department of Commerce draws on a number of sources to assemble a comprehensive listing of foreign investment activities in the US. The ITA reports provide the compiled list of transactions.

One is added to each of the foreign investment variables before I take logs, to prevent undefined observations for the cases where no new foreign investment occurred.

Since a number of the investment transactions do not include reported transaction values, I replace missing values with values predicted by a simple prediction equation that

Table A5.1 FDI disaggregated by function

	% of transactions	Weighted % of transactions
A. Full sample		
Manufacturing	0.52	0.59
Service	0.20	0.20
Resource	0.10	0.13
Trade	0.18	0.07
B. Transactions before 1985		
Manufacturing	0.54	0.52
Service	0.21	0.18
Resource	0.06	0.19
Trade	0.20	0.10
C. Transactions from 1985 and on		
Manufacturing	0.51	0.60
Service	0.19	0.21
Resource	0.12	0.11
Trade	0.17	0.07

Notes: Percentage of transactions shows the frequency of the transaction. Weighted percentage of transactions weights the transaction type by value, effectively breaking the categories to percentages of expenditure in each area. The percentages may not sum to 100 per cent, due to rounding.

Table A5.2 Manufacturing FDI disaggregated by transaction type

	% of transactions	Weighted % of transactions
A. All Manufacturing transactions		
Merger and acquisition	0.47	0.78
New plant	0.22	0.09
Plant expansion	0.12	0.08
Joint venture	0.07	0.04
Other	0.09	0.01
B. Manufacturing Transactions before 1985		
Merger and acquisition	0.46	0.61
New plant	0.11	0.17
Plant expansion	0.25	0.14
Joint venture	0.06	0.03
Other	0.08	0.02
C. Manufacturing Transactions from 1985 and on		
Merger and acquisition	0.47	0.79
New plant	0.21	0.08
Plant expansion	0.13	0.07
Joint venture	0.09	0.04
Other	0.10	0.01

Notes: Percentage of transactions shows the frequency of the transaction. Weighted percentage of transactions weights the transaction type by value, effectively breaking the categories to percentages of expenditure in each area. The percentages may not sum to 100 per cent, due to rounding.

uses nation, year, US state, transaction type and two-digit SIC industry dummy variables. In Swenson (1999), I experiment with different methods of controlling for missing values. Since none affected the underlying identification of product level substitution, and overall complementarity, I conclude that the estimated effects from the foreign investment series are not sensitive to the treatment of missing values. The foreign investment transactions data are also used to construct instruments for foreign investment. To gauge the attractiveness of the US as an investment location, I created a variable that measured foreign investment by other countries.

Trade data

The trade data are based on US Department of Census, Department of Commerce data on US imports, as compiled by Feenstra (1996). As with foreign investment data, I converted the data to constant 1992 dollars before I performed any of the aggregations.

Transportation costs

Transportation costs were constructed using the trade data described above. Transport cost = (CIF import value − customs import value)/(customs import value).

Macroeconomic variables

The real exchange rates and gross domestic product variables are taken from International Monetary Fund annual series data contained in the *International Financial Statistics*.

Notes

1 Other network ties have been found to exert their effects on foreign trade. Rauch (1996) shows that highly differentiated products that are not traded with a reference price or on an organized exchange are traded most intensively among countries that have links such as similar language or membership in a trading block. In addition, the trade volume of these products is more inhibited by distance than other products. Recent work on ethnic ties by Cassella and Rauch (1997) provides theoretical justification for how these ties may work. In a similar vein, evidence for the relationship between immigration and trade is reported in Gould (1994) and Head and Ries (1998).
2 Lipsey measures potential multinational ties by parent firm exports to affiliates, as contrasted with parent firm exports to unaffiliated parties in nine locations. The locations are the countries US, Japan, and Canada, and six broad regions that exclude the three countries.
3 Fahim-Nader and Zeile (1998) report that foreign mergers in the US rose from 17.8 billion dollars in 1991 to 64.3 billion dollars in 1997. Over the same time interval, total foreign investment rose from 25.5 billion dollars to 70.8 billion dollars in 1997 (p. 42).
4 *Mergers and Acquisitions*. March/April 1999, p. 16. The reported volume statistics exclude acquisitions of European targets by US buyers.
5 Dunning (1997b) notes that the large changes in firm *ownership* throughout Europe do not necessarily imply any fundamental changes in production location or in the identity of trading partners.

6 *The Economist*, 11 April 1998 (p. 82), reports the results of a survey done by Deloitte & Touche, Deloitte Consulting. Firms were asked how they would prefer to enter international markets: by combination or alliance including joint venture or merger, or by expansion of facilities or new facility creation. In all cases, the majority of firms indicated that they would prefer to enter by combination or alliance. These data were collected for the four developed regions (North America, Western Europe, Japan, and Australia and New Zealand). The same response was also associated with the cross-section of emerging markets (China, South-East Asia, Other East Asia, India and Pakistan, Brazil, Mexico, Other Latin America, Middle East, North Africa, Eastern Europe, and Former Soviet Union).

7 Horst (1972), Swedenborg (1979), and Brainard (1997) all provide empirical evidence on the industry and country factors that influence the degree of substitution between foreign affiliate sales and exporting.

8 Unlike some gravity treatments, I do not include US GDP in my specification. This is because the regression includes time dummies, which encompass the annual effects of US GDP as well as other annual effects that are captured in the time terms.

9 The FDI stocks are lagged for two reasons. First, lagging is appropriate if FDI plans and the set-up of FDI facilities require time before the effects on trade flows emerge. Second, lagged FDI stocks may mitigate simultaneity problems, as they are predetermined relative to trade flows.

10 Indirectly, financing constraints may create a link between imports and all types of foreign investment. In particular, if firms face financing constraints, then previous year imports represent earnings that the foreign countries may spend on investments, including FDI in the US.

11 Trade costs represent the weighted-average of product transportation costs. For countries the weights are country trade flows of the various products. For regions, the transportation costs are the weighted-sum of different products for the different countries in the region.

12 The coefficient for the effect of acquisitions on US exports is significant in Table 5.4, but not in Table 5.3.

13 The plant expansion coefficients are almost identical in Tables 5.3 and 5.4. However, the effects are not statistically significant in Table 5.4, since the standard errors are larger.

References

Blomström, M., Lipsey, R. E. and Kulchycky, K. (1988) 'US and Swedish direct investment and exports', in R. Baldwin (ed.),*Trade Policy Issues and Empirical Analysis*. Chicago: University of Chicago Press, pp. 259–99.

Blonigen, B. A. (1997) 'Firm-specific assets and the link between exchange rates and foreign direct investment', *American Economic Review*, 87: 447–65.

Blonigen, B. A. (2000) 'In search of substitution between foreign production and exports', *Journal of International Economics*, 53(1): 81–104.

Brainard, L. S. (1997) 'An empirical assessment of the proximity-concentration tradeoff between multinational sales and trade', *American Economic Review*, 87: 520–44.

Dunning, J. H. (1997a) 'The European internal market programme and inbound foreign direct investment', *Journal of Common Market Studies*, 35: 1–30.

Dunning, J. H. (1997b) 'The European internal market programme and inbound foreign direct investment: Part II', *Journal of Common Market Studies*, 35: 189–223.

Eaton, J. and Tamura, A. (1994) 'Bilateralism and regionalism in Japanese and US trade and direct foreign investment patterns', *Journal of the Japanese and International Economics*.

Fahim-Nader, M. and Zeile, W. J. (1998) 'Foreign direct investment in the United States', *Survey of Current Business*, June: 39–67.

Feenstra, R. C. (1996) 'US imports, 1972–1994: data and concordances'. NBER Working Paper No. 5515.

Froot, K. A. and Stein, J. C. (1991) 'Exchange rates and foreign direct investment: an imperfect capital markets approach', *Quarterly Journal of Economics*, 106: 1191–217.

Gould, D. M. (1994) 'Immigrant links to the home country: empirical implications for US bilateral trade flows', *The Review of Economics and Statistics*, 76: 302–16.

Head, K. and Ries, J. (1997) 'Overseas investment and firm exports', University of British Columbia Working Paper.

Head, K. and Ries, J. (1998) 'Immigration and trade creation: econometric evidence from Canada', *Canadian Journal of Economics*.

Horst, T. (1972) 'The industrial composition of US exports and subsidiary sales to the Canadian market', *American Economic Review*, 62: 37–45.

Knickerbocker, F. T. (1973) *Oligopolistic Reaction and Multinational Enterprise*. Boston: Division of Research, Graduate School of Business Administration, Harvard University.

Lipsey, R. E. (1995) Trade and production networks of US MNCs and exports by their Asian affiliates. NBER Working Paper No. 5255.

Lipsey, R. E. and Weiss, M. Y. (1981) 'Foreign production and exports in manufacturing industries', *Review of Economics and Statistics*, 63: 488–94.

Lipsey, R. E. and Weiss, M. Y. (1984) 'Foreign production and exports of individual firms', *Review of Economics and Statistics*, 66: 304–7.

Markusen, J. R. (1995) 'The boundaries of multinational enterprises and the theory of international trade', *Journal of Economic Perspectives*, 9: 169–89.

Rauch, J. E. (1996) 'Networks versus markets in international trade', NBER Working Paper No. 5617, June.

Scholes, M. S. and Wolfson, M. A. (1990) 'The effects of changes in tax laws on corporate reorganization activity', *Journal of Business*, 63: S141–64.

Sleuwaegen, L. (1985) 'Monopolistic advantages and the international operations of firms: disaggregated evidence from US based multinationals', *Journal of International Business Studies*, 16: 125–33.

Swedenborg, B. (1979) *The Multinational Operations of Swedish Firms: An Analysis of Determinants and Effects*. Stockholm: Industrial Institute for Economic and Social Research.

Swenson, D. L. (1994) 'The impact of US tax reform on foreign direct investment in the United States', *Journal of Public Economics*, 54: 243–66.

Swenson, D. L. (forthcoming) 'Foreign investment and the mediation of trade flows', Review of International Economics.

Yamawaki, H. (1991) 'Exports and foreign distributional activities – evidence on Japanese firms in the United States', *Review of Economics and Statistics*, 73: 294–300.

6

INTRA-FIRM TRADE AND MARKET STRUCTURE*

Stéphane Becuwe, Claude Mathieu and Patrick Sevestre

6.1. Introduction

Multinational firms (MFs) can be considered as major actors in the globalization movement of the world economy. Their importance can be appreciated through the increasing share of intra-firm trade[1] in the total trade of developed countries. Thus, for the United States, this share grew from 30 per cent in 1977 to 44 per cent in 1993 (see UN 1996). This evolution has caused a renewed interest of economists in the analysis of the behavior of MFs. However, the theoretical literature explaining the existence of intra-firm trade is still in its infancy (see nevertheless Horst 1971, 1973; Mainardi 1986; Cantwell 1994). In fact, the traditional analyses of international trade hardly justify such a type of trade, except for the contributions based on the theory of transaction costs (see for example Buckley and Casson 1985; Dunning 1988).

In a previous paper (see Becuwe *et al.* 1998) we pointed out the conditions under which intra-firm trade occurs when trade barriers exist and production costs are subject to uncertainty. Assuming a monopolistic structure of markets (as done by Horst 1971), we determined the impact of these trade barriers and production costs uncertainty on the intensity of intra-firm trade. In particular, we showed that, in such a context, exports and production abroad may be complementary for a MF, which uses its different production units as a means of limiting the impact of uncertainty on its production costs.

However, assuming a monopolistic structure of markets may be viewed as a too restrictive hypothesis. In the present paper, we propose to extend our previous analysis in considering that the number of MFs is not fixed on the markets/countries where these firms are present. We want to analyze the impact of the market structure (i.e. the number of MFs) on intra-firm trade flows both for each firm and at the level of the industry. This analysis is performed assuming that MFs have their parents

*We wish to thank S. Negassi and the participants of the 7th Sorbonne International Conference on 'MNE strategies: Location, Impact on Employment and Exports, Technological Spillovers' for their comments on a previous version of this article.

located either in the same country or in a different country. In the latter case, trade flows becoming bilateral, intra-firm trade is at least partially intra-industry trade. Consequently, we analyze to what extent the modifications of the market structure can affect the intensity of intra-industry trade between countries.

In the first section, we present the notation, the basic assumptions and the equilibrium concept underlying our model. In the second section, we determine the exports and sales equilibrium on each market when MFs have the same country/zone[2] origin and the conditions for this equilibrium to exist. We also show that when the number of multinationals increases, the volume of intra-firm exports realized by each firm always decreases while the volume of intra-firm trade in the whole industry can increase or decrease, depending on the relative value of the domestic and foreign sales elasticities with respect to the number of MFs, compared to the relative marginal production costs between parent firms and their subsidiaries. In the third section, we consider the case where parents are located in different countries. We show that in this case, a supplementary condition for the existence of an equilibrium is that parents have a lower marginal cost slope than their subsidiaries. Moreover, the variation of the total volume of intra-firm trade with respect to the number of MFs is always either positive or negative. In this case, transaction costs related to intra-firm trade appear to have an impact. Indeed, they distort competition in favor of parents and can amplify the reduction of total trade when the number of firms increases. Transaction costs also modify the relationship between the intensity of intra-industry trade and the number of MFs. The fourth section summarizes the main conclusions.

6.2. The model

We consider n MFs, each producing and selling the same homogeneous good in two different countries/markets on which Cournot competition prevails: the home country where the parent firms are located and the foreign country where their subsidiaries are. MFs are horizontally integrated and export from their parents to their subsidiaries, thus generating intra-firm trade. The geographical location of parent production is determined by the autarky situation. We first assume, in this basic model, that all firms have their parent in the same (domestic) country. When firms become MFs, all their affiliates are located in the same foreign country, denoted by an asterisk.

Even if the supplied good is homogeneous, the domestic and foreign markets are not integrated; the firms can identify two distinct inverse demand functions, one by country. Both inverse demand functions are assumed to be linear:

$$p = a - \sum_{i=1}^{n} D_i \tag{1.1}$$

$$p^* = a^* - \sum_{i=1}^{n} D_i^* \tag{1.2}$$

where p and p^* are the market prices, D_i and D_i^* the quantities sold by firm i at home and abroad, a and a^* two positive parameters.

MFs are assumed to maximize their global profits (parent plus affiliate), given by

$$\pi_i = p(D)D_i - \frac{c}{2}Q_i^2 + p^*(D^*)D_i^* - \frac{c^*}{2}Q_i^{*2} - t_i v_i X_i \tag{2}$$

where $D = \sum_{i=1}^{n} D_i$ and $D^* = \sum_{i=1}^{n} D_i^*$ are the global supplies on both markets, Q_i and Q_i^* the quantities produced by the parent of firm i and its affiliate, X_i the volume of its intra-firm trade, t_i a parameter that reflects the level of trade barriers due to internal transaction costs (incurred by the MF when it transfers specific assets – technologies, management – between its parent and its affiliate), but also to an *ad valorem* tariff and/or to transport costs; v_i is the transfer price fixed by firm i for its intra-firm trade.

Each MF then supports a total transaction cost of $t_i v_i X_i$. This total transaction cost is proportionate to trade barriers and to transfer prices. Thus, the optimal transfer price fixed by each firm should be zero. However, we will assume that v_i is bounded by a minimum value $\underline{v} > 0$, a value that will be the equilibrium transfer price, identical for all MFs. Such an assumption may be justified by tax laws in force in many countries, tax laws restricting the transfer price interval of MFs.

For each MF, parent exports must equal its subsidiary imports ($X_i = Q_i - D_i = D_i^* - Q_i^* = M_i^*$). Consequently, assuming that all parents are located in the same domestic country, exports of the product by this country ($X = \sum_{i=1}^{n} X_i$) correspond to the imports of the foreign country ($M^* = \sum_{i=1}^{n} M_i^*$).

Each MF faces two production cost functions, one by country. These functions are assumed to be quadratic since a condition for the parent to export to its affiliate is that the marginal domestic and foreign production costs are rising (see Horst 1973).[3] Moreover, we assume that firms share the same technology and the same input prices on each market but that these technologies and prices are different between countries ($c \neq c^*$).

6.3. Market structure and intra-firm trade with multinationals of the same country/zone origin

Given the hypotheses of the model, considering that all firms are identical is equivalent to assuming that they share the same average transaction cost ($t_i = t$). Because of the market segmentation, the level of sales in both countries, as well as the volume of intra-firm trade, can be all chosen independently, and the first-order conditions for a maximum profit of firm i are:

$$a - 2D_i - \sum_{i \neq j} D_j = cQ_i \tag{3.1}$$

$$a^* - 2D_i^* - \sum_{i \neq j} D_j^* = c^*Q_i^* \tag{3.2}$$

$$c^*Q_i^* = cQ_i + t\underline{v} \tag{3.3}$$

The first two conditions state that on each market, all MFs should equal marginal revenue and marginal production cost. The third condition equates the foreign marginal production cost to the intra-firm trade marginal cost, which is the sum of the domestic marginal production cost and the marginal transaction cost. Note that the verification of (3.3) does not imply necessarily $c^* > c$. But when this inequality holds, it is always optimal for each firm to produce more at home than abroad, i.e. $Q_i > Q_i^*$.

All MFs being identical, we can easily determine the symmetric Nash equilibrium, which for firm i corresponds to,

$$D_i = \frac{c(1 + c^* + n)(a + t\underline{v}) + c^*[a(1 + n) - a^*c]}{\omega} \tag{4.1}$$

$$D_i^* = \frac{c^*(1 + c + n)(a^* - t\underline{v}) + c[a^*(1 + n) - ac^*]}{\omega} \tag{4.2}$$

$$X_i = \frac{(1 + c + n)a^*c^* - (1 + c^* + n)ac - (1 + c + n)(1 + c^* + n)t\underline{v}}{\omega} \tag{4.3}$$

where $\omega = (1+n)(c+c^*+2cc^*+cn+c^*n)$. Quantities sold and exported as given by the above equations satisfy the second order conditions.[4] Consequently firm i has a maximum profit. However, the equilibrium will be effectively realized only if the quantities sold and exported are positive. From (3.3) we can easily deduce that exports X_i are positive if $c^*D^* > cD + t\underline{v}$. In other words, intra-firm exports exist when trade barriers are not too important and when the marginal production cost of quantities sold abroad by the MF is higher than the marginal production cost of the quantities sold at home. From (3.1) we get $D_i > 0$ if $a > cX_i$. As a is the maximal quantity that firms can sell on their domestic market, this means that the size of this market must be sufficiently large for domestic sales to exist. Otherwise, each MF prefers to export the whole of its domestic production although it keeps its domestic and foreign production units due to the increasing marginal costs. From (3.2), the optimal foreign sales are always positive when intra-firm exports between parents and affiliates exist. This result is consistent with the equality $D_i^* = Q_i^* + X_i^*$.

In the above, we have assumed that the export direction is from parents to affiliates. The symmetric case corresponds to $X_i < 0$ where parent firms are importers from their subsidiaries. In this case, the domestic sales of MFs are always positive and their foreign sales will exist under the condition that $a^* > -c^*X_i$. Note that as the good traded is homogeneous, no production unit can be importer and exporter as well.

Having specified the conditions of the equilibrium, we can now determine the impact of the market structure on sales and intra-firm trade. This impact is successively analyzed at the firm and industry levels.

First at the MF level, we have,

$$\frac{\partial D_i}{\partial n} \geq \text{ or } \leq 0 \tag{5.1}$$

$$\frac{\partial D_i^*}{\partial n} < 0 \tag{5.2}$$

$$\frac{\partial X_i}{\partial n} < 0^5 \tag{5.3}$$

Thus, an increased competitive pressure leads each MF to reduce the volume of its intra-firm trade and its quantities sold abroad. Note that this last result is similar to the one we would get for a market in autarky with domestic firms only. On the contrary, equation (5.1) shows that the variation in domestic sales of each MF is more ambiguous when the domestic market becomes more competitive. In this case, two opposite effects are at work, effects which are characterized by,

$$\frac{\partial D_i}{\partial n} = \frac{1}{1 + c + n} \left[\underset{(1)}{-D_i} \underset{(2)}{- c \frac{\partial X_i}{\partial n}} \right] \tag{5.4}$$

The first effect is negative since the demand addressed to each MF decreases as the number of firms increases. This is the same effect as the one playing on the foreign market. But the second effect is positive; it is equivalent to a trade diversion. From (5.3), we see that when the foreign competition intensifies, each MF exports and then produces less. That induces a decrease in its domestic marginal production cost which allows to sell additional quantities at home. Then, each MF reallocates a part of its domestic production from exports to its domestic market, which corresponds to a trade diversion. If the size of the foreign country is large, the volume of intra-firm trade is important and the second positive effect prevails over the first negative effect.

At the industry level, the evolutions of global domestic and foreign sales (D and D^*) and total exports (X) with respect to the number of firms are substantially different. Indeed, we have,

$$\frac{\partial D}{\partial n} > 0 \tag{6.1}$$

$$\frac{\partial D^*}{\partial n} > 0 \tag{6.2}$$

$$\frac{\partial X}{\partial n} \geq \text{ or } \leq 0 \tag{6.3}$$

Thus the signs of partial derivatives are now positive excepted for the derivative of the total intra-firm export function that may be negative (see Appendix 1.2). Consequently, the competitive pressure leads to increase the quantities sold on both markets, like in the autarky situation, and to a reduction in the volume of the total intra-firm trade as well. Intra-firm trade being balanced, we have, using (3.3),

$$\frac{\partial X}{\partial n} = X_i[1 + \varepsilon_{X_i/n}] \tag{6.4}$$

where $\varepsilon_{X_i/n}$ is the elasticity of the individual intra-firm exports with respect to the number of firms in the industry. From (6.4), we see that $\partial X/\partial n$ may be positive or negative, depending on whether $|\varepsilon_{X_i/n}| < 1$ or $|\varepsilon_{X_i/n}| > 1$. Unfortunately, we have only limited information about the possible values of this elasticity since we only know that $|\varepsilon_{X_i/n}| > 0$ because $\partial X_i/\partial n < 0$. In order to define a condition for which $|\varepsilon_{X_i/n}|$ is equal to 1, we can rearrange (6.4) as follows:

$$\frac{\partial X}{\partial n} = \frac{1}{n(c^* + c)}[c^* D^* \varepsilon_{D^*/n} - cD\varepsilon_{D/n}] \tag{6.5}$$

where $\varepsilon_{D^*/n}$ and $\varepsilon_{D/n}$ are respectively the elasticities of global foreign and domestic sales with respect to the number of MFs in the industry. To give a more precise interpretation of how the number of suppliers affects the equilibrium sales we can write both elasticities respectively as $\varepsilon_{D^*/n} = \varepsilon_{D^*/P^*}\varepsilon_{P^*/n}$ and $\varepsilon_{D/n} = \varepsilon_{D/P}\varepsilon_{P/n}$. These account for the usual price elasticity of demand and the elasticity of market price with respect to the degree of competition on the markets. From (6.5), it is easy to determine the condition for which we have $|\varepsilon_{X_i/n}| = 1$, that is,

$$\frac{c^* D^*}{cD} = \frac{\varepsilon_{D/n}}{\varepsilon_{D^*/n}} = \frac{\varepsilon_{D/P}}{\varepsilon_{D^*/P^*}} \frac{\varepsilon_{P/n}}{\varepsilon_{P^*/n}} \tag{7}$$

In other words, this condition states that the ratio of marginal production costs of quantities sold should equal the inverse ratio of sales elasticities. This result clearly shows that the partial derivative of total intra-firm export with respect to the number of firms may be positive or negative. More precisely, we have $\partial X/\partial n > 0$ (<0) when $c^* D^*/cD > (<) (\varepsilon_{D/n}/\varepsilon_{D^*/n})$. Then, it is more likely that the volume of intra-firm trade between both countries will increase with the number of multinationals in the industry when the marginal production cost in the foreign country[6] is high, relatively to the one in the domestic country and if the sales are more sensitive to a supply growth abroad than at home.

When expressions (6) are all positive, we can consider total intra-firm export and global foreign and domestic sales as complementary in the sense that the impact of a modification of n has the same sign for these three variables. Conversely, when $\partial X/\partial n < 0$, intra-firm trade is a substitute for global foreign and domestic sales because their variations with respect to n are of opposite signs.

When the number of MFs grows, condition (7) also leads intra-firm trade and foreign production to increase together, thus being complementary. Indeed, intra-firm trade is complementary to the foreign production of all the affiliates only if

$\partial X/\partial n$ is positive, because $\partial Q^*/\partial n$ is never negative as we have,

$$\frac{\partial Q^*}{\partial n} = \frac{c}{c^* + c}[D_i^* \varepsilon_{D^*/n} + D_i \varepsilon_{D/n}] > 0 \tag{8}$$

where both sales elasticities, $\varepsilon_{D^*/n}$ and $\varepsilon_{D/n}$, are always positive.

Up to now, we have assumed that all MFs have their parents located in the same country. This is obviously a rather strong assumption that we are going to relax. The questions we want now to answer are as follows: What is going on when parent firms do not have the same localization? More precisely, how could our main results about the relationship between market structure and intra-firm trade be modified? In particular, is the impact of the number of MFs on the volume of total intra-firm trade still ambiguous?

6.4. The case of a different location of parent firms

Assuming that the MF parents are located in different countries modifies the nature of intra-firm trade, which can now be to a greater extent an intra-industry trade, both countries being simultaneously exporters and importers of the same product. Moreover, the new localization of production requires that we precise the conditions for the existence of a solution where MFs have intra-firm exports and sell on both markets.

For the sake of simplicity, we suppose that firms of the same nationality/origin are identical to each other in every respect. Consequently, we have only two types of MFs, according to the origin of their parent, which have the following profit functions:

$$\pi_i = \left[a - \sum_{i=1}^{n} D_i - \sum_{j=1}^{n} D_j\right] D_i + \left[a^* - \sum_{i=1}^{n} D_i^* - \sum_{j=1}^{n} D_j^*\right] D_i^*$$

$$- \frac{c_i}{2}Q_i^* - \frac{c_i^*}{2}Q_i^{*2} - t\underline{v}X_i \tag{9.1}$$

$$\pi_j = \left[a - \sum_{i=1}^{n} D_i - \sum_{j=1}^{n} D_j\right] D_j + \left[a^* - \sum_{i=1}^{n} D_i^* - \sum_{j=1}^{n} D_j^*\right] D_j^*$$

$$- \frac{c_j}{2}Q_j^* - \frac{c_j^*}{2}Q_j^{*2} - t^*\underline{v}X_j^* \tag{9.2}$$

where firm i has its parent located on the domestic market, whereas firm j's parent produces in the foreign country. We still assume a quadratic structure for the production cost functions.

However, we allow these production costs to depend on the nationality of the parents and of the affiliates. Furthermore, we consider the number of parents n to be the same on each market, leading to $2n$ MFs in the industry. This number can be different between countries but the analysis then becomes more difficult without strongly affecting our results. We also suppose that MFs of a different nationality do not necessarily support the same transaction costs, due to trade policy differences across countries for example. Starting from this framework, we focus our attention on two polar cases, the other situations leading to very similar results but requiring more complex calculations. First, we consider that affiliates and parents share the same technology (the one available in the country where they are located), i.e. $c_i = c_j = c$ and $c_i^* = c_j^* = c^*$. Here, the two countries do not share the same technologies and, technological transfers inside MFs being either not possible or too costly, subsidiaries use local techniques by way of national technology spillovers, for example. As an alternative assumption, we consider that the technologies are identical for all parents, on the one, and for all affiliates, on the other, but are different between the parent and affiliate of each MF (in this case $c_i = c_j^* = c$ and $c_i^* = c_j = s$). That is, whatever their origin, the parents have the same technology but at the same time, the technological transfers inside the MFs are costly. This case can correspond to a situation where international spillovers exist but they are partially realized through direct investment/intra-firm trade (see Aitkin and Harrison 1994; Chung *et al.* 1996).

First case: country-specific technologies
In this case, one can show that the optimal quantities sold at home and abroad can be simultaneously positive while optimal intra-firm exports of the two types of MFs are either positive or negative, which is not in accordance with our assumption about the direction of trade, i.e. from parents to subsidiaries. To prove this last result, let us consider the first-order conditions with respect to the intra-firm trade, derived from the profit functions (9.1) and (9.2):

$$c^*(D_i^* - X_i) = c(D_i + X_i) + t\underline{v} \tag{10.1}$$

$$c(D_j - X_j^*) = c^*(D_j^* + X_j^*) + t^*\underline{v} \tag{10.2}$$

Assuming that intra-firm trade flows are realized towards subsidiaries is equivalent to $X_i > 0$ and $X_j^* > 0$. In fact, both constraints cannot be satisfied together with (10.1) and (10.2). Indeed, when these two conditions are simultaneously satisfied, their sum must also lead to an equality, that is,

$$(c + c^*)(X_i + X_j^*) + (t\underline{v} + t^*\underline{v}^*) = c(D_j - D_i) + c^*(D_i^* - D_j^*) < 0 \tag{10.3}$$

The difference between the optimal quantities sold by affiliates and that of rival parents is negative whatever the market, since we have sign$(D_j - D_i) =$ $-$sign$(c(1 + c^*)(t\underline{v} + t^*\underline{v}^*))$ and sign$(D_i^* - D_j^*) = -$sign$(c^*(1 + c)(t\underline{v} + t^*\underline{v}^*))$. In each country, the quantities sold by affiliates are lower than the sales of the rival parents. This result is a consequence of the transaction costs of intra-firm trade which makes sales abroad less profitable than domestic sales, other things being equal. Consequently, $(c + c^*)(X_i + X_j^*) + (t\underline{v} + t^*\underline{v}^*) < 0$, firms i and j not being able to have simultaneously intra-firm exports. Hence, it is impossible here for both constraints $X_i > 0$ and $X_j^* > 0$ to be simultaneously satisfied, contradicting our assumption about the direction of trade. Note that our demonstration holds whatever the trade policies of both countries and the level of transaction costs. The incompatibility between our assumptions and the verification of the first-order conditions is due to the fact that all MFs produce more in the country where the slope of the marginal costs is lower. Their trade flows then have the same direction between countries, some parents being incited to export and others to import from their subsidiaries according to their localization. Under these conditions, when technologies are assumed to be country-specific, intra-industry trade cannot be created by intra-firm trade.

Second case: parent vs. affiliate specific technologies
Assuming that parents and affiliates use different technologies and for simplicity that all MFs support the same marginal transaction cost, whatever their country of origin, the optimal sales and exports are:

$$D_i = \frac{cs(a - a^*) + (1 + 2n)[(c + cn + cs + ns)t\underline{v} + (c + s)a]}{\omega'} \quad (11.1)$$

$$D_j = \frac{cs(a - a^*) + (1 + 2n) + [-(c + cn + cs + ns)t\underline{v} + (c + s)a]}{\omega'}$$
$$(11.2)$$

$$D_i^* = \frac{cs(a^* - a) + (1 + 2n) + [-(c + cn + cs + ns)t\underline{v} + (c + s)a^*]}{\omega'}$$
$$(11.3)$$

$$D_j^* = \frac{cs(a^* - a) + (1 + 2n) + [(c + cn + cs + ns)t\underline{v} + (c + s)a^*]}{\omega'}$$
$$(11.4)$$

$$X_i = \{cs(a^* - a) + (1 + 2n)[(a^*s - ac)$$
$$- (1 + c + 2n + cn + s + cs + ns)t\underline{v}]\}/\omega' \quad (11.5)$$

$$X_j^* = \{cs(a - a^*) + (1 + 2n)[(as - a^*c)$$
$$- (1 + c + 2n + cn + s + cs + ns)t\underline{v}]\}/\omega' \quad (11.6)$$

where $\omega' = (1 + 2n)(c + 2cn + s + 2cs + 2ns)$. Before analyzing the impact of the market structure on intra-firm trade, we must determine the conditions under which the optimal quantities sold and exported are both positive. As $D_i > D_j$ and $D_j^* > D_i^*$, the conditions on the optimal sales require solely that D_j and D_i^* are positive together or equivalently that the following inequalities are verified:

$$(1 + 2n)(\phi t\underline{v} - (c + s)a) < cs(a - a^*)$$
$$< (1 + 2n)(-\phi t\underline{v} + (c + s)a^*) \quad (12)$$

where $\phi = c + cn + cs + ns$. In fact, (12) is effectively borne out if we have $\phi t\underline{v} - (c+s)a < -\phi t\underline{v} + (c+s)a^*$ or equivalently if $\phi t\underline{v} < ((c+s)(a+a^*))/2$. Note that when transaction costs are equal to zero, $(1 + 2n)(\phi t\underline{v} - (c + s)a)$ is always the lower boundary and $(1 + 2n)(-\phi t\underline{v} + (c + s)a^*)$ the upper boundary in (12).

Optimal intra-firm exports of both firms i and j must be also positive. It will be so if the following condition is satisfied,

$$(1 + 2n)(\phi't\underline{v} + (ac - a^*s)) < cs(a^* - a)$$
$$< (1 + 2n)(-\phi't\underline{v} + (as - a^*c)) \qquad (13)$$

where $\phi' = 1 + c + 2n + cn + s + cs + ns$. As previously, the validity of (13) is established when both boundaries are well defined or, in other words, if $\phi't\underline{v} < ((a^* + a)(s - c))/2$. This last condition calls for $c < s$. Then, intra-firm exports will exist if the marginal production cost slope is lower for the parent firms than for affiliates. Furthermore, under these conditions, optimal sales and trade are all positive.

Now, let us have a look at the influence of the market structure on the volume of the optimal sales and trade. Analyzing first this influence at the firm level, we obtain results very similar to the previous case where all MFs had the same origin:

$$\frac{\partial D_i}{\partial n} \geq \text{ or } \leq 0 \qquad (14.1)$$

$$\frac{\partial D_j^*}{\partial n} \geq \text{ or } \leq 0 \qquad (14.2)$$

$$\frac{\partial D_i^*}{\partial n} < 0 \qquad (14.3)$$

$$\frac{\partial D_j}{\partial n} < 0 \qquad (14.4)$$

$$\frac{\partial X_i}{\partial n} < 0 \qquad (14.5)$$

$$\frac{\partial X_j^*}{\partial n} < 0 \qquad (14.6)$$

Again, the increase in competitive pressure reduces the quantities sold abroad and the intra-firm trade of each MF, whatever its origin (see Appendix 2.1). On the other hand, when markets become more competitive, the evolution of domestic sales remains ambiguous.

However, $\partial D_i/\partial n$ can be now expressed as follows:

$$\frac{\partial D_i}{\partial n} = \frac{1}{1 + c + n}\left[-D_i - c\frac{\partial X_i}{\partial n} - \frac{\partial n D_j}{\partial n}\right] \qquad (15)$$

where nD_j is the global sales of the affiliates on the domestic market. Besides the demand and trade diversion effects, respectively negative and positive, we now have a new competition effect that corresponds to the impact of a competitive pressure variation on the quantities sold on the domestic market by the affiliates as a whole. As this third effect may be positive or negative, it can strengthen either the demand effect or the trade diversion effect.

Then if $\partial nD_j/\partial n$ takes a sufficiently low value, MF i is incited to increase its domestic sales despite the growth in the number of firms since the transaction costs are sufficiently large to distort competition in disfavor of the affiliates located on its market. The same reasoning holds to determine the sign of $\partial D_j^*/\partial n$.

Second, the impact of the number of firms on the global sales of parents and affiliates and on the total exports is substantially different in comparison to the previous case where all parents were located in the same country. Indeed, we now have the following partial derivatives with respect to n:

$$\frac{\partial D_O}{\partial n} > 0 \tag{16.1}$$

$$\frac{\partial D_O^*}{\partial n} > 0^7 \tag{16.2}$$

$$\frac{\partial D_F^*}{\partial n} \geq \text{ or } \leq 0 \tag{16.3}$$

$$\frac{\partial D_F}{\partial n} \geq \text{ or } \leq 0 \tag{16.4}$$

$$\frac{\partial X}{\partial n} \geq \text{ or } \leq 0 \tag{16.5}$$

$$\frac{\partial X^*}{\partial n} \geq \text{ or } \leq 0 \tag{16.6}$$

where D_O (resp. D_O^*) is the global sales of the parents on the domestic (resp. foreign) market, D_F (resp. D_F^*) the global sales of the affiliates on this (resp. foreign) market and X (resp. X^*) the exports of domestic (resp. foreign) country. The impact of the number of firms on the global sales abroad, i.e. D_F and D_F^*, will be positive for low levels of the average transaction cost and/or weak constraints imposed on the transfer prices by governments. As shown in Table 6.1, low values of tv do not sufficiently amplify the competitive pressure upon the parents on their market to reduce the global sales of the rival subsidiaries. This table also shows that the partial derivatives, $\partial D_F/\partial n$ and $\partial D_F^*/\partial n$, can have opposite signs, as long as the domestic and foreign markets have different sizes. More precisely, the impact of the number of firms on the sales of the subsidiaries will be negative in the smallest country, since competitive pressure and transaction costs are mutually reinforced in this country.

Table 6.1 Conditions on $t\underline{v}$ determining the signs of $\partial D_F/\partial n$ and $\partial D_F^*/\partial n$

Partial derivatives of D and D* with respect to n	Conditions on $t\underline{v}$
$\dfrac{\partial D_F}{\partial n} \geq 0$ and $\dfrac{\partial D_F^*}{\partial n} \geq 0$	$0 \leq t\underline{v} \leq \dfrac{(a+a^*)(\beta-cs\alpha)}{2\theta}$ [a]
$\dfrac{\partial D_F}{\partial n} < 0$ and $\dfrac{\partial D_F^*}{\partial n} < 0$	$\dfrac{(a+a^*)(\beta-cs\alpha)}{2\theta} < t\underline{v}$ [a]
$\dfrac{\partial D_F}{\partial n} < 0$ and $\dfrac{\partial D_F^*}{\partial n} \geq 0$	$\dfrac{a\beta-a^*cs\alpha}{\theta} < t\underline{v} \leq \dfrac{a^*\beta-acs\alpha}{\theta}$ [b]
$\dfrac{\partial D_F}{\partial n} \geq 0$ and $\dfrac{\partial D_F^*}{\partial n} < 0$	$\dfrac{a^*\beta-acs\alpha}{\theta} < t\underline{v} \leq \dfrac{a\beta-a^*cs\alpha}{\theta}$ [c]

With
$\alpha = c - 4cn^2 + s + 2cs - 4sn^2$,
$\beta = (s+2sn)^2 + cs(1+2n)(2+4n+3s+2sn) + c^2(1+4n+4n^2+ 3s+8sn+4sn^2+2sn^2)$,
$\theta = (1+2n)^2(c^2+2c^2n+2c^2n^2+cs+3c^2s+4cns+4c^2ns+cs^2+ 2c^2s^2+2ns^2+4cns^2+2n^2s^2)$.
a   This condition can be statisfied since $\beta > cs\alpha$.
b   Both inequalities are consistent if $a^* > a$.
c   Both inequalities are consistent if $a^* < a$.

The dependence of total exports on n depends, as in (6.5), on the comparison between the ratio of marginal costs and the ratio of sales elasticities since we have,

$$\frac{\partial X}{\partial n} = \frac{1}{n(c+s)}[sD_F^*\varepsilon_{D_F^*/n} - cD_O\varepsilon_{D_O/n}] \tag{17.1}$$

$$\frac{\partial X^*}{\partial n} = \frac{1}{n(c+s)}[sD_F\varepsilon_{D_F/n} - cD_O^*\varepsilon_{D_O^*/n}] \tag{17.2}$$

In this framework, the conditions for having $\partial X/\partial n > 0$ are more restrictive than in the previous case where all parents were located in the same country. When both conditions $(sD_F^*/cD_O) > (\varepsilon_{D_O/n}/\varepsilon_{D_F^*/n})$ and $(sD_F/CD_O^*) > (\varepsilon_{D_O^*/n}/\varepsilon_{D_F/n})$ are satisfied, the volume of total intra-firm exports increases with the number of MFs in the industry if the partial derivatives $\partial D_F^*/\partial n$ and $\partial D_F/\partial n$ are positive.[8] When they are negative, the competitive pressures are reinforced by the transaction costs effect, so that the volume of total exports always decreases when the number of MFs increases.

Moreover, as MFs now have a different origin, intra-firm exports lead to intra-industry trade between countries. It appears likely that the intensity of this trade will be affected by the variations of n. To evaluate the intensity of the bilateral intra-industry trade, we can use the index (GL) proposed by GRUBEL and LLYOD:

$$GL = 1 - \frac{|a-a^*|\omega'}{(1+2n)[(a+a^*)(s-c) - 2(1+2n)\phi't\underline{v}]} \tag{18}$$

Two cases are to be considered here:

- first, both countries have identical sizes. In this case, the whole of the intra-firm trade is intra-industry trade whatever the number of MFs;
- second, the countries have different sizes and the intensity of intra-industry trade then depends on the number of MFs.

In this last case, the evolution of GL with respect to n can be either positive or negative since we have,

$$
\text{sign}\left[\frac{\partial GL}{\partial n}\right] =
\begin{cases}
\text{sign}\left[\dfrac{\partial X}{\partial n}X^* - \dfrac{\partial X^*}{\partial n}X\right] & \text{if } a > a^* \\[2ex]
\text{sign}\left[\dfrac{\partial X^*}{\partial n}X - \dfrac{\partial X}{\partial n}X^*\right] & \text{otherwise}
\end{cases}
\tag{19}
$$

In fact, when the transaction costs are low, an increase in the number of MFs increases the intensity of intra-industry trade while with high transactions costs, this intensity decreases. As before, transactions costs distort competition in favor of parents. Thus, when these costs become stronger, they may decrease not only the volume of bilateral trade but also its intensity.

6.5. Conclusion

In this paper, we have analyzed the evolution of trade realized inside MFs and the intensity of intra-industry trade according to the competitive degree of markets. We adopt a framework where not only this competitive degree can vary but also the localization of parents can differ. First, we show that more competitive pressure on the markets does not systematically increase the volume of trade between countries. This is a relatively robust result of our model since it is obtained whatever the country of origin of multinationals. In this context, total intra-firm exports between countries can decrease when the number of MFs increases if the ratio of domestic over foreign marginal cost is lower than the ratio of foreign over domestic elasticities of sales to the number of MFs. Moreover, we show that the quantities produced by subsidiaries can be complementary to intra-firm trade, for example, they can have the same positive evolution with respect to the number of MFs. From this point of view, our analysis is consistent with recent empirical works (see for example Barrell and Pain 1999) that highlight a positive relationship between exports and direct investments even when trade barriers exist.

Second, we show that intra-industry trade does not systematically exist when MFs have a different origin, in particular if technologies used by firms are country-specific. In this case, MFs produce, indeed, in the country with the most efficient technology and trade is then unilateral. On the contrary, if the technology is parent versus subsidiary specific, intra-industry trade appears. In this context, the intensity of this type of trade will be affected by the number of MFs only if markets have a different size. Under this condition, the intensity of intra-industry trade increases with the number of MFs when transactions costs are low; otherwise these costs will distort competition in favor of the domestic production.

Appendix 1

All parents have the same localization.

1.1 In this framework, we must consider the evolutions of quantities exported and sold abroad by the firm i with respect to n; the sign of $\partial D_i / \partial n$ being determined from (5.4).

• First, let us show that $\partial X_i / \partial n < 0$. As shown by (4.3), X_i is the ratio of two functions that depend on n. Then we have,

$$X_i = \frac{f(n)}{g(n)}$$

These two functions being always positive by hypothesis, the derivative of their ratio has the following sign:

$$\text{sign}\left(\frac{f(n)}{g(n)}\right)' = \text{sign}(\log(f(n))' - \log(g(n))')$$

where,

$$\log(f(n))' = \frac{a^*c^* - ac - (2 + c^* + c + 2n)t\underline{v}}{(1 + c + n)a^*c^* - (1 + c^* + n)ac - (1 + c + n)(1 + c^* + n)t\underline{v}}$$

and

$$\log(g(n))' = -\frac{2((c^* + c)(1 + n) + c^*c)}{(1 + n)(c^* + c + 2c^*c + c^*n + cn)}$$

A priori, the difference between these two derivatives may be positive or negative; it depends on the value of a^*, amongst other things. The higher this value, the more likely it is that the sign of $(f(n))' - (g(n))'$ is positive. Considering the upper value of a^*, i.e. the one for which (4.1) is just equal to zero,

$$a^* = \frac{(1 + c^* + n)(a + t\underline{v})}{c^*} + \frac{a(1 + n)}{c}$$

we obtain,

$$\text{sign}(\log(f(n))' - \log(g(n))') = -\frac{(1 + c + n)(a(c^* + c) + ct\underline{v})}{a(1 + n)(c^* + c + 2c^*c + c^*n + cn)} < 0$$

Hence $\partial X_i / \partial n$ is always negative.

• Second, it is now easy to show that (5.2) is negative. Indeed, from (3.2) we can express D_i^* as,

$$D_i^* = \frac{a^* + c^* X_i}{1 + c^* + n}$$

Consequently, the partial derivative of D_i^* with respect to n has the following form,

$$\frac{\partial D_i^*}{\partial n} = \frac{c^* ((1 + c^* + n)(\partial X_i / \partial n) - X_i - a^* c^*)}{(1 + c^* + n)^2}$$

Knowing $\partial X_i / \partial n < 0$, we can easily deduce that $\partial D_i^* / \partial n < 0$.

1.2 Now let us prove that n has a positive impact on the global quantities sold at home and abroad.

- First, let us show that $\partial D / \partial n > 0$.

From (3.1) we can deduce that,

$$D_i = \frac{1}{1 + c + n}(a - c X_i)$$

whence,

$$D = \frac{an - cn X_i}{1 + c + n}$$

Remembering that all MFs are identical, we have $D = \sum_{i=1}^{n} D_i = n D_i$, like for D^* and X. The partial derivative of D with respect to n gives,

$$\frac{\partial D}{\partial n} = \frac{1}{1 + c + n} \left[(1 + c) D_i - cn \frac{\partial X_i}{\partial n} \right]$$

Since $D_i > 0$ and $\partial X_i / \partial n < 0$, we can conclude that $\partial D / \partial n > 0$.

- Second, let us show that $\partial D^* / \partial n > 0$.

From (3.2), D^* can be expressed in the following form,

$$D^* = \frac{a^* n + c^* n X_i}{1 + c^* + n}$$

Then,

$$\frac{\partial D^*}{\partial n} = \frac{1}{1 + c^* + n} \left[(1 + c^*) D_i^* + c^* n \frac{\partial X_i}{\partial n} \right]$$

By hypothesis, $D_i^* > 0$ and we have shown that $\partial X_i / \partial n < 0$. Consequently, we are faced with an uncertainty about the sign of $\partial D^* / \partial n$, this expression being constituted of positive and negative terms. However, all the terms where a^* is present, are positive. Taking then the lowest value of a^*, i.e. the one for which $X_i = 0$, we have,

$$\frac{\partial D^*}{\partial n} = \frac{(ac + t\underline{v})(1 + 2c^* + n + c^* n)c + acc^*(1 + n + c^* n)}{c^*(1 + c + n)\omega} + \frac{(1 + n)t\underline{v}}{\omega} > 0$$

Then this expression will be also positive for some greater value of a^*. Consequently, $\partial D^* / \partial n$ is always positive.

Appendix 2

A different localization of parents and parent- or affiliate-specific technologies.

2.1 Let us show that the derivatives of intra-firm trade and foreign sales of firms i and j with respect to n are negative; the sign of $\partial D_i/\partial n$ and $\partial D_i^*/\partial n$ being justified from (15).

- First, let us demonstrate that $\partial X_i/\partial n$ and $\partial X_j^*/\partial n$ are both negative. From (11.5), we see that X_i is the ratio of two functions. Then, as previously, we can write,

$$\text{sign}\left(\frac{\partial X_i}{\partial n}\right) = \text{sign}\left(\frac{f(n)}{g(n)}\right)' = \text{sign}(\log(f(n))' - \log(g(n))')$$

where,

$$\log(f(n))' = (2((a^*s - ac) - (1 + c + 2n + cn + s + cs + ns)t\underline{v})$$
$$- (1 + 2n)(2 + c + s)t\underline{v})/(cs(a^* - a) + (1 + 2n)((a^*s - ac)$$
$$- (1 + c + 2n + cn + s + cs + ns)t\underline{v}))$$

and

$$\log(g(n))' = \frac{2((c + 2cn + s + 2cs + 2ns) + (1 + 2n)(c + s))}{\omega'}$$

In fact, $\log(g(n))'$ is always positive. On the contrary, the sign of $\log(f(n))'$ is ambiguous due to the presence of a positive term, a^*s, all the other terms in the numerator of $\log(f(n))'$ being negative and its denominator being positive by hypothesis. But if we take the highest value of a^*, e.g. the value for which $D_i = 0$, we have,

$$\log(f(n))' - \log(g(n))' = -(2a(1 + c + 2n)(c + s) + [2ns(1 + 2n)$$
$$+ c^2(3 + 4n + 2s) + c(2 + 6n + 4n^2 + s + 4ns)]t\underline{v})/$$
$$\omega'(a + nt\underline{v}) < 0$$

Since this difference is negative for high values of a^*, it will also be the case when the foreign country has a smaller size. Then, $\partial X_i/\partial n$ is always negative. Using the same procedure, it is easy to show that $\partial X_j^*/\partial n < 0$.

- Second, let us show that $\partial D_i^*/\partial n < 0$ and $\partial D_j/\partial n < 0$. From (11.3), we have,

$$D_i^* = \frac{a^* + sX_i - nD_j^*}{1 + n + s}$$

whence,

$$\frac{\partial D_i^*}{\partial n} = \frac{1}{1 + n + s}\left[\left(s\frac{\partial X_i}{\partial n} - \frac{\partial D_O^*}{\partial n}\right)(1 + n + s) - D_i^*\right]$$

We know that $\partial X_i/\partial n < 0$ and $D_i^* > 0$. Moreover, we are going to show that $\partial D_O^*/\partial n > 0$. Consequently, $\partial D_i^*/\partial n$ is negative. The same demonstration holds for $\partial D_j/\partial n < 0$.

2.2 Now we must demonstrate that n has a positive impact on the quantities sold by parents on their respective domestic markets. In other words, we must show that $\partial D_O^*/\partial n > 0$ and

$\partial D_O/\partial n > 0$, the sign of $\partial D_F^*/\partial n$ and $\partial D_F/\partial n$ being justified in text (see Table 1) and the one of $\partial X^*/\partial n$ and $\partial X^*/\partial n$ being determined by conditions (17.1) and (17.2).

The partial derivative of D_O^* with respect to n is such as,

$$\frac{\partial D_O^*}{\partial n} = \frac{-acs\alpha + a^*\beta + \theta t\underline{v}}{\omega'^2}$$

where,

$$\alpha = c - 4cn^2 + s + 2cs - 4n^2 s$$

$$\beta = (s + 2ns)^2 + cs(1 + 2n)(2 + 4n + 3s + 2ns)$$
$$+ c^2(1 + 4n + 4n^2 + 3s + 8ns + 4n^2 s + 2s^2)$$

$$\theta = (1 + 2n)^2(c^2 + 2c^2 n + 2c^2 n^2 + cs + 3c^2 s + 4cns + 4c^2 ns$$
$$+ cs^2 + 2c^2 s^2 + 2ns^2 + 4cns^2 + 2n^2 s^2)$$

When $\alpha < 0$ or equivalently if $2cs < (c + s)(1 + 2n)(2n - 1)$, $\partial D_O^*/\partial n$ is positive since $\beta > 0$ and $\theta > 0$ are always verified. But, α may also be positive. In this case, $-acs\alpha < 0$ and the sign of $\partial D_O^*/\partial n$ becomes indeterminate. However, if we consider the highest value of a, e.g. the one for which (11.3) is equal to zero, then $\partial D_O^*/\partial n > 0$. Consequently, this partial derivative is always positive. The same process allows us to show that $\partial D_O/\partial n$ is likewise positive.

Notes

1 Intra-firm trade is defined as the transactions of good realized inside multinationals, between parents and subsidiaries or between subsidiaries themselves.
2 By now on, we shall adopt the common team of country, although our analysis is probably more relevant in terms of zones/regions (e.g. NAFTA, Europe, etc.)
3 Note that when production costs are uncertain this condition does not hold, the MF using its two production units to reduce risks (see Becuwe *et al.* 1998).
4 The Hessian matrix of second derivative of firm i profit function is negative definite since assuming that the slopes of marginal costs are positive, the principal minor of the Hessian are successively negative and positive.
5 See Appendix 1.1 for the demonstration.
6 More rigorously, $c^* D^*$ is the marginal production cost of the affiliates when these produce all foreign sales or in other words when there is no intra-firm trade between countries since $c^* D^* = c^* Q^* + c^* X$.
7 See Appendix 2.2.
8 $\varepsilon_{D_O/n}$ and $\varepsilon_{D_O^*/n}$ are no longer crucial for the analysis since $\partial D_O/\partial n$ and $\partial D_O^*/\partial n$ are always positive.

References

Aitken, B. and Harrision, A. (1994) 'Do domestic firms benefit from foreign direct investment? Evidence from panel data', Policy Research Working Paper, World Bank.

Barrell, R. and Pain, N. (1999) 'Trade restraints and Japanese direct investment flows', *European Economic Review*, 43: 29–46.

Becuwe, S., Mathieu, C. and Sevestre, P. (1998) 'Commerce intra-firm, coûts de production aléatoires et barrières aux échange', *Revue Economique*, 49: 581–91.

Buckley, P. J. and Casson, M. (1985) *The Economic Theory of the Multinational Enterprise.* London: Macmillan.

Cantwell, J. (1994) 'The relationship between international trade and international production', in D. Greenaway and L. A. Winters (eds), *Survey in International Trade.* Oxford: Blackwell.

Chung, W., Will, M. and Yeung, B. (1996) 'Foreign direct investment and host country productivity: the case of the American automotive components industry', Working Paper University of Michigan School of Business Administration.

Dunning, J. H. (1988) *Explaining International Production.* New York: Harper Collins.

Horst, T. (1971) 'The theory of the multinational firm: optimal behavior under different tariff and tax rates', *Journal of Political Economy*, 79: 1059–72.

Horst, T. (1973) 'The simple analytics of multinational firm behavior', in M. B. Connolly and A. K. Swoboda (eds), *International Trade and Money.* London: Allen and Unwin.

Maindardi, S. (1986) 'A theoritical interpretation of intra-firm trade in the presence of intra-industry trade', in D. Greenaway and P. K. M. T. Tharakan (eds), *Imperfect Competition and International Trade: The Policy Aspects of Intra-Industry Trade.* Brighton: Wheatsheaf Press.

UN (1996) 'World investment report: investment, trade and international policy arrangements', *Conference on Trade and Development*, Geneva.

Part III

MULTINATIONAL FIRMS, LINKAGES AND SPILLOVERS EFFECTS

7

LINKAGES, MULTINATIONALS AND INDUSTRIAL DEVELOPMENT

Amy Jocelyn Glass, Vasilios D. Kosteas,
and Kamal Saggi

7.1. Introduction

It has been frequently noted that flows of foreign direct investment (FDI) have increased rapidly during the past decade. While much of the global stock of FDI exists within developed countries, recent evidence indicates that flows to developing countries have increased substantially: in 1997, developing countries received 37.2 per cent of the global flows of FDI (UNCTAD 1998). Furthermore, given the relatively small economic size of these economies, even a small amount of foreign investment can account for a large percentage of their total investment and therefore generate a significant impact. For example, in 1996, the total stock of inward FDI as a percentage of the gross domestic product in developing countries equaled 48.6 per cent (UNCTAD 1998).

Multiple market forces are behind the observed growth in FDI: reduction in costs of communication has eased the constraints on global rationalization of production and the information technology revolution has created markets for many new products and services. Increased world trade in services has further contributed to global FDI flows since services often require suppliers to have a physical presence in a market. However, changes in the market environment do not capture the whole story.

Policy initiatives have also played a central role: many countries have gone further than simply removing barriers to inward FDI and have taken a more pro-active approach toward attracting FDI through the use of fiscal and financial incentives. This new, more favorable, policy environment in many developing and formerly communist countries contrasts sharply with historical attitudes toward multinational firms in these countries.

The spread of multinational firms was often viewed with suspicion and mistrust in such countries, particularly in those that pursued a strategy of import substitution. An important aim of import substitution policies was to encourage indigenous industrial development. Hostility toward multinationals was based on the perception that the entry of such firms was detrimental to domestic industrialization. The infant industry argument, or some derivation of it, often served as an intellectual justification for such policies.

However, a parallel tradition in development (at least among academic discussions) took a more optimistic view. In this tradition, multinationals were (and are) seen as agents that increase competition in the host economy, transfer modern technology, and help achieve a more efficient allocation of resources. The recent wave of liberalization of trade and FDI policies suggests that the optimistic view of FDI seems to be gaining the upper hand. One manifestation of this trend of liberalization is the proliferation of bilateral investment treaties across countries: there now exist 1,513 bilateral investment treaties among countries, compared with fewer than 400 at the beginning of 1990 (UNCTAD 1998). Of course, the failure of import substitution as a strategy for development is a crucial reason behind this remarkable turnaround in policies in many developing countries.

Within the more optimistic view of FDI, a frequently cited benefit of inward FDI is that it pushes forward the process of industrial development by creating *linkages* with the rest of the economy. In this paper, we explore the argument that FDI encourages industrial development through linkages. First, we discuss the relevant economics literature that has attempted to formalize the concept of linkages. Second, we discuss the existing empirical evidence regarding linkages. In our first task, we begin by tracing the intellectual development of the idea of linkages by noting the debt owed to Hirschman (1958) who provided a concrete definition of the fundamental concepts. Next, we provide a discussion of some of the more recent theoretical analyses of the concept of linkages. Then, we discuss empirical evidence on linkages in light of the insights yielded by theory. Finally, we comment on the findings of both types of literature and note the policy implications of these findings.

7.2. Fundamental concepts

In a classic work, Hirschman (1958) developed the concepts of backward and forward linkages and analyzed their importance for economic growth. In his own words:

> The setting up of an industry brings with it the *availability of a new expanding market for its inputs* whether or not these inputs are supplied initially from abroad.

This enhanced market exerts a backward pressure for establishing industries that supply the new entrants. He calls this process *backward linkage* effects:

> Every non-primary activity will induce attempts to supply through domestic production the inputs needed in that activity.

Similarly, *forward linkage effects* are created when one industry uses another industry's outputs as its inputs:

> Every activity that does not by its nature cater exclusively to final demands
> will induce attempts to utilize its outputs as inputs in some industries.

The sum of the backward linkage effect and the forward linkage effect gives the total linkage effect, which can be seen as the growth in new industries induced from establishing an industry. Hirschman was careful on the issue of backward linkages: he noted that linkages between parent and satellite industries are unlikely to be as important as those formed with larger industries that have a lower probability of forming.[1]

Another important point made by Hirschman was that multiple industries are likely to have a greater linkage effect when taken together, compared to simply adding up the individual effects. The presence of two or more industries may create enough demand to surpass the threshold required for establishing new industries, whereas the presence of only one of them would not.[2] Taking all of these industries together may provide enough incentive to create yet others. This cumulative effect may explain much of the acceleration of industrial growth seen early on in the development process.

Regarding empirical implementation, Hirschman suggested that the importance of linkages in an economy could be approximated by the percentage of inputs purchased from other industries for backward linkages and the percentage of output sold to other industries for forward linkages. Industries with strong linkages in both directions (such as petroleum products and chemicals) can be distinguished from those with predominately forward linkages (such as metal mining and agriculture) and those with predominately backward linkages (such as grain mill products and leather products). In this sense, Hirschman's scheme for development planning preceded and foresaw the recent debate regarding industrial targeting.[3]

Hirschman argued that part of the difficulty for underdeveloped economies is a lack of interdependence and linkages. Consequently, the development process must commence with industries that cater to final demand. This requirement leaves two possibilities: transformation of either primary goods or semi-manufactures into final products. Since the latter may provide stronger possibilities for linkages, Hirschman suggests that governments in such countries should assist industries involved in intermediate activities since these have strong potential for creating both backward and forward linkages.

Clearly, an accurate accounting of expected linkage effects is crucial for any plan to encourage investment in industries with the strongest linkages. Hirschman's suggested method for proceeding on this front was to use input–output data from more advanced countries with already existent industries to represent the linkages expected to form in some lesser-developed country. However, any extrapolation across countries runs the risk of error. For example, technologies adopted in lesser-developed countries might use a different mix of inputs, especially if other parameters (such as factor endowment ratios and trade policies) are not the same across countries. Many of the failures of development prescriptions stem from failing to account for idiosyncrasies across countries.

The entry of firms, especially large multinational firms in developing countries, may expand the total output of an industry through increased scale, enhanced competition, technology diffusion to local rivals, or general training of workers. This expansion in output of an industry may play a crucial role in bringing the scale of existing industries up to levels sufficient to generate backward and forward linkages needed for industrial development. As we shall see next, the theoretical economics literature on multinationals has indeed advanced this argument.

7.3. Multinationals and linkages: theory

The recent surge in the literature on industry linkages and international trade provides several concrete models of concepts originating in the development literature. In a recent paper, Rodríguez-Clare (1996a) takes up Hirschman's concept of linkages and develops a formal model to analyze the effects of multinationals on economic development. He relies on three premises to develop a model of the linkage concept. First, a greater variety of inputs leads to higher production efficiency, as captured by assuming a love of variety for inputs in the production of final goods (a weaker form of Hirschman's assumption that certain inputs were necessary for production). Second, market size limits the available variety of specialized inputs due to inputs being produced with increasing returns to scale (related to Hirschman's specification of a minimum economic size). Third, proximity of supplier and user is required, since domestic firms must buy all of their inputs locally (to ensure that domestically produced inputs are essential to developing an industry in final goods). Under such circumstances, an economy will exhibit multiple equilibria: a good equilibrium with high wages (which coincides with the production of complex final goods and a wide variety of inputs) and a bad equilibrium with low wages (which coincides with the production of simple final goods and a small variety of inputs). If the number of varieties of the intermediate good exceeds a threshold, then a country specializes in producing the more complex good. Since profits are zero due to the assumption of free entry, the higher wages in the good equilibrium imply that it Pareto dominates the bad equilibrium.

To give multinationals a role in the process of industrial development, Rodríguez-Clare supposes that two economies exist with one in the bad equilibrium (a developing country) and the other in the good equilibrium (a developed country).[4] Under this scenario, firms in the high-wage economy may wish to take advantage of the cheap labor overseas by establishing a plant in the host country, while maintaining headquarters at home to enjoy access to the wide variety of specialized inputs available there.[5] The crucial assumption is that specialized inputs cannot be exchanged internationally through arm's-length transactions and thus cannot be used by a firm unless it operates in the country where the inputs are produced. Consequently, only multinationals can combine the wide variety of specialized inputs from the developed country with the cheap labor from the developing country.[6]

Rodríguez-Clare develops a statistic called the *linkage coefficient* to address the effect of multinationals on the host economy. The linkage coefficient measures the ratio of employment generated in upstream industries by a firm to the labor hired directly by that firm. A *positive linkage effect* arises if the multinational has a higher linkage coefficient than domestic firms. A positive linkage coefficient implies that an increase in the number of multinationals results in a greater variety of intermediate goods produced locally, which in turn increases the productivity of domestic firms and the domestic wage.[7]

Positive linkages are most likely to result when the good that multinationals produce is more complex, the communication costs between the headquarters and the factory are higher, and the source and host countries are more similar in terms of the variety of intermediates produced. The cost of communication is modeled as an iceberg-type transportation cost: a fraction of the composite input (produced from specialized source inputs) melts *en route* from the source headquarters to the host factory. An increase in the cost of communication between the factory and headquarters causes a firm to purchase more goods locally, and hence raises its linkage coefficient. In addition, since the multinational is only able to purchase more inputs locally if they are produced, the linkage coefficient is increasing in the variety of intermediate goods produced in the host economy. Since firms using a greater variety of inputs tend to establish plants in countries with a smaller variety of intermediates, an implication of this analysis is that developing countries may not enjoy substantial linkages because multinational firms import their inputs from the source country.

This model operates under the principle of full employment, and the idea that foreign firms compete directly with domestic firms (hence creating a negative relationship between the number of firms in one country and another). In truth, underdeveloped countries do not possess full employment. A multinational may hire labor from the ranks of the unemployed, or from other industries that then replace their departed workers by drawing from the previously unemployed. In such a setting, not only the wage but the total wage bill (the wage times employment) should contribute to domestic welfare.[8] A multinational's presence could generate large benefits by increasing employment, even if wages increase only slightly.

Furthermore, the existence of multiple final goods industries would further complicate the scenario, since one would have to know from which industry the labor is being displaced. Consider three industries, A, B, C, which have linkage coefficients in descending magnitude. If a multinational enters in industry B, then it may have a negative impact on the host economy if it draws labor from industry A. However, the converse will hold if the addition of this firm draws labor from industry C. Which scenario is more likely?

What happens if we allow multinationals to pay a higher wage than local firms do?[9] This query is not merely of theoretical concern: multinationals are indeed often observed paying higher wages than local firms, especially in developing countries (see Aitken *et al.* 1996). Can the added labor income be enough to offset a mild negative linkage effect? While such questions are beyond the scope of Rodríguez-Clare's model, their importance can hardly be overstated.

In another interesting paper, Markusen and Venables (1999) construct a model with linkages to address the potential for cumulative causation in industrial development – the ability of the formation of an upstream industry to generate the later formation of a downstream industry. The entry of multinationals affects the host economy in two potentially opposing directions. On one hand, multinationals replace domestic firms through a *competition effect*: the entry of multinationals lowers the price index for the final good, which causes the exit of domestic producers of final goods to restore equilibrium. On the other hand, multinationals may create conditions beneficial to local industries through a *linkage effect*: the entry of multinationals may raise the demand for intermediates, which causes the domestic production of intermediate goods to expand.[10]

An important variable for assessing the linkage effect is the *input–output coefficient*, which measures the ratio of the intermediate required relative to the per unit total input requirement of the downstream industry.[11] Whether this ratio for the multinational firms exceeds the ratio for the domestic firms influences whether the linkage effect is positive. The two ratios may differ due to differences in technology (the multinational firms may use more intermediates relative to primary factors than do domestic firms) or differences in sourcing (multinationals may source from abroad). If this ratio is greater for multinational firms than for domestic firms, then the multinational uses local intermediate goods more intensively than the domestic industry. Thus, this ratio is the analogue to Rodríguez-Clare's employment-based measurement.

The Markusen–Venables model also exhibits multiple equilibria. Starting from the good equilibrium where the domestic economy already supports its own upstream and downstream producers, multinational activity can generate various consequences depending on the relative strengths of the competition and linkage effects. In general, the competition effect decreases the number of domestic firms (both upstream and downstream), while the linkage effect may increase both if multinationals use intermediates more intensively than domestic firms do. The various consequences are most easily understood by considering a few special cases. These cases are chosen to illustrate how the characteristics of the multinational investment project and of the domestic industry influence the magnitude and direction of the effects.

First, suppose multinationals source no intermediates locally. Then, the linkage effect must reduce the number of domestic firms (both upstream and downstream), which reinforces the competition effect. Second, alternatively assume that multinational production merely displaces foreign firms serving the domestic market through exports. Such a scenario arises if foreign firms decide to switch to being multinationals, a common occurrence (and hence not merely a theoretical exercise). Then, the competition effect is zero, and provided the multinationals source some intermediates locally, the linkage effect increases the number of domestic firms (both upstream and downstream).

Third, instead of assuming intermediate goods are near perfect substitutes so that the forward linkages, whereby additional upstream firms (through enhanced variety) induce entry of downstream firms, are shut down. Then, multinational firms purely displace domestic downstream firms, so the number of domestic downstream firms falls although the number of domestic upstream firms may rise. This last case illustrates the role of the love of variety for intermediates in inducing forward linkages and hence cumulative causation in industrial development.

Even starting with no initial domestic production (the bad equilibrium), backward linkages generated by multinational firms may be strong enough to induce the development of a domestic upstream industry. The domestic economy would be observed having its own upstream industry but not yet its own downstream industry (only multinational production). Forward linkages may then induce the development of a domestic downstream industry. Ultimately, the multinational presence serves as a catalyst to the development of the entire domestic industry. The expansion of domestic production may be so strong that it eventually drives the multinational out of the host country, as occurred in the bicycle and personal computer industries in Taiwan.

Matouschek and Venables (1999) takes a deeper look at the interaction between competition effects and backward linkages created by the entry of a multinational firm into the local market. They analyze the effects of investments in the downstream and then the upstream industry. They break the overall effect of multinational entry into two parts: an initial production effect and a feedback effect. The *initial production effect* is the immediate change in local production: the multinational production alters the output levels of domestic firms (through crowding out) in that industry as well as in upstream production. The number of downstream firms adjusts to restore zero profits, but the number of upstream firms is held constant in determining this piece of the overall effect. Next, the *feedback effect* occurs once changes in the upstream industry impact the downstream sector through changes in the price of upstream varieties (which are felt as cost changes to those downstream). Here, entry and exit of upstream firms affect both the variety of intermediates available as well as the intensity of competition.

The initial production effect in the downstream industry depends on two important parameters: relative local supply and the measure of local substitutes. The *relative local supply* is the ratio of the additional local supply generated by the foreign investment project relative to the local supply generated by a local firm. It depends on the export orientation (of the project and the local firms) and the extent that the project is import replacing. Relative local supply is decreasing in the export orientation of the multinational relative to local firms. If the project sells less of its output locally than do local firms (and the project is not import replacing), then the relative local supply is less than unity because the project is more export oriented than local firms.

Relative local supply is also decreasing in the extent that multinational output merely replaces imports of the downstream good from foreign countries. If the multinational has the same export orientation as local firms, then relative local supply is unity if the multinational's output does not displace any imports from abroad but zero if it fully displaces them (sells the same amount locally through FDI as it did before through trade). The initial production effect can be negative; as if the project sells all its output locally while local firms export some of their output and the project displaces no imports.

The *local substitutes* index states the number of units of local sales by local firms that are displaced by one unit of local sales by the foreign investment project. A value of zero means that local firms compete in completely different markets, while a value of one means local firms compete in the same market segment. Intermediate values between zero and one indicate the degree of competition.

Consider different possible values for these two parameters to illustrate their impact. When local substitutes take a value of one (compete in same market) and relative local supply is zero (multinational sales merely displace imports, or no multinational production is sold locally, for example), then the initial production effect is simply the foreign investment project's own production: no crowding out of local firms occurs in the downstream market. On the other hand, if relative local supply is one (such as if the project sells the same amount locally as one local firm but does not displace any imports), then no initial production effect results: multinational production fully crowds out local production so local production in the downstream market is unchanged. Hence, the initial production effect is decreasing in the relative local supply. Similarly, the initial production effect is also decreasing in the local substitutes index.

The initial production effect in the upstream industry depends on the level of *relative local sourcing*, which is the project's usage of local inputs per unit of output relative to the usage by local firms. A value of one means the project uses local inputs to the same degree as local firms, while a value of zero means the project buys all of its inputs from abroad (or uses none). The initial production effect in the upstream industry is increasing in relative local sourcing but decreasing in relative local supply. Putting the initial production effects in the upstream and downstream industries together, the initial production effect of the project is larger, the larger the export orientation or import replacement of the project, the lesser the degree that the project competes directly with local firms, and the larger the usage of local intermediate goods by the project.

In the next round, the feedback effect captures inter-industry effects generated by the project. Positive feedback effects are possible because increases in the demand for upstream goods induce the entry of upstream firms (which in turn causes entry of downstream firms due to reduced costs). Characteristics of each industry also affect the magnitude of the feedback effect. The feedback is greater if the upstream industry has a greater degree of imperfect competition. Backward linkages result in forward linkages, like the cumulative causation described in Markusen and Venables (1999) and initially seen in Rodríguez-Clare (1996a).

146

If the initial production effect is zero and relative local sourcing is unity, the project generates no feedback effect.

Feedback effects strengthen welfare gains: the reduced input costs lead to a reduced price for the final good and hence welfare benefits through consumer surplus. A relatively export-oriented project generates even greater welfare gains, which may help explain the export performance requirements that multinationals often face in developing countries. A welfare reduction will occur if the project has a relative local sourcing coefficient less than one and is export oriented. The more the output expansion and welfare gain, the higher the elasticity of demand, the greater the potential for expansion of sales at the expense of imports, and the greater the potential for expanding exports in the downstream industry.

Next, consider investing in a project in the upstream industry. Such an investment will lower the price of inputs for the downstream industry, increasing the demand for upstream production. There is also a substitution effect, where the lower price for one intermediate may reduce demand for others. However, more downstream firms enter due to higher profits (the feedback effect), which may offset the substitution effect. Additionally, if local industry supply is perfectly elastic, then there is no net result. Forward linkages require an initial production effect upstream in order to affect the downstream industry.

Furthermore, forward linkages are decreasing in both local substitution and export orientation. If the former equals one, or if all output is exported, then there are no forward linkages. Finally, larger welfare gains result if the downstream industry is more open to international trade and competition or if the upstream industry is more imperfectly competitive.

So far, three different models have proposed three different linkage measurements. To recapitulate, Rodríguez-Clare's statistic depends on the relative local job creating capabilities of multinational and domestic firms. Markusen and Venables use the competition effect to determine whether multinationals crowd out local firms and the input–output coefficient to compare the use of locally produced intermediate goods across multinational and local firms. Finally, Matschusek and Venables use two similar measures, relative local supply and relative local sourcing, to capture the crowding out of local production or imports and the demand resulting for locally produced intermediate goods. Rodríguez-Clare examines linkages in a general equilibrium setting where the emphasis is on wage effects, while the other two conduct their analyses in partial equilibrium where the emphasis is on price effects.

The last approach is somewhat more appealing as it provides a more complete view of how linkages affect the local economy. For empirical purposes, the relative local sourcing and Markusen–Venables indices are the easiest to quantify. The others involve job or demand creation, which can be analyzed theoretically using a *ceteris paribus* assumption, but would be difficult to implement empirically. The competition or crowding out effects may be apparent *ex post* (for assessing existing projects), but would be hard to determine *ex ante* (for assessing planned projects, such as for host country approval).

Other theoretical papers consider the role linkages play in trade liberalization (such as Krugman and Venables 1995, 1996, Venables 1996; Puga and Venables 1996, 1997; Baldwin 1999). None of these models contains FDI: instead of foreign firms becoming multinational, these models have concurrent exit of foreign firms and entry of domestic firms to shift production into the domestic economy.

In Krugman and Venables (1995), if transportation costs are sufficiently low, the presence of backwards and forwards linkages leads to agglomeration and a core–periphery dichotomy with its resultant wage gap. As costs fall to zero, the two economies again see production in both sectors and a convergence of wages. The other papers build off these results. Puga and Venables (1996) show that when cost linkages outweigh demand linkages, the upstream industries will be the first to flee the domestic economy, and the industries with weaker linkages will lead the exodus.[12] Extending these models to allow for FDI would seem to be productive avenues for future research.

7.4. Empirical evidence on linkages

Schive (1990) provides some empirical work on linkages from FDI in Taiwan. Since his work precedes the theoretical models discussed above, he does not use the above-mentioned measures. Nevertheless, his study shows that FDI in Taiwan tended to concentrate in industries with strong backward linkages. Initially, enterprises controlled by non-Chinese investors tended to import more and form enclaves, with little interaction with the rest of the economy. Over time, however, these firms tended to increase the percentage of inputs that they bought domestically. He postulates that perhaps these firms need time to determine which local suppliers could provide for their needs and points to evidence showing that those firms which set up shop later tended to import a lesser percentage from the start. Perhaps this shift occurred because later entrants had time to observe and learn from the behavior of earlier entrants. However, this learning effect may tell only part of the story. It is also likely that foreign firms begin to buy more local inputs due to a domestic learning effect: domestic suppliers may also need time to determine the needs of foreign firms and to learn to supply those needs at competitive prices. Thus, the later entrants enjoyed a better selection of locally produced inputs from which to choose.

Furthermore, Schive's observation that foreign-based non-Chinese firms tended to import a higher percentage of their inputs than domestic firms may not capture the full picture. Foreign firms could also use a higher level of inputs per unit of output, so that the resulting linkages effect may be stronger than the corresponding effect for Chinese foreign firms. Borrowing from Rodríguez-Clare's linkage coefficient concept, foreign firms might also create more jobs depending on the types of inputs they buy, despite their higher tendency to import. For example, if inputs demanded by multinationals require more labor per unit of output than those demanded by local firms, then the multinational's demand may actually create more jobs upstream than local firms.

Three other case studies precede the recent theoretical papers on linkages and FDI. Stewart (1976) studies linkages in a random sample of manufacturing firms located in the Limerick Mid-West Region of the Republic of Ireland. Stewart measures linkages in several different ways: backwards national linkages (BNL) are defined as the sum across firms of total inputs minus imports plus wages paid to employees at the plant (pre-tax). Similarly, backward regional linkages (BRL) are defined as the sum of inputs bought in the region plus the local wage. Finally, the difference between sales and exports is called forward national linkages (FNL) while forward regional linkages (FRL) equal regional sales across firms. The author notes that there are indeed several flaws with these measurements. First, the effect of wages in BRL may be overstated due to taxes. Second, redistribution of resources (labor and capital) results when a foreign firm replaces a domestic one. In this case, since there was high unemployment in this region during the survey period, this redistribution may not prove a significant issue in terms of labor. Furthermore, these measures also ignore secondary effects, which are captured by the cumulative causation analysis developed in Markusen and Venables (1999) and advanced by Matouschek and Venables (1999). The new theory and the linkage measurements developed take some of these effects into account, showing immediately how older empirical studies may benefit from the new theory. His analysis concludes that foreign firms fail to develop either backwards or forward linkages. Irish firms generate larger linkages as a percentage of output compared to foreign firms, but fewer of them are regional. He proposes that fiscal incentives and the region's characteristics attract firms that are less likely to develop linkages. In 1964, regional linkages as a percentage of output were as follows: 39.3 per cent for US firms, 22.1 per cent for British firms, and 27.4 per cent for Irish firms. In 1970, the figure for US firms had fallen to 28.7 per cent, comparable to the 29.5 per cent for Irish firms, both of which were paltry, compared to the 44.9 per cent witnessed with British firms.

British firms provide an excellent example of the general trend that multinationals tend to buy more locally as time goes on, while the behavior of US firms runs counter to it.[13] The British firms also illustrate the benefits of proximity to the host country, despite the claim by Rodríguez-Clare that proximity lowers communication costs and hence decreases the level of local purchasing. This counter result may well be due to some of the dynamics referred to in the Taiwanese example. Irish suppliers, by having a closer connection with the British than the US firms, both in terms of geography and the cultural spillover that results, may find it easier to determine the needs of British suppliers as opposed to US firms. British firms may likewise find it easier than US firms to purchase from Irish suppliers due to proximity. In addition, US firms may have a better selection of intermediates to choose from in their own domestic market owing to the larger size of the US market.

The Irish experience has also been studied by Barry and Bradley (1997) who find that foreign factories are much more likely to import their inputs than are local factories.[14] This result again casts doubt on the proposition that multinationals generate significant local linkages. However, Barry and Bradley also find that foreign firms have a higher productivity than domestic plants.[15] Furthermore, those industries with high levels of FDI tend to have higher wages.

Lim and Fong (1982) examine Singapore, starting in the early 1960s when there were few linkages because US tariffs (placed only on the value added) created the incentive for intra-firm trade. They conducted three case studies of long-established, export-oriented, multinational firms in Singapore's electronics industry.[16] Their conclusion was that, with limited government interference (as in Singapore), export-oriented multinationals can indeed create linkages. In a recent book, Moran (1998) provides anecdotal evidence strongly suggestive of extensive backward linkages from FDI in the Mexican auto industry. Within five years of the initial investment, there were 300 domestic producers of parts and accessories, of which 110 had annual sales of more than one million dollars.[17]

These case studies present some evidence that FDI results in linkages, especially backward linkages, since multinationals often locate simple manufacturing operations in developing countries to take advantage of low local wages. However, none of these studies provides a rigorous econometric study to help determine whether any of these trends or results is statistically significant. Certainly much more rigorous work, taking advantage of the new measurements developed in recent research, would add significant value to the empirical literature analyzing linkages and multinationals.

7.5. Conclusions

In this paper, we have provided a selective survey of the theoretical and empirical literature on linkages from FDI. At present, there does not exist a strong connection between theory and empirical evidence. Part of the problem may simply be that it is difficult to empirically implement the theoretical models. However, much of the advances in the theoretical modeling of linkages are relatively recent, so most empirical work pre-dates the formal theory.

In general, there is strong theoretical support for the idea that FDI can play a crucial role in industrial development by generating backward and forward linkages in the host economy. On the empirical side, the evidence is mixed. While some studies support the linkage effects of FDI, others fail to find such effects. However, much of the existing empirical evidence does not correspond directly to the theory and therefore should not be viewed as a direct test of existing theories. A fresh attack on the problem of measurement of linkages needs to be undertaken using the issues identified by modern theory.

Finally, linkages are but only one of the potential channels through which FDI impacts a host economy. Any policy formulation based primarily on the notion of linkages would be misguided. Increased competition, technology transfer, increased access to world markets due to spillovers to local firms, and worker training are some of the other channels through which FDI can benefit the host economy, and such benefits can be realized despite the absence of linkages. Hence, policy formulation should be based on a more holistic view of FDI.

Notes

1 Satellite industries are characterized by a strong locational advantage (established close to the parent industry), having as their predominant input the output of the parent industry, and possessing a smaller minimum economic size than the parent industry.

2 Thus, an economy may be subject to coordination problems, leading to the possibility of multiple equilibria: only if agents can successfully coordinate their investments will industrialization result in the economy. Such coordination problems have often been argued to lie behind development traps. See Rodríguez-Clare (1996b) for a formal model of such traps.

3 The main question in this debate is whether, through clever use of various policy instruments, a government can increase domestic welfare by biasing investments in an economy toward industries that generate stronger spillovers (or linkages) for the rest of the economy.

4 The two countries are assumed too small to affect international prices (or alternatively, the two final goods are perfect substitutes so that their relative price remains fixed).

5 The analysis should also apply to shifting production within countries, from an advanced to a backward region, provided labor supplies are immobile across regions.

6 The justification for this assumption is that relying on suppliers from abroad involves excessive coordination costs. Producer services such as banking and consulting are clear examples.

7 Hence, an increase in any parameter that increases the multinational's linkage coefficient benefits the host economy. Furthermore, positive linkage effects could push the number of varieties above the threshold, and shift the host economy from the bad to the good equilibrium. In this case, the backward linkages are strong enough to induce forwards linkages, creating a new downstream industry.

8 Alternatively, the wage minus the reservation wage times employment to account for the value of leisure.

9 See Glass and Saggi (1999) for a model in which a multinational's strategy of paying higher wages than domestic competitors has important welfare implications.

10 Again, intermediate goods are non-tradable, although their results should persist provided intermediate goods are not perfectly tradable.

11 The supply of primary factors is infinitely elastic, released from a perfectly competitive rest of the economy.

12 In a subsequent paper, Puga and Venables (1997) introduce the hub-and-spoke scenario of trade, where the hub has trading agreements with each of the spokes but the spokes have no such relationship with each other. Because the hub has lower costs and a larger demand (again linkages are the primary forces), trade liberalization results in a shift of production to the hub.

13 In a detailed study of Puerto Rico's experience between 1948 and 1963, Weisskoff and Wolff (1977) found evidence that linkages do grow over time.

14 O'Malley (1995) discovers that while foreign firms in Ireland have a lower backward linkage per unit of output, they possess a higher backwards linkage per employee, which is the statistic proposed by Rodríguez-Clare (1996a).

15 Incidentally, the fact that foreign-owned plants are more productive than domestic ones is perhaps the most robust finding of the empirical literature on FDI. For example, see Haddad and Harrison (1993) and Aitken and Harrison (1997).

16 The authors propose that linkage creation is determined by a three-step process. The first step involves determining whether there would be foreign or local sourcing of inputs. Next, the issue is whether to produce them in house or to purchase them locally. The final step determines the form of the direct relationship between buyer and independent seller.

17 Most interestingly, investments by foreign car manufactures were followed by invest-ments by foreign firms who made automobile parts. Foreign producers also transferred technology to such domestic suppliers: industry best practices, zero defect procedures, and production audits were introduced to domestic suppliers thereby improving their productivity and the quality of their products. See also Lall (1985) for similar evidence regarding India's trucking industry.

References

Aitken, B. and Harrison, A. (1999) 'Do domestic firms benefit from direct foreign investment? Evidence from Venezuela', *American Economic Review*, 89: 605–18.

Aitken, B., Harrison, A. and Lipsey, R. (1996) 'Wages and foreign ownership: a comparative study of Mexico, Venezuela, and the United States', *Journal of International Economics*, 40: 345–71.

Baldwin, R. (1999) 'Agglomeration and endogenous capital', *European Economic Review*, 43: 253–80.

Barry, F. and Bradley, J. (1997) 'FDI and trade: the Irish host-country experience', *Economic Journal*, 107: 1798–811.

Glass, A. and Saggi, K. (1999) 'Multinational firms and technology transfer', Ohio State University wp #97-04 and World Bank Policy Research Paper #2067.

Haddad, M. and Harrison, A. (1993) 'Are there positive spillovers from direct foreign investment? Evidence from panel data for Morocco', *Journal of Development Economics*, 42: 51–74.

Hirschman, A. (1958) *The Strategy of Economic Development*. New Haven: Yale University Press.

Krugman, P. and Venables, A. (1995) 'Globalization and the inequality of nations', *Quarterly Journal of Economics*, 110: 857–80.

Krugman, P. and Venables, A. (1996) 'Integration, specialization, and adjustment', *European Economic Review*, 40: 959–67.

Lall, S. (1985) *Multinationals, Technology, and Exports: Selected Papers*. New York: St. Martins Press.

Lim, L. and Pang, E. (1982) 'Vertical linkages and multinational enterprises in developing countries', *World Development*, 10: 585–95.

Markusen, J. and Venables, A. (1999) 'Foreign direct investment as a catalyst for industrial development', *European Economic Review*, 43: 335–56.

Matouschek, N. and Venables, A. (1999) 'Evaluating investment projects in the presence of sectoral linkages: theory and application to transition economies', London School of Economics, *Mimeo*.

Moran, T. (1998) *Foreign Direct Investment and Development*. Washington, DC: Institute for International Economics.

O'Malley, E. (1995) 'An analysis of secondary employment associated with manufacturing industry', Economic and Social Research Institute GRS No. 167.

Puga, D. and Venables, A. (1996) 'The spread of industry: spatial agglomeration in economic development', *Journal of the Japanese and International Economies*, 10: 440–64.

Puga, D. and Venables, A. (1997) 'Preferential trading agreements and industrial location', *Journal of International Economics*, 43: 347–68.

Rodríguez-Clare, A. (1996a) 'Multinationals, linkages, and economic development', *American Economic Review*, 86: 852–73.

Rodríguez-Clare, A. (1996b) 'The division of labor and economic development', *Journal of Development Economics*, 49: 3–32.

Schive, C. (1990) *The Foreign Factor: The Multinational Corporation's Contribution to the Economic Modernization of the Republic of China*. Stanford: Hoover Institution Press.

Stewart, J. (1976) 'Linkages and foreign direct investment', *Regional Studies*, 10: 245–58.

UNCTAD (1998) *World Investment Report: Trends and Determinants*. New York: United Nations.

Weisskoff, R. and Wolff, E. (1977) 'Linkages and leakages: industrial tracking in an enclave economy', *Economic Development and Cultural Change*, 25: 607–28.

8

LOCAL PROCUREMENT BY JAPANESE MANUFACTURING AFFILIATES ABROAD*

René Belderbos, Giovanni Capannelli and Kyoji Fukao

8.1. Introduction

The potential benefits of Foreign Direct Investment (FDI) in terms of technology transfer and spillovers to the host economy are enhanced through increased vertical linkages with the local economy. Increased vertical linkages, as measured by the local content of manufacturing operations, provide a number of benefits to the host economy. If increased local content is achieved by sourcing materials and components from local suppliers, it may involve transfer of know-how to, and promote growth of, the local supplying industry. If local content is increased, on the other hand, through increased vertical integration of manufacturing operations (by producing more components in-house), it may be associated with an upgrading of employee skills, in particular if the production of components is more technology and know-how intensive. In either case, increased vertical linkages are likely to enhance the local employment and trade balance effects of the investment project. In addition, since integration is achieved through country-specific investments in building up relationships with the local economy, highly integrated foreign firms are less likely to divest in the future and the long-term viability of FDI increases.

Japanese firms are often found to be less inclined to establish such vertical linkages but to rely on imports of components and materials from Japan (Graham and Krugman 1990; Froot 1991; Murray *et al.* 1995). A number of explanations have been put forward to account for this pattern. It has been argued that Japanese firms' lower local procurement may be caused by the relatively

*This research was conducted as part of the project 'Economic Analysis Based on MITI Survey Data' in liaison with the Institute of International Trade and Industry (ITI) and sponsored by the Japanese Ministry of International Trade and Industry (MITI). We are grateful to the ITI for the data compilations. We are also grateful to Ashoka Mody, David Wheeler, and Krishna Srinivasan for providing us with the Business International data. René Belderbos' research was funded by a fellowship from the Royal Netherlands Academy of Arts and Sciences.

recent establishment of their manufacturing plants, in comparison with European or US firms (e.g. Graham and Krugman 1990; Westney 1996). Since it takes time to establish relationships with local suppliers and to secure reliable delivery of components, the later 'vintage' of Japanese affiliates may leave them still more dependent on existing suppliers in Japan. Another explanation relates to a more idiosyncratic practice of Japanese firms: the reliance on long-term relationships with suppliers in vertical keiretsu (e.g. Mason and Encarnation 1994). Hackett and Srinivasan (1998) argue that Japanese firms face higher supplier switching costs because of their relationship-specific investments associated with the intensive use of cooperative-subcontractor relationships with established Japanese suppliers, in particular suppliers within vertical keiretsu. This implies that Japanese firms are less eager to switch to local suppliers for their overseas manufacturing operations. The empirical findings in Hackett and Srinivasan (1998) suggest that Japanese firms are less than US firms inclined to invest in countries imposing strict local content requirements on foreign investors, in accordance with the hypothesis of higher switching costs. A third possible explanation relates to the motivation for the rapid increase in Japanese overseas investments in the late 1980s and early 1990s. In industries responsible for a major share of Japanese foreign investment, such as electronics, machine tools, and automobiles, an important motive has been to 'jump' trade barriers erected against Japanese exports. There is convincing evidence that voluntary export restraints, high tariff levels, and antidumping measures have induced investments substantially over and above levels which would have been reached in the absence of such trade policies, in particular in the EU (Belderbos 1997b; Blonigen 1998; Barrell and Pain 1999). If investments are merely a response to trade barriers, they are not a first best managerial decision based on manufacturing cost and efficiency. Limiting investment to relatively simple assembly tasks while sourcing components from abroad may be the most cost-effective response. In particular, when trade policy measures are seen as temporary (e.g. given the five-year duration limit for antidumping measures), firms may also wish to limit resource commitment, facilitating the relocation of investment when measures have expired. Hence, the role of restrictive trade policies in motivating Japanese investments may also contribute to the explanation of the observed lower level of vertical linkages (Belderbos 1997a).

There is evidence from antidumping procedures that Japanese 'tariff jumping' investments in the EU indeed involved the establishment of simple assembly plants with limited vertical linkages. The Commission of the European Communities (CEC) considered the establishment of these plants an attempt to circumvent antidumping measures, and amended its antidumping law in 1987 in response. The amended law required the plants to source at least 40 per cent of components from other countries than Japan in order to avoid paying new antidumping duties. The amended antidumping law appears to have been administered as a local content rule (e.g. Belderbos and Sleuwaegen 1997). In general, local content rules in various guises have been affecting foreign investors, and in particular Japanese investors, in the United States and the EU. In the United States, local content rules embedded in rules of origin regulated with the establishment of the North American Free Trade Association (NAFTA) have affected the less integrated manufacturing operations of foreign-owned firms. The NAFTA rule of origin for automobiles, for example, implies that cars assembled in NAFTA countries can only be traded duty-free within the region if at least 62.5 per cent of value added is generated within the trade bloc. This rule *de facto* affected the operations of Japanese firms in a discriminatory way (Lopes-de Silanes *et al.* 1996). In both the US and the EU, subsidies granted by regional governments to (foreign) investors are often made conditional on direct and indirect employment generation. Implicitly or explicitly these conditions establish required local content levels. In Asia, several countries have instituted formal local content requirements for foreign investors, while others have made preferential investment status conditional on local content, or have put informal pressure on foreign investors to extend their vertical linkages (Japan Machinery Center for Trade and Investment 1997; Commission of the European Communities 1998). The popularity of local content rules among policy makers has also influenced a now substantial body of literature analyzing the welfare effects of local content rules under various market structures (e.g. Richardson 1993; Belderbos and Sleuwaegen 1997; Lopes de Silanes *et al.* 1996). However, there has been no empirical investigation of the actual impact of such rules, with the exception of Hackett and Srinivasan (1998).

In this paper we try to shed some light on the determinants of vertical linkages established by Japanese multinationals abroad in order to establish the validity of the different explanations for Japanese firms' behaviour. We analyze the determinants of the local procurement ratio (the value of local procurement over the value of total procurements) at the micro level, that is, at the level of individual affiliates, using affiliate-level data from MITI's 1992 survey among Japanese multinational firms. We focus on the local procurement part of local content because our main interest in this paper are the effects of local supplier relationships and supplier networks within keiretsu on procurement behaviour. These primarily affect the importance of local procurement transactions versus imports from Japan, but impacts intra affiliate value added less. The local procurement ratio includes procurements from locally owned firms, which are likely to be associated with greater technology transfer and the stimulation of local entrepreneurship (e.g. Lim and Fong 1983).[1] Hence, the potential benefits of FDI to host economies are arguably most enhanced if extended vertical linkages take the form of increased local procurement.

In the paper, we develop an empirical model, informed by transaction cost theory and the literature on supplier relationships and strategic sourcing, and test it on data for 272 Japanese manufacturing affiliates wordwide active in the electronics industry. The electronics industry is the largest Japanese investor and makes extensive use of subcontracting relationships outside and within vertical keiretsu. However, empirical research on Japanese subcontracting relationships to date has almost solely been concerned with the automobile industry. The empirical model examines Japanese firms' behaviour by including explanatory variables at the parent, affiliate, and country levels. The 'vintage' effect is taken into account by including a variable measuring the operating experience of the affiliate. The effect of supplier relationships within vertical keiretsu is measured by estimating for each investing parent firm the intensity of transactions within the vertical keiretsu in Japan. The effect of trade policy measures is measured at the affiliate level, by utilizing a question in the MITI survey concerning the different motivations for establishment of the affiliates. Local content regulations are captured in a similar way and also at the country level using a strictness of regulation index provided in a survey by Business International Corporation. In addition, a number of controlling variables are included, such as establishment mode, sales strategy and parent firm R&D intensity.

The remainder of this paper is organized as follows. The next section reviews the literature on international sourcing, local procurement and supplier and subcontracting relationships. Section 8.3 develops hypotheses concerning the determinants of the local procurement ratio of affiliates' manufacturing operations and describes the empirical model. Section 8.4 presents the results and Section 8.5 concludes.

8.2. Previous literature: local procurement, Japanese supplier networks and local content rules

We are not aware of any recent systematic empirical analysis of the vertical linkages of foreign-owned firms in host economies. There is a research tradition on local procurement by foreign firms in the economic geography literature. O'Farrell and O'Loughlin (1981), for instance, statistically analyzed local procurement levels of foreign-owned affiliates in Ireland. In a more recent study, Turok (1993) investigated local sourcing by foreign- (including Japanese) owned firms in the Scottish electronics industry ('Silicon Glenn') in 1992 and concluded that the level of vertical linkages was low.[2] The only recent attempt to provide a more comprehensive explanation of local sourcing decisions in this tradition is Reid (1995), but this study is primarily concerned with the effect of Just In Time (JIT) delivery systems on the spatial clustering of suppliers. Reid found that the use of JIT systems by 239 Japanese-owned manufacturing plants in the US is positively associated with the proportion of material inputs procured at the county level (but not at the state or national levels).

Recent empirical work on Japanese FDI has explored the role of supplier and subcontractor linkages in the decision to invest abroad and the location of investments. Belderbos and Sleuwaegen (1996) found that vertical linkages between firms are an important factor in the decision to invest in Asia: subcontractor firms within vertical keiretsu are more likely to invest in Asia if the parent firm operates a large number of plants (a 'regional core network') in the region. Using location data on Japanese manufacturing affiliates in the United States, Head et al. (1995) found that Japanese plants were more likely to be set up in a state, the greater the number of existing Japanese plants in that state in the same industry.

157

The existence of plants set up by parent firms or suppliers in the same vertical automobile keiretsu exerted an additional positive effect on the location decisions by firms in the keiretsu. Horiuchi (1989) and Cusumano and Takeishi (1991) report that Japanese automobile manufacturers actively assist their keiretsu component suppliers to set up plants near their assembly operations abroad.

Empirical work on Japanese subcontracting and buyer–supplier relationships has primarily been concerned with establishing the role of risk sharing as well as the correlation between relationship-specific investments and the performance of suppliers and assemblers. These studies have focused on the automobile industry. Asanuma and Kikutani (1992) and Okamuro (1995) provide evidence that the intensity of long-term supply relationships is positively correlated with the stability of performance. Dyer (1995) finds evidence that automobile assemblers are more profitable, the greater is the proximity (spatial clustering) of their suppliers. Proximity is associated with suppliers' dedicated investments in production facilities, greater sharing of know-how and more intense communication. These are found to be correlated with faster design changes, improved quality and increased return on investment. For the consumer electronics industry, Capannelli (1997) found that technology transfer by Japanese assembly firms to their input suppliers is positively related to specific investments to enhance respectively the former's technological capability and the latter's absorptive capacity, and negatively related to the bargaining power of suppliers. The effectiveness of technology transfer was found to be greater in case of lower-end production inputs.

Studies of component procurement and supply chain management in the strategic management literature have also focused on the relationship between sourcing strategies and firm performance. Kotabe and Omura (1989) examined sourcing strategies of a group of foreign (including Japanese) multinational firms in the United States and found that the extent of internal sourcing of major components was positively related to US market performance of the product. Murray *et al.* (1995) surveyed 104 foreign-affiliated manufacturing affiliates in the United States in 1993 and found weak evidence that reliance on non-standardized components and internal sourcing was related to better market performance as measured by sales growth. They also reported significant differences in procurement behaviour between European- and Japanese-owned affiliates in the United States in 1991. Japanese affiliates sourced a significantly smaller share of the value of components in the United States and combined a greater reliance on non-standardized components with significantly higher levels of intra-firm sourcing.

Another research tradition has been concerned with formal analysis of the welfare and strategic effects of local content requirements (e.g. Belderbos and Sleuwaegen 1997; Jie-A-Joen *et al.* 1998; Richardson 1993). The effect of local content requirements is found to depend, among others, on the market power of local parts suppliers, the cost competitiveness and level of vertical integration of local competitors in the assembly industry and whether the requirements induce FDI in component production. Despite the wealth of theoretical studies, the only empirical study of the effect of content regulations is

Hackett and Srinivasan (1998). Their finding that local content regulations exert a significantly negative effect on Japanese FDI would imply that, on balance, the negative effect on FDI in assembly industries is much stronger than any positive effect on FDI by assemblers and related suppliers in local components production to satisfy the requirements. However, they also found a positive and significant effect of the stock of Japanese FDI on new investments. This is consistent with the finding of strong agglomeration economies by Head *et al.* (1995) and may in fact measure a partly offsetting positive effect on FDI by subcontractors in response to previous investments by assemblers facing local content regulations.

8.3. Data, empirical model and hypotheses

In this section we develop an empirical model explaining the local procurement ratio of Japanese manufacturing affiliates. Since the dependent variable (LOCPRO) is restricted within the interval [0,1], two-limit Tobit analysis is used to relate the local procurement ratio to a set of explanatory variables. The data on Japanese affiliates are drawn from MITI's 1992 Basic Survey among Japanese multinational enterprises and report on operations in the fiscal year through March 1993. A representative number of 272 affiliates in the electronics industry had sufficient information on the local procurement ratio and the explanatory variables. Further details on the data selection as well as the definition of the dependent and explanatory variables are provided in the appendix. Means and standard deviations of variables are also provided there. Below we will discuss the hypotheses and corresponding explanatory variables. We distinguish determinants at the parent firm, affiliate and country level. These are discussed in turn below.

8.3.1. Parent firm level determinants

We posit that the R&D intensity of the parent firm (R&DINT) has an impact on the local procurement ratio of its foreign affiliates. R&D-intensive firms make greater use of proprietary designs and in-house know-how. They possess more intangible assets related to manufacturing capabilities of non-standardized high-technology components and are less likely to transfer component production to external suppliers. Hence, foreign affiliates are expected to be more dependent on procurement of non-standard components from the parent firm and first-tier suppliers in Japan. We expect a negative sign of R&DINT.

Japanese firms differ in the intensity of long-term cooperative subcontracting and supplier–assembler relationships (e.g. Sako 1992; Dyer 1995). Firms that are members of a large vertical keiretsu with a substantial number of related component manufacturers will make particularly intensive use of these relationships. Intra-keiretsu procurement is based on long-term relationships characterized by intensive interaction between supplier and assembler involving dedicated investments in equipment and human resources and requiring the implementation of JIT

159

delivery and total quality control systems. There is evidence that these relationships enhance performance and reduce risk (Dyer 1995; Asanuma and Kikutani 1992; Okamuro 1995). Since the assembler–supplier system is one of the bases for competitiveness of Japanese firms, they have followed a strategy to emulate it abroad. In practice, however, it has proven difficult to involve locally owned suppliers in such relationships (Hiramoto 1992). The supplier switching costs are higher for keiretsu firms given the sunk investments in existing relationships with Japanese suppliers (Hackett and Srinivasan 1998). Supplier networks have therefore often been replicated abroad through the establishment of overseas manufacturing plants by existing Japanese manufacturers of parts and components, in which they were often assisted by the 'core' firm of the keiretsu (Belderbos and Sleuwaegen 1996). The consequences of keiretsu membership for the local procurement ratio of overseas manufacturing affiliates are not unambiguous. On the one hand, keiretsu members firms' higher switching costs may lead to a greater continuing reliance on supplies of inputs from long-standing suppliers located in Japan. On the other hand, if the suppliers follow the assembler abroad, keiretsu firms may be able to reach higher local procurement ratios than independent firms. Hence, we are not able to sign the effect of keiretsu membership a priori.

Since there are substantial differences in the importance of supplier networks within different vertical keiretsu, membership of a vertical keiretsu as such is not a very distinctive characteristic. Instead, we devised a measure of the *intensity* of supplier–assembler relationships within keiretsu. We used Toyo Keizai's publication 'Nihon no Kigyou Guruupu' (Japanese corporate groups) to establish for each Japanese investor whether it belonged to a vertical keiretsu. Then we proxied the intensity of supplier–assembler relationships for keiretsu members by taking the ratio of the size (measured by paid-in capital) of all keiretsu-affiliated manufacturing firms ('kogaisha' and 'kankeigaisha') to the size of the 'core' firm of the keiretsu in Japan. We call this variable KEIRINT (keiretsu intensity). KEIRINT reaches higher values the more the 'core' firm relies on components sourcing from other manufacturers within its keiretsu. The values for KEIRINT corresponded well to our intuition concerning the strength of supplier networks, with for example, the highest ratios for Matsushita and Fujitsu and the lowest for Sharp.

8.3.2. Affiliate level determinants

At the affiliate level, the experience in manufacturing in a country is likely to be an important determinant of local procurement. Finding suitable local suppliers and establishing links with these firms is a time-consuming process, in particular if the suppliers have to adapt to the demands of the Japanese assemblers in terms of quality and delivery schedules. In other cases, re-design of the product is necessary to allow for the use of locally made standardized components. As foreign firms learn through time how to develop relationships with local suppliers and how to adapt products to local markets, local procurement is expected to increase. O'Farrell and O'Loughlin (1981) found a positive effect of operating experience on the level of local procurement by foreign-owned affiliates in Ireland, but Reid (1995) could not establish a similar effect for Japanese firms in the United States. One reason for the latter result may be that no distinction was made between greenfield establishments and acquisitions. In case the Japanese investor acquired the local affiliate, it is natural to assume that the affiliate is relatively deeply embedded in the local economy at the time of the acquisition. Hence, the number of years of operation under Japanese ownership is not likely to have an important additional impact on local procurement.[3] We include two experience variables, EXPER_GRE and EXPER_ACQ. EXPER_GRE measures the number of years since operations started in newly established (greenfield) manufacturing affiliates; EXPER_ACQ measures the number of years since acquired affiliates came under Japanese control. Because we expect a relatively strong increase in local procurement in the first few years of operating in the host country and a smaller effect of additional years of experience for older affiliates, we include EXPER_GRE and EXPER_ACQ in logarithmic form. We hypothesize a positive effect of EXPER_GRE but no effect of EXPER_ACQ.

The entry mode is likely to have an impact on vertical linkages in the host economy. Acquired affiliates are likely to have higher local procurement ratios given their pre-acquisition embeddedness in the local economy as locally owned firms. We also expect that joint ventures facilitate higher levels of local procurement than wholly owned affiliates. This is because the local joint venture partner or its related firms may have accumulated expertise in either electronics components manufacturing or components procurement from local suppliers. Taking the wholly owned greenfield affiliate as the base case, we include two dummy variables in the model, ACQUIS in case the affiliate was acquired, and JV in case the affiliate was established as a joint venture with a local partner. We hypothesize positive signs for both variables.

A feature of the overseas operations of Japanese electronics firms is a certain dichotomy between affiliates producing for export markets and affiliates primarily selling on the local market. The sales strategy may have an important impact on procurement behaviour of the affiliate. If the affiliate's primary markets are local, it is more likely to adapt products to local tastes and circumstances, which involves local procurement or local development of components. Furthermore, affiliates selling price sensitive products on the local market are also more vulnerable to currency swings if they rely on imports from Japan. Third, if the affiliate is located in less developed countries and sells locally, it will produce and sell relatively mature and low-priced products. In that case, the importance of cost reduction combined with the greater availability of low-cost standard components produced locally will have a positive impact on local procurement. In sum, we expect that affiliates with higher local sales ratios also reach higher local procurement ratios. We include LOCSALES, the percentage of affiliate turnover destined for the local market and expect a positive sign. In addition, this positive effect may be smaller the more developed the host economy. Therefore, we also include the cross-effect of LOCSALES and GDPCAP and expect a negative sign.

The motivation for establishment of the affiliate is likely to affect sourcing strategies. If the main motivation for setting up the manufacturing affiliate was to circumvent trade barriers, the investment was not a first best managerial decision based on manufacturing cost and efficiency. Limiting investment to relatively simple assembly tasks while sourcing components from abroad may be the most cost-effective response. In particular, when trade policy measures are seen as temporary (e.g. given the five-year duration limit for antidumping measures), firms may also wish to limit their resource commitment, facilitating the relocation of investment when measures have expired. Hence we expect less extensive local procurement in case restrictive trade policies induced manufacturing investments. The level of trade barriers varies substantially across products (e.g. tariffs) and trade protection is often targeted at specific products (e.g. VERs, antidumping).[4] Hence the role of trade barriers should be measured at the product or affiliate level. We could not obtain detailed product information for the affiliates but we could measure 'tariff jumping' motivation directly, by utilizing a question in the MITI survey concerning the motivation for the affiliate's establishment. If the affiliate chose 'trade friction' from among the alternatives, the dummy variable TARJUMP takes on the value 1. A negative sign is expected.[5]

8.3.3. Country level determinants

The first country characteristic affecting local procurement is the availability of locally established component suppliers. We include the variable SUPPLIERS, which measures the dollar value of electronic parts and components production in each country in 1992 and is expected to have a positive effect on local procurement.

The extent to which Japanese suppliers play a role in the local components industry will also affect vertical linkages. By using long-standing suppliers from Japan established near the overseas manufacturing base, firms can avoid switching costs and emulate best practice in Japan. There may also be important economies of agglomeration once a substantial number of Japanese suppliers have set up local manufacturing affiliates. For instance, reduced input costs can result from increased specialization and training of local personnel. We include the variable JSUPPLIERS, which is a measure of the role of Japanese firms in the local components industry and expect a positive sign. Since the presence of Japanese suppliers is most likely to allow keiretsu firms to avoid switching costs, keiretsu members are expected to increase their local procurement most. We include the cross-effect of JSUPPLIERS and KEIRINT and expect a positive sign. JSUPPLIERS is defined as the number of Japanese plants producing electronic components and materials in the country, divided by SUPPLIERS. A comprehensive data source on Japanese electronics production abroad (Denshi Keizai Kenkyujo 1993) was used to calculate plant counts. To incorporate differences in plant scale, we counted each component manufactured in multicomponent plants separately.

The cost advantage of using a local network of suppliers also depends on the quality of the infrastructure. A good infrastructure facilitates physical transport of components within the country and communication between assembler and suppliers. The quality of infrastructure has been found to exert a significantly positive impact on inward investment (Wheeler and Mody 1992; Hackett and Srinivasan 1998). As a proxy for the quality of infrastructure we include the variable INFRA, which measures the number of telephone lines per capita (ITU 1995). We expect that the quality of infrastructure primarily moderates the effect of SUPPLIERS. Hence we include SUPPLIERS * INFRA.

An important issue is to what extent local content rules are able to increase local procurement by (foreign-owned) firms. We include a country variable, LCR, which measures the severity of local content regulations in host countries. LCR is taken from a survey among US multinational firms conducted by Business International Corporation (1989) and measures the severity of such regulations on a scale between zero and ten. We expect a positive sign. As noted before, a certain level of local content or local procurement is often required if investing firms wish to benefit from tax grants and other incentive schemes offered by national and regional authorities in the United States and Europe. In less developed countries there often is a similar preferential treatment of foreign investment projects contingent on local content (amongst other requirements). Malaysia, for instance, grants 'Pioneer status' (entitling to tax exemptions) to investments which meet a number of conditions, among which local content requirements (Commission of the European Communities 1998). These incentive schemes and their conditions vary per investment project, introducing a degree of discretion in the application of local content rules. This implies that there could be an important firm-specific element in local content regulations. We therefore also include a measure of local content requirements at the level of the individual *affiliate* in addition to the country variable LCR. LCR_AFF is a dummy variable taking the value one if the affiliate indicated in the MITI survey that local content rules are affecting its manufacturing operations.

8.4. Empirical results

The results of five models explaining the local procurement ratio of Japanese affiliates are presented in Table 8.1.

Model 1 first tests the explanatory power of the independent variables if Japanese supplier linkages and keiretsu membership are not taken into account. All explanatory variables with the exception of the two variables related to local content rules (LCR and LCR_AFF) have the expected sign. As hypothesized, R&DINT has a negative sign, but its coefficient is not significant in Model 1. The operating experience of newly established affiliates EXPER_GRE is positive as predicted and significant at the 10 per cent level. The estimated coefficient implies that a doubling of experience years (equal to roughly 10 years' extra experience in the sample mean) leads to an increase in the local procurement ratio of 0.03 points.[6] 'Clearly, this magnitude of the experience effect is rather small and the results

Table 8.1 Determinants of the local procurement ratio of Japanese affiliates: Tobit results

	Model 1	Model 2	Model 3	Model 4	Model 5
R&DINT	−0.512	−0.764*	−0.751*	−0.714*	−0.652
	−1.283	−1.871	−1.829	−1.764	−1.616
log EXPER_GRE	0.034*	0.043**	0.043**	0.031*	0.032*
	1.843	2.343	2.333	1.728	1.757
log EXPER_ACQ	0.036				
	0.860				
ACQUIS	0.112	0.336***	0.333***	0.274***	0.262***
	0.525	3.383	3.353	2.799	2.687
JV	0.047	0.030	0.030	0.038	0.044
	1.437	0.927	0.932	1.206	1.376
LOCSALES	0.195***	0.163***	0.161***	0.172***	0.166***
	3.159	2.630	2.588	2.829	2.756
LOCSALES * GDPCAP	−0.004	−0.001	−0.001	−0.003	−0.003
	−0.913	−0.315	−0.301	−0.564	−0.574
TARJUMP	−0.089**	−0.094**	−0.093**	−0.092**	−0.089**
	−1.983	−2.116	−2.085	−2.101	−2.039
SUPPLIERS * INFRA	0.042*	0.035	0.035	0.042*	0.045*
	1.702	1.450	1.460	1.726	1.882
LCR	−0.010	−0.007	−0.007	−0.008	−0.011
	−0.868	−0.558	−0.568	−0.696	−0.954
LCR_AFF	−0.036	−0.033	−0.033	−0.018	−0.020
	−0.970	−0.900	−0.899	−0.504	−0.544
KEIRINT		0.062*	0.055	0.057*	0.005
		1.933	1.331	1.791	0.111
JSUPPLIERS		0.002**	0.002*		
		2.241	1.755		
KEIRINT * JSUPPLIERS			0.001		
			0.269		
JSUPPLIERS * DRATIO				0.011***	0.007*
				3.159	1.697
KEIRINT * JSUPPLIERS * DRATIO					0.013*
					1.690
CONSTANT	0.228*	0.081	0.083	0.090	0.110*
	1.918	1.293	1.318	1.491	1.800
Loglikelihood	−12.229***	−8.040***	−8.000***	−5.620***	−4.202***
Observations	272	272	272	272	272

*,**,*** = significant at the 10, 5, and 1 per cent level, respectively. The omitted entry mode dummy is Greenfield with full ownership.

can only provide partial support for the 'vintage effect' explanation for Japanese firms' procurement behaviour. The coefficient of experience for acquired affiliates, EXPER_ACQ, is positive but not significant. Hence, the hypothesis that operating experience plays no role for acquired firms cannot be rejected. This finding shows the importance of making a distinction between entry modes when assessing the impact of experience in the host economy. Although the coefficient of the ACQUIS dummy is relatively large, the estimated variance is substantial as well and the coefficient is not significant. This is likely to be due to a high degree of multicollinearity with EXPER_ACQ (see below). The coefficient of the joint venture dummy JV is positive as expected but not significant.

Local sales orientation of the affiliate (LOCSALES) has the hypothesized positive effect and is highly significant. The cross-effect with GDPCAP has the predicted negative sign, but fails to reach conventional significance levels. The negative and significant coefficient of the TARJUMP dummy confirms that affiliates set up to circumvent trade barriers establish fewer linkages with host country suppliers. This negative effect is relatively large: tariff jumping motivation reduces local procurement by 0.09 points. This result provides support for the hypothesis that the role of trade barriers in inducing Japanese FDI contributes substantially to the explanation of Japanese firms' relatively less developed vertical linkages.

The value of electronics parts production based in the host country (SUPPLIERS) moderated by the quality of the host country's infrastructure (INFRA) has a positive and significant impact on local procurement. The strictness of local content regulations in the host country, LCR, has a counter-intuitive negative sign but is not significant. The same applies to the indicator of affiliate-specific local content rules, LCR_AFF. There may be a number of reasons for these counter-intuitive results. Affiliates with relatively low levels of local procurement could be more likely to be affected by affiliate-specific local content rules. This introduces a negative correlation between LCR-AFF and *ex-ante* local procurement, which may be only partly offset by the positive effect of the specific regulations invoked.[7] Also, it is likely that the investing firms' response to local content rules may be to increase in-house production of parts and components rather than to increase procurement from host country suppliers. This is because local content rules tend to be strictest in countries where the local supply base is less developed.[8] Hence, local content rules may be effective in increasing local content, but the results suggests that they are not effective in increasing local procurement and in promoting the development of local suppliers.

Model 2 introduces two new explanatory variables: keiretsu intensity (KEIRINT) and the measure of the importance of Japanese manufacturers in the host countries' supply base (JSUPPLIERS). EXPE_ACQ is omitted since the hypothesis that there is no experience effect for acquired affiliates was confirmed. Overall, the fit of the model improves markedly compared with Model 1, with the loglikelihood increasing sharply. R&DINT now is negative and significant (at the 10 per cent level). The dummy for acquired affiliates, ACQUIS, is significant at the 1 per cent level and has a major impact on local procurement. It can be calculated that an acquired affiliate has an impressive 0.30 points higher local procurement ratio compared with newly established wholly owned affiliates, *ceteris paribus*. Both variables related to Japanese supplier linkages also have the expected sign and are significant. The positive and significant (at the 10 per cent level) effect of KEIRINT suggests that firms that have built up intensive supplier linkages within vertical keiretsu operate affiliates with higher local procurement ratios. In addition, local procurement ratios increase with the relative importance of local component manufacturing activities set up by Japanese firms (JSUPPLI-ERS). On the other hand, the effect of SUPPLIERS * INFRA is reduced and becomes insignificant. Since we expect that the positive effect of keiretsu intensity works through increased procurement from related Japanese firms, we added the cross-effect of KEIRINT and JSUPPLIERS in Model 3. Its sign is positive as expected, but its coefficient is not significant. With the cross-effect included, the estimated coefficient of KEIRINT becomes insignificant, while the coefficient for JSUPPLIERS remains significant at the 10 per cent level.

The results of Models 2 and 3 demonstrate the importance of existing Japanese supplier relationships both within and outside keiretsu for procurement behaviour abroad. However, the insignificant effect of the cross-term of keiretsu intensity and the indicators of Japanese supplier presence is puzzling. Given the higher switching costs of keiretsu firms, we expected that the positive effect of keiretsu membership on local procurement works primarily through increased procurement from keiretsu member firms. One possible reason for the insignificant result in Model 3 may be the definition of JSUPPLIERS. This does not take into account an observed dichotomy in market strategy of Japanese electronic component producing affiliates. In particular in Asia, there are affiliates that almost solely focus on export markets or re-exports to Japan (for instance in case of assembly and testing of semiconductors). The components that are manufactured do not match demand in the local electronics industry. If there are systematic differences in the share of such export-oriented affiliates across countries, it will be difficult to estimate a robust effect of the importance of the relevant Japanese supplier base in conjunction with the keiretsu intensity of assemblers. In Models 4 and 5 we therefore test as an alternative (but narrower) hypothesis that the size of the local Japanese supplier base with a *local market orientation* has a positive impact on the local procurement ratio of Japanese manufacturing affiliates. We multiply JSUPPLIERS with DRATIO, the weighted average share of sales by Japanese electronic component producing affiliates in the host country directed to the host country market (MITI 1994).

In Model 4, JSUPPLIERS * DRATIO has the predicted positive effect and is highly significant. In addition, the indicator of the size of the local supplier base, SUPPLIERS * INFRA, now becomes significant at the 10 per cent level, while the fit of the model further improves compared with Model 2. These results suggest that the sales orientation of Japanese component manufacturers indeed is an important moderating factor in explaining local procurement. In Model 5, the cross-effect of KEIRINT and JSUPPLIERS * DRATIO is positive and significant at the 10 per cent level. JSUPPLIERS * DRATIO and SUPPLIERS * INFRA also remains significant at the 10 per cent level, but KEIRINT becomes insignificant. Hence, if we control for the sales orientation of Japanese suppliers, the results do confirm that the primary effect of keiretsu membership on local procurement is through its interaction with locally established Japanese suppliers. Non-keiretsu investors also reach higher local procurement ratios in case of a stronger presence of Japanese suppliers (given the positive effect of DRATIO * JSUPPLIERS), but this effect is significantly smaller than for firms with intensive keiretsu supplier relationships. These findings are consistent with the hypothesis that keiretsu members are able to increase local procurement by replicating existing supplier linkages within keiretsu networks overseas. Although higher local procurement ratios by Japanese keiretsu firms are likely to benefit the host economy, the implication is also that these benefits do not extend to locally owned suppliers.

8.5. Conclusions

We examined the determinants of the extent to which Japanese firms establish vertical linkages in host economies, by analyzing the local procurement ratio of 272 Japanese manufacturing affiliates in the electronics industry. Our purpose was to determine the validity of three different hypotheses concerning the relatively low levels of local procurement reached by Japanese investors as revealed in previous, comparative work. There was limited evidence for the 'vintage effect' hypothesis that lower levels of local procurement by Japanese firms abroad are a result of their relatively rapid and late internationalization in the second half of the 1980s. In newly established affiliates, operating experience had a significant but rather small positive effect on local procurement. We did not find evidence that vertical keiretsu ties are responsible for stronger reliance on Japanese imports and lower local procurement. On the contrary, a robust result was that affiliates whose parent belongs to a vertical keiretsu with intensive intra-keiretsu supplier relationships reach significantly *higher* local procurement levels. We found initial evidence for the notion that membership of a vertical keiretsu facilitates this achievement of higher local procurement levels through coordinated investments in overseas manufacturing operations by the 'core' firm and its suppliers within the keiretsu. Keiretsu firms were found to achieve higher local procurement levels in case of a large presence of Japanese suppliers, provided that these locally established Japanese suppliers sell on the local market. The results supported the third hypothesis that Japanese affiliates that were set up in response to trade barriers (such as antidumping duties) establish less extensive vertical linkages.

No evidence was found that the strictness of local content regulations in the host country impacts on local procurement levels, suggesting that increases in local procurement are primarily achieved through intra-affiliate component production and not through increased procurement from host country suppliers. Hence, local content rules appear not to be an effective tool in developing the local supply industry. The size of the local supplier base moderated by the quality of (telecommunications) infrastructure was found to have a positive and significant impact on local procurement. At the same time, a greater relative presence of Japanese firms in the local supplier base (in particular, Japanese firms with

167

local market-oriented operations) was found to facilitate higher local procurement levels. The latter result suggests that non-keiretsu firms also face supplier switching costs and benefit from the local availability of Japanese-made parts and components.

The establishment mode of the affiliate was found to have a major impact on vertical linkages. Greenfield affiliates recorded significantly lower local procurement ratios than acquired affiliates, due to the latter's pre-acquisition embeddedness in the local economy. The sales strategy of the affiliates was also found to affect local procurement behaviour. Affiliates that sell a larger share of output on local markets recorded higher local procurement. A local sales orientation makes it more likely that products are adapted and re-designed to suit local consumer demand, in the process of which the availability of local supply sources will be taken into account. The parent firm's R&D intensity was found to negatively affect local procurement. R&D-intensive firms make greater use of non-standardized and technology-intensive proprietary components, often developed and produced by the firm in Japan. This makes them more reliant on imports of components from their Japanese operations.

We conclude that the importance of a 'tariff jumping' motivation for Japanese manufacturing investment is the most likely candidate to explain the observed lower levels of vertical linkages of Japanese firms. The results also suggest that another factor, which has not been emphasized previously, could be important: Japanese firms' traditionally strong reliance on greenfield establishments, rather than acquisitions, to expand manufacturing operations abroad. To our knowledge, the comparative studies of local procurement have not made a distinction between acquired affiliates and greenfield affiliates or joint ventures. An interesting subject of future research is to examine whether Japanese firms are still found to be less integrated into host economies after controlling for a possible different distribution of foreign affiliates over entry modes.

Appendix: data sources, data selection and variable definitions

Our data on local procurement of overseas manufacturing affiliates of Japanese electronics firms were taken from MITI's Fifth Basic Survey on Foreign Direct Investment (MITI 1994) and concern fiscal year 1992 (the year ending 31 March 1993). The MITI survey includes a total of 618 foreign manufacturing affiliates in the electronics and electrical industries. Affiliates are included in the survey if the Japanese firm owns at least 10 per cent of equity.[9] Unfortunately, for a relatively large number of subsidiaries, the information on local procurement was incomplete. In addition, for a number of affiliates no information was available on one or more of the explanatory variables. This reduced our sample to 272 affiliates. The definitions of the variables and the data sources used are given in Table A8.1. Means and standard deviations of the variables are provided in Table A8.2.

Table A8.1 Variable description and data sources

Variable	Description	Source
LOCPRO	Local procurement to sales ratio: local procurement/(total sales−import of finished goods).	1
R&DINT	Parent firm R&D ratio : Parent firm R&D expenditure *100/total sales.	1,5,6
KEIRINT	Intensity of supplier–assembler relationships within the vertical keiretsu in Japan: Paid-in capital of the core keiretsu firm's manufacturing-related companies in Japan/paid-in capital of the core keiretsu firm. Core firms have at least 250 billion Yen in sales.	2
ACQUIS	Affiliate came under control of the Japanese firm through an acquisition or capital participation.	1
JV	Affiliate was originally established as a joint venture with a local firm and was not wholly owned by 1993.	1
CONSUMER	Affiliate produces consumer electrical and electronic goods.	1
TELCOMP	Affiliate produces telecommunications and computer equipment.	1
PARTS	Affiliate produces electronic or electrical parts.	1
EXPER_GRE	Operating experience (greenfield affiliates and joint ventures): number of years of production since acquisition until March 1993.	1
EXPER_ACQ	Operating experience (acquired affiliates): number of years of production since start of operations until March 1993.	1
LCR_AFF	Affiliate-specific local content requirements. Dummy variable. Takes value 1 if affiliate reports that it faced such requirements.	1
LCR	Strictness of local content regulations in the host country measured on a scale between 0 and 10.	4
LOCSALES	Local sales ratio of the affiliate: sales in host country/total sales.	1
SUPPLIERS	Production value of the host country's electronic components industry (in billion dollars).	3
JSUPPLIERS	Presence of Japanese-owned suppliers in the local supply industry: cumulative number of electronic components produced by Japanese-owned plants in the host country/SUPPLIERS. Each component produced in multi-product plants is counted separately.	3,7
INFRA	Quality of infrastructure: number of telecommunication lines/million inhabitants.	8
GDPCAP	Host country's GDP per capita (in 1000 dollars).	8
DRATIO	Average local sales ratio of Japanese electronic component manufacturing affiliates established in the host country.	1

Sources
(1) MITI, Fifth Basic Survey on Foreign Direct Investment, 1994;
(2) Touyou Keizai Shinpousha, Nihon no Kigyou Guruupu, 1990;
(3) Elsevier Science Publishers, Yearbook of World Electronics Data, 1995;
(4) Business International Corporation, Country Assessment Service, 1989;
(5) Touyou Keizai Shinpousha, Japan Company Handbooks, 1992;
(6) Ministry of Finance, YuukaShouken Houkokusho (Financial Reports of Listed Firms), 1993;
(7) Denshi Keizai Kenkyuujo, Kaigai Seisan Shinshutsu Kigyou Joukyou: Ichiran Kunibetsu to Hinmokubetsu (Foreign Production: Overview by Country and Product), 1994;
(8) International Telecommunication Union, World Telecommunication Development Report, 1995.

Table A8.2 Means and standard deviations of variables

Variable	Mean	St. Dev.
LOCPRO	0.27	0.22
R&DINT	5.16	3.49
EXPER_ACQ	1.22	4.66
EXPER_GRE	9.67	8.09
ACQUIS	0.10	0.30
JV	0.28	0.45
LOCSALES	0.50	0.38
LOCSALES * GDPCAP	6.97	8.10
TARJUMP	0.12	0.33
SUPPLIERS * INFRA	0.58	1.01
LCR	2.69	1.49
LCR_AFF	0.17	0.38
KEIRINT	0.31	0.45
JSUPPLIERS	11.33	14.90
KEIRINT * JSUPPLIERS	3.70	9.84
JSUPPLIERS * DRATIO	3.57	4.00
KEIRINT * JSUPPLIERS * DRATIO	1.18	2.85

Notes

1 Unfortunately, our data do not allow us to distinguish between local procurement from locally owned versus Japanese-owned firms. The MITI data do allow for a distinction between procurements from suppliers owned by the same parent firm as the affiliates ('intra-group procurement' in the MITI terminology), which is a narrower definition than intra-keiretsu procurement. However, there is no distinction between procurements from third-country, Japanese or locally-owned suppliers and the question on intra-group procurement has a low response rate.

2 Only 12 per cent of components were supplied from Scotland and another 30 per cent from the rest of the United Kingdom (Turok 1993).

3 It is even conceivable that under Japanese ownership a restructuring of manufacturing activities takes place that involves a switch to the use of Japanese-made components.

4 In case of antidumping, duties are firm-specific.

5 We also included a set of four industry dummies representing sub-classes of the electronics industry to control for industry specific differences in local procurement (due to for instance differences in transport costs). The coefficients of these dummies never reached statistical significance and the dummies were left out in the results reported in Table 8.1.

6 The coefficients in the two-limit Tobit model cannot be directly interpreted as magnitudes of the effect of the explanatory variables. We calculated the impact effects (derivatives) of the explanatory variables in the conditional mean (see Greene 1997). Because the predicted values of local procurement do not reach the censoring limits often, the calculated derivatives do not deviate substantially from the coefficients reported in Table 8.1. The coefficients reported in the tables can therefore be interpreted as rough estimates of impact effects.

7 In our data set, the (*ex post*) correlation coefficient between LCR_AFF and the local procurement ratio LOCPRO is negative (-0.12).

8 The correlation coefficient between SUPPLIERS and LCR is -0.22 and the correlation coefficient between SUPPLIERS and LCR_AFF is -0.16.

9 The same threshold is used by the US Department of Commerce in its Benchmark Survey among US multinational firms. In practice, only two affiliates in our final sample registered a Japanese equity stake of less than 25 per cent. Seven more affiliates were owned less than 40 per cent.

References

Asanuma, B. and Kikutani, T. (1992) 'Risk absorption in Japanese subcontracting: a microeconometric study of the automobile industry', *The Journal of the Japanese and International Economies*, 6: 1–29.

Barrell, R. and Pain, N. (1999) 'Trade restraints and Japanese direct investment flows', *European Economic Review*, forthcoming.

Belderbos, R. (1997a) *Japanese Electronics Multinationals and Strategic Trade Policies*. Oxford: Oxford University Press.

Belderbos, R. (1997b) 'Antidumping and tariff jumping: Japanese firms' FDI in the European Union and the United States', *Weltwirtschaftliches Archiv*, 133: 419–57.

Belderbos, R. and Sleuwaegen, L. (1996) 'Japanese firms and the decision to invest abroad: industrial groups and regional core networks', *Review of Economics and Statistics*, 78: 214–20.

Belderbos, R. and Sleuwaegen, L. (1997) 'Local content rules and vertical market structure', *European Journal of Political Economy*, 13: 101–19.

Blonigen, B. (1998) 'Foreign direct investment responses of firms involved in antidumping investigations', Working Paper, Department of Economics, University of Oregon.

Business International (1989) *Country Assessment Service*. Business International Corporation.

Capannelli, G. (1993) 'Transfer of Japanese electronics industry to Malaysia', *Keizai Bunseki (The Economic Analysis)*, 129: 67–118.

Capannelli, G. (1997) 'Buyer–supplier relations and technology transfer, Japanese consumer electronics', *International Review of Economics and Business*, 44: 633–62.

Caves, R. (1995) *Multinational Enterprise and Economic Analysis*, 2nd edition. Cambridge, MA: Cambridge University Press.

Commission of the European Communities (1998) 'Sectoral and trade barriers database', http://mkaccdb.eu.int/mkdb/mkdb.pl.

Cusumano, M. A. and Takeishi, A. (1991) 'Supplier relations and management: a survey of Japanese, Japanese-transplant, and US auto plants', Paper MITJP 91-07, Center for International Studies, Massachusetts Institute of Technology.

Denshi Keizai Kenkyuujo (1994) 'Kaigai seisan shinshutsu kigyou joukyou: ichiran kunibetsu to hinmokubetsu (Foreign production: overview by country and product)', *Denshi Jouhou*, October 1994, Publication No. 673, Denshi Keizai Kenkyuujo, Tokyo.

Dyer, J. (1996) 'Specialized supplier networks as a source of competitive advantage: evidence from the auto industry', *Strategic Management Journal*, 17: 271–91.

Froot, K. (1991) 'Japanese foreign direct investment', Working Paper No. 3737, National Bureau of Economic Research, Cambridge, MA.

Fukao, K., Izawa T., Kuninori, M. and Nakakita, T. (1994) 'R&D investment and overseas production: An empirical analysis of Japan's electric machinery industry based on corporate data', *BOJ Monetary and Economic Studies*, 12: 1–60.

Graham, E. and Krugman, P. (1990) *Foreign Direct Investment in the United States*. Washington, DC: Institute for International Economics.

Greene, W. (1997) *LIMDEP Version 7.0: User's Manual and Reference Guide*. Bellport, NY: Econometric Software Inc.

Hackett, S. and Srinivasan, K. (1998) 'Do supplier switching costs differ across Japanese and US multinational firms?', *Japan and the World Economy*, 10: 13–32.

Head, K., Ries, J. and Swenson, D. (1995) 'Agglomeration benefits and location choice: evidence from Japanese manufacturing investments in the United States', *Journal of International Economics*, 38: 223–47.

Hiramoto, A. (1992) 'Subcontracting strategies of Japanese companies in Europe and Asia – a case study of the electronics industry', in S. Tokunaga, N. Altmann and H. Demes (eds), *New Impacts on Industrial Relations: Internationalization and Changing Production Strategies*. Munchen: Deutsches Institut fur Japan Studien.

Horiuchi, T. (1989) 'The flexibility of Japan's small and medium-sized firms and their foreign direct investment', in K. Yamamura (ed.), *Japanese Investment in the United States: Should We Be Concerned?* Seattle, WA: Society for Japanese Studies, University of Washington.

International Telecommunication Union (1995) 'World telecommunication development report 1995', Geneva.

Japan Machinery Center for Trade and Investment (1997) 'Ajia no keizai hatten to boueki toushi jou no mondaiten (Economic growth and government interventions on trade and investment in Asia)', *Mimeo*, Nihon Kikai Yushutsu Kumiai.

Kotabe, M. and Omura, G. (1989) 'Sourcing strategies of European and Japanese multinationals: a comparison', *Journal of International Business Studies*, 113–30.

Lim, Y. C. and Fong, P. (1982) 'Vertical linkages and multinational enterprises in developing countries', *World Development*, 7: 585–95.

Lopez-de-Silanes, F., Markusen, J. R. and Rutherford, T. F. (1996) 'Trade policy subtleties with multinational firms', *European Economic Review*, 40: 105–1627.

Mason, M. and Encarnation, D. (eds) (1994) *Does Ownership Matter: Japanese multinationals in Europe*. Oxford and New York: Oxford University Press.

MITI (Japan Ministry of International Trade and Industry) (1994) *Kaigai Toushi Tokei Souran (Basic Survey on Foreign Direct Investment No. 5)*. Tokyo: Okurashou Insatsukyoku.

Murray, J. Y., Wildt, A. R. and Kotabe, M. (1995) 'Global sourcing strategies of US affiliates of foreign multinationals', *Management International Review*, 35: 307–24.

Okamuro, H. (1995) 'Changing subcontracting relations and risk sharing in Japan: an econometric analysis of the automobile industry', *Hitotsubashi Journal of Economics*, 36: 208–18.

O'Farrell, P. N. and O'Loughlin, B. (1981) 'New industry input linkages in Ireland: an econometric analysis', *Environment and Planning*, 13: 285–308.

Reid, N. (1994) 'Just-in-time inventory control and the economic intergration of Japanese-owned manufacturing plants', *Regional Studies*, 29: 345–55.

Richardson, M. (1993) 'Content protection with foreign capital', *Oxford Economic Papers*, 45: 103–17.

Sako, M. (1992) *Prices, Quality, and Trust: Inter-firm Relations in Britain and Japan.* Cambridge: Cambridge University Press.

Turok, I. (1993) 'Inward investment and local linkages: how deeply embedded is 'Silicon Glenn', *Regional Studies*, 27: 401–17.

Westney, E. (1996) 'Japanese multinationals in North America', in L. Eden (ed.), *Multinationals in North America*. Calgary: The University of Calgary Press.

Part IV

MULTINATIONAL FIRMS, STRUCTURE AND DIFFUSION OF TECHNOLOGY AND INNOVATION

How globalization is structured

9

THE EFFECTIVENESS OF INTELLECTUAL PROPERTY RIGHTS*

An exploration of French survey data

Emmanuel Combe and Etienne Pfister

9.1. Introduction

Economic research in the field of patents can broadly be divided into three lines of investigation. In works such as those described by Griliches (1990), patents mainly serve as a measure of inventive activity and technological progress in general – and whether this measure is appropriate or not remains indeed a debate in itself. The second line of research, described in Van Dijk (1994) and Deffains (1997), aims at building an optimal patent system; thus, it focuses on the trade-off between increasing the incentives to innovate (and thus dynamic social efficiency) and maintaining an adequate level of competition in the post-innovation period.

The third line of research is more broad in its scope as it seeks to understand and measure the use and effectiveness of patents in protecting the rents from innovation. Beginning with the early empirical work of Edwin Mansfield (Mansfield *et al*. 1981; Mansfield 1986), this field of research has grown at a steady pace since the beginning of the 1980s. Theoretical models have focused on the many aspects of patents: how they may modify the incentives to innovate (Gilbert and Newbery 1982), how they may signal significant technological advances and deter further research (Fudenberg *et al*. 1983) and alternatively, how they may open new avenues of research through disclosure of new scientific discoveries (Choi 1990); how patents are enforced by firms against infringers (Lanjouw and Lerner 1996).

*We are grateful to the French Ministry of Industry (SESSI) for providing us with the data. We also acknowledge the financial support from both 'Programme Les Enjeux de l'Innovation', 5233/66 (CNRS) and 'Programme: La Compétitivité Internationale de l'Industrie Française', 02/1998 (CGP). Finally, we wish to thank Rémy Barré, Bruno Deffains, Jenny Lanjouw, Bruno van Pottelsberghe, Reinhilde Veugelers and other participants at the 1999 Sorbonne conference on multinational firms for their comments on an earlier version.

Empirical works have either tried to provide theoretical support to the above models (Cockburn and Henderson 1995; Lerner 1995; Lanjouw and Schankerman 1997) or sought to measure the effectiveness of patents against imitators, most frequently by using survey data (Levin *et al.* 1987; Cohen *et al.* 1997).

The main conclusions of survey data are the following:

- Patents are generally held to be only mildly effective against imitations. More precisely, they often rank behind alternative appropriation tools such as secrecy, lead-time, product/process complexity, complementary sales or manufacturing capabilities and so on.[1] Moreover, according to the Cohen *et al.* study, there is some evidence that despite efforts to improve patent systems in industrialized countries, the relative efficiency of patents has decreased compared to secrecy (at least in the United States). (In the older study made by Levin *et al.* patents came ahead of secrecy for product innovations; the opposite is true in the Cohen *et al.* survey.) The only consistent exception to the conclusion that patents are broadly ineffective against imitators appears to be the pharmaceutical industry, where patents are ranked as the most effective appropriation mechanism for product innovations (less so for process innovation).
- Another conclusion reached by these studies is that process patents are generally held to be less effective than product patents, presumably because of the disclosure effect induced by patents. Since product innovations are disclosed anyway through commercialization, disclosure is not considered an important limitations for product patents.
- Patent effectiveness varies greatly between industries, a result that matches patent propensity differences between industries. Unfortunately, explaining these inter-industry differences has never been thoroughly undertaken. The most plausible assumptions regarding these inter-industry differences range from the nature of innovation itself (some may be more easily imitated; others may be more easily distinguished from imitations by the courts) to the firms' and industries' characteristics (entry barriers, large size of the firms and so on).

The present paper clearly belongs to that third line of research. More precisely, we analyze the results of two surveys[2] of the French Ministry of Industry (SESSI). The first one is built on the famous Yale study of Levin *et al.* (1987), and seeks to evaluate the motivations, effectiveness and limitations of patents against imitators. Results are presented in Section 9.2. As far as possible, given the sample and surveys differences, we try to compare our results with those of Cohen *et al.* obtained for the United States. The second survey considers the limitations of the intellectual property systems in different world regions (France, Europe, United States, Japan, Asia, Other countries). It is especially focused on the limitations related to how patents are enforced. Indeed, in the framework of the TRIPs agreement, less developed countries, which traditionally relied on a very imperfect intellectual property system, are supposed to improve their standards of protection to minimum levels. However, as many experts have argued, the imperfections of the patent system may stem not so much from the legislation itself as from how this legislation is enforced. More generally speaking, the survey provides a first try at comparing the limitations of different intellectual property systems. Results are presented in Section 9.3.

9.2. The effectiveness of patents in a domestic context

9.2.1. Sample

Realized in 1993, the SESSI 'appropriation survey' regroups qualitative information on 1,797 French firms. It was sent to a representative sample of French manufacturing firms. Leaving out non-innovative firms leads to a sample of 1,000 innovative firms. Non-innovative firms were taken out from the sample both because the reliability of their answers was questionable and because we expect them to have only scant knowledge about the patent system and other appropriation strategies.

We first merged our sample of innovative firms from the SESSI survey with the 1993 EAE database (SESSI) and got a sample of 950 firms. Annual 1993 sales in our sample vary from 6,882,000 FF to 183,585,598,000 FF with an average of 1,321,523,220 FF. Employment varies from twenty employees to 118,575, with an average of 1,011.[3] For the present qualitative results, we exclusively work from the standpoint of our 1,000-firm sample, which gets further reduced because of non-answers. Our sample is classified into either two-digit industries or three-digit industries.

9.2.2. Effectiveness of appropriations tools

As in Brouwer and Kleinknecht (1998), the effectiveness of patents and other appropriation means is measured on a subjective five-point scale, ranging from zero (low effectiveness) to four (high effectiveness).[4] Table 9.1 gives the mean score for each appropriation tool for the 721 responding firms of our sample.

Two conclusions can be drawn from the table:

- On average, patents are more effective for product innovations than for process innovations. Levin et al. (1987), Cohen et al. (1997) and Brouwer and Kleinknecht (1998) draw similar conclusions from American and Dutch data, respectively.[5]
- Secrecy is more effective than patents for process innovations and the opposite is true for product innovations; Levin et al. (1987) obtained similar results.

To compare our results with those of previous studies, we consider the ordering of three alternative appropriation strategies, patents, secrecy and lead-time. These appear in all studies. Moreover, as suggested in an earlier footnote, lead-time

179

Table 9.1 What is the effectiveness of these mechanisms to prevent or deter competitors from imitating your new products/processes? (*N* = 721)

Appropriation strategy	Mean score			
	Product innovation N = 721	Process innovation N = 721	Product innovation N = 31	Process innovation N = 31
Patent	2.23	1.57	3.00	2.67
Secrecy	1.95	2.69	2.29	2.87
Technical complexity	2.06	2.31	2.35	2.96
Frequent innovation	1.45	1.01	1.45	1.01
First mover advantage	2.50	1.79	2.16	1.45

Table 9.2 Lead-time vs. secrecy vs. patents

	Our study	Cohen	Brouwer	Levin
Product patents				
1st	Lead-time	Lead-time	Lead-time	Lead-time
2nd	Patent	Secrecy	Secrecy	Patent
3rd	Secrecy	Patent	Patent	Secrecy
Process patents				
1st	Secrecy	Secrecy	Lead-time	Lead-time
2nd	Lead-time	Lead-time	Secrecy	Secrecy
3rd	Patent	Patent	Patent	Patent

'Cohen' stands for Cohen *et al.* (1997); 'Brouwer' stands for Brouwe and Kleinknecht (1998); 'Levin' stands for Levin *et al.* (1987).

tends to regroup some of the other appropriation strategies, such as experience economies, complementary manufacturing and marketing capacities. Our results appear in Table 9.2.

For product patents, our results contrast with those of Cohen *et al.* (1997) or Brouwer and Kleinknecht (1998), since patents come ahead of secrecy for product innovations. For process patents, we obtain results close to those obtained in Cohen *et al.* (1997): secrecy ranks ahead of first mover advantages and patents. In the Levin *et al.* and Brouwer and Kleinknecht (1998) studies, first mover advantage dominated secrecy, which on its turn dominated patents. (In our study, as in Brouwer and Kleinknecht, however, process complexity ranks ahead of patent protection.)

We also computed the mean scores for the part of our sample that had similar average size as that of Cohen (see Table 9.1). Although the number of firms is quite low (31), the results are striking: product patents rank ahead of any alternative appropriation mechanism with a mark of 3.00. Then comes product complexity, secrecy, lead-time and frequent innovations. For process patents, process complexity comes first, followed by secrecy, patents (2.67), lead-time and frequent innovations. Thus, we get the feeling that, compared to small firms, large firms are more satisfied with their patents and with process/product complexity and less with lead-time. This certainly contrasts with the results obtained by Cohen *et al.* (1997), for whom patents were always behind secrecy and lead-time. (However, as stressed in endnote 3, the different scales used in the two surveys preclude any straightforward conclusion as to the respective effectiveness of the French and American patent systems. Rather, we would conclude that we find no evidence of lower effectiveness for the French patent system.)

The effectiveness of appropriation strategies can also be evaluated at the industry level. Table 9.3 shows the mean score of patents per industry. Apart from the clothing industry, patents are more effective for product innovations than for process innovations; they appear particularly effective in the electrical and electronic equipment, mechanical equipment and electric and electronic components; we also observe that the patent score for the pharmaceutical industry is significantly above the average, as in all previous studies of patent effectiveness. In unreported tables, we also observe:

- that some industries display slightly abnormal features: for example, the product/process complexity is ranked very high in the chemicals, both for product and process innovations;
- that, for product innovations, lead-time is ranked in first position in 61 per cent of the industries while patents are ranked first in only 28 per cent of the industries; overall, product patents rank second in our study while they come behind all alternative appropriation mechanisms in Cohen *et al.* (1997). For process innovations, secrecy is ranked first in more than 64 per cent of the industries. High pace of innovation is never considered as the most effective way to deter imitation.

Compared to the Cohen *et al.* survey, we get similar results. They concluded that patents were most effective in the drug industry, the medical equipment industry and the specific purpose machinery industry. We agree with these results for the drug industry and for medical equipment. We do find that patents are more effective for special purpose machinery, but not that effective; instead, we find particularly high scores for the toy industry, non-ferrous metals and boiler-making. More generally, we find that patents are more often ranked as the most important appropriation tool than in the Cohen *et al.* survey, a difference which could be due to the differences either in alternative tools or in the effectiveness measurement.

For process patents, we find that they are much more effective than average for non-ferrous metals, farm machinery, drugs, toys and specific purpose machinery, while the Cohen *et al.* survey found that they were most effective for petroleum, drugs and medical equipment.

Table 9.3 Mean score for patents per industry (showing industries with more than ten firms)

Industry (N = 39)	Mean score product innovations	Mean score process innovations
Clothing	1.16	1.57
Leather and shoes	2.08	1.85
Printing and publishing	1.00	0.94
Pharmaceuticals	3.54	2.76
Household appliances	2.69	1.20
Soaps and perfumes	2.22	1.11
Furniture	1.66	1.37
Toys	3.00	2.00
Cars	2.00	1.64
Autoparts	2.55	1.30
Planes and aerospace	2.75	1.68
Boiler-making	3.09	1.49
Mechanical equipment	2.36	1.40
General purpose machinery	2.34	1.38
Farming equipment	3.28	2.28
Specific purpose machinery	2.77	2.00
Electrical engines	2.64	1.41
Phones and communications equipment	2.80	1.45
Medical equipment	3.00	1.78
Measurement equipment	2.32	1.94
Glass	2.53	1.64
Construction materials	2.00	1.20
Spinning and weaving	0.81	0.54
Textiles	1.50	1.50
Material and stitch	1.37	1.28
Wood	0.77	1.00
Paper	1.90	1.72
Paper and carton products	2.30	1.88
Organic chemicals	2.29	1.82
Miscellaneous chemicals	2.00	1.80
Caoutchouc	2.62	1.17
Plastics	2.30	1.62
Steel	2.06	1.16
Non-ferrous metals	3.00	2.80
Foundry	1.73	1.04
Metals work	1.78	1.19
Metallic products	2.36	1.65
Electrical equipment	2.70	1.28
Electronic components	2.00	1.81
Mean score	2.24	1.53

9.2.3. The incentives to patent[6]

The SESSI survey is also concerned with the reasons for patenting. Accordingly, only firms that have already patented an innovation at least once answered this question. We get a sample of 548 firms for product innovations and 376 firms for process innovations. Due to such a reduction in size, we computed mean sales and employees to see whether this sample was significantly different from that we have been working on so far. Merging survey data with quantitative data slightly decreases the sample size. For example, for process patents, we have only 359 firms instead of 386 and for product patents, we get 524 firms instead of 548. Looking at the sample of firms answering questions on their motivations for product patents, we get mean 1993 sales of 2,184,321,240 FF and a mean 1993 employment level of 1,590. The figures for the initial sample were respectively 1,321,523,220 and 1,012. The 'new' is thus significantly of higher 'size' than the initial sample. Indeed, considering the sample of firms that have been taken out because they did not report any product patent deposits, we get mean sales of 260,241,150 FF and mean employees of 300. The picture is similar for process innovations. For the resulting sample, we get mean 1993 sales of 2,922,169,880 FF and a mean 1993 employment level of 2,017. Once more, the 'new' sample is thus of significantly higher 'value' than the initial sample. Indeed, considering the sample of firms that have been taken out because they did not report any process patent deposits, we get mean sales of 349,218,400 FF and mean employees of 401.

We can thus conclude that firms that answered the questions on patent motivations (that is, that patented an innovation at least once) are significantly larger than those that did not.

Eight motivations are considered by the survey (see Table 9.4). We could only compute whether firms cited or did not cite these motivations.

Imitation deterrence is the most important reason for patenting, both for product and process innovations.[7] Other motivations such as revenues from licence contracts, access to foreign markets and concerns for performance measurement are much less frequently cited. More than 50 per cent of patenting firms seek to enhance their negotiation power and/or to avoid a trial for imitation and it increases to 73 and 76 per cent respectively for our sample with similar average size as Cohen's *et al.* (very large firms). Moreover, the motivation of license revenues is cited by

Table 9.4 Do you patent your innovations in order to ...? (per cent of firms citing the reason)

Incentives	Products (%)	Process (%)
Deter imitation	92	80
Enhance negotiation power	56	54
Avoid a trial for imitation	53	48
Gain license revenues	25	28
Gain access to foreign markets	23	24
Measure the performance of research teams	17	16

$N = 548$ for product patents
$N = 376$ for process patents.

66 per cent (products) and 72 per cent (process) of these firms. This ordering is very similar to that of Cohen *et al.*, although their survey includes an important motivation not accounted for by ours: patent deposits to prevent other firms from patenting.

9.2.4. *Patent imperfections*

The SESSI survey also seeks to evaluate the respective importance of four patent imperfections: deposit costs, defence costs, the ease of inventing around, and patent disclosure. Each firm rates each limitation on a scale from 0 to 4. Table 9.5 gives the mean score for each limitation.

For both patenting and non-patenting firms, the ease of inventing around is ranked as the most important imperfection of patents. Using a 7-point scale, Levin *et al.* reaches a similar conclusion. An interesting result is that, compared to the Cohen *et al.* survey, firms in our sample are less sensitive to disclosure and more to cost reasons. This could be because of the smaller average firm size in our sample. It could also explain the higher score of patents over secrecy (compared to the Cohen *et al.* study). Indeed, when we use the sample of similar average size as the Cohen sample (very large firms), we do get a higher mean score for disclosure (1.58) and lower mean scores for patent costs (1.54 for deposit and renewal costs and 1.35 for enforcement costs) and for the ease of inventing around (1.61).

Firms that never patented their innovations have a higher mean score for the ease of inventing around than patenting firms; accordingly, they also worry less about patent costs and disclosure. In an unreported table, looking at the distribution of patent limitations across industries, we confirm these results: more often than not, disclosure is the least important of the four patent limitations, while the ease of inventing around often comes first.

Table 9.6 gives the correlation between each of the patent drawbacks highlighted by the survey and the log of sales.

We find that patent limitations are significantly and negatively correlated with size, but with only a low magnitude, not exceeding 20 per cent . Once more these results are slightly different from those obtained by Cohen *et al.*: working on a by-industry basis, they find a negative and high correlation coefficient for both

Table 9.5 To what extent do patents for your innovations suffer from the following limitations?

Patent imperfections	Overall mean score (N = 984)	Mean score for patenting firms (N = 599)	Mean score for non patenting firms (N = 385)
Deposit and renewal costs	2.28	2.28	2.28
Defence costs	1.83	1.90	1.70
Ease of inventing around	2.40	2.20	2.71
Patent disclosure	1.29	1.39	1.13

Table 9.6 Correlation between log of sales and patent limitations

Limitations	Deposit costs	Defence costs	Inventing around	Disclosure
Correlation rate	−0.16600*	−0.09556*	−0.16451*	0.08191**
	(5.1418)	(2.9323)	(5.0944)	(2.5104)

$N = 935$
*significant at the 1 per cent level
**significant at the 5 per cent level.

Table 9.7 Correlation between log of sales and patent limitations (for firms that deposited a patent)

Limitations	Deposit costs	Defence costs	Inventing around	Disclosure
Correlation rate	−0.22950*	−0.17687*	−0.19151*	0.07555
	(4.1516)	(3.1640)	(3.4355)	(1.3340)

$N = 599$
*significant at the 1 per cent level.

deposit and defense costs, while ease of inventing around does not display any significant correlation with size. To get a better comparison with their sample, we restricted our sample to firms that have deposited a patent both for product and process innovation. This results in a higher average firm size, closer to that of the Cohen *et al.* sample. Table 9.7 shows the results.

Thus, once we only account for firms that have deposited a patent, defense costs become much more correlated with size, as in the Cohen *et al.* survey. However, disclosure is no longer correlated with size.

9.2.5. Conclusion

The results from the Appropriation survey conducted by the SESSI first confirm the findings of previous studies. Patents are less effective than lead-time for product innovation and less effective than lead-time and secrecy for process innovations. Results vary greatly between industries. Patents are more effective in the pharmaceutical industry. The main motivations to patent innovations are deterring imitators, but other strategic motivations, such as avoiding trials and enhancing negotiation power, seem to gain ground, especially for large firms.

The survey also exhibits differences with previous, American-based studies. First, we note that disclosure is less of a limitation in the present study than in the Cohen *et al.* survey. Patent deposit and enforcement costs seem to matter more. We show that these differences are due to differences in sample size. Ours has a smaller average size. Since patent deposit and enforcement costs seem to be more important for smaller firms, they appear to be more important in our sample. Indeed, when one builds a sample of comparable average size to that of Cohen *et al.* the importance of patent costs decreases while that of disclosure increases.

Using this sample of very large firms (comparable to the Cohen *et al.* sample), we find another striking result: product patents are rated as the most effective appropriation tool, a result that starkly contrasts with the Cohen *et al.* study, where patents were ranked among the least effective of all appropriation tools. Given survey differences, we cannot, however, unambiguously infer that the French patent system is rated as more effective by French firms; rather, we would conclude that we cannot find any statistical evidence pointing to an alleged superiority of the American system over the French one. To probe this question (and other matters) more deeply, we now study survey data that comprise information on both the French and American intellectual property systems.

9.3. The effectiveness of intellectual property systems: interregional differences

9.3.1. Sample

This survey was realized in 1997 by the SESSI. The sample consists of 1,199 firms. Questions hinged on whether the firm has tried to apply for an intellectual property right (patent, trademark, model) in different markets (France, Rest of Europe, United States, Japan, Rest of Asia, Other countries).

Mean turnover is 530,604,150 FF, mean number of employees is 390. Thus, the average sample size is rather small, smaller indeed than the sample presented in Section 9.2. To have a broad measure of the internationalization of the firms in our sample, the Table 9.8 gives the exports/turnover ratio.

9.3.2. Internationalization and intellectual property rights strategies

Table 9.9. reports the intellectual property titles owned by the firms in our sample, by country and by way of acquisition (firm or group). It also presents the percentage of firms that intended to get an intellectual property title, but finally aborted the process.

Models are less used than patents or trademarks; this is not surprising as models are designed for very specific types of discoveries. One can observe that the percentage of firms with a patent is higher than that with a trademark, except for the rest of Asia and other countries.

Table 9.8 The exports/turnover ratio

<5%	*>5% et <25%*	*>25% et<50%*	*>50%*
41%	27%	17%	14%

Table 9.9 Intellectual property titles

Country	Patent			Trademark			Model			Any title			Aborted		
	Total	Firm	Group	Total	Firm	Group	Total	Firm	Group	Total	Firm	Group	Total	Firm	Group
France	36.2	31.7	16.1	34.5	29.9	14.3	16.8	14.6	5.6	52.1	46.1	21.4	3.5	3.0	1.0
EU	30.3	25.9	15.2	24.4	20.4	12.3	10.5	8.4	5.3	39.6	33.7	19.6	1.75	1.6	0.3
USA	19.8	15.8	10.8	16.2	12.7	9.6	6.3	4.5	4.3	25.6	20.4	14.0	1.2	1.2	0.15
Japan	14.9	11.6	9.0	12.6	9.8	7.7	4.7	3.2	3.5	20.1	15.8	11.2	1.1	0.9	0.3
Asia	11.3	8.7	7.4	12.1	9.0	7.7	4.1	2.6	3.2	17.6	13.6	10.2	0.7	0.6	0.1
Others	12.5	9.7	7.4	13.1	10.0	7.3	4.2	2.8	2.9	19.5	15.5	10.2	0.3	0.2	0.1
At least one country	37.1	32.0	17.8	35.2	30.2	15.8	17.1	14.8	6.1	52.8	46.2	23.7	4.9	4.6	1.2

For deposits made by groups, the sample consists in the 658 firms that are affiliated to a group. For both firms and groups, we calculated the percentage on the basis of the overall sample, not on the basis of the sample of firms that have deposited any property right in the country. Thus the table reads like this: in the USA, 16.2 per cent of the overall sample (firms or groups) have deposited a trademark. 12.7 per cent of the overall sample reported a trademark deposit made by a firm. 9.6 per cent of the firms affiliated to a group reported a trademark deposited by that group.

Table 9.10 Russian dolls

Strategy	No deposits	France	France/ EU	Fr./EU/ Others	Others	EU	EU/ Others	France/ Others
%	47.2	12.5	10.6	28.5	0.2	0.2	0.2	0.5

Here, 'others' includes 'USA, Japan, Asia and other countries'. The table reads like this: 12.5 per cent of our sample have a title in France; 10.6 per cent have a title in both France and the EU.

It is evident from the table that French firms have a higher tendency to own intellectual property rights first in France, then in the EU, then in other industrialized countries and then in emerging or developed countries. This is even more evident in Table 9.10: the percentage of French firms that have made a deposit outside France without having made a deposit in France itself is always below 1 per cent and the percentage of firms that make a deposit in France and then in other countries, EU excluded, is only 0.5 per cent.

This is true for both groups and independent firms; however, as distance from the home market increases, the percentage of deposits made by groups decreases as well, but less than the percentage of deposits made by firms themselves. Thus, it would seem that firms tend to rely more on their respective group for deposits made in far-off countries. This is especially visible in Table 9.11: the share of titles owned by firms affiliated to a group exceeds by far the share owned by independent firms; this could be due to the fact that affiliated firms are more innovative. But the share of titles owned by affiliated firms increases for foreign countries. Thus, there seems to be a strategic role of groups in the process of filing at least in foreign countries, if not at home. This is also evident when one looks at the aborted filing process: on average, those firms belonging to a group are less prone to abandon a filing process than non-affiliated firms. Generally speaking, 5 per cent of the firms have aborted a filing process in at least one country; however, most abortions occur in the home market, not in foreign markets: that is, as firms get more internationalized, they are less prone to give up the filing process.

Let us now look at the internationalization strategies of firms. Table 9.12 reports the internationalization strategies of these firms. Looking at whether firms are present in the different foreign markets, we see that our firms are mostly present in the EU, then in the US and then in other countries (Table 9.12). When considering only the sample of firms that have a title in the respective markets, unsurprisingly, the percentage of firms present in the market increases. Thus, the path of deposits follows that of internationalization. Looking at the different modes of presence, exports are the main strategy, followed by foreign direct investment and license contracts. For Japan, the figures for FDI are lower than average because of the barriers to FDI.

Interestingly enough, one can observe that, for Europe, protection without an economic interest in the market is very rare, less so for other foreign markets. Admittedly, this could mean that protection for far-off foreign countries is sought before entering a market.

Table 9.11 Deposits per country: independent and affiliated firms

Country	Patent			Trademark			Model			Any title			Aborted[a]		
	Total	Firm	Group	Total	Firm	Group	Total	Firm	Group	Total	Firm	Group	Total	Firm	Group
France	36.2	22.1	77.9	34.5	27.4	72.6	16.8	28.9	71.1	52.1	30.5	69.5	6.7	12.1	4.4
EU	30.3	15.4	84.6	24.4	17.1	82.9	10.5	13.5	86.5	39.6	19.6	80.4	4.4	12.9	2.4
USA	19.8	11.4	88.6	16.2	12.4	87.6	6.3	10.5	89.5	25.6	14.4	85.6	4.9	9.1	4.2
Japan	14.9	11.2	88.8	12.6	14.0	86.0	4.7	12.3	87.7	20.1	14.6	85.4	5.4	2.8	5.8
Asia	11.3	9.6	90.4	12.1	14.5	85.5	4.1	6.1	93.9	17.6	14.7	85.3	3.8	9.7	2.8
Others	12.5	12.0	88.0	13.1	17.3	82.7	4.2	9.8	90.2	19.5	15.9	84.1	1.7	0.0	2.0
At least one country	37.1	11.8	78.2	35.2	16.9	73.1	17.1	28.3	71.7	52.8	30.1	69.9	9.3	13.7	7.5

In this Table, as opposed to Table 9.9., percentages are calculated on the basis of the overall sample (total), but also on the basis of the sample of firms that do own a title (Firm and Group). Thus, the table reads like this: 16.2 per cent of the overall sample own a trademark in the US; among these, 12.4 per cent are owned by non-affiliated firms, while 87.6 are owned by firms belonging to a group.

a for non-affiliated firms (number of firms that have aborted a filing process)/(number of firms that have deposited a title) *100; for affiliated firms (number of firms that have aborted a filing process/number of firms have deposited a title) *100. For the total (total number of firms that have aborted a filing process/total number of firms that have deposited a title) *100.

Table 9.12 International strategies

Country	Presence		Exports			License			Foreign direct investment		
	% of firms with a title	% of sample	% of firms with a title	% of firms present in the market	% of sample	% of firms with a title	% of firms present in the market	% of sample	% of firms with a title	% of firms present in the market	% of sample
EU	94.3	38.2	85.5	90.6	34.6	7.4	7.6	2.9	32.2	33.6	12.8
USA	83.7	21.9	71.7	85.9	18.8	7.5	8.7	1.9	27.7	32.3	7.1
Japan	83	17.0	73.9	89.2	15.2	10	11.8	2.0	17.4	20.6	3.5
Asia	86.3	15.5	75.8	88.2	13.7	9.9	11.3	1.7	25.6	29.0	4.5
Others	85.9	16.9	77.3	90.1	15.3	11.1	12.8	2.2	24.4	28.1	4.7

The table reads: 7.4 per cent of firms owning a title in the EU are present in this market through a license contract.

9.3.3. The limitations of the intellectual property rights system:
an international comparison

Table 9.13 presents the limitations of the intellectual property system of different world regions, as viewed by French firms. These limitations can be broadly
divided into three categories: (1) tariffs-related limitation; (2) limitations related
to enforcement of the patents; (3) limitations regarding the institutional environment. The limitations are rated on a scale from 1 to 3 (1 = weak; 3 = strong).
Respondents also had the possibility of answering that they did not feel concerned by the question. However, unreported statistical work revealed that this
variable may have induced confusion in the minds of the respondents for some
types of questions; for example, it is possible that some firms answered that they
did not feel concerned about litigation costs precisely because these costs are too
high and prevent them from suing the infringers. Hence, we shall focus on the
ratings.

For France, the main limitations are related to the litigation process and to the
costs of counselling. Institutions play only a minor role. The EU displays similar
results, except that patent costs are more of an obstacle. This is unsurprising since
European patents are notoriously more expensive than national patents. A very
interesting result is that the costs of litigation and of counselling are held to be
more important obstacles in the USA than anywhere else in the world. On the other
hand, these investments may be worthwhile since the level of damages awarded
is considered to be less of a limitation in the USA than anywhere else. Japan is
characterized by high deposit costs; other costs are also rated as important, but
they have lower ratings than in the United States. As for the rest of Asia, cost-
related reasons are rated as less important than in Japan, but more than in France;
above all, firms complain of their inability to detect and sue infringers, and then
to receive an appropriate level of compensation. Legislation itself, the subject of
much debate in the TRIPs agreement, appears to be only a minor obstacle. It can
be noted that both institutional limitations and discrimination, while kept to low
levels in other countries, reach their peak for Asia.

9.3.4. The limitations of intellectual property rights:
an econometric specification

We are now interested in the determinants of IPR limitations. In particular, we wish
to see whether size, the affiliation to a group or the different modes of presence in
the foreign country are of any empirical relevance. These are all firm-specific data
and in this exploratory analysis, we concentrate on the obstacles most likely to
vary with size, such as detection, litigation, damages awarded and discrimination
against foreign firms.

To build an appropriate set of data, we merged our information on obstacles and
firms into a single database and added dummies for each region (EU, US, Japan,
Asia and others). We considered only obstacles rated as significant by firms.

Table 9.13 The limitations of intellectual property systems in the world

Obstacles	Fr. (658 firms)		UE (489 firms)		USA (319 firms)		Japan (251 firms)		Asia (217 firms)		Others (237 firms)	
	Rating	% of firms for whom this is not a concern	Rating	% of firms for whom this is not a concern	Rating	% of firms for whom this is not a concern	Rating	% of firms for whom this is not a concern	Rating	% of firms for whom this is not a concern	Rating	% of firms for whom this is not a concern
Tariffs												
Deposit	1.61	0	1.87	0	1.88	0	1.94	0	1.81	0	1.77	0
Renewal	1.56	0	1.73	0	1.77	0	1.80	0	1.67	0	1.97 (184)	15
Counsels	1.97	36	2.03	34	**2.17**	35	2.12	36	2.06	38	2.04	39
Litigation	1.90	67	1.90	65	**2.19**	63	1.98	67	1.92	65	1.95	65
Effectiveness												
Detection	1.79	49	1.76	49	1.76	51	1.73	48	**2.01**	48	1.95	49
Litigation capability	1.94	70	1.87	71	1.84	72	1.85	74	**2.22**	66	2.24	71
Insufficient damage awarded	1.80	77	1.75	77	1.54	75	1.76	78	**2.08**	72	2.00	74
Discrimination			1.47	83	1.68	80	1.86	80	1.96	77	1.90	78
Assurance	1.73	74	1.73	74	1.69	75	1.75	76	1.87	75	1.74	72
Institution												
Legislation	1.36	0	1.39	0	1.36	0	1.38	0	1.38	0	1.31	0
Counsels in France	1.24	47	1.38	51	1.19	53	1.29	52	1.28	57	1.28	54
Counsels abroad	NA	NA	1.28	76	1.32	75	1.44	71	1.43	72	1.19	73
Intermediary in France	1.51	60	1.43	67	1.36	74	1.44	75	1.60	78	1.43	74
Intermediary abroad	NA	NA	1.43	86	1.44	88	1.55	88	1.60	87	1.39	86

Using an ordered logit specification the equation we test for is:

$$\text{Obstacle intensity} = f(\text{PRE};\text{EXP};\text{LIC};\text{FDI};\text{GROU};\text{SIZE};\text{DEU};$$
$$\text{DUSA};\text{DJAP};\text{DASI};\text{DAUT})$$

Where:

Obstacle intensity: is an ordered qualitative variable ranging from 1 to 3, reflecting the intensity of the different obstacles under study: detection, litigation capability, level of damages awarded and discrimination.

PRE: is a dummy variable indicating whether the firm is commercially present in the foreign market (whatever the strategy – exports, license or foreign direct investment);

EXP: is a dummy variable that takes the value of one if the firm exports to the region and zero otherwise;

LIC: is a dummy variable that takes the value of one if the firm sells license contracts to firms in the region and zero otherwise;

FDI: is a dummy variable that takes the value of one if the firm has foreign direct investment in the region and zero otherwise;

GROU: is a dummy variable that takes the value of one if the firm is affiliated to a group in both 1994 and 1997; it takes the value of zero if the firm does not belong to a group at these two dates;

SIZE: is the logarithm of turnover of the firm in 1997;

DEU, DUSA, DJAP, DASI and DAUT: are dummy variables that take the value of one when the data considered is taken from our data set on the EU, the USA, Japan, Asia or other countries (respectively). DEU is used as the region of reference.

Econometric results are presented on Table 9.14. The fit of our model is very low, but sufficient to discriminate the empirical relevance of our firm-level data against the country effects. Overall, they show that the mode of presence in the foreign country is never significant, with the exception of licensing in the case of litigation capability. Size and commercial presence in the foreign country are almost always negatively correlated with the intensity of the obstacles faced by the firm. Overall, the obstacles faced by firms seem more country-specific than firm-specific.

9.3.5. Conclusion

The SESSI survey on international protection of intellectual capital brings forth the following results:

- The distribution of intellectual property rights of French firms neatly matches the distribution of their interests: France, the rest of EU and then the rest of

Table 9.14 The firm-level determinants of the obstacles to IPR effectiveness

	Detection capability	Litigation capability	Insufficient damages	Discrimination
PRE	−1.094*	−0.884	−2.303*	−0.412
	(0.419)	(0.599)	(0.776)	(0.684)
EXP	−0.346	−0.001	−0.159	−0.637
	(0.244)	(0.368)	(0.409)	(0.425)
LIC	0.010	0.561*	0.086	−0.069
	(0.226)	(0.288)	(0.320)	(0.327)
FDI	−0.082	0.177	−0.163	−0.150
	(0.174)	(0.224)	(0.242)	(0.275)
SIZE	−0.100*	−0.096**	−0.124*	0.108
	(0.045)	(0.053)	(0.061)	(0.070)
GROU	−0.223	−0.365**	−0.206	−0.265
	(0.154)	(0.199)	(0.224)	(0.274)
DUSA	−0.050	−0.090	−0.650*	0.379
	(0.200)	(0.259)	(0.304)	(0.341)
DJAP	0.059	−0.129	−0.208	0.629**
	(0.217)	(0.292)	(0.332)	(0.375)
DASI	0.773*	0.806*	0.770*	1.006*
	(0.220)	(0.278)	(0.305)	(0.359)
DAUT	0.444*	0.839*	0.506**	0.959*
	(0.214)	(0.284)	(0.301)	(0.350)
No. of firms	767	433	370	297
χ^2	47.31	31.90	42.77	24.06

* and ** respectively denote the 5 and 10% levels of significance.

the world. It is very rare to find a firm that owns some title in the EU or in the rest of the world and that does not have a title in France.

- Belonging to a group seems to be an important determinant of whether the firm has obtained protection or of whether it has abandoned the filing process.
- Looking at the main limitations of these intellectual property rights, one should stress the impact of the costs of litigation and of the costs of counselling (especially in the USA), except for emerging Asian economies, where firms are more concerned with detecting and suing the infringers, as well as with obtaining appropriate compensation for the lost profits. Asia is also outlined for its institutional deficiencies and its discrimination policy, even though these latter problems seem less acute.
- Using an ordered logit specification, we concentrate on some of these obstacles – those most likely to be firm-dependent – to show that obstacles to IPR effectiveness seem much more country-specific than firm-specific. An interesting point, though, is that in concordance with previous studies, they seem to decrease with size or when the firm is commercially present in the country (see Lanjouw and Schankerman 1997).

9.4. Conclusion

The present paper presents statistical results on two surveys of the SESSI/French Ministry of Industry. Both relate to the topic of industrial property rights, a subject that is much debated in both industrialized and developing countries. The survey of French firms on the effectiveness of patent protection shows that patents remain a very imperfect appropriation tool. The effectiveness of patents against imitators depends on the industry, the type of innovation and plausibly, on the type of the firm. Comparing our results with the most recent American survey, we find no evidence supporting the alleged comparative ineffectiveness of the French patent system. The second survey on international IPR strategies confirms the intuition that IPR deposits closely match the geographical distribution of activities. This survey also shows that obstacles to IPR effectiveness remain very high in Asia and originate mainly from a lack of enforcement ability (too few competent courts, low damages, and so on). The higher costs of enforcement in the US are another interesting result. Finally, we show that the differences in the obstacles faced by firms are more country- than firm-specific. Further research should seek to relate the survey data to quantitative data so as to build more convincing empirical settings.

Notes

1 It is problematic that some of the proposed alternatives are sometimes ill-defined: what is, for example, the difference between 'lead-time' and 'moving quickly down the learning curve' in the Levin *et al.* study? Similarly, aren't 'complementary sales efforts' and 'complementary manufacturing efforts' mere inputs in lead-time strategies?

2 These surveys are available on request from the authors.

3 It is interesting to note that the average firm in our main sample is of a smaller size than that in the Cohen *et al.* (1997) sample (mean sales of $4.44 billion and mean number of employees of 21,817). It is also smaller than the average firm in the Levin *et al.* (1987) survey, but it is likely to be larger than that in the Brouwer and Kleinknecht study, which comprises firms with fewer than twenty employees. As will become clear from the next paragraphs, it became very interesting to frame our sample so as to get a sample the same average size as that of the Cohen sample. Unfortunately, the resulting sample was only of thirty-one firms (with mean sales of FF 26.5 billion).

4 Levin *et al.* (1987) use a 7-point scale while Cohen *et al.* (1997) use a 5-point scale, where response categories correspond to the percentage of innovations for which each appropriability mechanism had been effective in protecting their competitive advantage from innovations during the prior three years. While this scale is less subjective than ours or Levin's, it cannot reflect skewness in the value of protected innovations; as Cohen *et al.* do recognize (p. 5 of their paper), a firm find patents to be effective for only 10 per cent of its innovations, but these 10 per cent may also be the most profitable innovations.

5 We also calculated the mean score for patenting firms only. The main difference from the above table is that the mean score for patents is higher for patents and processes, reaching 2.82 and 1.92 respectively.

6 Only the Cohen *et al.* (1997) study gives results on the motivations to patent.

7 Similar results are obtained with industry classification. Deterring imitation is cited as a reason for patenting in 97 per cent of the industries for product innovations and in 92 per cent of the industries for process innovations.

References

Brouwer, E. and Kleinknecht, A. (1998) 'Innovative output and firm's propensity to patent: an exploration of a firm's propensity to patent', *Research Policy*, 1998–2004.

Choi, J. (1991) 'Dynamic R&D competition under "hazard rate" uncertainty', *RAND Journal Of Economics*, 22: 597–611.

Cockburn, I. and Henderson, R. (1995) 'Racing to invest? The dynamics of competition in ethical drug discovery', *Journal of Economics and Management Strategy*, 3: 481–519.

Cohen, W., Nelson, R. and Walsh, J. (1997) 'Appropriability conditions and why firms patent and why they do not in the American Manufacturing sector', Working Paper, Carnegie Mellon University.

Deffains, B. (1997) 'Progrès scientifique et analyse économique des droits de propriété intellectuelle', *Revue d'Economie Industrielle*, 79: 95–118.

Fudenberg, D., Gilbert, R., Stiglitz, J. and Tirole, J. (1983) 'Preemption, leapfrogging and competition in patent races', *European Economic Review*, 1: 3–31.

Gilbert, R. and Newbery, M. (1982) 'Preemptive patenting and the persistence of monopoly', *American Economic Review*, 72(3): 514–25.

Griliches, Z. (1990) 'Patents as economic indicators: a survey', *Journal of Economic Literature*, 28: 1661–707.

Lanjouw, J. and Lerner, J. (1996) 'Preliminary relief: theory and evidence from patent litigation', NBER Working Paper No. 5689.

Lanjouw, J. and Schankerman, M. (1997) 'Stylized facts of patent litigation: value, scope and ownership', NBER Working Paper No. 6297.

Lerner, J. (1995) 'Patenting in the shadow of competitors', *The Journal of Law and Economics*, 38(2): 463–96.

Levin, R., Klevorick, A., Nelson, R. and Winter, S. (1987) 'Appropriating the returns from industrial research and development', *Brookings Papers on Economic Activity*, 3: 783–820.

Mansfield, E., Schwartz, M. and Wagner, S. (1981) 'Imitation costs and patents: an empirical study', *Economic Journal*, 91: 907–18.

Mansfield, E. (1986) 'Patents and innovation: an empirical study', *Management Science*, 32: 173–8.

Taylor, C. and Silberston, Z. (1973) *The Economic Impact of the Patent System: A Study of the British Experience*. Cambridge University Press.

Van Dijk, T. (1994) 'The economic theory of patents: a survey', *MERIT Research Memorandum*.

10

THE INNOVATIVE ACTIVITIES OF MULTINATIONAL FIRMS IN ITALY*

Giovanni Balcet and Francesca Cornaglia

10.1. Global technology: definitions and theoretical issues

The notion of technological globalization is far from being clearly defined: indeed, it has been employed in different contexts with different meanings.

It is widely recognized that a general relationship exists between technological change and globalization: the widespread impact of new information and communication technologies may be considered, along with the processes of deregulation, as a prerequisite for globalization processes in industry, services and especially in finance (Balcet 1999). Moreover, the new technologies have created the conditions for the spread of inter-firm networks, that characterizes what has been called 'alliance capitalism' (Dunning 1997) and represents another crucial dimension of globalization. However, technological globalism is much more than a prerequisite. According to Archibugi and Michie (1997), three main definitions may be considered.

The exploitation and transfer of technological innovation in international markets
This is not at all a new phenomenon: it is at the core of the mechanism described, since the 1960s, by the well-known product-life-cycle model (Vernon 1966, 1979). In that model, dynamic interrelations between innovators and followers explain both the direction and the evolution over time of international trade flows, as well as the crucial decision of innovative exporting firms to become multinational, via foreign direct investments (FDIs).

*University of Turin, Italy. This paper is part of a wider research project on Technological Globalization in Italy. The research group also includes Rinaldo Evangelista (CNR) and Giulio Perani (ISTAT). In the final version of this paper, Giovanni Balcet wrote Sections 10.1, 10.2 and 10.6; Francesca Cornaglia Sections 10.3, 10.4 and 10.5. The authors thank the participants at the Seventh Sorbonne Conference on the Multinational Enterprise held in Paris in June, 1999, for their useful comments. Financial support by the Italian Ministry of University and Scientific Research is acknowledged.

Empirical evidence on trade patterns and patent distribution shows a positive correlation in most advanced countries between R&D intensity of industrial sectors, export performance and FDI flows, as well as considerable growth of the international exploitation of innovations.

International technological cooperation and networking

A second dimension of technological globalism refers to the creation of international inter-firm partnerships and research-oriented networks that have developed since the 1980s. They involve both national and multinational firms, as well as government agencies and academic centres. Partner firms may be vertically connected, or operating in the same industry.

In this case, interesting questions arise as to why rival companies tend to cooperate while at the same time competing and why they should share their rent-creating knowledge in strategic R&D-intensive areas. The explanations proposed by economic literature focus on the shortening of the product life cycle, on the need for sharing the high risks of huge research projects and on the dynamics of research-based competition (Balcet 1990). Indeed, a concentration of joint ventures and cooperative agreements has been observed in new sectors, such as information and communication technologies and biotechnologies, including a growing number of research joint ventures (Dunning 1997).

International location of R&D activities by multinational firms

A third definition refers to the internationalization of the R&D activities within the multinational enterprise (MNE). These strategic activities, which generate new technologies, have been traditionally considered as highly centralized in the multinational headquarters in the home country. However, since the 1980s a new decentralization trend has developed. Some authors have found evidence of increasing shares of R&D located outside the home country by MNEs (Dunning 1993; Cantwell 1994). Not only has incremental R&D been decentralized in order to adapt products to local needs and requirements, but some MNEs have also located abroad segments of basic research. In high-tech industries, new FDIs have been made aiming at acquiring new technologies and building networks for international sourcing of scientific and technological resources.

In this respect, FDIs can be considered a formal instrument for organizing transfers of technology (along with joint ventures and other contractual agreements), as opposed to spontaneous spillovers deriving simply from proximity, and the exploitation of unintended externalities (Antonelli 1999; Mariani 1999).

It should be pointed out, however, that the international spread of technological capabilities may be not only the result of strategic choices of the MNE, but also the indirect outcome of international acquisitions of innovative firms, aimed at different goals, such as market penetration. Evaluation of the extent and implications of these relatively new trends is still controversial. It has been observed that a vast majority of patented innovations are still developed in the home country of big multinational corporations (Patel 1997). Moreover, multinationals tend to decentralize new technologies mainly outside their core business.

In this paper, reference will be made to this last and narrower definition of technological globalism, i.e. the location abroad of innovative capabilities by and within MNEs, as measured by the usual basic technology indicators. An attempt will then be made to explore empirical evidence in the case of foreign multinational affiliates in Italy.

Multinational innovative strategies reflect the interaction of firm-specific advantages with locational factors (Dunning 1997): technological knowledge and innovative capabilities may be embedded in the firm's organization, but at the same time they are localized in a given territory (Antonelli 1999). How these two dimensions interact is a major analytical issue. Three relevant approaches in economic literature can be identified, the first stressing the role of company-specific advantages, the second and third the locational advantages.

Company-specific technological resources

A first approach underlines the close relationship between the process of technological innovation and the firm's organization, human resources, routines and capabilities, given the tacit and not codified nature of most advanced technologies. The role of organizational learning and organizational innovation are then emphasized, as well as path-dependency in innovative processes within the firm (Ciborra 1992).

National systems of innovation

A second approach, on the contrary, stresses the role of national systems of innovation. According to this point of view, innovative firms exploit the advantages connected with country-specific technological externalities. In particular, scientific institutions and infrastructures, including universities and public research centres, as well as technological policies play a central role mainly at a national level (Lundvall 1992). It should be noted that multinationals can be attracted by technological capabilities abroad, while exploiting internationally generated innovations in the home country technological system.

Technological districts

A third approach looks at the 'localized technological change' processes (Antonelli 1995). It focuses on technological externalities and spillovers at infra-national level which give rise to technological districts of related firms. From this point of view, the processes of diffusion and percolation of innovations, based on location-bound advantages, are as important as their first introduction by pioneer innovators. In the French tradition of regional studies, the notion of *milieu innovateur* points to the synergies and spillovers created by a specific local technology-rich environment (Maillat 1995).

These three approaches are not necessarily incompatible with each other. Indeed, the multinational enterprises not only produce new technological knowledge in their home countries, but also search for scientific and technological resources abroad, which are country-specific and localized. In so doing, they interact with local institutions, and internalize new technologies within their organizations. This search explains FDIs, acquisitions and joint ventures in technological districts, where private and public innovative capabilities are concentrated.

In other words, path-dependency may result at the level of an individual company, because innovative capabilities are embedded in its organization, human resources and routines. At the same time, innovations may be embedded in a given territory or district, where technological opportunities and externalities arise.

The relevant question, therefore, is: to what extent is the spreading of technology a spontaneous and unintended process of spillover? Should technological knowledge be considered a public good? To what extent, on the contrary, is it the outcome of formal and contractual mechanisms requiring complementary investments and transaction-specific costs? (Antonelli 1999). If the latter is true, FDIs and multinational operations are by definition a main instrument to create efficient technology transfers.

It should also be noted that all the above-mentioned approaches acknowledge the importance of international networks of alliances and cooperative intra-firm agreements. In several high-tech sectors, such as telecommunications and software, network externalities are a primary source of competitiveness and global technological standards shape the markets.

Moreover, governments too may deeply influence inter-firm alliances, imposing global standards as part of their strategic industrial policies (Mytelka 1991). Factors influencing centralization or decentralization of R&D activities by multinational firms are both firm-specific and country-specific (OECD 1997). Factors encouraging R&D centralization in the multinational home country include:

- economies of scale and synergies within the parent company;
- insufficient scale of R&D facilities abroad;
- low technology intensity and lack of technological opportunities of the sector;
- little need to adapt products to local requirements;
- high transaction costs of coordinating and controlling international R&D projects;
- need for protection of intellectual property and easy imitation;
- lack of highly-skilled personnel in the host country;
- lack of a sound scientific infrastructure.

Conversely, the international spreading and decentralization of innovative activities are impelled by the following factors:

- need to adapt products to local conditions;
- good local scientific infrastructure;
- size of foreign affiliates;
- high R&D intensity of the sector in the host country;
- strategies of international location of R&D by direct competitors;
- MNE's capacity to manage efficiently complex research systems and networks;

200

- acquisitions of firms with complementary or similar R&D capabilities abroad;
- high cost of domestic research;
- local regulations and constraints (OECD 1997).

Multinational technological strategies will therefore result from a complex set of factors, including firm-specific organization and resources, and from the comparison of locational advantages and disadvantages on a global or macro-regional scale. Our hypothesis is that two main patterns of multinational behaviour tend to emerge in the localization of research activities abroad.

Multi-domestic pattern
The bulk of R&D activities is concentrated in the multinational headquarters and in the home country, as predicted by the classic product-life-cycle model (Vernon 1966). The share of R&D located abroad is low, and due almost exclusively to the adaptation of local production to local needs, regulations and market characteristics. R&D is therefore largely user-oriented and contextual to the production of foreign affiliates.

Internationally integrated pattern
The share of R&D activities located abroad is relevant and research units are part of international networks, organized on a macro-regional or global base. In this case, multinational R&D activities tend to be general purpose, unconnected to local manufacturing, needs or characteristics. In particular, technology-oriented acquisitions and joint ventures tend to follow agglomeration patterns and to exploit internationally the local innovative and human resources, developing technological specializations and competences in specific sectors and niches.

In Section 10.6 these different patterns will be applied to the empirical evidence regarding Italy on the basis of clusters of foreign affiliates in various industries.

10.2. Technological globalization in Italy

How does this *problématique* apply to Italy? Our starting point may be the macro-sectoral distribution of foreign affiliates in Italy. As expected, according to Pavitt's classification, most employment is concentrated in scale-intensive sectors, where MNEs are generally strongly represented. The most interesting feature is that about a quarter of total employment in foreign affiliates in 1997 was in science-based sectors. This share, however, has been sharply decreasing: from 31.4 per cent in 1985 to 29.0 per cent in 1991 and 24.1 per cent in 1997 (see Table 10.1A), suggesting that Italy has decreasing appeal in high-tech industries.

If this data is compared with the structure of employment in Italian affiliates abroad (Table 10.1B), the outlook shows strong contrasts: science and technology-based industries account for less than 10 per cent of total employment abroad. This is usually considered a consequence of the structural weakness of Italian firms in R&D-intensive activities (Begg *et al.* 1999). Specialized suppliers, too, are less

Table 10.1 Employment in foreign affiliates in Italy and affiliates of Italian firms abroad, by macro-sectors (at year-end)

	1985	%	1991	%	1997	%
A. Foreign affiliates in Italy						
Scale-intensive industries	207,258	44.4	232,675	45.1	283,093	50.5
Science and technology-based industries	146,644	31.4	149,516	29.0	134,965	24.1
Specialized suppliers	86,156	18.4	94,865	18.4	111,322	19.9
Traditional industries	31,758	6.8	44,329	8.6	31,058	5.5
Total industry	467,121	100.0	515,965	100.0	560,438	100.0
B. Affiliates of Italian firms abroad						
Scale-intensive industries	183,233	75.0	359,980	65.3	395,073	65.2
Science and technology-based industries	23,965	9.8	60,364	10.9	55,015	9.0
Specialized suppliers	17,802	7.3	46,235	8.4	61,147	10.1
Traditional industries	19,188	7.9	84,986	15.4	95,031	15.7
Total industry	244,188	100.0	551,565	100.0	606,266	100.0

Source: Cominotti *et al.* 1999.

able to invest abroad, because of their small average size, although they are highly export-oriented. At the same time, the share of foreign production in traditional sectors grows significantly over time, thanks to recent cost-saving relocations to low-cost areas, such as Eastern Europe. This means a convergence process of the pattern of foreign production with the Italian trade pattern, where traditional industries account for a very high share of total exports (Balcet 1997). This is peculiar to Italy, among OECD countries.

However, given the lack of reliable statistics on the technological content and innovative intensity of the activities carried out by foreign multinationals, until now not much was known about the nature of their innovative activities in Italy. In particular, it was not known whether their prevailing strategy was to manufacture in the country on the basis of imported technologies and knowledge, in order to penetrate the large domestic market and/or to export to other EU countries, or whether, on the contrary, they decentralized significant R&D activities to their Italian affiliates, therefore actively contributing to the development of the country national innovation system. In other words, it was not known which pattern of internationalization of technology, as described in the previous section, was dominant in Italy. Limited empirical evidence and case studies at the firms' level could support both hypotheses. In some cases, R&D facilities have been created by MNEs in high-tech sectors (e.g. IBM Italia). In other cases, R&D-intensive Italian firms have been acquired by their foreign competitors (e.g. the pharmaceutical industry), which have inserted Italian R&D divisions into international networks, coordinated by foreign regional or global headquarters.

Crucial questions are, therefore, still open regarding the impact of technological spillovers from foreign affiliates, as well as the industrial concentration and size pattern of innovative activities by multinational firms. To what extent is R&D finalized to adapt products to the requirements of the domestic market? What proportion of decentralized R&D comes from acquisitions of pre-existing R&D and production facilities of Italian firms? In other words, is it the result of explicit global technological strategies, or a side-product of market-oriented strategies?

Other issues concern the interaction of MNEs with localized technology change in specialized industrial districts, which are peculiar to the Italian economy (Balcet 1995). Is there any interaction between such systems of SMEs, able to create externalities in limited areas, and technology transfers by multinational enterprises?

The policy implications of such questions are relevant: how much and how do multinationals contribute to the national system of innovation and local districts? How do they react to change in the policies and institutions? Finally, how could specific attractivity policies affect their behaviour?

10.3. The basic innovative indicators of foreign affiliates in Italy

A first attempt to shed light on these issues can be made by matching two existing databases:

- the ISTAT (Italian National Statistical Institute) database on innovation activities by Italian industrial firms in 1992. It was compiled via questionnaires to over 22,000 firms with more than twenty employees. A new survey was carried out in 1998 and the results will be available in 1999.
- the Reprint database of Milan Polytechnic, sponsored by the CNEL (National Council of Economy and Labour), on the activities of foreign affiliates in Italy and of Italian affiliates abroad. This database, updated every two years, identifies the nationality of foreign firms on the basis of the ultimate beneficiary and includes both majority-owned and minority-controlled affiliates. The 1992 survey accounted for 1,500 foreign industrial affiliates in Italy.

Seven hundred and twenty-three foreign industrial affiliates, with a total of 271,000 employees included in both databases, have been identified. They represent a significant sample for a first insight into this topic, and for systematic comparison of their behaviour with that of domestic firms. Tables 10.2–10.9 summarize some of the first results, which are to be considered preliminary and to be investigated further.

Table 10.2 gives the absolute values of R&D expenditure, by industry and firm size, compared with R&D performed by foreign affiliates. For total manufacturing, the share of foreign R&D on total R&D is estimated at 23.1 per cent. This figure, which represents a major increase of our knowledge of the role of foreign multinationals, should be compared with the figure noted in 1994 in certain OECD

Table 10.2 R&D expenditure of foreign affiliates and Italian firms (millions of lire and percentage)

	R&D foreign affiliates (A)		R&D all Italian firms (B) (millions of lire)	A/B (%)
	Millions of lire	%		
Firm size (employees)				
*20–99	26,166	1.46	499,314	5.2
100–499	177,001	9.89	920,924	19.2
500 plus	1,587,381	88.65	6,322,834	25.1
All	1,790,548	100	7,743,072	23.1
Industries				
Food, beverages, tobacco	3,288	0.18	126,522	2.6
Textiles, clothing, leather, footwear	5,666	0.32	115,326	4.9
Paper	3,461	0.19	22,600	15.3
Printing and publishing	203	0.01	31,909	0.6
Refined petroleum, nuclear fuel	7,217	0.40	39,035	18.5
Chemical products	87,492	4.89	484,787	18.0
Rubber and plastics products	9,316	0.52	75,005	12.4
Non-metallic mineral products	9,334	0.52	81,191	11.5
Basic and fabricated metals	10,881	0.61	194,549	5.6
Non-electrical machinery	87,490	4.89	649,884	13.5
Office and computing machinery	241,714	13.50	680,329	35.5
Other electrical equipment	31,164	1.74	255,763	12.2
Radio, Tv and communication equipment	851,422	47.55	1,248,107	68.2
Scientific instruments	26,365	1.47	187,528	14.1
Motor vehicles	27,589	1.54	1,704,306	1.6
Other transport equipment	12,670	0.71	441,694	2.9
Other manufacturing	1,748	0.10	63,302	2.8
Pharmaceuticals	373,527	20.86	806,255	46.3
All	1,790,548	100	7,743,072	23.1
Pavitt macro-sectors				
High-tech	1,505,324	84.07	3,285,209	45.8
Scale-intensive	149,961	8.38	2,640,527	5.7
Specialized suppliers	117,008	6.53	882,343	13.3
Traditional	18,256	1.02	934,993	2.0
All	1,790,548	100	7,743,072	23.1

Source: Elaborated from Istat, Survey on Technological Innovation 1992, and Reprint database.

countries (OECD 1997):[1]

United Kingdom: 18.5%
Germany: 16.4%
France: 14.9%
Sweden: 12.6%
Netherlands: 17.4%

Spain: 32.7%
Canada: 37.6%
USA: 13.4%

Multinationals contribute more than could be expected to the national R&D activity in Italy, especially if compared to other European countries. It should be noted that in 1992 foreign affiliates accounted for about 10 per cent of total employment in Italian manufacturing (Cominotti and Mariotti 1994).

In the main OECD countries, R&D by foreign affiliates is highly concentrated in a few industries: computers and information technology, pharmaceuticals and electrical equipment, chemicals and the car industry.

In the case of Italy, this feature is accentuated by a strong industry composition effect. The industries showing the higher values of this ratio are telecommunications equipment (68.2 per cent), pharmaceuticals (46.3 per cent), and office and computing machinery (35.5 per cent). As a consequence, foreign affiliates represent 45.8 per cent of total R&D expenditure in the high-tech macro-sector, according to Pavitt's classification, because of a strong composition effect. On the other hand, the contribution of foreign affiliates to the R&D activity in scale-intensive industries is particularly low. The contribution of foreign affiliates also grows with the size of the firm: their share is 25.1 per cent in firms with over 500 employees.

In Table 10.3, the industry structure of both foreign affiliates and all Italian firms is related to three indicators of innovative activities:

- R&D expenditure over sales;
- R&D expenditure per employee;
- the share of 'innovative firms' – i.e. the firms which introduced innovations in 1990–92 against the total number of firms.

Considering the whole manufacturing sector, it can be observed that the basic R&D/turnover ratio is higher for foreign than for domestic firms (1.7 against 1.0). Similarly, the share of foreign-owned firms defined as 'innovative' is 58 per cent, compared with 32 per cent for Italian firms.

Foreign firms' R&D intensity (R&D/turnover) is higher in five industries: the most research-intensive sector (telecommunication equipment), three low-tech sectors (textiles, clothing and footwear; oil refineries; non-metallic minerals), and one intermediate sector (non-electrical machinery). In significant technology-intensive industries, such as pharmaceuticals and computers, domestic firms have higher R&D ratios than foreign affiliates, even if the latter represent very high shares of total R&D expenditure (46 per cent in pharmaceutical and 35 per cent in computers: see Table 10.2). This paradox could be explained by considering that foreign affiliates, besides local production, play a crucial role in marketing other products imported from abroad. Therefore their sales are much higher than local production. This means that not all Italian R&D facilities and laboratories are necessarily connected with Italian production; in some cases they could be part of an

Table 10.3 Innovation indicators of foreign affiliates and national firms in manufacturing

	R&D/turnover		R&D/employees		Innovative firms/total	
	Foreign affiliates (%)	Domestic firms (%)	Foreign affiliates	Domestic firms	Foreign affiliates (%)	Domestic firms (%)
Firm size (employees)						
20–99	0.50	0.29	1.84	0.6694	39.0	29.0
100–499	0.62	0.56	2.36	1.4468	63.0	50.2
500 plus	2.34	1.61	8.74	6.3514	84.9	75.6
All	1.77	1.00	6.61	3.0268	58.0	32.3
Industries						
Food, beverages, tobacco	0.04	0.21	0.19	0.8825	40.7	30.8
Textiles, clothing, leather, footwear	0.33	0.17	0.64	0.3454	28.2	19.4
Paper	0.18	0.21	0.55	0.5172	51.7	37.5
Printing and publishing	0.01	0.21	0.04	0.5392	38.1	38.3
Refined petroleum, nuclear fuel	0.04	0.03	1.57	1.6979	54.5	37.2
Chemical products	0.77	1.54	3.26	5.0450	52.6	44.1
Rubber and plastics products	0.27	0.57	0.59	1.2626	50.0	41.5
Non-metallic mineral products	0.35	0.30	0.78	0.6739	57.9	28.9
Basic and fabricated metals	0.24	0.36	0.63	0.8390	51.8	33.8

Non-electrical machinery	1.11	1.07	2.47	2.5288	68.2	48.1
Office and computing machinery	2.62	4.54	17.39	26.9767	100.0	60.5
Other electrical equipment	0.75	0.82	1.72	2.2938	66.0	37.4
Radio, Tv and communication equipment	9.25	6.12	20.95	12.1081	87.5	56.9
Scientific instruments	1.93	2.80	4.34	5.3030	74.1	48.8
Motor vehicles	0.63	4.53	2.32	10.7506	80.8	42.5
Other transport equipment	2.15	2.79	6.14	5.1469	66.7	35.7
Other manufacturing	0.35	0.35	1.00	0.7528	46.2	25.6
Pharmaceuticals	3.35	4.86	14.00	16.2533	74.1	49.3
All	1.77	1.00	6.61	3.0268	58.0	32.3
Pavitt macro-sectors						
High-tech	4.83	5.41	17.01	12.3693	78.6	52.2
Scale-intensive	0.33	0.96	1.64	3.8038	56.2	36.6
Specialized suppliers	1.06	1.03	2.37	2.4819	66.9	44.5
Traditional	0.14	0.41	0.44	1.0665	39.9	25.0
All	1.77	1.00	6.61	3.0268	58.0	32.3

Source: Elaborated from Istat, Survey on Technological Innovation 1992, and Reprint database.

international – European or global – network. The ratio of imports/sales of foreign affiliates would be most useful to verify this hypothesis, but unfortunately this data is not yet available. R&D per employee confirms with some small differences the results emerging from the R&D/turnover index.

If one looks at the macro-sectors à la Pavitt, the average higher R&D intensity of local firms versus foreign affiliates is confirmed both in the high-tech industries and in scale-intensive and traditional industries. This means the overall result for total industry (1.7 vs. 1.0) is mainly due to a composition effect: multinationals are much more concentrated in high-tech activities than Italian domestic firms.

These figures also suggest a strong positive correlation between innovation indicators and firm size. As expected, larger firms invest more in R&D activities. Foreign affiliates are more R&D intensive than Italian ones in all size classes, but in the case of medium-sized firms, ranging from 100 to 500 employees, the gap is narrower. The gap is larger for bigger firms, with more than 500 employees and for smaller, with fewer than 100 employees. If the R&D per employee ratio is observed, foreign affiliates show higher values in all size classes.

In Table 10.4, total innovative expenditure (including R&D, patents, licenses and technological payments) and total innovative investments (i.e. fixed capital incorporating process innovations) over sales are related to structural variables of both foreign affiliates and domestic firms.

In traditional sectors, such as textiles/clothing, Italian firms make more innovative expenditure than foreign firms, but absolute values are quite low. The same indicator is higher for foreign affiliates in certain capital-intensive industries (such as refining), as well in machinery, electrical equipment and 'other transportation equipment'. In the case of telecommunications equipment, the value of this index confirms the high innovative propensity observed through the R&D/turnover ratio. Moreover, bigger firms show higher values, especially if they are foreign-controlled.

The second indicator – total innovative investments over sales – may be considered a significant indicator of the ability to acquire new incorporated technology, and to adapt and customize innovation. Typically, for Italian SMEs this source of innovation tends to be more important than R&D. Indeed, domestic firms show higher innovative investment/turnover ratios than R&D/turnover ratios (see Tables 10.3 and 10.4), while the opposite is true for foreign affiliates.

The highest values of innovative investments are observed in the motor vehicles sector, followed by other scale-intensive industries, such as basic metals and paper. If reference is made to Pavitt's taxonomy, in scale-intensive and traditional sectors, both domestic and foreign firms show higher innovative investments ratios than R&D ratios. On the contrary, in the high-tech macro-sector, R&D is the dominant way of innovating. The behaviour of domestic and foreign firms diverges in the specialized producers sector, where the former show higher R&D ratios, and the latter higher innovative investments ratios.

Table 10.4 Innovative expenditure and investment

	Total innovative expenditure/turnover		Innovative investments/ turnover	
	Foreign affiliates (%)	Domestic firms (%)	Foreign affiliates (%)	Domestic firms (%)
Firm size (employees)				
20–99	0.94	0.67	1.08	1.21
100–499	1.11	1.14	1.48	1.15
500 plus	3.11	2.15	1.41	1.77
All	2.44	1.51	1.42	1.48
Industries				
Food, beverages, tobacco	0.09	0.40	0.80	0.72
Textiles, clothing, leather, footwear	0.50	0.51	0.56	0.77
Paper	0.37	0.54	1.81	2.37
Printing and publishing	0.04	0.62	1.41	1.97
Refined petroleum, nuclear fuel	0.15	0.10	0.90	0.32
Chemical products	1.29	1.87	0.97	1.58
Rubber and plastics products	0.55	1.25	0.92	1.62
Non-metallic mineral products	0.70	0.80	1.25	1.66
Basic and fabricated metals	0.60	0.92	3.05	2.83
Non-electrical machinery	2.07	1.98	1.07	0.98
Office and computing machinery	4.06	5.61	0.82	0.57
Other electrical equipment	1.85	1.47	1.77	1.05
Radio, TV and communication equipment	10.69	9.95	1.23	2.24
Scientific instruments	2.68	4.11	0.49	1.17
Motor vehicles	2.04	5.05	8.02	6.29
Other transport equipment	6.47	5.85	0.92	2.21
Other manufacturing	0.50	0.66	1.05	1.02
Pharmaceuticals	4.00	6.14	1.03	1.15
All	2.44	1.51	1.42	1.48
Pavitt macro-sectors				
High-tech	6.03	8.12	1.00	1.68
Scale-intensive	0.71	1.31	1.88	2.10
Specialized suppliers	2.14	1.89	1.40	0.93
Traditional	0.25	0.65	0.77	0.91
All	2.44	1.51	1.42	1.48

Source: Elaborated from Istat, Survey on Technological Innovation 1992, and Reprint database.

10.4. Export orientation and characteristics of foreign investors

The share of exports of total sales of foreign affiliates is always a crucial indicator in order to analyze multinational strategies. Table 10.5 gives data on the

Table 10.5 Export intensity

	Export/turnover			
	Foreign affiliates		Domestic firms	
	Innov. (%)	Total (%)	Innov. (%)	Total (%)
Firm size (employees)				
20–99	19.65	18.37	21.91	18.36
100–499	24.39	22.80	25.70	23.38
500 plus	23.31	23.03	15.79	15.91
All	23.46	22.72	18.46	18.27
Industries				
Food, beverages, tobacco	9.05	8.67	7.74	8.50
Textiles, clothing, leather, footwear	42.54	42.51	32.21	27.61
Paper	36.60	24.86	16.71	15.41
Printing and publishing	10.10	6.92	5.58	5.10
Refined petroleum, nuclear fuel	4.11	4.02	4.21	4.21
Chemical products	17.30	17.12	23.34	22.83
Rubber and plastics products	40.04	37.76	34.63	28.68
Non-metallic mineral products	25.08	18.79	20.67	16.78
Basic and fabricated metals	36.55	33.18	23.63	20.09
Non-electrical machinery	51.43	48.61	44.60	42.03
Office and computing machinery	39.97	39.97	27.36	12.57
Other electrical equipment	28.40	36.24	15.73	14.07
Radio, TV and communication equipment	20.77	20.62	27.54	26.22
Scientific instruments	27.76	25.31	34.12	30.47
Motor vehicles	39.13	38.47	34.49	33.21
Other transport equipment	25.82	31.59	35.96	33.08
Other manufacturing	59.82	42.73	32.80	30.84
Pharmaceuticals	13.34	14.57	17.67	15.87
All	23.46	22.72	18.46	18.27
Pavitt macro-sectors				
High-tech	24.75	24.52	30.22	27.78
Scale-intensive	17.79	17.14	16.73	16.12
Specialized suppliers	45.74	46.17	31.17	28.67
Traditional	21.40	18.31	12.93	15.91
All	23.46	22.72	18.46	18.27

Source: Elaborated from Istat, Survey on Technological Innovation 1992, and Reprint database.

export-orientation of foreign affiliates, compared with that of domestic companies, according to the 'innovative' or 'non-innovative' nature of the firm.

Foreign affiliates are in general more export-oriented than domestic firms, and the gap is larger for innovative firms (23.5 per cent against 18.5 per cent) than for non-innovative firms (19.1 per cent against 17.9 per cent). It must be stressed that innovative foreign affiliates are significantly more export-oriented than non-innovative affiliates.

Small and medium-sized innovative domestic firms are significantly more export-oriented than foreign affiliates. This interesting result partly reflects the industrial structure and international trade pattern of Italy, dominated by dynamic smaller firms: as in the case of specialized suppliers, such as non-electrical machinery producers, and the textiles – clothing industry within traditional sectors. However, these figures do not fully reflect the Italian trade pattern, because, on the whole, traditional sectors show a lower than average export intensity, while science-intensive activities have higher values. Foreign affiliates in high-tech industries are slightly more export-oriented than the average (e.g. computers), but less than specialized suppliers.

The very strong orientation to export that characterizes foreign, especially innovative producers of machinery must be stressed. The performance of foreign firms in the textiles–clothing and rubber–plastic sectors is also relevant.

In order to completely understand the multinational strategies in Italy, it would be most useful also to analyze their import orientation.[2] Further insight into the orientation towards exports or the domestic market, within different patterns of foreign affiliates, will be given in Section 6, on the basis of industry clusters.

Looking at the country of origin of foreign multinationals, identified as ultimate investors (Table 10.6), it can be seen that American affiliates are more R&D intensive than European ones. It should be noted that in terms of employment, among the 'other countries', Japanese affiliates represent less than 3 per cent of total foreign affiliates in Italy. American and other non-European affiliates seem more domestic-market oriented than European multinationals.

Non-control participations[3] show higher values than majority-owned participations. This outcome is interesting because it could reflect the presence of research-oriented joint ventures, and contrasts with the traditional hypothesis of a correlation between the propensity to make joint ventures and the maturity of a given industry. However, it should be noted that, according to the Reprint database, minority-owned affiliates represent less than 18 per cent of total employment in foreign affiliates in 1992 (Cominotti and Mariotti 1994). They also show high innovative expenditure and innovative investment ratios.

Minority participations show remarkable export orientation, notwithstanding the conflicts that could arise between international marketing strategies of joint ventures and parent companies. Finally, more recently built-up affiliates show higher R&D intensity than older ones.

10.5. Intra-group international technology flows

Table 10.7 shows the share of foreign-owned firms involved in international intra-group inflows or outflows of technology. Only 13.1 per cent of foreign affiliates receive intra-group technological inflows. The shares, however, vary greatly according to sectors and firm size. In the case of foreign affiliates, the ratio grows to 27 per cent for bigger firms, to 80 per cent in the computer industry and to 24.1 per cent in the pharmaceutical industry. This trend is confirmed by

Table 10.6 Innovation indicators of foreign affiliates by country of origin, type of ownership and year of investment

	R&D/ Turnover (foreign affiliates) (%)	Innovative firms/total (foreign affiliates) (%)	Total innovative expenditure/turnover (foreign affiliates) (%)	Innovative investments/turnover (foreign affiliates) (%)	Export/Turnover	
					Innovative foreign affiliates (%)	Foreign affiliates (%)
Countries						
European Union	1.79	57.3	2.54	1.77	26.09	26.13
Other European countries	1.45	56.4	2.14	1.39	26.60	23.12
USA	2.04	59.9	2.66	0.89	21.25	19.29
Other countries	0.65	59.2	1.13	1.80	18.02	19.25
All	1.77	58.0	2.44	1.42	23.46	22.72
Type of ownership						
CTR	1.33	57.5	1.98	0.91	21.53	21.08
MIN	4.04	59.8	4.88	3.98	32.88	32.26
NA	0.36	62.5	0.70	0.50	15.92	6.96
All	1.77	58.0	2.44	1.42	23.46	22.72
Year of investment						
Before 1982	1.47	60.2	2.12	1.25	22.14	21.16
After 1981	2.83	54.4	3.66	2.00	28.54	27.08
NA	0.73	65.4	0.98	0.90	19.42	27.73
All	1.77	58.0	2.44	1.42	23.46	22.72

Source: Elaborated from Istat, Survey on Technological Innovation 1992, and Reprint database.

Table 10.7 Share of firms involved in intra-group technology inflows and outflows

	Inflows (%)	Outflows (%)
Firm size (employees)		
20–99	6.7	6.4
100–499	13.0	12.7
500 plus	27.0	29.4
All	13.1	13.3
Industries		
Food, beverages, tobacco	5.1	8.5
Textiles, clothing, leather, footwear	2.6	2.6
Paper	17.2	17.2
Printing and publishing	4.8	0.0
Refined petroleum, nuclear fuel	18.2	9.1
Chemical products	15.8	15.8
Rubber and plastics products	5.9	14.7
Non-metallic mineral products	15.8	13.2
Basic and fabricated metals	7.2	10.8
Non-electrical machinery	14.5	12.7
Office and computing machinery	80.0	60.0
Other electrical equipment	17.0	19.1
Radio, TV and communication equipment	20.8	20.8
Scientific instruments	7.4	14.8
Motor vehicles	15.4	11.5
Other transport equipment	16.7	16.7
Other manufacturing	7.7	15.4
Pharmaceuticals	24.1	16.7
All	13.1	13.3
Pavitt macro-sectors		
High-tech	22.3	19.6
Scale-intensive	13.4	12.8
Specialized suppliers	14.2	14.2
Traditional	5.8	9.2
All	13.1	13.3
Countries		
European Union	13.6	15.8
Other European countries	6.4	6.4
USA	17.5	11.3
Other countries	4.1	10.2
All	13.1	13.3
Type of ownership		
CTR	14.0	13.9
MIN	8.8	10.8
NA	6.3	6.3
All	13.1	13.3
Year of investment		
Before 1982	16.0	14.3
After 1981	9.7	12.1
NA	7.7	11.5
All	13.1	13.3

Source: Elaborated from Istat, Survey on Technological Innovation 1992, and Reprint database.

the distribution based on taxonomy: the high-tech macro-sector shows a ratio of 22.3 per cent, compared to an average value of 13.1 per cent. It is noteworthy that foreign affiliates originate technology outflows of a similar size to inflows, especially in high-tech industries (19.6 per cent of firms).

Even if these shares are an approximate indicator, they are lower than one would expect and seem to suggest that Italian affiliates are only marginally involved in international intra-group flows of new technologies. In most industries, Italy appears as a relatively peripheral location within multinational technological networks. However, this outcome confirms the presence of some multinational R&D facilities integrated in international networks and not only oriented to the needs of local production.

Tables 10.8 and 10.9 disaggregate the same data according to the geographical origin or destination (Europe or the rest of the world). As expected, inflows from Europe concern higher shares of foreign firms than inflows from the rest of the world (mainly from the US; see Table 10.8). They are more frequent in the case of larger affiliates (500 employees and more) and in technology-intensive industries. The highest ratio is found in the computer industry (80 per cent).

Similarly, a remarkable share of foreign affiliates is involved in outflows of technology to Europe and to a lesser extent to the rest of the world (Table 10.9). In this case, too, a strong concentration in big affiliates and in high-tech industries can be observed. The highest value is again observed in the computer industry. This last observation seems to suggest that for a few specific technologies, R&D capabilities set up in Italy by foreign affiliates, having reached a high level of development, are able to originate intra-group exports of technology.

10.6. Research intensity and clusters of multinational affiliates

This is a first attempt to shed light on the innovative activities of foreign multinationals in Italy. A primary finding is that such activities are relevant in quantitative terms, as measured by R&D intensity and by other basic indicators. Indeed, in 1992, 23 per cent of total industrial R&D in Italy was made by foreign affiliates, while in the same year they accounted for less than 10 per cent of total industrial employment (Cominotti and Mariotti 1994). Therefore, their impact on the Italian system of innovation should not be underestimated.

In order to explain this data, it has been pointed out that a double composition effect takes place: a strong industry composition effect, and a firm size effect. First, this result is fully consistent with the industry distribution of foreign affiliates, concentrated in science and technology-intensive sectors (24 per cent), even if this share is decreasing in the long term. This high penetration of foreign firms, mainly through acquisitions, could originate in the structural weakness of Italian firms in most high-tech sectors (Begg *et al.* 1999), rather then by the technological attractiveness of Italy.

Table 10.8 Share of firms involved in intra-group technology inflows from Europe and the rest of the world

	Inflows from Europe (%)	Inflows from the rest of the world (%)
Firm size (employees)		
20–99	6.0	1.9
100–499	10.3	4.8
500 plus	22.2	14.3
All	10.8	5.4
Industries		
Food, beverages, tobacco	5.1	0.0
Textiles, clothing, leather, footwear	2.6	0.0
Paper	17.2	3.4
Printing and publishing	4.8	0.0
Refined petroleum, nuclear fuel	18.2	9.1
Chemical products	12.6	8.4
Rubber and plastics products	5.9	0.0
Non-metallic mineral products	10.5	7.9
Basic and fabricated metals	7.2	0.0
Non-electrical machinery	8.2	9.1
Office and computing machinery	80.0	40.0
Other electrical equipment	14.9	6.4
Radio TV and communication equipment	20.8	4.2
Scientific instruments	7.4	0.0
Motor vehicles	15.4	3.8
Other transport equipment	0.0	16.7
Other manufacturing	0.0	7.7
Pharmaceuticals	20.4	13.0
All	10.8	5.4
Pavitt macro-sectors		
High-tech	19.6	9.8
Scale-intensive	11.7	4.8
Specialized suppliers	8.8	8.8
Traditional	5.2	0.6
All	10.8	5.4
Countries		
European Union	13.1	2.9
Other European countries	6.4	1.3
USA	9.0	14.7
Other countries	4.1	0.0
All	10.8	5.4

Source: Elaborated from Istat, Survey on Technological Innovation 1992, and Reprint database.

A second factor explaining our findings is the larger size of foreign affiliates compared to Italian firms; in fact this variable is strongly related to the innovativeness of firms. In order to better appreciate the contribution of foreign affiliates to Italian innovative capabilities, however, other factors must be taken into consideration.

Table 10.9 Share of foreign affiliates involved in intra-group technology outflows to Europe and the rest of the world

	Outflows to Europe (%)	Outflows to rest of the World (%)
Firm size (employees)		
20–99	5.6	1.9
100–499	10.6	4.5
500 plus	27.8	11.9
All	11.8	4.8
Industries		
Food, beverages, tobacco	8.5	0.0
Textiles, clothing, leather, footwear	2.6	0.0
Paper	17.2	3.4
Printing and publishing	0.0	0.0
Refined petroleum, nuclear fuel	9.1	9.1
Chemical products	14.7	5.3
Rubber and plastics products	14.7	2.9
Non-metallic mineral products	13.2	2.6
Basic and fabricated metals	10.8	0.0
Non-electrical machinery	8.2	7.3
Office and computing machinery	40.0	40.0
Other electrical equipment	14.9	12.8
Radio, TV and communication equipment	20.8	12.5
Scientific instruments	14.8	0.0
Motor vehicles	11.5	3.8
Other transport equipment	0.0	16.7
Other manufacturing	7.7	7.7
Pharmaceuticals	16.7	7.4
All	11.8	4.8
Pavitt macro-sectors		
High-tech	17.9	8.9
Scale-intensive	12.4	3.4
Specialized suppliers	9.5	9.5
Traditional	8.7	0.6
All	11.8	4.8
Countries		
European Union	15.0	3.6
Other European countries	6.4	1.3
USA	7.3	9.0
Other countries	8.2	6.1
All	11.8	4.8

Source: Elaborated from Istat, Survey on Technological Innovation 1992, and Reprint database.

As pointed out in previous sections, in many high-tech, as well as in several scale-intensive industries (e.g. computers, scientific instruments, motor vehicles, chemicals), R&D intensity of foreign affiliates (measured by R&D over sales) is lower than that of domestic firms. Moreover, the data shows that in most industries

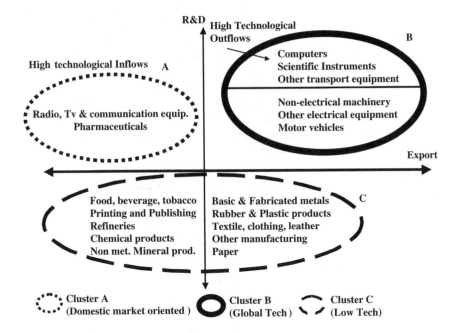

Figure 10.1 Cluster analysis.

foreign affiliates are only marginally involved in intra-group international flows of technology. Therefore, in the case of Italy, different typologies and diversified strategies of multinationals emerge with respect to innovative behaviour.

In some sectors the prevailing market-orientation of multinational operations in Italy goes along with the location of relevant R&D facilities, aiming to adapt the range of products to domestic market features. In other sectors, on the contrary, high innovation indicators go along with high export intensity and intra-group outflows of technology.

A cluster analysis permits identification of relevant typologies of foreign multi-national firms in Italy. The clusters have been constructed by comparing indicators of innovativeness and export-orientation of foreign affiliates of a given sector, with the average of foreign affiliates in all industrial sectors (see Fig. 10.1).

- A first group of industries includes communication equipments and pharma-ceuticals (cluster A): R&D intensity and intra-group technology inflows are higher than average, while export intensity is lower. The main strategy of MNEs in this case seems to be access to the Italian domestic market, mainly through acquisitions, and the exploitation of innovative advantages created abroad and transferred from the home country or from other affiliates to Italy.

- A second group of high-tech industries, on the contrary, shows higher export-intensity indicators than average (cluster B). In the case of computers, scientific instruments and other transport equipment, higher than average intra-group technology outflows can be observed. This cluster includes MNEs with European or global strategies, which are able to export both innovative goods and new technologies from Italy. In this case, R&D activities are not only connected to the local manufacturing units, but are also related to international research networks. IBM Italia is a relevant example of this typology.
- Finally, cluster C includes relatively low R&D-intensive industries, both export and local-market oriented.

If reference is made to the patterns of localization of research activities abroad by MNEs, as pointed out in Section 10.1, it can be seen that cluster A corresponds to the traditional domestic market-oriented and 'product-life-cycle' type operations, with limited adaptive R&D connected to the local productive units (*multi-domestic pattern*). Pharmaceutical affiliates of European multinationals are a typical example of this first pattern.

On the contrary, in the industries in cluster B, regional or global strategies and organizational configurations seem to prevail; they are mainly oriented to the European markets, able to produce innovations and export new goods and, to some extent, also new technologies (*internationally integrated pattern*). Computers and office machinery give the best examples of this second pattern, which could also be called the *IBM model*.

An extension of research to the number of patents granted to foreign affiliates could improve comprehension of this issue, as well as a dynamic assessment of their growth performances, related to their innovative effort.[4] However, a satisfactory explanation of the results presented here needs in-depth analysis within each of these clusters of the strategies and performances at firm and at group level.

Notes

1 A caveat must be raised about the comparability of this data, which in some cases refer to samples of enterprises.
2 This data will be available in the future, thanks to the integrated Istat firm-level database.
3 Control and non-control participations are defined on a case by case basis, considering not only ownership of shares, but also effective control.
4 Assessment of the evolution of the innovative activities of foreign affiliates in the period 1992–98 will be possible when ISTAT publishes the new survey results.

References

Antonelli, C. (1995) *The Economics of Localized Technological Change and Industrial Dynamics*. Boston: Kluwer.
Antonelli, C. (1999) *The Microdynamics of Technological Change*. London: Routledge.

Archibugi, D. and Michie, J. (1997) 'The globalisation of technology: a new taxonomy', in D. Archibugi and J. Michie (eds), *Technology, Globalisation and Economic Performance.* Cambridge: Cambridge University Press, pp. 172–197.

Balcet, G. (1990) *Joint Ventures Multinazionali.* Milano: Etas Libri.

Balcet, G. (1997) 'International relocations strategies of Italian firms', in P. Buckley and J. L. Mucchielli (eds), *Multinational Firms and International Relocation.* Cheltenham, UK: Edward Elgar, pp. 71–89.

Balcet, G. (1999) 'La globalizzazione, al di là dei miti', *Il Mulino*, 1: 26–40.

Begg, I. Dalum, B. Guerrieri, P. and Pianta, M. (1999) 'The impact of specialization in Europe', in J. Fagerberg, P. Guerrieri and B. Verspagen (eds), *The Economic Challenge for Europe: Adapting to Innovation-Based Growth.* Cheltenham, UK: Edward Elgar, forthcoming.

Cantwell, J. (1994) *Transnational Corporations and Innovatory Activities.* London: Routledge.

Ciborra, C. (1992) 'Innovations, networks and organisational learning', in C. Antonelli (ed.), *The Economics of Information Networks.* Amsterdam: North Holland, pp. 91–102.

Cominotti, R. and Mariotti, S. (1994) *Italia Multinazionale 1994.* Milano: Etas Libri.

Cominotti, R. Mariotti, S. and Mutinelli, M. (1999) *Italia Multinazionale 1998.* Rome: Documenti CNEL.

Dunning, J. (1993) *Multinational Enterprises and the Global Economy.* Wokingham: Addison.

Dunning, J. (1997) *Alliance Capitalism and Global Business.* London: Routledge.

Longhi, C. and Quéré, M. (1993) 'Innovative networks and the technopolis phenomenon: the case of Sophia-Antipolis', *Environment and Planning*, 11.

Lundvall, B. (1992) *National Systems of Innovation.* London: Pinter.

Maillat, D. (1995) 'Territorial dynamic, innovative milieus and regional policy', *Entrepreneurship and Regional Development*, 7.

Mariani, M. (1999) 'The regional–global patterns of R&D activity', *AISSEC Conference*, Siena, June.

Mytelka, L. (1991) *Strategic Partnership. States, Firms and International Competition.* London: Pinter.

OECD (1992) *Technology and Economy, The Key Relationships.* Paris.

OECD (1997) 'Internationalisation of industrial R&D: patterns and trends', OECD Statistical Working Party, Group of National Experts on Science and Technology Indicators, Paris.

Patel, P. (1997) 'Localised production of technology for global markets', in D. Archibugi and J. Michie (eds), *Technology, Globalisation and Economic Performance.* Cambridge: Cambridge University Press, pp. 198–214.

Vernon, R. (1966) 'International investment and international trade in product cycle', *Quarterly Journal of Economics*, 8: 190–207.

Vernon, R. (1979) 'The product cycle hypothesis in a new international environment', *Oxford Bulletin of Economics and Statistics*, 41: 255–67.

11

INNOVATIVE STRATEGIES AND KNOW-HOW FLOWS IN INTERNATIONAL COMPANIES*

Some evidence from Belgian manufacturing

Reinhilde Veugelers and Bruno Cassiman

11.1. Introduction

With a global business environment where the pace and scope of changes in technological know-how and consumer taste are unprecedented, managing the innovative
process has become more central in today's corporations. Innovation strategies
require increasingly more global sourcing: sensing new market and technology
trends worldwide, while adequately responding to them through generating new
ideas which are then implemented around the world (e.g. Bartlett and Ghoshal
1997). These tendencies imply a changing role of innovations in international
companies, with important implications for the role of subsidiaries in recognizing
the potential of innovations and exploiting them. Global sourcing and implementing innovations require finding an organizational structure that allows activities to
be effectively coordinated and linked on a global scale, leading to important flows
of know-how within and around MNEs.

This paper tries to assess empirically how technology flows are structured in
international firms. Belgian company data from the Eurostat Community Innovation Survey are used, which allow us to map national and international technology
transfers and acquisition of know-how used by different types of companies such
as subsidiaries of MNEs, headquarters of Belgian MNEs, Belgian exporting firms,
or local firms. First, by analyzing the innovation strategies of different types

*Paper prepared for the 7th Sorbonne International Conference on 'MNE strategies: Location,
Impact on Employment and Exports, Technological spillovers', Paris I. Comments from B. van
Pottelsberghe and other participants at the Conference are gratefully appreciated. Bruno Cassiman
acknowledges support from a TMR grant on Foreign Direct Investment and the Multinational
Corporation (FMRX-CT98-0215). The authors are grateful to DWTC and IWT for providing
the data.

of firms, the data allow us to check to what extent trends towards truly global transnational technology sourcing have materialized in a small, but traditionally very open economy, such as Belgium. Second, we determine which modes of information sourcing are most effective to access know-how. At the same time, we distinguish the relative importance of international versus national information sources to the firms. Third, we discuss the importance and directionality of internal technology transfers within MNEs. This allows us to classify subsidiaries according to the relative weight of technology transfers from headquarters to subsidiaries and from subsidiaries to headquarters. The autonomy to source externally, the importance of local external sources and the mechanisms used to transfer externally sourced know-how feature prominently in this classification of subsidiaries.

While all types of international firms, including subsidiaries, are found to be innovation active, companies which are part of an international group, affiliates but especially headquarters, have the widest innovation strategy, relying on internal as well as external technology sources. These external sources are located nationally as well as internationally and are accessed through buying strategies as well as cooperation. In addition, internal transfers and intra-group cooperation are quite pervasive in these companies, although the evidence for transfers from headquarters to subsidiaries is stronger than for the reverse flow from subsidiaries to headquarters. The analysis further points to the importance of reciprocity in know-how flows, through the prevalence of cooperation which relies on mutual exchange. Nevertheless, foreign affiliates have a relatively lower frequency of cooperation with external partners that are located internationally. This indicates that, in line with the low strategic importance of the Belgian market, foreign affiliates that have a leading role in globally linked innovations are on average not (yet) pervasive for Belgium.

The outline of the paper is as follows. In the next section we briefly review the literature. Section 11.3 lays out the research agenda and discusses the data set. In Section 11.4 we present the main results of our analysis on the innovation strategy of manufacturing firms located in Belgium. Finally, Section 11.5 concludes.

11.2. Changing innovative strategies of transnational companies

In the traditional literature on multinationals, following the seminal work of Dunning (1988), multinational activities originate out of the R&D activities of the firm. To exploit the fruits from these intangible assets beyond the home market, rather than selling technology internationally through licensing, firms may prefer to set up or acquire affiliates in host markets. The latter mode allows the multinational to appropriate more benefits from its innovations, given the high transaction costs involved when transferring technology through market mechanisms. The result is internal transfers of know-how from headquarters to subsidiaries. This is the '*center-for-global*' innovations in the Bartlett and Ghoshal (1997) terminology, with emphasis on a centralized R&D function, based on centrally located generic knowledge.

The affiliative structure, with a direct geographic link between markets and production, leaves room for a role for the subsidiaries in incremental innovations: adjusting products and processes to (changing) local needs: the '*local-for-local*' types of innovations with a strongly decentralized R&D. Motives for R&D decentralization relate to market proximity where it is important to be close to 'lead users' and adapt products and processes to local conditions. Supply-related motives relate to the creation and renewal of core capabilities by allowing access to a wider range of scientific and technological skills. While adjusting products and processes to local specificities, subsidiaries create location-specific knowledge, often through incremental innovations. These incremental innovations are generated in the local market and are associated with local knowledge flows.

Rather than seeing the geographic dispersion of MNEs as a result of knowledge creation, the emphasis in the literature has more recently shifted towards seeing the geographic dispersion of MNEs as a source for, rather than a result of, knowledge creation. Companies need to be responsive to market and technology opportunities and threats worldwide, to generate innovations which are implemented on a global scale (Bartlett and Ghoshal 1997). Since the pace and scope of technological and market change result in the increasing importance of external sources of technology, subsidiaries become important as vehicles to access (local) external sources. International R&D units are more and more engaged in cross-border interactions, both across units within the MNE and between units and external partners (Westney 1997). The subsidiary, using location-specific know-how, can continually reassess and upgrade know-how on core products and technologies to provide a basis for new generations of innovative products used throughout the organization, thus contributing to the generation of central generic knowledge. Bartlett and Ghoshal (1997) distinguish two possible innovative processes in this new view. In '*locally leveraged*' innovations, the know-how generated in one subsidiary is transferred across the company to benefit other subsidiaries. Units are engaged in worldwide learning from each other and therefore location-specific knowledge must flow from one location to another. In '*globally linked*' innovations, resources and capabilities of all units are pooled within the MNE to jointly create innovations, which can be used by all units. This strategy builds on exploiting synergies from combining complementary know-how: central generic knowledge with location-specific knowledge or location-specific knowledge from multiple locations. In the Ronstadt (1977) terminology, these are the global technology units, while Pearce and Singh (1992) label these as the internationally interdependent labs, whose role is in the long-term basic research of the group, and who will have close collaboration with other similar labs.

Which role subsidiaries play in the innovative process of the MNE depends on the level of technological capabilities and the strategic importance of the host market. On the one extreme, subsidiaries can play a purely implementing role for projects where they hold low levels of technological expertise and low strategic importance in the market. In this case the technology transfer is one of pure import into the local market. As soon as the location holds a high level of technological capability for a particular innovative project, it can be assigned a contributing role to develop generic central know-how or even play a more crucial leading role as a 'centre of excellence', with a 'global product mandate' (Rugman and Poynter 1982). In those cases, the transfers of know-how are multiplex, with the subsidiary responsible for sourcing know-how in other units of the MNE (including the headquarters), but also accessing external sources. These third parties can be found in the local environment, if the technological capability of the subsidiary follows from being embedded in a 'national innovation system', but third parties can be sourced across the globe.

In summary, the recent literature suggests a shift towards subsidiaries that are R&D active, not just in incremental, adaptive innovations, based on development activities, but rather in drastic innovations, creating basic generic know-how, where the subsidiary is as active as headquarters in external linkages. Know-how needs to flow across units and locations. This requires working on effectively linking R&D units, mobility and transfer of people, building long-distance interpersonnal communication and providing adequate reward systems and responsibilities (Westney 1997; Bartlett and Ghoshal 1997).

Empirical evidence on know-how flows within multinational organizations has never been abundant. Recent studies can easily show the transfers of know-how from parents to affiliates, but find less conclusive support for the reverse direction, from subsidiaries to headquarters. Fors (1997) finds home R&D to influence significantly host output growth, while host R&D fails to influence significantly home output growth. Frost (1998), using USPTO data for 1980–90, found evidence for the importance of headquarter patents for the innovations of subsidiaries. But patent data provided only limited evidence for the transfer of know-how from subsidiaries to headquarters. In addition, subsidiaries were using external sources, which were localized, i.e. proximity mattered a lot: patents from subsidiaries cited other entities located in the same state.

Case or survey-based evidence confirms that MNEs are increasingly engaged in cross-functional learning from different sites.[1] Pearce and Singh (1992), using an international sample, find that although 44 per cent of sample subsidiaries report that they predominantly function as internationally interdependent labs (IILs), on average 60 per cent regularly worked to adapt to local markets. Seventy per cent developed new products for local markets, while 45 per cent developed new products also used in other markets. The authors conclude that on average adapting is still an important task, but development of products also used in other markets is becoming more widespread (see also Pearce 1999). They found little evidence that subsidiaries have a role in basic research through wider programmes. The 'supervised freedom' granted to subsidiaries leads to less feedback back to the parent. The level of integration within the MNE of subsidiaries' innovative strategies often depends on historical factors, such as mergers and acquisitions, the type of industry (science versus market based), as well as home market characteristics such as size and technological competence (Niosi 1999).

Changing innovative strategies will not only affect the internal know-how transfers within multinational firms, but also the flows of know-how to and from external sources. Traditionally, subsidiaries of MNEs are seen as vehicles for the international diffusion of technology, transferring know-how to the local economies. Mansfield and Romeo (1980) found that two-thirds of UK firms indicated that their technological capabilities were raised by technology transfers from US firms to their overseas subsidiaries. But only 20 per cent felt this effect was of importance. While MNEs may or may not generate positive spillovers on host economies, at the same time they extract know-how from the host economy. Evidence for technology sourcing as motive for FDI for Japanese companies investing in the US is provided by Kogut and Chang (1991), and for the US and Japan in the EC by Neven and Siotis (1996). Survey results for R&D labs located in the US indicate the importance of access to human capital and technological expertise as a major location motive (Serapio and Dalton 1993; Florida 1997).

MNEs need not be present in the local market to access local sources. Technology is transferred through other channels than subsidiaries, such as licensing, purchase of equipment, international movement of personnel and other informal channels. Teece (1992) and Mowery (1992) stress that alliances can, in particular, be an effective and superior mechanism for linking external sources. Related to the question of whether a local presence through affiliates is necessary for know-how diffusion is the question of whether spillovers are local or not. If networks are mainly informal and tacit, then embeddedness is important and spillovers will be localized. Jaffe *et al.* (1993), using patent data, show that proximity matters and that being close to an external source increases the impact of spillovers from that source on own know-how.

11.3. Research agenda and data

An increasing emphasis on international sourcing within international companies to successfully implement global innovative strategies is profoundly influencing the pervasiveness of technology flows, internally within international companies, but also externally between international companies and other relevant third parties in the local or global environment. This paper tries to characterize empirically how technology flows within and around different types of companies in a host economy. Figure 11.1 represents the different elements. A local firm in the host economy can be an independent (domestic) firm or can be part of an international group (MNE). If part of an international organization, the local firm, being an affiliate or a headquarter company, can receive transfer from other parts of the MNE, headquarters or affiliated companies. These affiliates or headquarters can be located in the same country or in different countries. At the same time the firm can transfer or sell technology to other parts of the international organization.

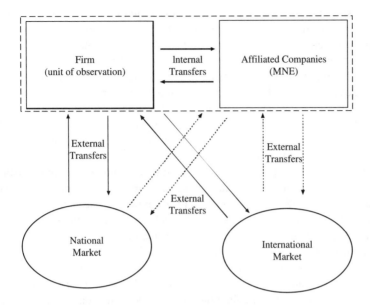

Figure 11.1 National and international technology flows.

The firm can also access technology from external sources and transfer technology externally. All these transactions can be at the local or international level. Although the affiliated companies can also source and transfer technology to an international or national external source, these flows are not studied here because of lack of information.

The paper tries to address whether firms with different international strategies (local firms, exporting firms, headquarters and subsidiaries of MNEs) have different innovation strategies. For each type of firm, the following patterns are examined and compared:

- What are the important technology sources for innovation?
  Are they internal or external? Are they national or international?
- Is technology transferred?
  Are these transactions internal or external? national or international?

Such analysis allows us to consider, among other things, whether subsidiaries of MNEs get their technology inputs from headquarters? From local external sources? From global external sources? Whether subsidiaries transfer their know-how to headquarters or other parts of the company? From which type of firm the local economy is more likely to benefit: subsidiaries, headquarters, or exporting firms? Comparing MNEs with exporters allows us to assess whether the mode of internationalization has an impact on know-how flows. Comparing headquarters and subsidiaries allows us to study the impact on the local economy simultaneously as a host as well as a home to international firms.

The analysis draws on innovation data for the Belgian manufacturing industry that were collected as part of the Community Innovation Survey conducted by Eurostat in the different member countries in 1993. The survey intended to develop insights into the problems of technological innovation in the manufacturing industry and was the first of its kind organized in many of the participating countries. A representative sample of 1,335 Belgian manufacturing firms was selected and the 13-page questionnaire sent out to them. The response rate was higher than 50 per cent (748). The researchers in charge of collecting the data also performed a limited non-response analysis and concluded that no systematic biases could be detected (Debackere and Fleurent 1995).

The survey allowed companies to be identified based on their size and innovativeness, but also on their international linkages: their export-intensity, whether they belonged to an international group, with foreign or local headquarters. It contained, next to questions on motives and problems of innovations, questions on the importance of internal and external information sources for innovation, the use of different mechanisms to acquire technology (nationally and internationally), the use of different mechanisms to transfer technology (nationally and internationally), and the use of cooperation in R&D with different types of partners (nationally and internationally). As such, the data allow us to characterize a firm's innovative strategy based on the following decisions: the technology make or buy decision, the technology sell decision and the decision to cooperate in R&D. In view of the reciprocity that lies at the basis of most cooperative agreements, we take cooperation to be a simultaneous buy and sell transaction.

While this study uses direct survey evidence on the occurrence of technology acquisition and transfers, it provides less evidence on the size of these flows and their impact on other economic variables and hence may be critized for subjectivity. To the best of our knowledge, the only alternative attempt to trace know-how flows *within* and *across* firm boundaries is the use of patent information, more particularly an analysis of citations to previous patents, see for example, Frost (1998) for the USPTO data. However, with a vast amount of information transferred without writing it down in patent applications or even in formal contracts, we consider resorting to more qualitative data like the EUROSTAT/CIS data an important source of information on firms' innovation strategy.

11.4. Results

Section 11.4.1. presents a classification of international strategies. Section 11.4.2 discusses, for each type of international firm, innovative strategies in terms of make, buy, sell and cooperate. The national versus international dimensions of technology flows through buy, sell and cooperate are detailed in Section 11.4.3. Section 11.4.4 presents a typology of foreign subsidiaries on the basis of transfers to and from affiliated firms.

11.4.1. A characterization of the sample

The companies in the sample could be identified according to their international involvement:

- SUB when the company is a subsidiary of an international group. Within this classification we will make a distinction between FSUB, subsidiaries with foreign headquarters, and BSUB, subsidiaries of an international group with Belgian headquarters.[2]
- HQ when the company is the headquarters of an international group. Given our sample, this means that the headquarters are located in Belgium.
- EXP when the company is independent or part of a Belgian group without foreign affiliates, but exporting more than 50 per cent of their production abroad.
- LOC when the company is independent or part of a Belgian group without foreign affiliates and exporting less than 50 per cent of their production abroad.

With 44 per cent of the total number of companies being local, the sample displays a dichotomy in international scope. Of the sample companies, 32 per cent are subsidiaries, most of which are foreign (28 per cent), and 4 per cent are in the HQ category. One-fifth of the companies have an exporting profile (EXP).[3] This distribution is very typical for a small and open economy such as Belgium, with little own multinationals but a pervasiveness of foreign affiliates and exporting firms. With respect to the industry distribution, local firms are over-represented in food, textiles, wood and paper and other industries, but under-represented in chemicals and electronics. Foreign subsidiaries, on the other hand, are over-represented in these sectors. Headquarters and Belgian subsidiaries are mainly found in chemicals and (non-ferrous) metals and textiles.

Size is strongly and significantly correlated with the type of international involvement. Seventy five per cent of local companies have less than 50 employees. With almost two-thirds in the category of >250 employees, headquarters and subsidiaries are over-represented in the largest size category. The majority of exporting companies (53 per cent) are found in the mid-sized category, between 50 and 500 employees.[4]

In line with the industry distribution and size correlation, an international strategy is also strongly associated with innovation. While 48 per cent of local companies are innovative (i.e. claimed to have introduced new or improved products and processes between 1990 and 92 and reported a budget for innovation), for exporting firms competing in international markets this percentage is 72 per cent. Members of an international group are even more innovative: all headquarter-type firms are innovative, while 85 per cent of subsidiaries are innovative. This last number indicates that innovation appears as an important subsidiary-level function, although the percentage is smaller than the, comparably sized headquarter type of companies. It furthermore remains to be investigated whether this innovation derives from implementing existing centralized know-how, or relies on locally generated know-how, a topic that will be analyzed in the next section. In the remainder, the sample will be restricted to innovative companies only, since the survey only provides information on knowledge flows for this subsample.[5]

11.4.2. Innovative strategy by degree of international involvement

A firm can rely on a combination of different strategies to manage its innovation process and engage in innovation. We will distinguish between knowledge inputs into the innovation process and knowledge outputs from the innovation process. With respect to knowledge inputs, we analyze two sources. First, firms can do R&D in-house and develop their own technology, which we label as the firm's MAKE decision. A second alternative strategy is to acquire technology externally, the BUY decision. Within the BUY decision a firm can acquire new technology which is *embodied* in an asset that is acquired, such as new personnel or (parts of) other firms or equipment. Alternatively, new technology can also be obtained *disembodied* such as in blueprints through a licensing agreement or by outsourcing the technology from an R&D contractor or consulting agency. While buying allows access to more specialized resources, it introduces market transaction costs. Another knowledge sourcing strategy is to absorb existing technology without any explicit involvement from the innovator. Freely available information or involuntary spillovers from innovators can be used by companies in their innovation process.

As part of its innovation strategy, the firm also decides on knowledge outputs through the transfer and sale of knowledge or technology to interested parties. Given the importance of information flows towards an economy, we will also analyze this part of the innovation strategy for the different types of firms.

A more hybrid form of obtaining knowledge and developing new technology is through cooperative agreements between firms or other research institutions. As compared to market transactions and internal development, cooperation allows a faster, less costly and lower risk mode of accessing new technology, while exploiting partner complementarity and actively managing the transfers of know-how between partners (Pisano 1990). The inherent reciprocity, which can be considered a simultaneous technology sell transaction, allows the risks of partner opportunism to be managed, reducing transaction costs (Oxley 1997). We will thus consider an innovation strategy that includes cooperation as evidence of simultaneous buy and sell activities of the firm (see Teece 1992; Mowery 1992).

11.4.2.1. Innovation strategy: make, buy, sell and cooperate

With the exception of the strategy of capitalizing on involuntary spillovers, the different sourcing strategies could be empirically identified. Given the lack of available data at the project level, the make, buy, sell and cooperate decisions are studied at the firm level. Identification of the presence of an innovation strategy and whether this innovation strategy includes make, buy, sell or cooperate, is based

Table 11.1 Innovation strategies of Belgian manufacturing firms

	Total (%)	LOC (%)	EXP (%)	HQ (%)	SUB (%)
N	494 (100%)	158 (32%)	104 (21%)	30 (6%)	202 (41%)
MAKE	**80**	**61**	**81**	**100**	**93**
BUY	**74**	**67**	**65**	**90**	**81**
DEMB	65	55	50	87	77
EMB	44	46	39	57	43
SELL	**44**	**27**	**29**	**83**	**59**
DEMB	42	24	27	80	58
EMB	26	15	13	53	38
COOP	**44**	**22**	**38**	**67**	**61**

Notes

MAKE = innovative companies that have own R&D activities and have a positive R&D budget.

BUY = innovative firms acquiring technology through licensing and/or through R&D contracting and/or through consultancy services (DEMB) and/or purchase of another enterprise and/or hiring skilled employees (EMB). We disregarded the 'embodied' purchase of equipment, mainly because too many firms responded positively on this item. The reported results are not affected by the inclusion or not of purchase of equipment in the buy option. Probably not all of them interpreted the question as buying equipment with the explicit purpose of obtaining new technologies and as an alternative to developing the technology internally (see also Evangelista *et al.* 1997).

SELL = innovative firms selling technology through licensing and/or through R&D contracting and/or through consultancy services (DEMB) and/or purchase of another enterprise and/or hiring skilled employees (EMB).

COOP = innovative firms that have cooperation in R&D, where both parties have an active involvement.

only on whether these strategies have been used or not. Information on budgets was incomplete and unreliable. Table 11.1 presents the results.

At the firm level, innovative companies typically combine internal and external sources of innovation, witness the high percentage of companies making technology (80 per cent), as well as the high percentage of firms buying technology (74 per cent). All firms that are cooperating in R&D also have own R&D activities.

Compared to local firms, all types of international firms have a significantly higher probability of having own R&D activities, especially firms belonging to international groups (HQ and SUB). These latter firms are also significantly more active in acquiring and selling technology as well as in R&D cooperation. Exporting companies are relatively less engaged in acquiring and selling technology, as well as in cooperative agreements, in comparison to subsidiaries and headquarters. Although a majority of innovative local companies have own R&D activities, they are, in comparison to international firms, relying relatively more exclusively on externally acquired technology.

Hence, in comparison to local and exporting companies, being part of an international group is most associated with combining internal and external sources for innovation. When buying technology, both disembodied and embodied technology acquisition is pursued. Embodied purchase is mainly through personnel.

Interesting to note is that subsidiaries are most active in disembodied purchase of technology and relatively less through embodied purchase, as compared to headquarters. With acquisition of technology so pervasive among companies which belong to international groups, it remains to be investigated whether this external sourcing is local or global, a topic discussed in Section 11.4.3. But it is already important to note that 47 per cent of the technology acquisition by headquarters is internal acquisition within the group, while for subsidiaries this is 56 per cent.

In order to start understanding whether Belgium gains from its openness, the other side of the transaction market should be considered as well, namely the supply of know-how. The table shows that 44 per cent of all innovative companies in the sample are engaged in selling know-how. This number is considerably lower than the number of companies acquiring know-how, but varies for the different types of companies. While the lowest numbers are for innovative companies which are local or exporting, 83 per cent of headquarters are involved in selling know-how. Subsidiaries, although comparable in size, are significantly less involved in selling technology, albeit that more than half of them are engaging in know-how sales. For companies belonging to an international group, intra-company transactions are quite pervasive: 90 per cent of headquarters sell technology to affiliated companies, while this percentage is 60 per cent for the opposite transaction, when subsidiaries sell to other group members. This is consistent with a *central-for-global* or *local-for-local* innovation strategy, where the headquarters are more active in supplying the subsidiaries with technological expertise, rather than the subsidiaries increasing the knowledge pool at the central R&D lab.

Selling technology is complementary to buying technology: 40 per cent of all innovative companies buy and sell technology at the same time. Both buying and selling technology at the same time is much less obvious for local and exporting firms; typically only one-quarter combine buying and selling technology. This percentage is much higher for headquarters and subsidiaries (resp. 80 per cent and 54 per cent). The complementarity in buying and selling technology is also apparent in the higher frequency of cooperation for headquarter or subsidiary firms. More than 60 per cent of these companies have at least one cooperative agreement.

11.4.2.2. *Importance of external sources*

While the analysis thus far has detailed how international companies are actively accessing external sources, it remains to be examined how important these sources are in the innovative process of these companies. The CIS survey data allow us to assess the importance of internal and external sources of technological information for innovative companies. The respondents were asked to rate the importance to their innovation strategy of different information sources for the innovation process on a 5-point Likert scale (from unimportant (1) to crucial (5)). In order to manage the answers to these many questions, we aggregated the answers by averaging the scores on related variables. Table 11.2 summarizes the different categories.

Table 11.2 Sources of information for the innovation process

Internal Information Sources: INTERN	Information within the company
Internal Information Sources: INTGR	Information within the group
External Information Sources	
From Vertically Related Firms: LINK	Information from suppliers
	Information from equipment suppliers
	Information from customers
From Competitors: COMP	Information from close competitors
From Research Institutes: SCIENCE	Information from universities
	Information from public research institutes
	Information from technical institutes
Freely Available Information: GINFO	Patent information
	Specialized conferences, meetings, publications
	Trade conferences, seminars

Table 11.3 Importance of information sources for the innovation process[a]

	Total (%)	LOC (%)	EXP (%)	HQ (%)	SUB (%)
INTERN	72	62	69	87	79
INTGR	36	17[b]	25[b]	37	57
LINK	45	40	49	60	45
COMP	33	30	26	47	36
SCIENCE	4	4	1	0	5
GINFO	17	12	10	33	23

Notes

a The percentage of companies rating the various sources as very important to crucial (i.e. a score of 4 or 5).

b Only very few local and exporting firms are part of a group. The average score of INTGR for these types is therefore not very revealing.

The percentage of companies rating the various sources as very important to crucial (i.e. a score of 4 or 5) is reported in Table 11.3 for the various international categories.

Sources internal to the company (INTERN) are in all cases most important for innovation. The headquarters especially score high on this item. Subsidiaries, given their comparable size, rate this source as less important as compared to headquarters, although it is still their most important technology information source. For subsidiaries, sources internal to the group (INTGR) are very important. This source is ranked second, which is not the case for the other companies. In particular, headquarters find suppliers and customers more important as an information source. These results are again consistent with the *central-for-global* innovation strategy of MNEs and correspond to the results of Pearce and Singh (1992), who also found 77 per cent of subsidiaries to indicate own ideas, approved by the parent, to be a regular source of project ideas. Only 13 per cent indicated suggestions from parent labs as a regular source, but 70 per cent rated them as an occasional source.

Table 11.4 Cooperative agreements by type of partner[a]

	Total (%)	LOC (%)	EXP (%)	HQ (%)	SUB (%)
COOPLink	28	13	25	50	38
COOPComp	7	3	9	13	8
COOPScienc	28	12	23	57	39
COOPIntgr	24	2[b]	4[b]	53	47

Notes

a   COOPLink: at least one cooperative agreement with suppliers or customers.
    COOPComp: at least one cooperative agreement with competitors.
    COOPScienc: at least one cooperative agreement with universities, public or
    private research institutes.
    COOPIntgr: at least one cooperative agreement within the group.

b   Only very few local and exporting firms are part of a group. The average score
    for these types is therefore not very relevant.

Among external information sources, the vertically related customers and suppliers in particular are important sources of information. For all types, this is the most important external source, followed by competitors. Interesting to note is the low importance of research institutes, with only 4 per cent rating them to be very important or crucial. Although this source is not crucial, it is still on average moderately important.[6] A sectoral differentiation is typical here, depending on the science-based nature of the technology used.

One mechanism through which external sources may be accessed is cooperative agreements. As reported in Table 11.4, disentangling different types of cooperative partners for the various firm types confirms the importance of inter-group cooperation for headquarters and subsidiaries, confirming that cooperative agreements perform an important knowledge transfer function. For subsidiaries, this is the most important type of cooperative agreement. Similarly we observe that vertically linked companies are most important as external partners for the other firm types. Somewhat unexpectedly, research institutes are important cooperative partners, especially for the headquarter firms. All this suggests that research institutes cannot be neglected as an external source, but that on average they tend to be only moderately important to the innovativeness of companies.

In summary, although internal and external information sources are important to subsidiaries, their higher share of within-group sources and their lower share of within-company and external sources in comparison to headquarters suggest that the role of subsidiaries in generating global innovations is on average for the Belgian economy not pervasive. Along with Frost (1998) and Pearce and Singh (1992), these results support the importance of headquarters for subsidiaries, while the evidence of transfer of know-how from subsidiaries to headquarters is more limited, witness the lesser importance of within-group sourcing for the HQ type. The lesser importance of science as a source of information indicates that, on average, the Belgian science system does not seem to be a crucial location factor for subsidiaries.

11.4.3. National versus international innovation strategies

Given that information exchanges are such an important element in the innovation strategy of firms, especially for the internationally involved companies, it remains to be investigated whether these exchanges are national or international. At the same time, this should reveal the directionality of these information flows for internationally active companies. In addition, policy makers attempt to maximize the knowledge in-flows to the local economy. We are in a position to analyze which parts of the innovation strategy and which type of firm are more likely to generate these kinds of information flows.

11.4.3.1. National versus international technology acquisition

When buying technology, both national and international sources are used, albeit that international transactions are used more than national transactions. Table 11.5 presents the results. On average 57 per cent of companies buy technology internationally, and 53 per cent buy nationally. For local companies and exporting companies, the prevalence of national overrules the international transactions. Interesting to note is the position of subsidiaries. For every foreign affiliate that buys technology nationally, there are 1.5 foreign affiliates that buy technology internationally, the highest ratio among all types of companies.

Disentangling disembodied and embodied acquisition of technology is important, since the embodied acquisition is typically hypothesized to be more localized than the disembodied purchase. The results support this hypothesis. International disembodied transactions are used more than national disembodied transactions. Only for local companies does the prevalence of national transactions in disembodied acquisition slightly overrule international transactions. Interesting to note is

Table 11.5 National and international technology acquisition

	Total (%)	LOC (%)	EXP (%)	HQ (%)	SUB[a]	
					FSUB (%)	BSUB (%)
BUY NAT	**53**	**56**	**48**	**67**	**50**	**55**
DEMB NAT	38	39	29	57	42	34
EMB NAT	35	42	34	40	27	41
BUY INAT	**57**	**39**	**43**	**80**	**76**	**66**
DEMB INAT	54	37	40	77	73	62
EMB INAT	20	11	12	33	29	31

a Because our sample consists of firms located in Belgium, we need to distinguish between foreign and Belgian subsidiaries in order to disentangle the national versus international elements of the innovation strategy without exaggerating the national transactions of Belgian subsidiaries, which might just reflect transfers between headquarters and their Belgian subsidiaries, or, the international transactions of foreign subsidiaries, which might also reflect transfers between foreign headquarters and their subsidiaries located in Belgium.

the position of subsidiaries, who have the strongest international orientation in disembodied buying of technology. Contrary to the profile of disembodied purchase, there are more companies that buy embodied technology nationally (35 per cent) than internationally (20 per cent). The national orientation is again highest for the local companies. Only for foreign subsidiaries are there more companies that acquire technology embodied internationally than nationally.[7]

In conclusion, although a majority of companies are acquiring technology nationally, the local embeddedness should not be overrated, since international technology acquisition is even more prevailing, especially disembodied technology acquisition through licensing. Only embodied acquisition through personnel has clearly a more national orientation. The international orientation of external sourcing is less pronounced for the local companies, but most pronounced for the headquarters and subsidiaries of foreign companies. For the case of foreign subsidiaries this result puts in perspective the importance of local external technology sourcing as a motive for a foreign presence through embedded affiliates in Belgium. The high percentage of international technology acquisition for headquarters suggests that having own affiliates abroad is conductive to acquiring technology internationally. Exporting firms do not appear to be more successful at acquiring technology internationally compared to local firms. This puts doubt on exporting as an effective mechanism for knowledge acquisition.

To better understand the role of international technology acquisition in the innovative strategies of affiliates, it is important to assess the extent to which these international flows are received from within the company, typically from the headquarters, or are truly external, originating from third parties. For companies belonging to an international group, the survey data allow us to assess whether national and international acquisition is internal to the group or not. Of headquarters that acquired technology internationally, 42 per cent reported internal acquisitions within the group, i.e. transfers from subsidiaries to headquarters. This indicates the importance of headquarters in sourcing technology through its foreign subsidiaries according to a '*locally leveraged*' or '*globally linked*' innovation strategy.[8] Of foreign affiliates located in Belgium and acquiring technology from abroad, 66 per cent indicated international internal transfers within the group, from sister or typically parent companies. The higher percentage of internal acquisition for subsidiaries compared to headquarters underscores, in line with Frost (1998), the importance of headquarters or other leading sister companies as sources for innovation within subsidiaries located in Belgium. While there is strong evidence for substantial internal transfers, the direction is mostly from headquarters to subsidiaries.

11.4.3.2. National versus international technology sale

While the evidence on the selling of technology, presented in Section 4.2.1, indicates the importance of MNEs as vehicles for technology diffusion, it remains

Table 11.6 National and international technology sale

	Total (%)	LOC (%)	EXP (%)	HQ (%)	SUB	
					FSUB (%)	BSUB (%)
SELL NAT	**17**	**18**	**11**	**13**	**17**	**31**
SELL DEMB NAT	15	16	8	13	15	31
SELL EMB NAT	8	9	8	10	6	14
SELL INAT	**39**	**17**	**25**	**77**	**56**	**69**
SELL DEMB INAT	37	16	23	73	55	62
SELL EMB INAT	22	9	10	47	32	55

to be investigated whether these transfers occur nationally in the host market or internationally.

Table 11.6 shows that technology transactions that remain in the local market are relatively less frequent: only 17 per cent of innovative companies have transferred technology locally, versus 39 per cent of innovative companies selling internationally.[9] The majority of transactions by innovative companies in the Belgian sample are international transactions, mostly disembodied. While there are about as many local companies selling technology nationally as well as internationally, the international orientation of transactions is highest for the headquarters. Also, for foreign subsidiaries, the international orientation is more pronounced. In contrast to the embodied acquisition of know-how which was mostly localized, the embodied transfer of know-how is strongly international: for every company transferring know-how embodied nationally there are 2.7 companies transferring know-how embodied internationally, an effect which is due to the Belgian MNEs and foreign subsidiaries. This result suggests a strong international mobility of the Belgian workforce employed within these firms.[10]

Given this strong prevalence of international know-how flows in international groups, it is interesting to check whether these transfers remain within the group. Of headquarters that transfer technology internationally, 91 per cent report internal international transfers, while this figure is 81 per cent for foreign subsidiaries and 85 per cent for Belgian subsidiaries. These high numbers again reflect the importance of internal transfers crossing national boundaries within MNEs and reflect that MNEs are an important channel for international technology diffusion. We find that Belgian subsidiaries play an important role for foreign sister companies, consistent with the '*globally linked*' innovation strategy.

To conclude, the embodied and disembodied transfer of know-how to the local economy is quite restricted. As we discuss next, the international focus in buying and selling strategies contrasts with the more national focus observed in technological cooperation. The hope is that such cooperation is an effective mode of transferring know-how to the local economy.

11.4.3.3. National versus international cooperation

Although the evidence for local embeddness in technology sourcing so far is not very strong for foreign subsidiaries, there are other modes through which companies can access externally available know-how. Cooperating in R&D can be used to source as well as transfer technology externally. Section 11.4.2.1 has already indicated that cooperation is quite pervasive among innovative companies, especially for those companies belonging to an international group. The survey allows us to check whether partners in cooperation are national or international, as well as affilated companies or independent third parties.

Table 11.7 reveals that most companies, especially those belonging to an international group, combine national and international cooperation, albeit that more companies are engaged in cooperation with national partners than with international partners. For local companies the national orientation is somewhat higher, and for HQ this is somewhat smaller, but these differences are not significant. It is interesting to note that headquarters tend to be more engaged in cooperative agreements than subsidiaries. Given their technology transfer function, we find this difference to be more important internationally.

The type of partner differs between national and international cooperative agreements in R&D. The national orientation of alliances is highest for vertical alliances. On the one hand, this indicates that proximity might be more important to benefit from a cooperative agreement with suppliers or customers. On the other hand, this might just be the result of the availability of partners. The national orientation of alliances is lowest for research, leaving the largest category of external partners for international alliances to be research institutes.

Although more than one-third of innovation-active foreign affiliates have vertical alliances with national partners, it is the type of company that has the lowest share of local vertical partners in national cooperation. Similarly for national cooperation

Table 11.7 National and international cooperation

| | Total (%) | LOC (%) | EXP (%) | HQ (%) | SUB | |
					FSUB (%)	BSUB (%)
COOP NAT	**36**	**13**	**30**	**57**	**53**	**55**
COOP NAT link	26	11	22	50	35	45
COOP NAT science	21	8	16	47	28	38
COOP NAT comp	6	3	9	13	6	14
COOP NAT intgr	—	—	—	37	35	38
COOP INAT	**32**	**11**	**20**	**60**	**49**	**52**
COOP INAT link	14	6	10	33	19	17
COOP INAT science	18	7	15	37	24	38
COOP INAT comp	2	1	2	7	2	7
COOP INAT intgr	—	—	—	40	27	31

with research institutes, foreign affiliates have the lowest share of local research partners in national cooperation. So again we find little evidence for MNEs using foreign affiliates to access the local science system in Belgium. For companies belonging to an international group, cooperation with affiliate firms is quite pervasive. For the foreign subsidiaries, affiliated companies are the most frequent partners, especially in international cooperation, reflecting that these subsidiaries have a function in locally leveraged or globally linked innovations. This is also the case for headquarters that transfer technology to their international affiliates through cooperative agreements.

In summary, headquarters and Belgian subsidiaries are as active in national as in international alliances and with several different types of partner: vertically related firms, research institutes and affiliates of the same international group. Foreign affiliates are also active in alliances, even somewhat more in national than international alliances, but the scope of their different types of partner is more restricted, with a larger share of affiliated companies. All this seems to suggest that for foreign affiliates located in Belgium the emphasis is more on a 'contributing' role in the global innovative strategy of their parent, with specific tasks for globally linked innovation projects, but less of a 'leading' role on average, because this would involve more cooperation with third parties, nationally and internationally. The absence of a leading role corresponds to the low strategic importance of the local Belgian market. Export-oriented companies are least cooperative (only 38 per cent have cooperative agreements), with the strongest national orientation. All this suggests that exports are not the most straightforward internationalization mode that is conductive to international cooperation, as it also was not for buying technology.

11.4.4. A typology of foreign subsidiaries

The analysis so far has compared companies that differ in their international strategy: local and exporting firms versus headquarters and affiliates. As the theoretical literature strongly suggests, the large group of foreign affiliates cannot be treated as one homogeneous block, when describing their innovative activities. Zeroing in on the foreign subsidiaries only, the information available in the survey on internal transfers of information within multinational groups allows us to classify foreign subsidiaries according to their role in the MNE's innovative strategies. Once subsidiaries have been identified according to this role, the classification can then be used to look for possible differences in innovative strategies with regard to buying and selling know-how and cooperating in R&D. Any difference in the local orientation when buying and selling know-how can be particularly helpful in assessing which type of foreign subsidiaries are attractive for the host economy.

Figure 11.2 shows that of the 208 subsidiaries present in the sample, there are 23 per cent which are not innovative active, 17 per cent of which are innovative active but have no own R&D, that is rely exclusively on buying (6 per cent). For these companies we have no information on transfers received. Compared to the total sample, this is a relatively low percentage, suggesting that affiliates are most

Innovation-active foreign subsidiaries with internal R&D (MAKE) (n=208)

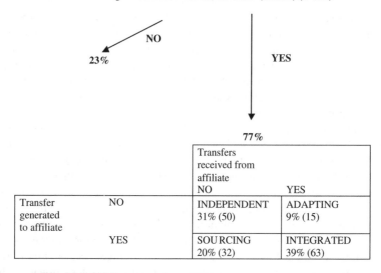

| | | Transfers received from affiliate | |
		NO	YES
Transfer generated to affiliate	NO	INDEPENDENT 31% (50)	ADAPTING 9% (15)
	YES	SOURCING 20% (32)	INTEGRATED 39% (63)

Figure 11.2 Typology of foreign subsidiaries.

likely to have their own innovative capacities. The 160 subsidiaries that have an own R&D capacity (MAKE) can be classified according to whether or not they receive know-how from within the group and/or whether they generate transfers of know-how to the group. Companies are classified on 'Transfers received from affilates' as YES when they report that from the know-how they received, internal within-group sources were accessed AND when these internal group sources were at least moderately important to the innovative process of the subsidiary.[11] For the variable 'Transfers generated to affiliates', only information on the occurrence of such transfers was available, not on the importance of these transfers.

About 31 per cent of foreign subsidiaries receive no transfers and also generate no transfers to the group. These are labelled as *independent* or autonomous subsidiaries. These affiliates, quite important in number, may be older, longer-established subsidiaries that traditionally have built up an independent 'local for local' innovative strategy. Apparently, their parents, when implementing a truly global innovative strategy, still have an important task to integrate the local know-how process in the central know-how process. Only 9 per cent of foreign subsidiaries receive internal transfers, but do not generate any internal transfers. These are the typical *adapting* subsidiaries, implementing 'central for global' innovations while adjusting them to the local market. This low number does not suggest that adapting is not important, but that it is less important as the main innovative activity of affiliates. Subsidiaries that have a role as sensors, scanning technological developments to direct global innovations, receive no internal transfers, but generate transfers to affiliated companies. These *sourcing* subsidiaries account for

20 per cent in the sample. The largest group of affiliates is the one that simultaneously receives and generates internal know-how transfers: 39 per cent of foreign affiliates are thus labelled as *integrated*. The two-way internal flows in which they are engaged could indicate a leading role in 'locally leveraged' or even 'globally linked' innovations, but a contributing role, with specific tasks in 'globally linked' innovations, could also fit into this characterization.[12]

Another important mode through which transfers of know-how can materialize are cooperative agreements among affiliated companies. Consistent with the classification, one would expect independent subsidiaries to be the least engaged in such alliances and the integrated subsidiaries the most. Also, for sourcing and adapting subsidiaries such alliances can be an integral part of their innovative strategy, albeit that the intensity of know-how flows between partners need not be equal in all directions. As expected, the independent subsidiaries are significantly less likely to be engaged in such alliances as compared to the other affiliates. Only 34 per cent of them have intra-firm alliances, as compared to 47 per cent for all subsidiaries.

Having classified subsidiaries according to their role in global innovations, it remains to be analyzed whether different types of subsidiaries use different innovative strategies. At the same time, the national versus international dimension in external technology buying, selling and cooperating may differ. Table 11.8 presents these results.

Not surprisingly, the sourcing and integrated affiliates have the highest frequency of locally buying technology. Similarly, the integrated affiliates also have the highest frequency of alliances with local external partners. Although more than half of the sourcing affiliates have alliances with local partners, this is not as high as expected, compared to the other types of subsidiaries. The independent and adapting affiliates are less actively engaged in accessing external local know-how: the independent affiliates are particularly under-utilizing cooperation with local partners, while the adapting affiliates are particularly less involved in the buying of local technology. The independent subsidiaries seem to be not only independent from their group, but also independent from external sources in general.

Table 11.8 National and international innovation strategies of foreign subsidiaries

	Independent (%)	Adapting (%)	Sourcing (%)	Integrated (%)	Total (%)
BUY NAT	46	33	53	56	50
BUY INAT	56	87[a]	78	86[a]	75
SELL NAT	4	7	28	25	18
SELL INAT	26	27	72[a]	84[a]	58
COOP ext NAT	36	53	53	60	51
COOP ext INAT	24	40	44	54	41

The Chi-squared independence tests are significant for all row variables at the 1 per cent level.
a Since the data do not allow to disentangle internal versus external BUY and SELL, these percentages are already high from internal BUY and SELL by the definition of the categories.

Cooperation with external partners located internationally reflects a discretionary power to scan worldwide for partners that are most complementary. Not surprisingly then, the integrated affiliates have the highest propensity to be engaged in such alliances and the independent the least. The international buying variable cannot disentangle internal and external transactions. As such, the score for adapting and integrated affiliates is high by definition, already based on internal transactions. But interesting to note is the high frequency of international buying for sourcing companies. Since, by definition, these are not internal transactions, this result suggests that the market that these subsidiaries are supposed to scan extends the Belgian market to include a wider, European, market. The international cooperative agreements of these companies should be likewise interpreted. Not surprisingly, the independent affiliates have the lowest frequency of buying technology internationally. Still, 56 per cent of them have acquired technology from an external partner which is internationally located.

An important question from a policy point of view is to find out which type of subsidiary is most attractive for the host economy in terms of being able to absorb most know-how from is. The integrated and the sourcing affiliates have the highest propensity to sell to local partners. In combination with the high frequency of allying with local partners, these companies constitute a serious source of accessible know-how for the local economy. The adapting and especially the independent subsidiaries are the least engaged in local transfer of technology. The independent subsidiaries, for which this lack of local selling comes on top of the low propensity to ally locally, are therefore the least interesting for the local economy in terms of transfers of know-how.

11.5. Conclusions

The EUROSTAT/CIS survey results for Belgium clearly indicate that internationally operating firms are more innovation active. But while all types of international firms, including subsidiaries, are found to be more innovation active, companies which are part of an international group, as affiliates but especially as headquarters, have the widest innovation strategy, relying on internal as well as external technology sources. Internal within-group transfers and intra-group cooperation are quite pervasive in these companies. In addition, they access not only local but also international external technology sources, through buying strategies as well as cooperative R&D agreements. While disembodied purchase of know-how (licensing) is most international, the embodied purchase of know-how through personnel mobility is most localized. Also for R&D contracting and R&D cooperation the local orientation is stronger. Hence, having a presence in the foreign market is more conducive to accessing foreign know-how through these mechanisms.

The evidence on the difference between headquarters and affiliates in their frequency of internal international buying and selling, and the importance of intra-group sourcing, suggests, in line with previous studies, that transfers from headquarters to subsidiaries are more frequent and important compared to the reverse flow from subsidiaries to headquarters.

The analysis further suggests an important role for reciprocity in know-how flows, through the prevalence of cooperation which relies on mutual exchange. In addition, there is a strong complementarity between selling and buying technology. Interestingly, those firms receiving know-how are also more likely to transfer know-how. In a companion paper, Cassiman and Veugelers (1999) show how companies that have access to international technology markets, either by directly buying technology internationally or through international cooperative agreements, are more likely to transfer know-how nationally through the direct sale of technology, but in particular through national cooperative agreements. This holds especially for the headquarters and subsidiaries. But the results presented here also strongly suggest a complementarity between technology transfers occurring internally within the MNE and transfers to the local economy. Foreign affiliates which are receiving internal know-how, when they are integrated in the multinational innovative process, are more likely to generate local transfers and to cooperate with local partners. Those affiliates that are operating most independently from their multinational structure are least likely to transfer know-how locally or to cooperate locally. This result suggests that a trend towards having subsidiaries playing a more integrative role in multinational innovations is not necessarily detrimental for the host economy, at least in terms of being able to benefit from the spillovers of this know-how.

Although most of these results are confirmed in econometric analysis, correcting for firm and industry characteristics (see Cassiman and Veugelers 1999), more work is needed to test the robustness of these results, before the results can be molded into firm conclusions for MNE's innovative strategies and host government's innovative policy. The Eurostat data allow us to compare results across EC countries. This would allow us to identify possible host market characteristics which, the literature suggests, influence the results. More importantly, the analysis should be extended beyond whether know-how flows occur or not, towards assessing the efficiency of such flows, and their impact on innovative performance and growth.

Notes

1 For some recent studies, see the Research Policy Special Issue on the Internationalization of Industrial R&D, 1999, 2–3.
2 Incorporating BSUB with their HQ group did not significantly alter the results of the analysis.
3 Note that also the HQ and the SUB category typically have a high export-intensity.
4 To compare, for the total sample, 43 per cent is in the <50 category, 24 per cent in the 50–250, 16 per cent in the 250–500 and 17 per cent in the >500 category.
5 Of the total 494 innovative companies, 32 per cent are LOC, 21 per cent are EXP, while 6 per cent are HQ and 41 per cent are SUB (35 per cent FSUB and 6 per cent BSUB).
6 The percentage of companies rating this source at least moderately important (i.e. a score of at least 3) is on average 25 per cent, but for headquarters, this percentage increases to 50 per cent.

7 The national–international ratio can be further detailed for the different modes of embodied and disembodied purchase. Most internationally oriented are licensing. R&D contracting is nationally as important as internationally. Only for foreign subsidiaries are there more companies outsourcing internationally than nationally. For embodied purchase of technology, the national orientation is solely due to the item personnel. For buying equipment and take-overs, international is more important than national. Hence, know-how acquisition through personnel mobility is the most localized.

8 None of the national acquisitions made by foreign affiliates are internal within the group. For Belgian headquarter companies, internal within-group transactions only constitute a limited 5 per cent of national acquisitions made by these companies. For Belgian subsidiaries this is 31 per cent, indicating important transfers from the headquarters, which happen to be located in Belgium.

9 Note the significantly higher local technology transfer by Belgian subsidiaries. Seventy-four per cent of these subsidiaries are, however, transferring technology internally, most likely to their headquarters.

10 Detailing the channels which are used most often to transfer know-how, we find that for international transactions, consulting is used most often, followed by personnel, informal contacts, licenses and R&D contracts. Of little importance is selling of companies and selling of equipment to transfer technology. For national transactions, personnel, consulting and informal contacts are most often used. There are no significant differences in the relative importance of these channels according to the type of firm.

11 When using as criterion for importance of internal group sources at least very important, a considerable number of integrated subsidiaries in particular shift to the sourcing category, leaving 33 per cent sourcers and 26 per cent integrated companies.

12 For the Belgian subsidiaries, we find that 74 per cent are engaged in transfers to affiliates, compared to 59 per cent of foreign subsidiaries, explained by their proximity to headquarters: only 19 per cent of the Belgian subsidiaries are classified as independent and 7 per cent as adapting, but 48 per cent are sourcing and 26 per cent integrated.

References

Bartlett, C. and Ghoshal, S. (1997) 'Managing innovation in the transnational corporation', in M. Tushman and P. Anderson (eds), *Managing Strategic Innovation and Change*. Oxford University Press, pp. 452–76.

Blomström, M. and Kokko, A. (1998) 'Multinational corporations and spillovers', *Journal of Economic Surveys*, 12: 247–77.

Cantwell, J. (1989) *Technological Innovation and the Multinational Corporation*. Basil Blackwell.

Cassiman, B. and Veugelers, R. (1999) 'Importance of international linkages for local know-how flows: some econometric evidence from Belgium', *Mimeo*.

Debackere, K. and Fleurent, I. (1995) 'De CIS-enquete voor Vlaanderen: een non-response analyse', Working Paper, *Vlerick Management School*, Gent, Belgium.

Dunning, J. (1988) 'The Eclectic paradigm of international production: a restatement and some possible extensions', *Journal of International Business Studies*, 19: 1–31.

Evangelista, R., Perani, G., Rapiti, F. and Archibugi, D. (1997) 'Nature and impact of innovation in manufacturing industry: some evidence from the Italian innovation survey', *Research Policy*, 26: 521–36.

Florida, R. (1997) 'The globalisation of R&D: results of a survey of foreign affiliated R&D labs in the US', *Research Policy*, 26: 85–103.

Fors, G. (1997) 'Utilization of R&D results in the home and foreign plants of multinationals', *Journal of Industrial Economics*, 45: 341–55.

Frost, A. (1998) 'The geographic sources of innovation in the multinational enterprise: US subsidiaries and host country spillovers, 1980–1990', Ph.D. Sloan School of Management, MIT.

Jaffe, A., Trajtenberg, M. and Henderson, R. (1993) Geographic localisation of knowledge spillovers as evidenced by patent citations. *Quarterly Journal of Economics*, 577–98.

Kogut, B. and Chang, S. (1991) 'Technological capabilities and Japanese foreign direct investment in the US', *Review of Economics and Statistics*, 401–13.

Mansfield, E. and Romeo, A. (1980) 'Technology transfer to overseas subsidiaries by US based firms', *Quarterly Journal of Economics*, 737–50.

Mowery, D. (1992) 'International collaborative ventures and US firms' technology strategies', in O. Grandstrand, L. Hakanson and S. Sjolander (eds), *Technology Management and International Business*. New york: Wiley, pp. 209–232.

Neven, D. and Siotis, G. (1996) 'Technology sourcing and FDI in the EC: an empirical evaluation', *International Journal of Industrial Organisation*, 14: 543–60.

Niosi, J. (1999) 'The internationalisation of industrial R&D: from technology transfer to the learning organisation', 28: 107–17.

Oxley, J. (1997) 'Appropriability hazards and governance in strategic alliances: a transaction cost approach', *Journal of Law, Economics and Organisation*, 387–409.

Pearce, R. (1999) 'Decentralized R&D and strategic competitiveness: globalised approaches to generation and use of technology in MNEs', *Research Policy*, 28: 157–78.

Pearce, R. and Singh, S. (1992) 'Internationalisation of R&D among the world's leading enterprises: survey analysis of organisation and motivation', in O. Grandstrand, L. Hakanson and S. Sjolander (eds), *Technology Management and International Business*. New York: Wiley, pp. 137–62.

Pisano, G. (1990) 'The R&D boundaries of the firm: an empirical analysis', *Administrative Science Quarterly*, 35: 153–76.

Rugman, A. and Poynter, T. (1982) 'World product mandate: how will multinationals respond?', *Business Quarterly*.

Serapio, M. and Dalton, D. (1993) 'Foreign R&D facilities in the US', *Research and Technology Management*, 33–9.

Teece, D. (1997) 'Capturing value from technological innovation: integration, strategic partnering and licensing decision', in M. Tushman and P. Anderson (eds), *Managing Strategic Innovation and Change*. Oxford University Press, pp. 287–306.

Westney, E. (1997) 'Multinational enterprises and cross-border knowledge creation', *Sloan Working Paper*, 159–97.

12

FOREIGN DIRECT INVESTMENT AS A TECHNOLOGY SOURCING STRATEGY*

The case of Korean multinationals

Luis Miotti and Frédérique Sachwald

12.1. Introduction

From the end of the 1980s onwards, Korean firms launched an impressive effort to invest abroad, which lasted for a decade. They invested massively in South-East Asia in order to compensate for increasing production costs in Korea. More surprisingly, they have also made large investments in North America and Western Europe, not only in cases when Korean exports faced trade barriers, but also in high-tech sectors. Outward direct investment (ODI) by latecomer firms from an emerging country in leading countries and in high-tech sectors does not fit well with the received theory of multinational companies. Indeed, according to the latter, one fundamental determinant of ODI is the possession of some competitive advantage, while Korean firms typically have no such advantages *vis-à-vis* American and European competitors.

This paper argues that in the context of globalization, multinationals have become much more common. As a consequence, multinational operations may not only aim at exploiting competitive advantages, but can also be part of a strategy to overcome weaknesses, and in particular to source technological resources abroad. The second section discusses this evolution and considers the relevant theoretical developments, and the third section tests this hypothesis for Korean ODI in the United States, which is a particularly relevant case. The conclusion considers implications for the theory of multinational firms.

*We acknowledge research assistance from Serge Perrin, who established the database on firms' investment which was originally in Korean. We thank Wang Yung-Joong for his help with respect to the data on firms' investments and Rajneesh Narula for his useful comments on an earlier version of the paper. This article has been written in the context of a research project on Korean outward direct investment at ifri, which is supported by the Korea Foundation and the results of which will be published as a book in late 1999.

12.2. Globalization and the theory of multinational firms

At a very general level, globalization may be characterized by two major trends, deeper and broader international economic integration.[1] One major channel for deeper integration is the expansion of foreign operations by multinational firms, while broader internationalization means that more countries are involved. Emerging countries have fully participated in globalization; they have become major actors in international trade from the 1970s onwards and have also generated new multinationals.

Section 12.2 considers the diversification of multinationals and the consequences for the theory of international production. It focuses on the role of competitive advantage as a determinant of foreign investment.

12.2.1. From ownership advantage to technology sourcing

The observation of American firms after World War II has had a deep and long-lasting influence on multinational theory. In particular, one early insight on the determinants of multinationality has been the proposition that firms need to possess specific competitive advantages to venture abroad (Hymer 1976). In the 1960s, such advantages, based on innovative and marketing capabilities, were mainly possessed by American firms, which wanted to make the most of them by accessing foreign markets (Vernon 1966).

12.2.1.1. European and Japanese multinationals

Since the 1970s, European and Japanese economies have largely caught up with the American economy. This macroeconomic evolution corresponds to the development of strong competitive advantages by European and Japanese firms and to their progressive multinationalization.[2] The historical experience of European and Japanese firms thus seems to correspond broadly to the general framework of analysis, according to which firms have to develop competitive advantages in their national environment before they venture abroad.

At the same time, European and Japanese firms have resorted to ODI to source technology from the US. Firms may resort to different organizational modes in order to transfer technology from a foreign country. They have traditionally bought licenses. More recently, they have also settled R&D laboratories in high-tech clusters and entered alliances with innovative foreign firms. European firms have extensively resorted to these modes of research cooperation and technology transfer in order to tap into the dynamic pool of American R&D resources.[3] This trend has been particularly strong in the fields of biotechnology (Sharp 1994; Shan and Song 1997) and electronics (Hobday 1994; Delapierre and Millelli 1994). At the end of the 1990s, European firms tend to acquire young innovative American firms in the fast-moving field of information technology. Telecommunication equipment companies such as Alcatel or Siemens, for example, acquired American firms to speed up their learning of Internet-related competencies.

The contribution of empirical tests to the issue of technology sourcing as a pull factor (Anand and Kogut 1997) may be considered as twofold.

First, tests on ODI by European and Japanese multinationals have not found as strong a support for the competitive advantage hypothesis as previous studies of American multinationals. This has been the case for both the goodwill and technology-based advantages,[4] but the discussion below focuses on the latter.

In the empirical studies on the determinants of Japanese investment in the US, results for R&D variables are mixed. Japanese firms' R&D intensity is positively related to their propensity to invest in the US (Hennart and Park 1994). However, the exact interpretation of this correlation is difficult. Indeed, R&D intensity is highly correlated between countries and it seems that FDI in the US tends to be directed to industries with strong R&D expenditures (Kogut and Park 1991; Anand and Kogut 1997). It is thus difficult to decide whether the correlation between R&D intensity and FDI is indicative of technology transfer or rather of technology sourcing. According to the internalization theory, Japanese firms should resort to greenfield and majority-owned ventures whenever they intend to transfer technology and know-how advantages to their affiliates in the US.[5] This hypothesis has been successfully tested in the case of American affiliates abroad (Gomes-Casseres 1989), but the influence of R&D spending on the mode of entry has proved difficult to establish in the case of Japanese multinationals. Some tests indicate that high R&D spending fosters full ownership (Hennart and Park 1993), but not others (Hennart 1991b). Sectoral studies suggest that in some industries, Japanese firms invested abroad in order to source technology – in chemicals and pharmaceuticals, for example (Sachwald 1995b).

A second category of empirical studies has tested the hypothesis of technology sourcing more directly. And here again, the results are ambiguous. One method has been to consider the sectoral difference of R&D intensity between home and host country as a proxy for technological advantage. According to this approach, if American firms show a higher share of R&D expenditures than Japanese firms, the latter are more likely to source technology in the United States in the corresponding sector. An empirical test covering the 1970s and 1980s suggests that this has been the case only when Japanese firms entered the US through joint ventures (Kogut and Chang 1991). Other entry modes, i.e. new plants and acquisition of local firms, were positively related to the sum of American and Japanese R&D intensity.

This same method has been applied to entries in the US by British, German and Japanese firms over 1974–91, with quite different results (Anand and Kogut 1997). The R&D difference variable is correctly signed but never significant, for none of the nationalities and none of the entry modes. The test shows that sectoral R&D intensity is positively and significantly correlated with investment in the US, and particularly strongly in the case of Japanese firms. Besides, the R&D intensity variable is not significant in the case of joint ventures, while it has a strong positive influence in the case of new plants. A similar empirical approach has been used for investment into the European Community between 1984 and 1989 (Neven and Siotis 1996). According to the authors, their results suggest that technology sourcing might be an important motivation for American and Japanese investment in Europe, while it is not the case for intra-European flows.[6]

The hypothesis of technology sourcing has been tested on Italian foreign entries between 1986 and 1993 (Mutinelli and Piscitello 1998). The average R&D intensity for the line of business of the foreign unit has a positive influence on the probability to enter with a joint venture rather than with a fully owned unit on foreign markets. The authors interpret this result as supporting the technology sourcing hypothesis. However, the variable has no significant impact when Italian firms invest in Western Europe and the case of North America is difficult to interpret.[7]

These contradictory results are disquieting. One possible explanation is that data was not sufficiently disaggregated. FDI between developed countries is intra-industry and a German pharmaceutical firm may have strong competitive advantages (and R&D intensity) and nevertheless invest in the United States in the field of biotechnology. A complementary explanation is that R&D intensity is not a good enough proxy for technological competencies, or rather for the attractiveness of the United States as a location for high-tech ventures and R&D operations.[8] Finally, it seems that technological sourcing might become more frequent in the context of globalization, which means that recent data might give different results.

12.2.1.2. . . . and Korean multinationals

Outward direct investment from emerging countries is largely directed towards neighboring developing countries. In 1996, for the major Asian developing home economies, more than half of the stock of ODI was located in other developing countries from the region (UN 1998). As a consequence, emerging multinationals are relatively small and concentrated in low-tech sectors.

Korean ODI only partially follows this pattern. During the 1990s, more than 40 per cent has been directed to North America and Europe.[9] Moreover, the *chaebols* are the main investors abroad and in 1998 large firms controlled 80 per cent of the stock of Korean ODI.[10] A substantial part of these investments is located in industrial economies and is concentrated in capital-intensive and technology-intensive sectors. In the 1990s, Korean firms have built a number of greenfield sites and have also bought into American and European firms.

Empirical analyses of Korean FDI in developed countries have built upon insights from the theory of the multinational company and from empirical studies on the Japanese case. They have focused on the role of barriers to trade, firms' specific capabilities and oligopolistic reactions.

The specific assets hypothesis does not seem to be relevant in the case of Korean investment in developed countries, at least with respect to its usual presentation. The intensity of marketing expenditures does not significantly influence Korean ODI in developed countries (Jeon 1992; Perrin 1997; Hoesel 1999). Neither do R&D expenses (Perrin 1997). Interestingly though, human capital[11] does have a positive influence on investment by Korean electronic firms in developed countries (Hoesel 1999). According to the results of the available empirical tests, it seems that

Korean firms have invested in developed countries mostly to jump over antidumping barriers to export. Large firms have been motivated to invest in the foreign markets where their exports were constrained. In such a context, Korean firms may invest in the United States and Europe to preserve their export markets, despite their not possessing assets on which to build strong competitive advantages over local firms.[12] Supposedly, their strategy is to try to compete on their low cost segment of the market.

Some of the Korean ventures in the United States do not correspond to the barrier jumping rationale since they are in high-tech sectors where local firms have world-class competitive advantages. In fact, a number of Korean firms have explicitly used investment abroad as part of their strategy to upgrade their technological capability (Kim 1997; Hoesel 1999). This technology pull factor in Korean ODI is explored below.

12.2.2. The theoretical puzzle

The diversification of multinationals implies a diversification in the motives for venturing abroad. This section argues that a growing number of firms are motivated by a *strategic gap*. This type of behavior is better accounted for by an evolutionary approach of the multinational than by the more established theoretical perspectives.

12.2.2.1. Multinationals and the theory of the firm

From the 1960s onwards, the theory of the multinational has built upon industrial economics, with its emphasis on the role of market structure and barriers to entry, and on international economics, with its emphasis on the interaction between national resource endowments and specialization. Since the 1970s, the analysis of multinationals has increasingly drawn from transaction cost theory to discuss international internalization and from economic geography to analyze the spatial distribution of activities. Besides, these different streams of thought have been very much influenced by the economics of innovation.[13] A major theoretical challenge has been to integrate these different streams into a single framework. As a consequence, multinational theory has developed as an 'eclectic discipline'.[14] Indeed, the 'eclectic paradigm' which has been developed by John Dunning from the mid-1970s onwards has provided a useful framework of analysis.

The eclectic paradigm is able to synthesize and accommodate different theoretical insights on multinational companies, such as the product cycle theory and the internalization theory. It has probably been better than other analysis at integrating some of the new phenomena which are related to globalization. John Dunning has proposed extensions, in particular to try to account for the maturing of multinationals and the development of complex networks (1993), or the increasing role of cooperative alliances in innovation and internationalization (1997). One problem with such extensions is that the clear-cut synthesis is progressively burdened with new variables and considerations, which means that it becomes less useful.[15] A second problem is that some of the new variables may actually be incompatible with the original insight. Such is the case with the introduction of some resource seeking strategies since the paradigm still considers *ownership advantage* as a preliminary condition or incentive for the internationalization of value added activities.[16] What is at issue here is the extent to which the resources which are sought abroad are necessary to compensate for a firm's weak competitive status, or rather marginal.

The above discussion on the evolution of multinationals' behaviour suggests that some ODI decisions are taken by firms which do not possess strong ownership advantages, except possibly the availability of funds. On the contrary, a number of ventures by European, Japanese and Korean multinationals have been motivated by the search for important complementary resources. This is the case in particular of R&D resources, which firms may badly need in order to compete, not only in a specific country, but in all their markets. In such cases, foreign ventures are pulled by a *strategic gap* rather than pushed by an *ownership advantage*.

In order to account for both the strategic gap and the ownership advantage motivations, it proves extremely useful to adopt a quite different perspective. The idea is to focus on the multinational as a firm rather than on the decision to invest abroad. This might appear to be just a twist, but it is indeed a major shift since it means that the theory of the multinational should build upon the theory of the firm.[17] Since we want to address the development of the competitive capabilities of multinationals in relation to their strategies, a logical reference is the evolutionary theory of the firm. The resource-based view of the firm from the strategy field is a particularly useful framework of analysis. It is essentially evolutionary in its logic, identifying the role of competence build-up and path dependencies for firms' strategies and growth.[18] More precisely, strategy can be considered as the set of actions firms devise to match their resources and capabilities with the evolution of the competitive environment.

The competence-based approach can be readily applied to multinationals. The multinational is a firm which draws from its internal resources and its environment to develop its competitive advantages through a path-dependent learning process. As a result, multinationals strongly depend on the resources and characteristics of their country of origin. This proposition is coherent both with the traditional ownership advantage analysis and with an evolutionary perspective.[19] However, as firms extend outward and learn international management, they may increasingly draw from foreign countries too. The whole idea of global management is to learn how to design efficient world networks to optimize resource identification and allocation. Because path dependency is a pervasive phenomenon, the learning process is difficult and multinationals feel the weight of their 'administrative heritage' in their attempt to become global companies (Bartlett and Ghoshal 1989).

The discussion of R&D capabilities has been central in the emergence of an evolutionary theory of the multinational corporation. Innovative capabilities have become crucial to firms' competitiveness in general. In such a context, multinationals use their global reach both to transfer their R&D advantage abroad and to leverage their own innovative performances (Cantwell 1989, 1995). Empirical studies have shown that multinationals still mostly rely on their home R&D base, but that they increasingly organize to tap into foreign countries' technological resources.[20]

In the case of leaders from the triad, this internationalization of R&D means both exploiting the rich pool of R&D resources from the home base and building networks to draw on foreign-specific capabilities, especially in world-leading clusters. In the case of latecomers or second-rate competitors, the role of foreign R&D resources may be much more central. It may actually be a crucial component of a catch-up strategy. This may have been the case for part of the chemical and pharmaceutical Japanese sectors in the 1980s and 1990s (Sachwald 1995a,b). This could also be the case for Korean firms, which strive to catch up in a number of high-tech sectors. In their catching-up strategy, they have resorted to various classical means, including high R&D expenses, foreign licenses, OEM contracts and cooperative agreements with foreign partners.[21] As they have become stronger competitors, they have had more difficulties in finding foreign partners willing to transfer up-to-date technologies to them. Moreover, in the 1990s, they have felt the need to come closer to the technological frontier. This is why they have turned to direct investment as part of their R&D strategies.

12.2.2.2. Sourcing competencies abroad

When firms invest abroad to gain access to certain foreign technological capabilities, they are faced with specific problems, which in turn require specific internalization solutions.

The internalization theory of the multinational has built up from transaction cost analysis in order to discuss the modes of organization of foreign operations. Most applications of the transaction framework have explored the internalization of one particular type of input, technological and managerial know-how, marketing services, raw materials or capital. A priori, the analysis can be applied equally to selling in foreign markets based on ownership advantages and to procuring abroad (Hennart 1991a). Moreover, it can span all types of organizational modes, from greenfield sites to foreign acquisitions and various types of joint ventures (Hennart 1991a; Sachwald 1998). Nevertheless, in the case of knowledge, most studies have focused on multinationals exploiting their innovative capabilities abroad.

As recalled above, technological resources have represented major ownership advantages for American multinationals. As a result, R&D and marketing expenditures have been found to correlate positively with both the propensity of American firms to invest abroad and their tendency to do so through wholly owned subsidiaries.[22] Full control may be the first best solution, but firms nevertheless tend to enter joint ventures whenever they badly need a foreign partner, as when they have little international experience, either in the sector of investment or in the host country. These incentives to share ownership have been quite clear in the case of Japanese firms, which internationalized very rapidly in the 1980s (Hennart 1991b; Sachwald 1995b).

When firms invest abroad to source technology, they want to integrate the acquired knowledge into their own pool of resources. This entails a complex learning process by which their personnel are exposed to new knowledge and methods. One organizational mode firms increasingly resort to is the creation of a new laboratory in a favorable foreign setting, such as a science park. The foreign unit is typically populated with both local researchers and engineers and personnel from the parent company. This solution is particularly adequate when the parent company looks for complementary resources, on a specific research or design area for example. European firms have resorted to it with biotechnology laboratories in the US and Japanese carmakers with technical and design centers in Europe. The parent company has to carefully devise the location and choose the personnel of such units (Kuemmerle 1997). In particular, the laboratory has to be sufficiently independent and related to the local scientific community, and at the same time related to the home-base lab. Besides the orgnizational difficulties, 'home-base-augmenting' laboratories need an incubation period before they can really benefit from their foreign environment and yield fruitful results (Florida 1998).

The *greenfield* laboratory is much less adequate when technological resources cannot be captured simply through location. This is the case in two sets of circumstances. First, when the resources are proprietary or *firm specific* rather than *location specific*.[23] Second, when the contribution of the parent company is weak in the relevant technological fields. The main reason is that in this case, the most important resources are located outside the firm and the latter cannot bring many interesting complementary resources – except for funds. Moreover, its way of doing business and of organizing research may be ill suited to the specific needs of the foreign researchers involved in the field. As a consequence, when a firm wants to tap into a foreign technological base in which it is comparatively quite weak, it must turn to existing foreign firms or laboratories. Besides, since the greenfield solution may take quite a long time to bear fruit, it is not adequate when technological change is rapid.

In such situations, acquisition is typically not the best mode of entry either. The reasons are the same as in the case of diversification in general; they basically relate to cultural factors, which may be of sectoral or national origin. A successful foreign laboratory or start-up may be destabilized by alien management methods or a new organization of its R&D which may not be tailored to its specific needs. As a result, the best researchers and engineers may quit after an acquisition. More generally, when the contribution needed from the foreign unit depends on continued commitment by its local employees, an outright acquisition is more risky.[24]

The mode of entry to source technology abroad is thus influenced by two sets of factors. The objective to control the knowledge and results created by a foreign unit logically constitutes an incentive to acquire full ownership. On the contrary, organizational factors related to the conditions of production of knowledge are conducive to partial ownership. Results from empirical studies suggest that organizational factors may have the strongest influence. While investing in the US, Japanese firms have resorted to joint ventures rather than acquisitions or outright control when they have diversified outside their main sector (Hennart 1991b) and when they were less technologically advanced than American firms (Kogut and Chang 1991).

This argument should be particularly relevant for latecomers eager to catch up with the technological frontier, as are Korean firms. Hence the main hypothesis which is tested below: when sourcing technology in the United States, Korean firms are more likely to resort to joint ventures and minority ownership than to full control. Conversely, when Korean firms have strong competitive advantages they should choose majority-owned modes of entry.

12.3. A direct test of technology sourcing

Technology sourcing is one of the determinants of Korean direct investment in the United States. According to the above discussion, such a behavior from Korean firms should focus on certain sectors and be implemented through a specific mode of entry.

12.3.1. Test design

12.3.1.1. Sample and dependent variable

The sample is taken from a Korean database which lists foreign manufacturing ventures by Korean firms as of 31 December 1997.[25] The database indicates the name and location of the venture, its activity (fabricated products), the amount of the investment and the controlled share of capital. This test only takes into account the ventures located in the United States. In 1997, the database recorded 452 Korean manufacturing ventures in the United States. Due to data constraints on some of the independent variables, the sample used in the test has 339 records.

The dependent variable is a dummy which captures the ownership status of each Korean venture. Since we want to identify the determinants of holding a minority shareholding, the dummy variable takes a value of one if the parent owns a minority shareholding and zero if the parent owns a majority.[26] In a number of previous empirical tests, the definition of joint venture was a share of equity between 5 and 95 per cent. However, 95 per cent seems much too high if one wants to deal with the issue of control, which is assured over 50 per cent, and often below.[27] We have not set a minimum threshold because of the possibility that Korean firms might resort to low shareholding in cases where they want to have technological listening posts. They could, for example, resort to venture capital arrangements. Small capital participation may also accompany technological cooperative agreements, which have become important channels to transfer technology and innovate.[28] In order to check for sensibility, the test is run for two different dependent variables, ENTRY50 and ENTRY30, which take the value of one when the Korean parent owns, respectively, less than 50 per cent and less than 30 per cent of the equity. Of the Korean ventures in the sample (27 per cent 339 cases), had a shareholding below the 50 per cent threshold and 19 per cent below the 30 per cent threshold.

Because of the binary nature of the dependent variables, the statistical estimation uses a logit specification. The regression coefficients estimate the impact of the independent variables on the probability that the American venture will be partially owned.

12.3.1.2. Independent variables

There are three types of independent variables: those that proxy the competitive advantage of American and Korean firms, those that reflect production characteristics of the manufacturing sector of the venture, and one variable which indicates whether the venture is located in a favorable cluster.

12.3.1.3. Competitive advantage

R&D data have proved particularly difficult to use in testing hypotheses about ODI (Kogut and Chang 1991). First and foremost R&D data tends to be highly aggregated, while in testing for technology sourcing one would want to be able to use very detailed categories. Second, R&D expenditures are correlated across countries, even when technological levels differ substantially. In Korea, for example, the rate of R&D expenditures is as high or higher than that of most advanced countries.[29] This reflects Korea's efforts to catch up in a number of fields, but it would be misleading to interpret the intensity of this effort as a sign of technological leadership. Third, national statistical methodologies may be different, which could partially explain the level of Korean R&D intensity (Kim 1997). Given these data problems, R&D intensity is used here as a sectoral characteristic and not as an indicator of competitive advantage – the variable is discussed below.

Instead of R&D intensity, competitive advantage is captured with a new method. It draws on the above analysis of the determinants of Korean ODI. Some of the Korean ventures in the US are due to constraints on exports. In this case, they should occur in sectors where Korea has a comparative advantage. But we also argued that some Korean ventures are attracted by the technological resources which are embodied in some American firms. In this second case, investment should take place in sectors where American firms tend to have a competitive advantage. The hypothesis is that firms' competitive advantages are related to the home country's comparative advantages.[30] The latter are proxied by the following indicators:

$$CAus_i = Xus_i/Xus/Xz_i/Xz$$
$$CAk_i = Xk_i/Xk/Xz_i/Xz$$

Xus and Xk are exports from the US and Korea respectively; Xz are exports from a reference zone including the following countries: Canada, France, Germany,

Table 12.1 Summary of independent variables and expected signs

Variable name	Description	Expected sign (+ encourages partial ownership or joint venture)
PULLus	Difference between US and Korea comparative advantage	+
RD	R&D-intensive sector	+
SI	Scale-intensive sector	−
LI	Labor-intensive sector	−
RI	Resource-intensive sector	+
MACH	Machinery	?
SW	Software	+
DIST	Distribution	+
CLUSTER	Venture located in a cluster	+

Ireland, Italy, Japan, Korea, Mexico, the Netherlands, Portugal, Spain, UK, and the US. This variable is particularly interesting because it can be calculated at a product level. Calculations use trade data from the OECD.[31]

An American comparative advantage, especially in high-tech sectors, should represent an incentive for Korean firms to source technology in the US. Conversely, when Korea has a comparative advantage, the usual analysis applies, i.e. either Korean firms will export to the US or they will enter the American market through greenfield investment. As a result, according to the above analysis, an American comparative advantage should increase the probability of joint ventures, while a Korean comparative advantage should increase the probability of majority-owned ventures. In the argument, American and Korean comparative advantages are used symmetrically; we use the difference as an indicator of the competitive pull of the United States (PULLus), which should influence positively the probability to observe joint ventures (Table 12.1).

$$PULLus_i = CAus_i - CAk_i$$

12.3.1.4. Sectoral characteristics

Comparative advantage variables capture locational factors. Sectoral characteristics are used to identify resources and competencies which Korean firms are likely to search for or, on the contrary, which they tend to master satisfactorily. We use the classification established by Pavitt (1984) and Guerrieri (1992) to capture the relevant characteristics.

Sectoral characteristics are identified with dummy variables indicating whether they are R&D intensive (RD), resource intensive (RI), labor intensive (LI), scale intensive (SI) or mostly produce specialized machinery (MACH). Since firms tend to resort to joint ventures when sourcing technology, Korean firms should rather choose minority shareholding in RD sectors (Table 12.1). LI sectors correspond to products for which Korea has a comparative advantage. As a result, Korean firms may have some competitive advantage and may want to exploit it through fully owned greenfield ventures. LI sectors should thus exhibit mostly majority-owned American ventures (negative coefficient in Table 12.1).

Theoretical arguments and empirical tests suggest that firms enter RD sectors through joint ventures (Gomes-Casseres 1985; Hennart 1991a). This is because the market for agricultural and mineral resources tend not to be competitive and because local firms are more likely to have privileged access to domestic supply than multinationals. RI should thus influence positively the probability of minority owned entries (Table 12.1).

Economies of scale may have two contradictory effects. High economies of scale mean that minimum efficient-scale production units are likely to be large and investment particularly costly. This could constitute an incentive to enter with a partner to run a joint venture. This argument is used in the literature on cooperative agreements and seems particularly relevant in sectors such as chemicals and the automobile industry.[32] However, according to a previous test by Hennart (1991b), the relative size of investment has not influenced Japanese firms' decision to choose joint ventures as opposed to majority ownership.[33]

The problem may be that Japanese firms had competitive advantage precisely in sectors where economies of scale are high, like the automobile or other assembly industries. Korean firms, especially the *chaebols*, have also gained considerable competencies in capital-intensive and SI sectors like steel, electronic consumer goods, electronic components or automobile. In such sectors, besides financial resources, firms need strong competencies in production know-how. This type of knowledge is embedded in people on the shopfloor, teams and the organization in general. It is only partly codifiable and has to be progressively taught to foreign personnel. As a consequence, it may be difficult to transfer abroad, which constitutes an incentive to look for control.[34] When they started to invest in industrialized countries Japanese companies tended to favor full control and greenfield sites (Sachwald 1995b). Korean companies seem to have the same preference. As a consequence, we would expect economies of scale to constitute an incentive for Korean multinationals to avoid minority ownership (Table 12.1).

We add two variables in order to better identify two different types of characteristics of some of the ventures in the database. SW is a dummy variable which takes the value of 1 when a venture produces software. This variable has been added because software is not well identified in the trade classification and has been aggregated with computers.[35] This could adversely affect the results since American firms have strong competitive advantages in software.[36] SW should be positively correlated with minority ownership (Table 12.1). DIST is a dummy variable which takes the value of 1 when the description of the activity of the venture includes sales or distribution. This is the case in particular in food and beverages as well as in furniture, where retailing may be involved. This may be important since a local partner is often considered useful to set up an efficient distribution network abroad. DIST should thus have a positive impact on the probability to enter with minority ownership (Table 12.1).

12.3.1.5. Locating in clusters

Insights from geographical and innovation economics can be used to analyze the location of overseas ventures. Market size and growth have long been identified as location factors. Similarly, when foreign investment is resource seeking, it will logically locate in countries endowed with natural resources or low-cost labor.

This logic can be applied to technology sourcing. The main hypothesis here is that Korean firms are sourcing technology in the United States because this country is one major contributor to world-class scientific research and innovation. Agglomeration hypothesis goes further in predicting the location of this type of investment. Indeed, if various types of agglomeration effects are such that competitive clusters emerge,[37] then such areas should be particularly attractive for foreign investors. Clusters may exist in various sectors, from tile to carpet or automobile manufacturing. However, agglomeration effects tend to attract much attention in R&D-intensive industries where universities and various public institutions have to interact closely with firms.[38]

Agglomeration effects are captured with a dummy (cluster) equal to one when the Korean venture is located in a state where a cluster has been identified for the product(s) it manufactures.[39] The dummy is 1, for example, when Korean firms have invested in microelectronics or golf equipment in California or in agricultural equipment in Illinois.

12.3.2. Results

Statistical results confirm both the pull effect of American technological resources and the pull specific effect of local clusters. The specific effect of each of the relevant variables is not correctly measured because of multicollinearity. We use a method based on the multiple correspondence analysis to deal with this collinearity problem.

12.3.2.1. The correlation matrix

Table 12.2 presents the correlation matrix; it shows two levels of shareholding by Korean parents and the independent variables discussed above. Most of the variables significantly influence the mode of entry as predicted in the above analysis. PULLus, RD, SW and CLUSTER have a positive impact on minority shareholding, while LI and SI have a negative impact. Effects are stronger on ENTRY30, which suggests that technology sourcing may be attempted through low shareholding.

Table 12.2 shows three types of intercorrelation among the independent variables. First, the variables which capture the attractiveness of an American location

Table 12.2 Correlation matrix

	ENTRY50	ENTRY30	CLUSTER	RI	LI	SI	MACH	RD	PULLus	DIST	SW
ENTRY50	1.00										
ENTRY30	0.80	1.00									
CLUSTER	0.26	0.31	1.00								
RI	0.00	−0.05	−0.15	1.00							
LI	−0.25	−0.28	−0.22	−0.24	1.00						
SI	−0.13	−0.14	−0.04	−0.20	−0.29	1.00					
MACH	−0.04	−0.03	−0.11	−0.15	−0.23	−0.19	1.00				
RD	0.39	0.47	0.44	−0.25	0.37	−0.30	−0.24	1.00			
PULLus	0.27	0.27	0.22	0.02	−0.34	−0.07	0.17	0.26	1.00		
DIST	0.05	−0.02	−0.02	0.32	−0.05	−0.02	−0.08	−0.12	0.10	1.00	
SW	0.11	0.16	0.30	−0.07	−0.11	−0.09	−0.07	0.30	0.09	−0.04	1.00

Shaded areas indicate significant correlations (95 per cent level).

are positively correlated. This is logical since they tend to be related to high-tech or high R&D sectors (PULLus, RD, CLUSTER and SW). Second, LI, which is strong in sectors where Korea has a comparative advantage, is negatively correlated with the variables indicating American attractiveness. Third, DIST is positively correlated with RI (see the discussion of DIST above).

Intercorrelation among the variables is a statistical problem which undermines the precision of the estimates. We use the multiple correspondence approach to cope with multicollinearity. The idea is to attempt to extract from the set of independent variables, a smaller set of truly independent sources of variation in the dependent variables. In order to apply this method, we first introduce new variables on the characteristics of the products. We use the OECD classification of technological levels according to R&D intensity[40] and another variable – Frontier – which tries to capture the fact that a product within a given sector is more technologically advanced or sophisticated. Frontier is only partially related to the technological level. For example, in the database, a venture which declares 'electric car' as its activity has been classified in the automobile sector and the Frontier dummy has been set to 1 to account for the very specific type of car involved. Such a configuration may happen in different sectors, and not necessarily in those where R&D intensity is the highest (as in the car example).

Appendix 1 gives the full correlation matrix including these new variables; in Appendix 2 a figure summarizes the main results of the multiple correspondence analysis. This analysis is used to identify three new factors (F1, F2, F3) which are linear combinations of the initial variables and which are used in a separate estimate. Factor 1 summarizes 48.8 per cent of the total information. It opposes ventures in high-tech and R&D-intensive sectors located in clusters to ventures in low-tech and labor-intensive sectors which are not located in clusters. Factor 2 summarizes 19.4 per cent of the information and Factor 3, 9.5 per cent. The first three factors thus summarize 77.6 per cent of the information. A fourth factor is strongly related to resource-intensive sectors. It accounts for only 7.7 per cent of the information. Moreover, as discussed above, RI sectors include ventures which may have a distribution activity. This is why separate regressions have been run without the observations for which RI is equal to 1.

12.3.2.2. Results and discussion

The results of the binomial logistic regressions are presented in Tables 12.3 and 12.4. Three regressions are presented for each entry level. Column 1 in Table 12.3 gives the results of the regression with the first set of variables discussed above (Table 12.1) and the full sample.

According to the classification used here, each sector is qualified as either RI, LI, SI, RD or as machinery. This means that all these dummies cannot be included simultaneously as independent variables. Resource-intensive sectors have been chosen as the reference situation; it is in a way included in the constant and the coefficients have to be interpreted against this reference.[41] For both entry levels, the

Table 12.3 Parameter estimates for binomial logit model: minority ownership vs. wholly-owned subsidiary

Variable name	Coefficient (z-statistic)					
	ENTRY 50			ENTRY 30		
	1. Full sample	2. If R1 = 0	3. Factors and variables if R1 = 0	1. Full sample	2. If R1 = 0	3. Factors and variables if R1 = 0
Constant	-1.890*** (-4.053)	-2.930*** (-6.516)	-2.154*** (-5.884)	-2.586*** (-4.487)	-5.304*** (-4.816)	-3.303*** (6.199)
PULLus	0.412** (2.507)	0.422** (2.439)	0.403** (2.286)	0.414** (2.172)	0.437** (2.174)	0.397** (2.036)
RD	1.072** (2.376)	2.165*** (4.622)	—	1.404*** (2.643)	4.206*** (3.868)	—
CLUSTER	0.514 (1.443)	0.333 (0.899)	—	0.642* (1.681)	0.325 (0.821)	—
LI	-1.056** (-2.042)	—	—	-2.535** (-2.302)	—	—
SI	-0.669 (-1.332)	0.410 (0.791)	—	-0.788 (-1.212)	1.833 (1.617)	—
MACH	-0.289 (-0.549)	-0.746 (1.360)	—	-0.070 (-0.111)	2.628** (2.311)	—
DIST	0.771 (1.111)	0.399 (0.332)	0.703 (0.583)	0.247 (0.284)	1.848 (1.381)	1.487 (1.140)
SW	-0.313 (-0.467)	-0.356 (0.722)	-0.353 (-0.525)	-0.058 (-0.086)	0.069 (0.103)	-0.068 (-0.100)
F1	—	—	1.858*** (5.266)	—	—	3.291*** (4.588)
F2			-0.178 (-1.855)			0.021 (0.034)
F3			-1.285** (-2.461)			-1.282* (-1.862)
Mc Fadden R^2	0.174	0.193	0.214	0.268	0.301	0.315
Probability (LR stat)	0.000	0.000	0.000	0.000	0.000	0.000

Table 12.4 Classification table for the 50 per cent and 30 per cent thresholds

True	Predicted values								
	1. Full sample			2. If $RI = 0$			3. Variables and factors if $RI = 0$		
	Majority owned	Minority owned	Total	Majority owned	Minority owned	Total	Majority owned	Minority owned	Total
ENTRY 50									
Majority owned	213	46	259	183	36	219	190	43	233
Minority owned	33	47	80	29	44	73	22	37	59
Total	246	93	339	212	80	292	212	80	292
Correct	213	47	260	183	44	227	190	37	227
% correct	86.59	50.54	76.70	86.32	45.00	77.74	86.62	46.25	77.74
ENTRY30									
Majority owned	254	38	292	214	31	245	214	31	245
Minority owned	19	28	47	19	28	47	19	28	47
Total	273	66	339	233	59	292	233	59	292
Correct	254	28	282	214	28	242	214	28	242
% correct	93.04	42.42	83.19	91.85	47.46	82.88	91.85	47.46	82.88

constant is highly significant, which means that the reference situation is clearly identified and the contribution of each of the variables included in the regression can be calculated (see below).

The model has a high overall explanatory power, for all three specifications, but it is better when ENTRY30 is the dependent variable. The explanatory power also increases when we correct for the adverse effect of multicollinearity (Column 3 for each entry level). Another way of measuring how well the model fits the data is to use it to classify observations. Table 12.4 shows that the model has a very good ability to classify the minority and majority ventures, whatever the precise threshold and the exact specification.

The predicted positive influences of the American pull factor and of R&D intensity are strongly supported by the regressions, at both levels of entry. So is the negative influence of labor intensity, which thus appears as an incentive to enter with majority-owned subsidiaries. The influence of CLUSTER is more fragile since it is significant for ENTRY30 only. This is in fact due to the statistical problem of multicollinearity discussed above. Table 12.2 indicates that CLUSTER is significantly and positively correlated with both ENTRY30 and ENTRY50. Table 12.5 also shows that CLUSTER significantly influences the probability of entering the US with a minority shareholding.[42]

For each level of entry, the third column in Table 12.3 gives the results of the regressions using the multiple correspondence correction. The regression in Column 2 with the sub-sample where the RI dummy is zero has been run for the sake of comparison with Column 3: it shows that the results are very similar. The conclusion from Regression 3, which is not affected by multicollinearity, is similar to that of regression 1: the choice of a minority shareholding is positively influenced by R&D intensity and American location advantage, both at the national and at the cluster level. According to Regression 1, the fact that a venture is in an RD sector increases the probability of observing a minority shareholding by 17.5 per cent, in comparison with the reference situation represented by the constant. That same probability increases by 7 and 5.5 per cent respectively for ventures located in a cluster and showing a positive American pull effect. Similarly, in Regression 3, when compared to the reference situation represented by the constant, Factor 1 increases the probability of observing a minority shareholding increase by 32.3 per cent; the American pull effect increases that probability by 4.4 per cent.

12.4. Conclusion

This paper is the first to directly test the hypothesis of technology sourcing by Korean multinationals, rather than starting with the usual hypothesis of competitive advantage and trying to explain paradoxical results. The results strongly support the hypothesis that Korean firms are attempting to tap into the American technological resources through minority ventures. Moreover, they clearly tend to locate these technology sourcing ventures in specific clusters where adequate resources and partners are concentrated. Taken together, the existence of multicollinearity and

Table 12.5 Chi-square test of the significance of CLUSTER

CLUSTER	≥ 50	<50	Total
ENTRY50			
NO	+++	− − −	
	216	61	277
	77.98%H	22.02%	100%H
	87.80%V	65.59%V	81.71%V
	63.72% T	17.99%T	
YES	−−−	+++	
	30	32	62
	48.39%H	51.61%H	100%H
	12.20%V	34.41%V	18.29%V
	8.85%T	9.44%T	
Total	246	93	339
	72.57%H	27.43%H	100%H
	100.00%V	100.00%V	100.00%V
Chi-2	Degree of freedom	Probability	
22.28	1	0.000	

Remarks
- +++ or −−− Significant, 99 per cent level.
- H: horizontal
  V: vertical
  T: total.

the corrected regression suggest that the American comparative advantage (both at the national and local levels) interact with R&D intensity in attracting Korean investments.

These empirical results are to be considered in the context of globalization, where multinational firms have become a much more heterogeneous crowd. As argued in the paper, in this new context, multinationals should not be considered such exceptional firms as during the post-world war period. Comparisons between American, European and Japanese multinationals have already suggested that national characteristics have a long-lasting impact on firms' advantages and behavior. The Korean case represents yet another source of heterogeneity since Korean multinationals are typically latecomers.

The paper discussed the evolutionary approach to multinationals. The empirical results are an incentive to further explore this approach, where multinational firms may be considered as sophisticated organizational modes to exploit and transfer location-bound resources, not only from the home country to foreign countries, but also the other way round. In this perspective, future research should consider foreign fully owned laboratories and equity ventures which firms use to procure or transfer technology internationally as well as non-equity research cooperative agreements. As indicated in the paper, a number of empirical observations suggest that they have become major channels of technology transfer, learning and innovation, both at the national and international levels.

Appendix 1: complete correlation matrix

	ENTRY50	ENTRY30	CLUSTER	Frontier	RI	LI	SI	MACH	RD	Ltech	Htech	MLtech	MHtech	PULLus	DIST	SW
ENTRY50	1.00															
ENTRY30	0.80	1.00														
CLUSTER	**0.26**	**0.31**	1.00													
Frontier	**0.33**	**0.38**	**0.23**	1.00												
RI	0.00	-0.05	**-0.15**	-0.10	1.00											
LI	**-0.25**	**-0.28**	**-0.22**	**-0.11**	**-0.24**	1.00										
SI	**-0.13**	**-0.14**	-0.04	-0.08	**-0.20**	**-0.29**	1.00									
MACH	-0.04	-0.03	**-0.11**	-0.05	**-0.15**	**-0.23**	**-0.19**	1.00								
RD	**0.39**	**0.47**	**0.44**	**0.30**	**0.25**	**0.37**	**-0.30**	**-0.24**	1.00							
Ltech	**-0.20**	**-0.27**	**-0.31**	**-0.18**	**0.37**	**-0.23**	**-0.22**	**-0.30**	**-0.47**	1.00						
Htech	**0.28**	**0.32**	**0.40**	**0.20**	**0.31**	**0.61**	0.04	-0.05	**0.69**	**-0.60**	1.00					
MLtech	**-0.14**	-0.10	-0.04	-0.05	0.08	**-0.45**	**0.13**	0.06	**-0.23**	**-0.29**	**-0.30**	1.00				
MHtech	0.00	0.01	-0.09	0.03	**-0.15**	0.01	**0.13**	**0.43**	-0.10	**-0.29**	**-0.30**	**-0.15**	1.00			
PULLus	**0.27**	**0.27**	**0.22**	0.07	0.02	**-0.23**	-0.07	**0.17**	**0.26**	**-0.36**	**0.26**	0.02	**0.12**	1.00		
DIST	0.05	-0.02	-0.02	-0.05	**0.32**	**-0.34**	-0.02	-0.08	**-0.12**	**0.13**	**-0.16**	0.02	0.02	0.10	1.00	
SW	**0.11**	**0.16**	**0.30**	**0.11**	-0.07	-0.05	-0.09	-0.07	**0.30**	**-0.14**	**0.24**	-0.07	-0.07	0.09	-0.04	1.00

Shaded areas indicate significant correlations (95 per cent level)

Appendix 2. multiple correspondence analysis

The first two factors in the multiple correspondence analysis

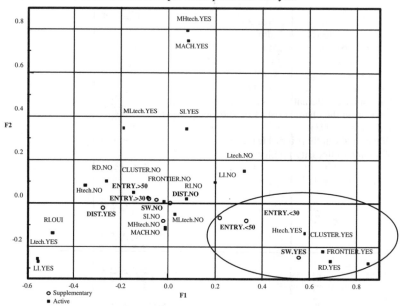

Remark: Factors 1 and 2 have been used to draw the axes. Dependent variables have been projected on the figure to show their proximity to independent variables.

Notes

1 On the dynamics of globalization, see in particular (Dicken 1992; Sachwald 1994b).
2 A number of European multinationals are much older, but extensive ODI from Europe, and in particular to the US, dates back to the 1970s.
3 On transatlantic cooperative agreements, see (Sachwald 1994a; Hagedoorn and Narula 1996; Hagedoorn 1998; Narula 1999).
4 For a review, see (Dunning 1993).
5 The choice of internal versus contractual technology transfer may depend on transaction costs or on the characteristics of knowledge, such as its degree of complexity (Kogut and Zander 1993).
6 However, the authors indicate that these results should be interpreted cautiously because of a multicollinearity problem.
7 The constant is not significant; the coefficient for R&D is significant and much lower than for the whole sample (which includes all countries).
8 This argument is expanded below about the Korean case.
9 Forty-nine per cent over 1981–90 and 43 per cent over 1991–97 (source: Bank of Korea).
10 Calculation based on the cumulated amount of ODI (Ministry of Finance 1998).
11 Proxied by the firm's average annual earnings by employee.
12 Or at least their competitive advantage is much less obvious than was that of Japanese firms when they massively invested in the US.
13 See below the discussion of the evolutionary theory of the firm.
14 This qualification is used by (Casson 1997) about *international business*. On the different issues and disciplines involved in the analysis of international production, see also (Cantwell 1991).
15 As an illustration, one can compare the summary tables of the paradigm provided respectively in (Dunning 1980, 1993, 1997).
16 This is not specific to the electric paradigm, since internalization theory (Hennart 1991a) or Ozawa's (1979) macroeconomic approach also rely on the existence of such conditions, even if they are not integrated in the analysis in the same way.
17 For an earlier version of this argument based on the analysis of cooperative agreements, see (Sachwald 1998).
18 See in particular (Penrose 1959; Teece *et al*. 1994).
19 For different contributions on the role of national factors in the formation of multinationals' competitive advantage (Vernon 1966; Muchielli 1985; Kogut 1988; Porter 1990).
20 A number of studies are based on data up to the mid-1990s (Patel 1993; Cantwell and Kotecha 1994, 1999; Papanastassiou and Pearce 1995; Zander 1997; Doremus *et al*. 1998).
21 On Korean firms latecomers' strategies, see in particular (Hobday 1995; Kim 1997; Hoesel 1999).
22 For reviews on these connected themes, see (Hennart 1991a; Dunning 1993).
23 The two are nevertheless related.
24 B. Gomes-Casseres (1989) reaches the same conclusion, but focuses on managerial shirking, which in turn raises the issue of governance. The above argument emphasizes organizational factors. For a similar opposition between the opportunist argument and the organizational argument with respect to ownership advantage transfer, see (Kogut and Zander 1993).
25 This base was the responsibility of the Bank of Korea until 1996 and has been maintained by the Korea Federation of Banks since then.

26 (Gomes-Casseres 1989) used the same convention, while Hennart (1991b) and Kogut and Zander (1993) have used the reversed convention (1 for majority shareholding).

27 The choice of a 95 per cent threshold may have been due to the fact that, originally, the issue was the determinants of 'wholly owned subsidiaries' rather than the reverse question. Then, the 95 per cent threshold was chosen without much discussion (Stopford and Wells 1972; Gomes-Casseres 1989; Hennart 1991b; Mutinelli and Piscitello 1998).

28 For different perspectives on this issue, see (Teece 1992; Hagedoorn and Narula 1996; Sachwald 1998); it is raised again in the conclusion below.

29 In 1996, the ratio of gross domestic expenditure on R&D to GDP was 2.79 per cent in Korea, 2.62 per cent in the US, 2.83 per cent in Japan and 2.32 per cent in France (OECD 1998). On Korean R&D expenditures and patents see also (Kim 1997).

30 This hypothesis corresponds to the arguments and results from different strands of literature: the theory of the multinational firm, the analysis of national systems of innovation and the evolutionary approaches of the firm.

31 International trade by commodities statistics, based on the Harmonized system (6,800 products).

32 See for example (Sachwald 1992, 1994a; Garrette and Dussauge 1995).

33 The amount of direct investment for each project was also used as an explanatory variable here, but the coefficient was not significant.

34 According to an empirical test by Kogut and Zander (1993) on a sample of knowledge transfers by Swedish multinationals, internal transfer to subsidiaries was chosen when knowledge was complex, difficult to codify and to teach.

35 Moreover, part of international exchanges in software are recorded as service flows.

36 On the software industry and competitive positions, see (Mowery 1996).

37 The literature on clusters and agglomeration factors is rapidly growing; in relation to competitiveness, see for example (Porter 1990, 1998).

38 In Silicon Valley, the complex networks or relationships are reinforced by the strong participation of venture capitalists.

39 Clusters have been identified from the list given by Michael Porter (1998).

40 According to R&D intensity, sectors are classified as low tech, mid-low tech, mid-high tech, or high tech (see the correlation matrix in Appendix 1).

41 Later on in the discussion, when RI will be set to 0, the reference situation will be LI = 1.

42 This same test is not presented for ENTRY30 since CLUSTER is significant in the regression; however, the chi-square test is also significant.

References

Anand, J. and Kogut, B. (1997) 'Technological capabilities of countries, firm rivalry and foreign direct investment', *Journal of International Business Studies*, 3rd Quarter.

Bartlett, C. and Ghoshal, S. (1989) 'Managing across borders. The transnational solution', Century Business.

Cantwell, J. (1989) *Technological Innovation and Multinational Corporations*. Basil Blackwell.

Cantwell, J. (1991) 'A survey of theories of international production', in C. Pitelis and R. Sugden (eds), *The Nature of the Transnational Firm*. Routledge.

Cantwell, J. (1995) *Technological Innovation Multinational Corporations and New International Competitiveness: The Case of Intermediate Countries*. Harwood Academic Publishers.

Cantwell, J. and Kotecha, U. (1994) 'L'Internationalisation des activités technologiques: le cas français en perspective', in [Sachwald 1994].

Casson, M. (1997) 'Economic theories of international business: a research agenda', in B. Toyne and D. Nigh (eds), *International Business, An Emerging Vision*. University of South Carolina Press.

Dicken, P. (1992) *Global Shift*. Paul Chapman Publishing.

Doremus, P., Keller, W., Pauly, L. and Reich, S. (1998) *The Myth of the Global Corporation*. Princeton University Press.

Dunning, J. (1980) 'Toward an eclectic theory of international production: some empirical tests', *Journal of International Business Studies*, Spring/Summer.

Dunning, J. (1993) *Multinational Enterprises and the Global Economy*. Addison-Wesley.

Dunning, J. (1997) *Alliance Capitalism and Global Business*. Routledge.

Garrette, B. and Dussauge, P. (1995) *Les stratégies d'alliances*. Editions d'Organisation.

Guerrieri, P. (1992) *Technology and Trade of the most Advanced Countries*. Roma: CNR.

Hagedoorn, J. (1998) 'Atlantic strategic technology alliances', in G. Boyd (ed.), *The Struggle for World Markets*. Edward Elgar.

Hagedoorn, J. and Narula, R. (1996) 'Choosing organizational modes of strategic technology partnering: international and sectoral differences', *Journal of International Business Studies*, 2nd Quarter.

Hennart, J.-F. (1991a) 'The transaction cost theory of the multinational enterprise', in C. Pitelis and R. Sugden (eds), *The Nature of the Transnational Firm*. Routledge.

Hennart, J.-F. (1991b) 'The transaction cost theory of joint ventures: an empirical study of Japanse subsidiaries in the US', *Management Science*, April.

Hennart, J.-F. and Park, Y.-R. (1993) 'Greenfield vs. acquisition: the strategy of Japanese investors in the United States', *Management Science*, September.

Hennart, J.-F. and Park, Y.-R. (1994) 'Location, governance and strategic determinants of Japanese manufacturing investment in the United States', *Strategic Management Journal*.

Hobday, M. (1994) 'The semiconductor industry', in [Sachwald 1995a].

Hobday, M. (1995) *Innovation in East Asia. The Challenge to Japan*. Edward Elgar.

Hoesel, R. van (1999) *New Multinational Enterprises from Korean and Taiwan*. Routledge.

Hymer, S. (1976) *The International Operations of National Firms*. MIT Press.

Jeon, Y.-D. (1992) 'The determinants of Korean foreign direct investment in manufacturing industries', *Welwirtschafliches Archiv*, Heft 3.

Kim, L. (1997) *Imitation to Innovation*. Harvard Business School Press.

Kogut, B. (1988) 'Country patterns in international competition: appropriability and oligopolistic agreement', in N. Hood and J.-E. Vahlne (eds), *Strategies in Global Competition*. Routledge.

Kogut, B. and Chang, S. (1991) 'Technological capabilities and Japanese foreign direct investment in the United States', *The Review of Economics and Statistics*.

Kogut, B. and Zander, U. (1993) 'Knowledge of the firm and the evolutionary theory of the multinational corporation', *Journal of International Business Studies*, 4th Quarter.

Kuemmerle, W. (1997) 'Building effective R&D capabilities abroad', *Harvard Business Review*, March–April.

Ministry of Finance (1998) 'Trends in international investment and technology inducement', Ministry of Finance and Economy, Republic of Korea.

Mowery, D. (ed.) (1996) *The International Computer Software Industry: A Comparative Study of Industry Evolution and Structure*. Oxford University Press.

Muchielli, J.-L. (1985) 'Les firmes multinationales: mutations et nouvelles perspectives', Economica.

Mutinelli, M. and Piscitello, L. (1998) 'The entry mode choice of MNEs: an evolutionary approach. *Research Policy*, No. 50

Narula, R. (1999) 'Explaining the growth of strategic R&D alliances by European firms', *Journal of Common Market Studies*, December.

Neven, D. and Siotis, G. (1996) 'Technology sourcing and FDI in the EC: An empirical evaluation', *International Journal of Industrial Organization*.

OECD (1998) Main Science and Technology Indicators, 2.

Ozawa, T. (1979) *Multinationalism: Japanese Style*. Princeton University Press.

Papanastassiou, M. and Pearce, R. (1994) in [Sachwald 1995b].

Patel, P. (1993) *Production localisée de technologie pour des marchés mondiaux*. Document de travail DSTI/EAS/STP/NESTI (93) 4, OCDE, Paris, avril.

Pavitt, K. (1984) 'Sectoral patterns of technical change: toward a taxonomy and theory', *Research Policy*, 13(6): September.

Penrose, E. (1959) *The Theory of the Growth of the Firm*. Basil Blackwell.

Perrin, S. (1997) 'Korean manufacturing investment in Europe: an empirical analysis of firm and industry-level influences', *Europe-Asie: les enjeux de l'interdépendance*, Colloque International, Université du Havre, 25–26 September.

Porter, M. (1990) *The Competitive Advantage of Nations*. The Macmillan Press.

Porter, M. (1998) 'Clusters and the new economics of competition', *Harvard Business Review*, November–December.

Sachwald, F. (1992) 'The role of co-operative agreements in the automobile industry', *Proceedings of the 18th European International Business Association*, The University of Reading, 13–15 December.

Sachwald, F. (ed.), (1994) *Les défis de la mondialisation. Innovation et concurrence*. Masson.

Sachwald, F. (ed.) (1995a) *European Integration and Competitiveness – Acquisitions and Alliances in Industry*. Edward Elgar.

Sachwald, F. (ed.) (1995b). *Japanese Firms in Europe*. Harwood Academic Publishers.

Sachwald, F. (1998) 'Cooperative agreements and the theory of the firm: focusing on barriets to change', *Journal of Economic Behavior and Organization*.

Shan, W. and Song, J. (1998) 'Foreign direct investment and the sourcing of technological advantage: evidence from the biotechnology industry', *Journal of International Business Studies*, 2nd Quarter.

Sharp, M. (1994) 'Transferts de technologie et politique de l'innovation: le cas des biotechnologies', in [Sachwald 1994b]

Teece, D. (1992) 'Competition, cooperation, and innovation: organizational arrangements for regimes of rapid technological progress', *Journal of Economic Behavior and Organization*.

Teece, D., Rumelt, R., Dosi, G. and Winter, S. (1994) 'Understanding corporate coherence. Theory and evidence', *Journal of Economic Behavior and Organization*.

UN (1998) *World Investment Report 1998*. United Nations.

Vernon, R. (1966) 'International investment and international trade in the product cycle', *Quarterly Journal of Economics*.

Zander, I. (1997) 'Technological diversification in the multinational corporation – historical evolution and future prospects', *Research Policy*, 26(2): May.

INDEX

backward: national linkages (BNL) 149; regional linkages (BRL) 148, 149
backward linkage effect 140, 141
backward linkages 145, 146, 150
Balance of Payments Appendices: French data 51
Barry, F. 149
Bartlett, C. 222
Belgian: exporting firms 220; science system 232, 237
bilateral investment treaties 140
Blomström, M. 47
Bradley, J. 149
Bureau of Economic Analysis (BEA) 5
Business International Corporation 157, 163

Cassiman, B. 241
CIS survey data 230
CNEL (National Council of Economy and Labour) 203
complementarity: hypothesis 89; key dimensions 45
Cournot competition 120

domestic employment 24, 26, 28, 35
domestic industry: downstream 145; upstream 145
Dyer, J. 158

econometric analysis: model 91; of panel data 96; results 92
employment within firms: effects of foreign production 18
EUROSTAT/CIS Survey 240

exports 44, 46–8, 51, 58, 65, 66, 84–91, 96, 101, 105; bilateral 71, 74; global 43, 87, 94; industrial 43, 45; intra-firm 86, 120, 122, 124–7, 130–1

feedback effect 145–7
Feenstra, R. C. 105
Fifth Basic Survey on Foreign Direct Investment 171
foreign affiliates 17, 28, 30, 31, 43, 46
foreign employment 6, 9, 27, 28, 32, 34
foreign investment 101, 102, 105–7, 113, 139; complementary effect 112; data 117; equation 107, 108; project 146; types 106, 108
foreign investors 209
foreign multinationals in Italy: innovative activities 214
foreign subsidiaries: *adapting* 238; *independent* 238; *sourcing* 238; typology 237
foreign venture: *ownership advantage* 249; *strategic gap* 249
forward: national linkages (FNL) 149; regional linkages (FRL) 149
forward linkage effects 141
forward linkages 145–7
France: comparison of trade and FDI 67, 85; import equations 65
French Directory of International Economic Relations (DREE) 86
French firms 62, 85, 86; FDI 84; FDI flows 51; multinational firms 84, 85

German firms 51
Ghoshal, S. 222
'global product mandate' 223

global technology 197
greenfield: affiliates 90; laboratory 251; sites 255; solution 251; ventures 246, 255
Gross Domestic Product (GDP) 6, 43, 47, 77, 84, 91, 105–8, 112–13

Haussman test 49, 61, 95
Head, K. 103
Heckscher and Ohlin, model 88
Hirschman's concept of linkages 142
horizontal FDI 90
horizontal investment 27

imports 47, 48, 58, 65, 66, 71, 74, 85, 90; bilateral 57; global 96; intra-firm 46, 86
increased vertical linkages: local employment 154; trade balance effects 154
Industrial Institute for Economic and Social Science Research (Stockholm) 47
industrial regional level: analysis of foreign and domestic employment 29; model 29
initial production effect 146
innovation strategies 228, 229; central-for-global 230, 231; cooperate 228; local-for-local 230
innovation strategy of firms: international 233; national 233
innovative process: globally linked 222, 234, 235, 239; locally leveraged 222, 234, 239
intellectual property rights 186, 188; French survey data 177; determinants 191; enforcement of the patents 191; limitation 178
intellectual property titles 186, 187
international growth and domestic employment: theoretical framework 25
international mobility, capital factor 88
International Trade Administration (ITA) 104
internationalization strategies of firms 186, 188
internationally integrated pattern, multinational behaviour 201
internationally interdependent labs (IILs) 223
inward FDI 44, 66, 69–71, 73–5, 81, 140
ISTAT (Italian National Statistical Institute) 203

Italian firms 25–7, 30, 32, 34, 35, 56; manufacturing firms 29
Italian multinational foreign affiliates: employment 32; local employment 32
Italian National Institute for Social Security: data set 27

Japanese affiliates, local procurement ratio 163–6
Japanese firms 156; foreign investment 155; Japanese exports 155; vertical keiretsu 155–7, 159, 160
Japanese foreign investments: antidumping law 155; vertical linkages 155–7
Just In Time (JIT) 157, 159

Kokko, A. 47
Korean direct investment in US, determinants: technology sourcing 252
Korean multinationals 244
Kotabe, M. 158

linkage coefficient concept 148 see Rodriguez-Clare
linkage effect: input–output coefficient 144
local procurement 159–62, 165; affiliate level determinants 160; country level determinants 162; parent level determinants 159
local substitutes index 146

macroeconomic complementarity 48, 51, 74; between trade and FDI 70
macroeconomic variables 57, 58, 91, 116
majority-owned affiliates (MOFAs) 5, 6, 8, 11, 21
manufacturing employment: foreign 10; overseas 10
Markusen, J. 146–7, 149
Markusen–Venables model 144
MFs, evolution of trade 131
MITI 47
MNC employment 6
'Mondialisation' 86
multi-domestic pattern, multinational behaviour 201
multinational behaviour, patterns 201

multinational enterprise (MNEs) 198–9, 201–3, 218, 221–5, 231, 235, 237, 241
multinational entry 145
multinational firms theory: eclectic paradigm 245, 248
multinationals: European 245, 246; Japanese 245, 246; Korean 244, 245, 247
multinationals and linkages: theory 142
Murray, J. Y. 158

Nash equilibrium 122
'national innovation system' 223
nonbank US multinational firms: employment 20, 21; gross product 19, 20
North American Free Trade Association (NAFTA) 156

OECD countries 45, 48, 49, 74, 91, 202, 205
Omura, G. 158
ordinary least squares (OLS) 92, 94, 95
outward direct investment (ODI) 69–71, 73–5, 244–9; flows 81
overseas manufacturing: affiliates, Japanese electronics 171; local procurement 171

parent firms: manufacturing, non manufacturing 15
patent: incentives 182; process 178, 180–3; product 178, 180–3
patent imperfections 184
patents economic research: inventive activity 177; optimal patent system 177
process innovation 181, 183, 185
product innovation 180, 181, 183, 185
production: affiliate 12, 13; foreign 5, 8, 12; overseas 5, 12; parent 5, 13
production in foreign affiliates: effects 26, 145

relative local sourcing 146
Reid, N. 157
Ries, J. 103
Rodríguez-Clare 142, 143, 144, 146, 148 149

science park 251
sectoral characteristics: labor intensive (LI) 254, 258; mostly produce specialized machinery (MACH) 254; R&D intensive (RD) 254; RD 258; resource intensive (RI) 254, 258; scale intensive (SI) 254, 258
SIC industries 104
simulated bilateral trade flows 49
single-region firms 31, 32, 34
spillovers 61, 70, 71; assessment of the magnitude 72; cultural 149; international 126; effects 89; national technology 126; Stewart studies 149
stocks of foreign investment: service 106; trade 106
substitution–complementarity debate 91
Swedish firms 3, 4

technological globalization: Italy 201
technology acquisition: disembodied 233, 234; embodied 233, 234; international 233, 234; national 233–4
technology sale: international 234, 235; national 234, 235
technology sourcing strategy 245; FDI 244
trade 44, 45, 47, 48, 51, 69, 85, 88–92, 101, 102, 105, 107; bilateral 45, 49, 51, 66; and FDI 62–87; foreign 26, 34, 35; global 84, 86, 87, 89, 91; inter-firm or arms length 86–92, 94, 119–21, 123, 126, 131; international 49, 84, 86, 119, 142; intra-firm 43, 85, 87; intra-industry 120, 127, 130–1; wholesale 43, 45; world 84
traditional general equilibrium: trade model 87
transaction cost theory 88
Turok, I. 157
types of foreign investment, commonalities 108

United States: economy 5–7; exports 105, 106, 109, 111; labor markets 4, 12
US and French industries: relationships between trade and FDI flows 43; database patterns 5
US employment: foreign employment 7, 9; manufacturing employment 9; in US affiliates abroad 7

US firms 4–7, 14, 18, 47, 101, 149;
manufacturing affiliates 9;
manufacturing MNCs 8–10;
multinational 4–6, 12, 48

Venables, A. 146, 147, 149
vertical investment 25, 26
Veugelers, R. 241

WTO working group 74

Yamawaki, H. 101, 103
'Yearly Enterprises Inquiry' (EAE) 86